# A CULTURAL HISTORY
# OF TRAGEDY

VOLUME 4

**A Cultural History of Tragedy**
*General Editor: Rebecca Bushnell*

**Volume 1**
A Cultural History of Tragedy in Antiquity
*Edited by Emily Wilson*

**Volume 2**
A Cultural History of Tragedy in the Middle Ages
*Edited by Jody Enders, Theresa Coletti, John T. Sebastian, and Carol Symes*

**Volume 3**
A Cultural History of Tragedy in the Early Modern Age
*Edited by Naomi Liebler*

**Volume 4**
A Cultural History of Tragedy in the Age of Enlightenment
*Edited by Mitchell Greenberg*

**Volume 5**
A Cultural History of Tragedy in the Age of Empire
*Edited by Michael Gamer and Diego Saglia*

**Volume 6**
A Cultural History of Tragedy in the Modern Age
*Edited by Jennifer Wallace*

# A CULTURAL HISTORY OF TRAGEDY

# IN THE AGE OF ENLIGHTENMENT

VOLUME 4

*Edited by Mitchell Greenberg*

BLOOMSBURY ACADEMIC
LONDON • NEW YORK • OXFORD • NEW DELHI • SYDNEY

BLOOMSBURY ACADEMIC
Bloomsbury Publishing Plc
50 Bedford Square, London, WC1B 3DP, UK
1385 Broadway, New York, NY 10018, USA
29 Earlsfort Terrace, Dublin 2, Ireland

BLOOMSBURY, BLOOMSBURY ACADEMIC and the Diana logo are trademarks of
Bloomsbury Publishing Plc

First published in hardback in Great Britain 2020
This paperback edition 2023

Copyright © Mitchell Greenberg and contributors, 2020

Mitchell Greenberg and contributors have asserted their right under the Copyright,
Designs and Patents Act, 1988, to be identified as the Authors of this work.

Series design by Raven Design

Cover image: *The Sacrifice of Isaac*, 1603 © Michelangelo Merisi de Caravaggio/Getty Images

All rights reserved. No part of this publication may be reproduced or transmitted
in any form or by any means, electronic or mechanical, including photocopying,
recording, or any information storage or retrieval system, without prior permission
in writing from the publishers.

Bloomsbury Publishing Plc does not have any control over, or responsibility for, any
third-party websites referred to or in this book. All internet addresses given in this
book were correct at the time of going to press. The author and publisher regret
any inconvenience caused if addresses have changed or sites have ceased to
exist, but can accept no responsibility for any such changes.

A catalogue record for this book is available from the British Library.

A catalog record for this book is available from the Library of Congress.

ISBN: HB: 978-1-4742-8805-7
Set: 978-1-4742-8814-9
PB: 978-1-3504-1679-6
PB Set: 978-1-3504-1692-5

Series: The Cultural Histories Series

Typeset by RefineCatch Limited, Bungay, Suffolk
Printed and bound in Great Britain

To find out more about our authors and books visit www.bloomsbury.com
and sign up for our newsletters.

# CONTENTS

LIST OF ILLUSTRATIONS vi
LIST OF GRAPHS viii
NOTES ON CONTRIBUTORS ix
SERIES PREFACE xi

Introduction: Definitions and Understandings: A Cultural History of Tragedy (and the Tragic) 1
*Mitchell Greenberg*

1 Forms and Media: The Evolution of French Tragedy in the Seventeenth and Eighteenth Centuries, from Scenic Cruelty to the Dramatic Poem 21
*Christian Biet*

2 Sites of Performance and Circulation: Tragedy in the Repertory of Molière's Troupe and its Successors, 1659–89 39
*Jan Clarke*

3 Communities of Production and Consumption 65
*Sylvaine Guyot and Clotilde Thouret*

4 Philosophy and Social Theory: From Political Tragedies to Tragic Politics 87
*Jonathan Strauss*

5 Religion, Ritual and Myth 107
*Juliette Cherbuliez and Christopher Semk*

6 Politics of City and Nation: A Short History of Scaffold Tragedy c. 1650–1800: How a Classic Trope Salvaged the Spectacle of Punishment in the Age of Sympathy 125
*Julie Stone Peters*

7 Society and Family: Tragedy and the Family 147
*John D. Lyons*

8 Gender and Sexuality: Sexuality and Gender in Enlightenment Tragedy 167
*Jennifer Row*

NOTES 187
BIBLIOGRAPHY 213
INDEX 231

# LIST OF ILLUSTRATIONS

## INTRODUCTION

| | | |
|---|---|---|
| 0.1 | Portrait of Pierre Corneille. | 6 |
| 0.2 | The actor Jean-Baptiste Britard, known as Brizard, in the role of old Horace in *Horace* by Pierre Corneille. | 8 |
| 0.3 | Sketch of the stage costume of the character Emilie in *Cinna* by Pierre Corneille. | 11 |
| 0.4 | Portrait of the poet Jean Racine. | 12 |
| 0.5 | Sketch for a stage costume from *Athalie* by Jean Racine, performance from 1779 at Comédie-Française. | 16 |
| 0.6 | Engraving featuring François-Marie Arouet, better known as Voltaire. | 17 |
| 0.7 | Engraving featuring John Dryden. | 19 |

## CHAPTER 1

| | | |
|---|---|---|
| 1.1 | Engraved illustration of Henry IV (1553–1610). | 26 |
| 1.2 | Engraving from "The Miseries and Misfortunes of War." | 30 |

## CHAPTER 2

| | | |
|---|---|---|
| 2.1 | Portrait of Jean-Baptiste Poquelin, known as Molière, by Nicolas Mignard. | 45 |
| 2.2 | Portrait of Marie Desmares La Champmeslé. | 51 |

## CHAPTER 3

| | | |
|---|---|---|
| 3.1 | 1787–8 Season Opening, *Iphigénie en Aulide*, followed by *La Feinte de l'amour* by Claude-Joseph Dorat. | 68 |
| 3.2 | *Les Comédiens-Français*, drawn by Antoine Watteau. | 71 |
| 3.3 | *David Garrick as Richard III*, drawn by William Hogarth. | 72 |
| 3.4 | *Théâtre Français, Mr Talma dans Brutus*, engraved by Adrien Godefroy. | 73 |
| 3.5 | *Sarah Siddons as Lady Macbeth*, by Staffordshire Pottery. | 75 |
| 3.6 | *Mlle Clairon couronne Voltaire sur la scène française*, engraved by Nicolas Dupin. | 79 |
| 3.7 | *Représentation d'une salle de spectacle avec des acteurs en scène*, drawn by Pierre-Alexandre Wille. | 82 |
| 3.8 | *The Pit Door at the Theatre Royal, Drury Lane, 1784*. | 83 |

## CHAPTER 4

| | | |
|---|---|---|
| 4.1 | Illustration of Louis XIV of France. | 90 |

LIST OF ILLUSTRATIONS vii

4.2  Title page of *Le Cid*, performed in Paris in 1637. 93
4.3  Portrait of Marie-Joseph Chénier. 99

## CHAPTER 5

5.1  Set design for Act 2 of Pierre Corneille's *Andromède*, as first performed on February 1, 1650. 113
5.2  Title page of *Oedipe*, performed for the first time on November 18, 1718. 119

## CHAPTER 6

6.1  *The Triumphs of Gods Revenge Against the Crying and Execrable Sinne of (Wilful and Premeditated) Murther.* 128
6.2  *The Idle 'Prentice Executed at Tyburn*, drawn by William Hogarth. 133
6.3  New gallows stage in front of the Old Bailey Courthouse and Newgate Prison, *c.* 1783. 139
6.4  Proposed scene of highwaymen at hard labor. 142
6.5  *The Tragic End of Marie Antoinette* 144

## CHAPTER 7

7.1  Frontispiece to the 1660 edition of *Nicomède*. 150
7.2  Title page of the first edition of *Aureng-Zebe*. 151
7.3  *Phèdre and Hippolyte*, illustrated by Charles Le Brun, engraved by Sebastien Leclerc. 155
7.4  Front page of *Le Philosophe sans le savoir*. 162

## CHAPTER 8

8.1  Illustration of Act 4 of *Iphigénie*. 170
8.2  Engraving for the frontispiece of the original 1643 version of *Polyeucte*. 179
8.3  The actor Lekain as Orosmane in the tragedy *Zaïre*, as performed in 1767. 185

# LIST OF GRAPHS

## CHAPTER 2

| | | |
|---|---|---:|
| 2.1 | Percentage of "main plays" that were tragedies. | 43 |
| 2.2 | Percentage of performances that involved tragedies. | 43 |
| 2.3 | Total number of performances of individual tragedies given by Molière's troupe, 1659–60 to 1672–3. | 48 |
| 2.4 | Total number of performances of individual tragedies given by the Guénégaud company, 1673–4 to 1679–80. | 52 |
| 2.5a | Number of performances of individual tragedies given by the Hôtel Guénégaud company and at the Comédie-Française, 1680–1 to 1688–9 (part 1). | 56 |
| 2.5b | Number of performances of individual tragedies given by the Hôtel Guénégaud company and at the Comédie-Française, 1680–1 to 1688–9 (part 2). | 57 |
| 2.6a | League table of relative popularities (top third). | 58 |
| 2.6b | League table of relative popularities (middle third). | 59 |
| 2.6c | League table of relative popularities (bottom third). | 60 |
| 2.7a | League table of tragedies performed privately, 1680–1 to 1688–9 (top half). | 63 |
| 2.7b | League table of tragedies performed privately, 1680–1 to 1688–9 (bottom half). | 64 |

# NOTES ON CONTRIBUTORS

**Christian Biet** is a professor at the University of Paris Nanterre, and Institut Universitaire de France. He has written on subjects such as performing arts, theatrical and drama aesthetics, and French studies. A specialist of French and English seventeenth- and eighteenth-century theater, and working on culture, literature, theater, and law in the early modern period, he has published several articles and books including: *Qu'est-ce que le théâtre?* edited with Ch. Triau (2006; English translation: *What is theatre?* 2019); *Théâtre de la cruauté et récits sanglants (France, XVI–XVIIe siècle), Tragédies et récits de martyres (France, fin XVI-début XVIIe siècle)*, edited with M.-M. Fragonard (2009; and *Le Théâtre du XVIIe siècle*, 2009).

**Juliette Cherbuliez** is Professor of French and Chair of the Department of French and Italian at the University of Minnesota. Her books include *The Place of Exile* (2005) and *In the Wake of Medea: Theater and the Arts of Destruction* (forthcoming). Her research addresses the relationship between theater and violence, spectatorship, history of the book, and women's writing. She has published on tragedy and violence, libertinism, early modern Paris, and seventeenth-century fans.

**Jan Clarke** is Professor of French in the School of Modern Languages and Cultures at Durham University. She works on all aspects of French seventeenth-century theater history, particularly stage and theater design and company organization, and is currently editing a volume on *Molière in Context*.

**Mitchell Greenberg** is the Distinguished Professor of Arts and Sciences in Romance Studies at Cornell University. He is the author of several studies on Baroque and Classical French and European culture: *Detours of Desire: Readings in the French Baroque* (1984), *Corneille, Classicism and the Ruses of Symmetry* (1986), *Subjectivity and Subjugation in Seventeenth Century Drama and Prose: The Family Romance of French Classicism* (1992), *Canonical States, Canonical Stages: Oedipus, Othering and Seventeenth-Century Drama* (1994), *Baroque Bodies: Psychoanalysis and the Culture of French Absolutism* (2001), and *Racine: From Ancient Myth to Tragic Modernity* (2010) as well as numerous articles and editions. His work incorporates psychoanalysis and cultural anthropology in the reading of early modern texts.

**Sylvaine Guyot** is Professor of Romance Languages and Literatures at Harvard University. She is the author of *Racine et le corps tragique* (2014) and *Racine ou l'alchimie du tragique* (2010), as well as the co-editor of a critical edition of Racine's *Théâtre complet* (2014). She has co-edited a special issue of *Littératures classiques* on "l'œil classique" (2013), a festschrift for Alain Viala, *Littéraire* (2018), and an online volume on theater studies and digital humanities, *The Eighteenth-Century Stage Online* (2019). Her book, *Les Scénographies de l'éblouissement*, is forthcoming from Garnier. She is a principal researcher of the *Comédie-Française Registers Project* and the founding director of the theater company La Troupe at Harvard.

**John D. Lyons** is Commonwealth Professor of French at the University of Virginia and *Chevalier de la légion d'honneur*. His studies of early modern French tragedy include *The Tragedy of Origins: Pierre Corneille and Historical Perspective* (1996), *Kingdom of Disorder: The Theory of Tragedy in Seventeenth-Century France* (1999), and most recently *Tragedy and the Return of the Dead* (2018). He is the editor of the *Cambridge Companion to French Literature* (2016) and the *Oxford Handbook of the Baroque* (2019).

**Julie Stone Peters** is the H. Gordon Garbedian Professor of English and Comparative Literature at Columbia University, where she teaches on a range of topics in the humanities, from drama, film, and media to law and culture. Her most recent book is *Theatre of the Book: Print, Text, and Performance in Europe 1480–1880*. She is currently working on a historical study of legal performance, theatricality, and spectatorship.

**Jennifer Row** is an assistant professor at the University of Minnesota in the department of French and Italian. Her research and teaching interests include early modern theater, queer theory, the history of sexuality, disability studies, and affect theory. Her book project, *Queer Velocities: Time, Sex and Biopower on the Early Modern Stage*, under review with Northwestern University Press, examines new affects and queer desires wrought by the staging of temporal intensities and the impact of such queer affects on an emerging biopolitics. She actively researches in disability studies, critical race theory, and theater and performance studies.

**Christopher Semk** is an independent scholar. He received his PhD from Indiana University in 2010. He has published on Bossuet and is the author of *Playing the Martyr: Theater and Theology in Early Modern France* (2017). He teaches French and Latin at the Ethel Walker School in Simsbury, CT.

**Jonathan Strauss** is Professor of French at Miami University, specializing in French literature and culture from 1800 to the present while focusing on issues of subjectivity, mortality, and life. He is the author of *Subjects of Terror: Nerval, Hegel, and the Modern Self* (1998); *Human Remains: Medicine, Death, and Desire in Nineteenth-Century Paris* (2012); *Private Lives, Public Deaths: Antigone and the Invention of Individuality* (2013); and has edited a volume of *diacritics* (*Post-Mortem: The State of Death as a Modern Construct*, fall 2000). He recently held a residential fellowship at the Society for the Humanities at Cornell and is currently completing a book on literary temporality in Balzac.

**Clotilde Thouret** is Professor of Comparative Literature at Lorraine University (Nancy, France). Her research focuses on early modern drama in England, Spain, and France, with particular emphasis on the relationships between theater and society, the theatrical experience (especially emotions), and the controversies on theater. She is the author of *Seul en scène. Le Monologue dans le théâtre européen de la première modernité (Angleterre, Espagne, France; 1580–1640)* (2010) and *Le Théâtre réinventé. La défense de la scène dans l'Europe de la première modernité* (2018). She is the co-editor of *Corps et interprétation (XVIe–XVIIIe siècles)* (2012, with Lise Wajeman) and the editor of *Le Dramaturge sur un plateau. Quand l'auteur dramatique devient personnage (XVIe–XXIe)* (2018). Since 2013, she has co-directed the project "The hatred of theatre" with François Lecercle (Labex Obvil, Sorbonne Université).

# SERIES PREFACE

A cultural history of tragedy faces a daunting task: how to address tragedy's influence on Western culture while describing how complex and changing historical conditions have shaped it over two and a half millennia. This is the first study with such an extensive scope, investigating tragedy's long-lived cultural impact and accounting for its material, social, political, and philosophical dimensions.

Since antiquity, tragedy has appeared in a myriad of forms, reinvented in every age. It has been performed as opera, dance, film, and television as well as live theater. From the beginning, concepts of tragedy have also surfaced in other literary genres such as narrative poetry and novels, as well as in non-literary forms, including journalism, visual art, and photography. Tragedy never appears in a vacuum: the conditions of performance and production and its communal functions always affect its form and meaning. Tragedy has never belonged solely to elite culture, and who creates and consumes these forms of tragedy also makes a difference. Not only has the status of tragedy's producers—the writers, actors, artists, and performers—evolved over time, but so has the nature of the audiences, viewers, and readers as well, all significantly affecting tragedy's aesthetic and social impact.

Tragedy also does more than simply represent or perform human catastrophe or suffering; it is a mode of thought, a way of figuring the human condition as a whole. Philosophers and social and cultural theorists from Plato to Lacan have long pondered the idea of the tragic, while in turn literary models have influenced philosophy, social thought, and psychoanalysis. Tragedy has always had a complex relationship with religion and ritual practices, both complementing and conflicting with religious orthodoxies concerning fate, the power of the gods, and the meaning of suffering. At the same time, since its earliest staging in fifth-century Athens as a civic as well as religious event, tragedy has both echoed and challenged relationships of power and political events in societies experiencing conflict or change.

While tragedy in all its versions has thus profoundly tapped into broad social, intellectual, and political movements, it has often represented those themes through individual experiences, ranging from the titanic sufferings of princes to the sorrows of ordinary men and women. While tragedy's themes of ambition, authority, transgression, and rebellion are grounded in religion and politics, its plots often play out through family relationships that both mirror and conflict with social and political norms. When tragedy thus engages familial and personal themes, it often involves tensions of gender and sexuality. Sexuality is a powerful driver of tragic catastrophe, when desire is granted its own kind of fatal power.

As with other *Cultural History* series, here the story of tragedy writ large is divided into volumes covering six historical periods from antiquity to modernity. Although the boundaries between those time are necessarily fluid, the volumes are divided as follows: 1. Antiquity (500 BCE–1000 CE); 2. Middle Ages (1000–1400); 3. Early Modern Age (1400–1650); 4. Age of Enlightenment (1650–1800); 5. Age of Empire (1800–1920), and 6. Modern Age (1920–present). While such a history naturally focuses on Western culture and history, at the end it also touches on tragedy's later post-colonial adaptations, which put its fundamentally Western concerns in a global context. Each volume has its own introduction by an editor or co-editors presenting an original and provocative vision of tragedy's manifestations in one historical era. Each volume also covers the same eight topics as the others in the *Cultural History*: forms and media; sites of performance and circulation; communities of production and consumption; philosophy and social theory; religion, ritual, and myth; politics of city and nation; society and family; and gender and sexuality. Readers may thus follow one topic over a wide historical span, or they may focus on all dimensions of tragedy in one period. Either way they read, they will be able to appreciate the power of tragedy to shape our understanding of human experience, and in turn, how tragedy has changed over time, both reflecting and challenging historical conditions.

*Rebecca Bushnell, University of Pennsylvania, General Editor*

# Introduction

## *Definitions and Understandings: A Cultural History of Tragedy (and the Tragic)*

MITCHELL GREENBERG

The period covered by this volume in the *Cultural History of Tragedy* series is bookended by two shockingly similar historical events: the beheading of a king. The aftermath of these two executions had, however, decidedly different historical repercussions. In the throes of the English civil wars Charles I was brought before parliament and charged with treason. He was found guilty and was subsequently beheaded on January 30, 1649. On the far end of our period, during the French Revolution's turn toward terror in 1793, the last French monarch of the Old Regime, Louis XVI, was also, after a heated debate, found culpable of the same crime ("of having committed a multitude of crimes to establish your tyranny, in destroying her freedom") and sentenced to death so that, in the words of Robespierre, the "State may live." With Louis' execution, some have argued, western civilization entered a radical new phase. On the political front, the demise of the French monarchy and the concomitant rise of English power re-established a balance in European culture which had seen the dominance, militarily, politically, and culturally of France in the preceding one hundred and fifty years. While there is no denying the many contributions of English, Spanish, and Germanic societies in the flourishing of dramatic culture during this period, the dominance of France with its central influence and with the imposition of French cultural and dramatic productions during our period will be the central concerns of the various chapters that make up this volume.

In a curious reversal, the execution of Louis XVI ended a centuries-long political regime that had, in one form or another, dominated the social and cultural lives of the emerging nation-states of Europe. The fall of the guillotine's blade had not only severed Louis' head from his body but had changed forever the symbolic order he represented. Europe was headed for a convoluted period of political, social, and economic change—a "revolution," and not simply another in a long series of "revolts." The changing politics of the state seems to have returned to the scene where the tragic execution of a king and the tragedies of so many fallen monarchs are joined by the ambivalent place of the scaffold ("échafaud" in French), a site of both execution and representation.

The system that the Revolution put an end to—absolutism—was an ideology that in its articulation was more resonant in its abstraction than other political terminologies and perhaps emptier too. It is a term that, nevertheless, appears capable of generating a proliferation of both conscious and unconscious associations by which and through which our culture constantly reinvents itself. For the majority of contemporary historians, absolutism was never an actually achieved political system. Rather, most tend to view it as an asymptotic ideological trajectory where changes in economy, politics, and religion constantly present different, sometimes congruent, but more often decidedly contradictory demands on the bureaucrats attempting to centralize royal policy in the emerging nation-states of early modern Europe. Although evolving over a period of more than two hundred years, absolutism remains more a process than a condition. The reality of absolutism is as elusive as it is evocative. Detached from any universal historical anchoring, the word drifts into the realm of myth, where fantasy and reality commingle.

What better art form to represent this realm of myth, of fantasies of death and desire, than the theater? And it is during this period that the theater experiences one of its greatest moments. Ever since the Renaissance, a long tradition had associated princely largesse with its manifestation in/as spectacle. The representation of the prince and his court is inextricably bound to a politics of spectacle, to the imaginary scenario that empowers. On a first level the importance of "spectacle" for sovereignty is a life that is theatricalized, where the sovereign is co-terminously both the privileged spectator and the most compelling spectacle of his realm (compare the spectacular scenarios of court life devised by and for James I, Philip IV, Charles I, Louis XIII, and Louis XIV). The image, the imaginary of power, is relayed through a spectacular dissemination and will be reproduced in those royal entrées that mark all the memorable events of a reign, in the extraordinary royal entertainments—the masques, the balls, the "Plaisirs de l'Ile Enchantée"—and in the construction, beginning with the Retiro palace in Madrid but reaching its apogee in Versailles, of a spectacular architecture in which the images of sovereignty are mirrored and produced.

Finally, and more important for our purposes, an indispensable link develops between the sovereign—spectacle and spectator—and the theater, a theater that (despite its on-again, off-again battle with religious and moral authorities) flourishes with stunning success in each of the three centralizing states of early modern Europe—England, Spain, and France. The theater enjoys one of its golden periods at the same time that absolutism establishes its hold on European political life. The questions, therefore, that we might ask in order to frame our discussion of the relation between the theater—and here we are speaking of its "noblest" form, "tragedy"—and its relation to the political, economic, and sexual transformations occurring during this moment of, if we are to believe Michel Foucault, enormous epistemological transitions, are: What is the relation between the emergence of the first "modern" absolutist states and tragedy? Why did tragedy become the privileged form of representation of the emerging absolutist states of Europe and why is it that this theater, whose splendor existed for a relatively brief moment, tended to be almost exclusively the theater of familial conflict—of the patriarchal family living in and under the dictates of the father/king? Finally, how can we articulate the "decline" in tragedy, its transformation into melodrama during the time of absolutism's waning, to see as the eighteenth century progresses those ideas that had been suppressed at absolutism's height re-emerge reinvigorated—I am speaking, of course, of the "Enlightenment"—at the same time that "tragedy" while eclipsed on the stage becomes central to the tragic scenes of revolutionary "terror"?

It must strike us as symptomatically telling that European literature of the medieval and Renaissance periods is singularly lacking in familial narratives. In order to encounter familial scenarios, we must return to ancient Greece, and to the tragedies of Aeschylus, Sophocles, and Euripides, to find a similar insistence on representing the human subject within the sexual-political confines of family. The great theatrical productions of the seventeenth and eighteenth centuries in England, France, and Spain introduced the family into modern Western literature as the privileged site of individual subjugation. In its plots and *peripeteia* we are called upon to witness the submission (and resistance) of every human child to those societal codes that pre-exist his or her entry onto the stage of social existence and which s/he must internalize in order to participate in communal existence. The family becomes the locus of tragic action at the same time that tragedy becomes the privileged form of representation in absolutist Europe. The conflation of family and tragedy, which at first might strike us as strange, becomes apparent when we consider the remarks of the French psychoanalyst André Green who in his now classic study, *The Tragic Effect: the Oedipus Complex in Tragedy*, tells us that:

> The family, then, is the tragic space par excellence, no doubt because in the family the knots of love—and therefore of hate—are not only the earliest, but also the most important ones. The tragic space is the space of the unveiling, the revelation of an original kinship relation.[1]

The familial scenarios of the seventeenth-century stage become the site where the sexual and political demands of society are most acutely represented in conflict with a "personal" desire that those demands paradoxically inform.

The hundred and fifty or so years that form the limits of our volume are moments of major historical change, fraught moments where no clear separations of epistemic systems are possible. It is during these moments that we see that the "place of the stage" (to borrow Steven Mullaney's resonant title) comes to the fore.[2] Mullaney discussing the ambivalent space of the actual geographical location of the theaters in Elizabethan England—neither in the jurisdiction of London nor in that of the neighboring boroughs—uses this geographic ambiguity to highlight the function of the theater as a locus of intermingling where the stage and the *parterre* remain both separate and connected, where the flux of spectator and actor make each a possible participant in both scenes and where, of course, conflicting worldviews, ideologies are in constant unrest. Although we know that the theaters of Paris and Madrid were not situated in the "no-man's land" of the English theaters but, rather, in the very centers of Madrid and Paris they, nevertheless, configure the same dialectical space that Mullaney's metaphor implies. The theater functions the most intensely as a dialectical space, where competing and contradictory ideologies act out for and through the audience a ritualized *mise en scène* of society's own internal struggles. As he so cogently puts it:

> Hegemonic culture is . . . a historical dynamic, an ongoing, diachronic negotiation between the old and the new. The dominant culture in any given period cannot hope to include or even account for all human aspirations and energies; present culture is continually limited, challenged or modified by culture past and culture yet to come.[3]

What these struggles might be for the tragedies of our period, although obviously numerous can, I will suggest, be reduced to the battles which a hegemonic discourse (absolutism) attempts to impose on an unruly, quite motley populace—that is the dominance of the concept of the "One"—the ruler, king, over what was a fractured society. In the societies of early modern Europe, emerging as they were from almost a hundred years of religious upheaval, of cosmic decentering of a universe that had for centuries seen the Earth as the center of that cosmos with "man" at its very heart (Copernicus, Kepler), and the discoveries of lands unheard of by the ancients, the possibility of chaos was ever-present. We hear the anxiety of chaotic dispersal resound across the continent from the sermons of Latimer to Louis XIV writing to his son in his

*Mémoires*.⁴ From this anxiety emerges a desire, an appeal to a centralizing, protective figure who would offer stability in a world that was seemingly whirling out of control. In the metaphoric (but also quite literal) appeal to the shining "body royal," this new leader, would subsume disparity in his own body and impose unity on difference. The monarch, in his person and persona, is made to incarnate the contradictory hopes and desires of his people—the desire of and appeal to the Absolute.

It strikes me that the political system that looked to the king as the embodiment of protective unity could not function unless it was underpinned by an entire metaphoric structure that equated the king both to God (the heavenly "father") and the father of each patriarchal family. In other words, a metaphoric chain uniting God the father with the king "father of his people" with the father of each individual family functioned to unite polity with family in a self-enclosed circuit of metaphoric patriarchy. In this way both the relation of the king to God and to his people were fused in the familial scenario of the Christian family. What this means, as Green, has implied is that the father/king becomes the target of both intense love but also of intense (unconscious?) hatred. That hatred which could never be directed towards the father (regicide/patricide was the most heinous of political crimes, punished most gruesomely), there had to be a substitute, an alternative paternal figure upon whom this hatred could be directed. It was the "prime ministers," the Richelieus, Mazarins, Buckinghams, and Olivares, who standing in for the monarch would be the recipients of the venom that could not be directed at the Father of the nation. It would seem, therefore, that the dynamics of politics and familial "sexuality" becomes the inspiration for the majority of tragedies in the period of absolutism's rise. Its fall will be, as we know, not so much metaphorical as quite brutally real.

Before going further, we must not forget what Franco Moretti has reminded us about the contradictions between the actual "real" political powers of the seventeenth-century monarch and the representations of that "ideal" as it was portrayed on the tragic stage:

> If the general culture of absolutism qualified the sovereign power it conferred upon the king with countless hesitations and uncertainties ... tragedy surrenders such power to him wholly and without the slightest reserve. In the world of tragedy the monarch is truly *absolute*. Tragedy, then, stages not the institutions of absolutism, but its culture, its values, its ideology.⁵

What Moretti means by "ideology" I suggest we understand in its most abstract definition, perhaps the famous definition of Louis Althusser where "ideology" is defined as "representing the imaginary relationship of individuals to their real conditions of existence," and where I will be equating "imaginary" with the unconscious.⁶

It is interesting to note the differences between the theatrical scenarios of England, those of Spain, and those of France. What is fascinating about the first two of these great producers of theater in the late sixteenth and early seventeenth centuries is that, unlike their colleagues in Italy and France, they do not seem ready to bend their practice to what will become the dominant mode in France. The controversies, scholarly arguments, and critical debates around the discovery and diffusion of Aristotle's *Poetics* did not seem to inhibit the most illustrious writers of Spain and England. In neither the works of the Elizabethans nor in those of Spain's "Golden Age" do we find the desire to conform to what will become the hallmarks of French neo-Classicism. Lope de Vega in his *Arte Nuevo de hacer comedias en este tiempo* (1609) had stated the case for Spanish dramaturgy. He begins his manifesto by first showing the world that he, as well as his learned Spanish colleagues, are well aware not only of the precepts of Aristotle's *Poetics* and the debates that swirled around its interpretations, but that they also are well acquainted with Horace, Cicero "e tutti quanti." Lope then goes on to state that the precepts of the ancients were well and good, but they were precepts for their time. He and his colleagues are writing for the public of their own time and that time requires more freedom, a language adapted to their public for a theater that must amuse and instruct on matters far removed from ancient Greece and Rome. In both English and Spanish theater (I realize I am speaking in great generalities), therefore, there seems to be no necessity for unity of plot, nor time, nor place. The plays of Lope de Vega, Calderón, Shakespeare, Marlowe, and Jonson roam freely around the world, include characters of mixed social stations, mingle scenes of comedy with those of horror.

One could, of course, say the same for the French theater of the late sixteenth and early seventeenth centuries. In the plays of Pierre du Ryer, Alexandre Hardy, Jean De Schelandre, and Théophile de Viau, in what is commonly referred to as "baroque" theater, we have many of the same elements—various subplots, disguises, kidnappings, rapes, and murders with no regard to any unity of time or place as those written in France's political rivals. Once, however, when politics begins to impose its centralizing dictates on France in the reign of Louis XIII whose prime minister Cardinal Richelieu orchestrates the monopolization of the major aspects of French society, things begin to change radically. French tragedy goes off in a decidedly different direction than the production of its rival nations. When the dominance, both military and cultural of France gains the upper hand in Europe, we will witness the imposition of French neo-Classicism with its own particular take on tragedy and tragic scenarios become the model for theatrical production across the continent and for more than a hundred years—at least.

Of Richelieu's many innovations, all of which aim at assuring the imposition of a centralized state on what had been a "mosaic" of provincial differences inherited from the feudal Middle Ages, perhaps the most lasting was his enforcing of "order" on the French language. What this essentially means is that Richelieu recognized the importance of "controlling" the language, of "purifying" it, of making it more "abstract," more capable of expressing "rationally" theoretical concepts. Richelieu sought out the most refined writers of the day and corralled them into working for the government. In order to solidify his hold on the arts and to convert them into an aesthetic system that both corroborated and constructed the tenets of political absolutism, Richelieu creates several national "academies" the foremost of which the "French Academy" was the first to be founded in 1635. The Academy had as it mission to oversee the "purification" of the French language and to pass aesthetic judgment on the various plays, poems, and "novels" submitted to it. In this way Richelieu sought both to dominate all artistic production in the kingdom while at the same time stifling any ideological and or stylistic dissent.

The Cardinal, himself, the author of spiritual and political treatises, was, most interestingly for our purposes, a great aficionado of the theater. Not only did he have the first "modern" theater "à l'italienne" built in his Parisian palace (the "palais cardinal," later the "palais royal"), but he was said to be the author of several works for the stage. He was, of course, a major patron of some of the most prominent dramatists of the day, including the dramatist who was to revolutionize French dramaturgy and whose influence was to be felt not only in France but across Europe—Pierre Corneille.

Corneille like many members of his class (lawyers, merchants, physicians, theologians) was educated by the Jesuits in his home town of Rouen. A Jesuit education was highly regarded because of its strong insistence on rhetoric, logic, and a sure knowledge of Latin and the Latin classics. The Jesuits had long relied on theatrical productions in their

FIGURE 0.1: Portrait of Pierre Corneille (Rouen, 1606–Paris, 1684), French dramatist and writer. Engraving. Photo by De Agostini Picture Library/De Agostini Picture Library/Getty Images.

education; at first plays in Latin on classical and biblical subjects were performed by the students, and later plays (in Latin) scripted in imitation of the ancients became common in the academic curriculum. We know that Corneille was quite a brilliant Latinist during his school days, and we can assume that it was in great part thanks to his education that his interest in the theater was initially kindled. Despite following his family's tradition in becoming a lawyer, Corneille's passion for the theater pushed him to try his hand at writing. Rouen was a major commercial and printing center with traveling theater troupes performing there regularly. After one performance, it is said, Corneille consigned an early play to one of these traveling companies that took the play (a comedy) to Paris where it was performed successfully. From then on Corneille continued to supply the Parisian stage with his comedies that met with greater and greater acclaim. It was in 1635, however, that Corneille first tried his hand at tragedy, with his version of the Medea myth.

*Médée*, Corneille's first tragedy was written at a critical moment in the debates about what a "proper" tragedy should be. Although *Médée* was not proper it did establish some of what will become the hallmarks of the great tragedies that would follow. It is interesting that for his first foray into tragedy Corneille chose one of the most resonant familial myths of ancient Greece, with at its center what one might call a conflict between civilization and savage nature. Medea, a princess of Scythia, a land which for the Greeks was situated at the confines of the known world, a land of savagery and magic, is first seduced by Jason in his quest for the golden fleece and then is brought back by him to Greek civilization—Argos. When a more tempting political opportunity appears to Jason—marriage into a powerful Greek dynasty—he abandons Medea, who had sacrificed all for him, to destitution and banishment. As we know, Medea with her supernatural powers will wreak havoc on the Greeks and murder the children she had with Jason. At the tragedy's end Medea, having brutalized the "civilized" society that betrayed her, flies away in her dragon-drawn chariot.

As Corneille last draws her in the penultimate scene of the tragedy, Médée is no longer the wife, no longer the mother, but she becomes again a mythic, supernatural force, a force that has destroyed the family which, as the basic unit of "civilized" life, should be seen as the triumph of nature over culture. More important, however, for the ideology of tragedy that will dominate French neo-Classicism, we are left with the image of this vengeful, irrepressible female force. Free and uncontainable, Médée, the wild woman, becomes the original object of desire and fear whose repression will constitute the political and sexual tension of the great tragedies to come. These tragedies reflecting the structures (and fears) of Classical patriarchy, always show these structures to be teetering on the brink of an abyss ready to fall into death and chaos.

Although *Médée* had only a tepid reception, Corneille's next play, *Le Cid* (1636) was a revolutionary triumph ushering in a radically new moment in theater history. The play, in its first iteration dubbed a "tragi-comedy," became in its second simply a "tragedy." While *Le Cid* was publicly acclaimed a masterpiece, its young hero seemingly embodying an entire (aristocratic) public's values and ideals, the play fared less well in the judgment of Corneille's rival playwrights. Perhaps envious of the enormous success of *Le Cid*, Corneille's learned challengers accused the play of being simply a plagiarized version of the Spaniard Guillén de Castro's *Las Mocedades del Cid* (1618), of not following the rules—the three unities of time, action, and place, and of ignoring both the dictates of verisimilitude and decency ("les bienséances"). The debates were so heated that Cardinal Richelieu stepped in to ask his newly formed Académie to resolve the quarrel. The play was submitted to the judgment of the academicians, their very first task as a state institution, and as academicians are wont to do, they hesitated, delayed, argued, and finally emitted a judgment on the play that was indecisive. Although they recognized the great general beauty of the play and the attractiveness of its hero, Rodrigue, they did reprimand the author for not respecting the "rules" especially his unrealistic timing of the various events of the drama. Finally, and most interestingly, for our purposes, their severest condemnation was for the female lead character, Chimène, whom they described as "too sensitive a lover and too unnatural a daughter," adding, "we must admit that her morals are at the least scandalous if not actually depraved."[7] In other words, Chimène, a new Medea, the recalcitrant avenger of her father's and her own honor, troubles the order both of the play and of the socio-political system that would have her conform to its precepts of what is acceptable (that is subservient) behavior in women.

Corneille did not bother responding to the judgment of the Academicians. Instead he returned to his home in Rouen and wrote a new play *Horace* (1640) that was not only another great success, but this time, a "perfectly" crafted neo-Classical tragedy. *Horace* marks yet another revolution in the (early) modern theater. Intriguingly for his first "regular" tragedy, Corneille abandons the universe of myth for the stage of history. From here on in it is ancient history rather than myth that will supply Corneille with the themes for his tragedies (myth will be called upon in his "machine plays"). *Horace* recreates a familial/political struggle that marks the initial triumph of Rome over herself/same neighbor Alba, thus setting Rome on the path to universal conquest. The political struggles of the tragedy's characters are played out (bloodily) within the confines of two families whose members are intertwined by marriage and love. *Horace* will most forcefully represent what has become known as the "Cornellian dilemma": that is, a situation where the demands of the state are in direct conflict with personal desires and where the hero, faced with an impossible choice between his love and his duty, always resolves to sacrifice his own feelings for the greater good of the state.

FIGURE 0.2: The actor Jean-Baptiste Britard, known as Brizard, in the role of old Horace in *Horace* by Pierre Corneille (1606–84). Engraving, France, seventeenth century. Paris, Bibliothèque Des Arts Decoratifs (Library). Photo by DeAgostini/Getty Images.

Corneille himself states in his *Discours de l'utilité et des partis du poème dramatique* (1660) that the real aim of tragedy must always be a political struggle, where love has only a very secondary place: "Tragedy's dignity requires a great affair of State or some nobler and more virile passion than love." ("La dignité [de la tragédie] demande quelque grand intérêt d'Etat ou quelque passion plus noble et plus male que l'amour.")[8] Politics rather than passion will be the central concern of his plays but "politics," we note, is immediately sexualized by his use of the term "mâle" (virile). For Corneille, tragedy which must always be "political" must always at the same time represent those virile virtues embodied in all of his heroes. What this means, of course, is that Cornellian tragedy will always have to constantly represent rather traditional gender roles where the female characters are always portrayed as "divided," never able to conform to the ideological imperatives of a world of the absolute, never one but always (at least) two.

Corneille continued to be the dominant force in French theater well into the reign of Louis XIV. After *Horace*, he wrote two other of France's most famous tragedies. The first, *Cinna ou la clémence d'Auguste*, represents a famous moment in Roman history when the emperor Augustus learns of a plot to assassinate him fomented by some of his most trusted and loved relations. While at first outraged and deeply wounded, Augustus is determined to have these traitors executed. Later, listening to the advice of his wife, Livie, he opts instead for clemency. Following Seneca (*De Clementia*) and Montaigne (chap. Xxiii of the first book of the *Essais*) Corneille uses this historic event to devise a new type of tragedy—a tragedy without bloodshed. This is not to suggest that the play shies away from violence, but, as required by the rules of propriety, the violence in the description of those scenes from the Roman civil wars that traumatized the protagonists of the plot against the emperor is always rhetorically reproduced in dialogue: it is recounted rather than represented.

What is new in *Cinna*, and what is perhaps so unsettling, is the greater subtlety Corneille brings to this, his second "Roman" tragedy. When we consider, for instance, that *Cinna* was composed at the same time as *Horace*, it does seem shocking that the two plays project a glaringly different representation of the tragic. Compared to *Horace's* white-hot fury, with its descent into the abyssal sacrifice of familial blood, *Cinna* appears as a strikingly "pallid" tragedy. For the first time in Corneille's dramatic oeuvre we are spectators at a tragedy that appears to skirt around the "tragic": there is no blood shed in this play, and no expiatory victim dies so that a new state may rise from this immolation.

It would, however, be an error to judge the tragic of *Cinna* on this basis. For here, in the most conflictual of plays, we witness Corneille's audacious redefinition of tragedy and the tragic. *Cinna* presents an insidiously clever articulation of a new tragic vortex. It is a vortex of rhetorical illusion which draws into its own center, in ever descending "spirals of power and pleasure" ("des spirales où plaisir et pouvoir se renforcent"), the diverse demands of sexuality and politics.[9] It produces a violence so great, yet so subtle, mutilation so total, that death can be omitted without in any way diminishing the shattering effect the play exercises on its audience. In *Cinna* Cornellian tragedy truly becomes "cosa mentale." By not giving in to his thirst for revenge, Auguste, who had up to now only been the "master of bodies," becomes the "master of hearts." He breaks out of a system of repetition that had condemned Rome to constantly replay her internal strife in dissension and fragmentation and thus constitutes a new order of history where because of his "generosity" his erstwhile plotters become his most devoted allies; instead of a renewal of Republican zeal, all is now sacrificed to the glory of the Monarch. Whether or not Napoleon was a good judge of the theater, and whether or not he was correct in interpreting Auguste's inviting Cinna to be his "friend," as the "feint of a tyrant," his judgment is emblematic of the trend that interprets *Cinna* as a classic demonstration of the seductions of totalitarianism.

Once again, however, we must remark that, in all of these plays (including the last of the four "great" tragedies, *Polyeucte*), the motivating dramatic tension of the plots revolves around politics and sexuality, where the heroines' refusal to accept masculine "logic" motivates the conflicting actions of their male counterparts. Camille in *Horace*, Emilie in *Cinna*, and Pauline in *Polyeucte* following Chimène in *Le Cid*, all, in one way or the other, represent the stumbling blocks, by their adamant refusal to toe the absolutist line, to accept the dictates imposed upon them by their societies. They threaten the stability of the world-order that, on one level, the plays seem to celebrate. These dangerous female characters will only grow in stature and destructive power as Corneille's career extends into the 1660s and 1670s (he dies in 1684). In his later tragedies, the male characters seem to lose their total self-control, their indestructible self-confidence. In fact, as one of the most important scholars of Corneille puts it, there seems to be an "inversion" of roles as the female characters (in *Rodogune, Pertharite, Nicomède, Suréna, Tite et Bérénice* to name only the most prominent) seem to become more decisive, more domineering, and more virile, while the male protagonists slip into indecision and weakness.[10]

Corneille remained a powerful presence in France and in Europe. The first translations of his plays appeared in England in the 1660s and certainly influenced the course of English discussions of "classical" art (Dryden). Translations quickly followed in German, Dutch, Spanish, and Italian. The influence of the French tragic stage spread across Europe, eventually replacing native traditions and imposing neo-Classicism as a European norm.

But, Corneille, although the most popular and successful dramatist was not alone, and certainly, as the century progressed and a new king and his reign replaced the old court of Louis XIII, another revolution in tragedy took center stage and challenged, for the first time, the pre-eminence of Pierre Corneille. It was not a challenge that Corneille and his supporters took lightly, and it was a dispute that not only engaged aficionados of the theater, but, in a state where politics, art, and religion were never clearly separated this confrontation, had social repercussions that affected a large part of the well-educated population.

Corneille was educated by the Jesuits and he remained faithful to them and their teachings throughout his life. The Jesuits, however, were only one part of the rather complicatedly diverse religious makeup of Counter Reformation France. In the seventeenth century, France was the battleground of varied Catholic orders vying for predominance in the general movement of religious reform. New religious orders, both for men and women, came into prominence and often into conflict. Perhaps the most famous of these religious controversies was described by the mathematician, philosopher, and consummate genius, Blaise Pascal. Pascal's family was intimately involved in one of the more austere Counter Reformation movements—Jansenism—that was to play a large role in the education and psychological formation of the man who was to become Corneille's greatest rival, Jean Racine.

Jansenism presented a rather somber view of the human condition that was radically at odds with the Jesuits. In one of the most famous theological treatises of the century, Pascal's *Lettres Provinciales* (1657), Pascal savagely (and comically) pits an orotund Jesuit defending his company's approach to human sin (unsurprisingly Jesuitical) against the more acerbic defender of Jansenism's approach to the same topic. Although the book is famous for being the first serious theological treatise written in French, what is more

FIGURE 0.3: Sketch of the stage costume of the character Emilie in *Cinna* by Pierre Corneille (1606–84). Engraving, seventeenth century. Paris, Bibliothèque Des Arts Decoratifs (Library). Photo by DeAgostini/Getty Images.

important, it seems to me, is the rather bleak vision one can glean from the debate, a vision of the human condition (without the belief in God) as a dire one. This tragic view of humanity is even more dramatically voiced in the enigmatic, quasi-"mystical" passages of Pascal's *Pensées* posthumously published in 1670. These "thoughts" on religion, on the condition of mankind cut off from a hidden God, alone in an infinite universe, miniscule beings in an unfathomable world, represents one of the greatest philosophical traditions of the seventeenth century, a tradition that will be embraced by philosophers and theologians up to the present day.

What is potentially of great interest to the "tragic" view of the human condition, a view that sees fallen man thrown into a world of divine absence, is its probable influence on the greatest of French tragic dramatists, Jean Racine, who was raised in the Jansenist

FIGURE 0.4: Portrait of the poet Jean Racine (1639–99). Found in the Collection of State Hermitage, St. Petersburg. Photo by Fine Art Images/Heritage Images/Getty Images.

community of Port Royal.[11] Jansenism derives its name from Cornelius Jansen, bishop of Ypres who published a dense theological treatise on Saint Augustine, the *Augustinus* (1640). This theological plea for a return to the teachings of Augustine and a more abstract spiritual relation to what was supposed to be a more "original" form of Christianity, with a rather pessimistic view of humanity's fallen nature, was almost from its initial publication the object of controversy and attack by the more established Church hierarchy. The royal government, in turn, did not look favorably at a dissident branch of Catholicism that struck many of the major Catholic leaders as heretical, preaching a form of austerity and predestination that seemed dangerously close to Protestantism. Even more dangerous in the eyes of the French state was the potential threat that this dissident doctrine posed to royal authority.

The Jansenists had a rather grim view of the human condition. Man was born predestined to damnation or (less probably) salvation. Only the mysterious workings of grace could save an individual living in a fallen world. The community of nuns and lay gentlemen of Port Royal des Champs (the central community of Jansenism before the establishment of a convent in Paris) was constantly under siege. At the same time the community managed for many years to attract a society of exceptionally learned men ("les solitaires de Port Royal") who, coming from the Parisian elite, chose a life of work and contemplation. They established near the monastery schools that introduced new forms of education, logic, and grammar. What this meant for the young Racine was an innovative, if strict, education in the humanities, in rhetoric, in dialectics, and most importantly, in ancient Greek. Racine was one of the few educated men of his day who actually had an excellent command of Greek. This enabled him to read, in the original, the works not only of the major philosophers, but the tragedies of Aeschylus, Sophocles, and Euripides. The latter, "the most tragic" of the ancients, became Racine's preferred model.

Racine's interest in the theater did not sit well with his former teachers at Port Royal. It was certainly a shock to his aunt who had been a "spiritual" mother to the young Racine during his years at Port Royal and who, when she learned of her nephew's engagement with the theater, begged him to give up these "worldly" pursuits that surely meant his eternal damnation and to return to the teachings of Port Royal. Racine's brutal response to his former teachers and to his aunt mark his break with Port Royal and his decision to pursue the theater as a means of making his way in this fallen world. But although the rupture with his past was violent and his career as a playwright and courtier glorious, the tragic view of life inherited from his past, the belief in man's inability to resist his fate (predestination), was nevertheless to play a central role in the tragic vision of Racine's seductive masterpieces which mark yet another revolution in the history of the theater.

In his celebrated essay, *On Racine*, Roland Barthes tells us that Racine is "the greatest French writer." Paradoxically, Barthes writes that Racine is a matchless dramatist because the Racinian text is "an empty critical cipher," "a blank space, eternally offering itself to interpretation."[12] How is it, we might ask, that tragedies written for a society so different from our own can still manage to attract and move theatergoers not only in France but world-wide? While Racine's great creations are surely of their time, they are not limited to the socio-political world for which they were initially created. It would be a mistake to read tragedy as the mere reflection of social reality. The theater critic, Anne Ubersfeld reminds us that such an interpretation contains at least two important critical fallacies:

> We must be mindful of two dangers: first of all considering the work merely in respect to its immediate connections, to its socio-political conditions, because that would be to subject it to what it isn't, to make of it a document rather than a production. Next would be to think there is an automatic relation between social structures and the works of art. ... That would be to imagine that social structures are simple and reducible to class relations or economic infrastructures, and it would be forgetting the infinite dialectical complexity of society on all its different levels.[13]

Perhaps the longevity of Racine's plays, stem from the seductive sonority of his verse coupled with tragic plots whose mythic echoes profoundly resonate in the audience's own "inner theater" of unconscious fantasies? Racine wrote seven profane tragedies between 1667 and 1677 dealing with subjects taken from Greek mythology, Roman history, and even, rather contemporary (although taking place in Constantinople geographically distant) events.[14] His tragedy was a revolutionary departure from the reigning plays of Corneille. Whereas the latter had made politics rather than romance the central concern of his tragedies, Racine, reflecting a new and different sensibility, a sensibility that found a profound echo in the new generation of theatergoers, creates a tragedy of passion, desire and death—or in more academic terms, "une tragédie galante."

*Andromaque*, Racine's first great tragedy was as revolutionary for its time (1668) as *Le Cid* (1636/7) was in its while laying out what will become the celebrated schema of all Racinian tragedy; character A loves character B who loves character C who, in turn, loves character D who is dead. In other words, we have tragic situations where any sort of reciprocated desire is blocked and where exacerbated frustration leads to aggression and death.

This is, of course, the situation in *Andromaque* where the title character, a prize of war, is loved by her captor, Pyrrhus whose father, Achilles had killed Hector, Andromaque's husband and who himself has already been promised in marriage to another, Hermione. Hermione, in turn is spurned by her fiancé and turns for revenge on her erstwhile aspirant, Oreste, doomed son of Agamemnon and Clytemnestra and leader of a Greek emissary sent to demand the surrender of Andromaque's son, Astyanax. The tragic crux of the play turns around the impossible situation in which Andromaque is placed by Pyrrhus: either marry him or have the son whom she rescued from the destruction of Troy turned over to Greeks to be killed. A coalition of Greek kingdoms fear that Astyanax will grow up and rekindle their long-held rivalry that a horrific war has recently ended. In the annals of theater history, we learn that one of Racine's innovations in seventeenth-century tragedy is his bringing onto the tragic scene a child, either a virtual one like Astyanax an actual one like Joas (*Athalie*), but this child who is brought onto the scene of tragedy is summoned forth to be sacrificed. All of Racine's tragedies turn around the possible immolation of a child thus returning the tragedies of Classical France to the very origins (some say) of tragedy—the participatory spectacle of sacrifice.

While the locus of Racinian tragedy is always the family, this familial space has become acute in its narrowness and intensity. Paradoxically Racine's heightening and intensification of the tragic locus corresponds to what we might call a step backward in representation. Racine leaves the world of history so successfully exploited by Corneille and returns, in his greatest tragedies (*Andromaque, Iphigénie, Phèdre*) to the archaic world of myth, but not just any myth; as Philip Lewis has so amply demonstrated, all of Racine's plays are linked genealogically to the foundational myth of Oedipus, his family, and his progeny, with all the varied consequences of this tragic destiny.[15] Even those historic tragedies *Britannicus* and *Mithridate* or the biblical tragedies *Esther* and *Athalie*, by conjuring up as they do the unconscious terrors of familial sexuality, seem to exceed the picturesque qualities of the historic scenario and to plunge us into the frightening and terrifying world of Oedipal fantasies.

Curiously, although we know that Racine had annotated a copy of Sophocles' *Oedipus Tyrannos* and had begun his own version of the tragedy he, unlike Corneille, never completed his own adaptation of the play.[16] Nevertheless the echoes of the Oedipus legend, which, as Marie Delcourt has written, is the "most complete political myth of the Greeks" ("le plus complet de tous les mythes politiques") in which the question of sovereignty—of how to achieve and retain sovereign power—obviously resonated for the subjects of a powerfully seductive absolute monarch.[17]

*Phèdre*, Racine's greatest tragedy and one of the West's supreme dramatic creations marks the apogee of French neo-Classicism. Basing himself on Euripides' *Hippolytus*, Racine rescripts the ancient myth into a tragedy of divine vengeance wreaked by Venus on the entire female line of the Sun. In order to punish the Sun for revealing her and Mars' illicit love affair to the laughter of all the Olympian gods, Venus puts a curse on all his female descendants. They are made to suffer from "unnatural" lust. In the case of Phèdre, the Sun's granddaughter, she is afflicted, notwithstanding all her best efforts to escape it, with a lustful passion for Hyppolite, her husband's son. Despite all her attempts to avoid the object of her unnatural desire, Phèdre is caught up in the inexorable web of the plot where the curse of the Gods, or destiny, or predeterminism, leads all of the major characters into a vortex of illicit passion and from there to their death. The moral and ethical dilemma posed by the play revolves around questions of predestination and freewill. Regardless of all her exertions, Phèdre appears from the very beginning doomed to her fate. Yet, in the convoluted dynamics of the plot, the question remains is she also guilty of an innocent's death?

The tragedy would seem to ask questions that are at the very heart of Jansenist theology. Does this, Racine's last profane tragedy, signal his return to Port Royal? Is Phèdre, "a Christian for whom grace was denied," or is the play rather, a Hellenizing tragedy of hubris? Containing some of the most seductively beautiful verses in the annals of French poetry, *Phèdre* is one of the very few works in the Western tradition that can rival the loftiest tragic creations of the Greeks. Racine's first biographer, his son Louis, writes that Racine also thought *Phèdre* his greatest work and compares it, interestingly, to Sophocles' *Oedipus*, telling us that "the character of Phèdre is like that of Oedipus' or those uncommon subjects that are not the creation of poets but rather must be supplied by either myth (legend) or history."[18] While trying to account for the latter play's lasting fascination, Freud writing in 1900 opines that "If *Oedipus Rex* moves a modern audience no less than it did the contemporary Greek, one the explanation can only be that its effect does not lie in the contrast between destiny and human will, but is to be looked for in the particular nature of the material on which that contrast is exemplified."[19] In other words, it is the matter of the tragedy, passion, calumny, and murder committed in the tightly restricted confines of the family that continues across the centuries and despite enormous social and political changes to resonate in contemporary audiences.

By the time Racine had reached the height of his art he along with other members of the French elite were engaged in a rhetorical battle with a new theatrical form that challenged the pre-eminence of "spoken tragedy." Opera, a new dramatic genre inherited from Italy, but reformed for French tastes by J.B. Lully, the official court composer of Louis XIV, had begun to rival, in popularity, the more traditional tragic productions. Lully with his librettist, Philippe Quinault, created some of the most popular dramatic productions of the latter seventeenth century. Taking their subject matter from both Greco-Latin mythology and from the courtly epics of the Italian tradition, their major operas aimed to rival the great works of Corneille and Racine. These "musical" ("lyrical") tragedies while treating serious, "noble" subjects, often did not have a typically "tragic" ending. Death did not necessarily haunt the stage of these tragedies. The "operas" did, nevertheless, enjoy—and this well into the eighteenth century when renewed by J.P. Rameau and later, when summoned to France, by C.W. Gluck—great favor both at court and in Paris. Nevertheless, for opera to attain a truly tragic dimension one would have to wait until the early 1800s and opera's triumph in the hands of Italian and German composers.

Racine and his allies had little truck with this new form of theater. Boileau mocked Quinault and defended the deep seriousness of the classic tragedy in his satires. Unfortunately, for the proponents of the great tradition of "spoken tragedy," after the triumph of *Phèdre*, Racine, for reasons we will never quite know, decided to abandon the theater. Did the Jansenist echoes we can perceive in *Phèdre*, signal a spiritual crisis in Racine? Was he determined to leave behind his too "worldly" pursuit of honors and applause, or had he simply achieved the goals he had always pursued—a secure position at the court and the favor of the king who bestowed upon Racine (and Boileau) the position of "historiographer?" Twelve years passed before Racine returned, at the request of Mme de Maintenon, to the theater. Louis' morganatic wife, Madame de Maintenon, had established at Saint-Cyr a school for the poor daughters of the aristocracy and she asked Racine to write some "edifying" plays based on biblical subjects to be performed by the young ladies. Racine took up his pen, once again. His two "biblical" tragedies, *Esther* (1689) and especially *Athalie* (1691) were performed by the young ladies of Saint-Cyr, the first a great court spectacle, the second in more restricted setting, and met with the general approbation of the court. These plays, however, had to wait until well into the eighteenth century before they were given a public performance. *Athalie*, considered by many to be one of Racine's greatest creations was not given a public performance until 1716, and *Esther* (where Racine introduced a chorus in imitation of ancient Greek tragedy) was performed for the first time in 1721.

FIGURE 0.5: Sketch for a stage costume from *Athalie* by Jean Racine (1639–99), performance from 1779 at Comédie-Française. Engraving, eighteenth century. Paris, Bibliothèque Des Arts Decoratifs (Library). Photo by DeAgostini/Getty Images.

Racine and Corneille (and here we may even include Corneille's younger brother Thomas [1625–1709], a successful playwright in his own right) continued to reign over the theater well after their deaths. Their fame and influence extended well beyond the borders of France, imposing the neo-Classical style with its plots that dealt with the tragedies of great kings and its imposition of the unities of time, place, and action, as well on the playwrights of England, Italy, Spain and as far away as Russia. In France, any new dramatist had to measure him (or her) self against these giants if they wished to gain any renown of their own.

Recently scholars of the period have underlined that "tragedy" was not the sole purview of the male writers who have traditionally been signaled out for their work. We now can appreciate the writings of several female playwrights whose dramas were performed on the Parisian stage to much acclaim. The most prominent "female tragic writers" were perhaps Marie-Catherine de Villedieu (1640–83), who besides her short novels wrote tragi-comedies and one tragedy (*Nitétis*), and Catherine Bernard (1662–1712) whose tragedies (*Laodamie* and *Brutus*) were quite successful on the Parisian stage and were produced well into the eighteenth century.

There are too many minor playwrights who created "tragedies" for the stage for us to go into any detail for each one. We should, however, mention if only in passing P.J. de Crébillon, a successful dramatist whose tragedies are known for their macabre and often violent peripeteia and who, for a time, was a rival to the next great French tragic dramatist, Voltaire.

FIGURE 0.6: Engraving from 1833 featuring François-Marie Arouet, better known as Voltaire (1694–1778). Photo by traveler1116/DigitalVision Vectors Collection/Getty Images.

François-Marie Arouet, who would take the pen name Voltaire by which he is remembered, was born in Paris in the twilight years (1694) of Louis XIV's reign. The period of his youth is marked by a disaffection of the French populace with the old king's ruinous attempts to impose French hegemony through wasteful wars and with what was seen by a new generation as a tiresome imposition of outdated and restricted religiosity. With the decline of the king, artistic and intellectual life no longer sought patronage at Versailles but rather in the capital. Paris became once again the center of intellectual discussions of novel theories of art, politics, and philosophy. The spirit of contestation that had been under Louis XIV's rule more or less contained, found new avenues of expression during the period of his decline. Under the government of his successors intellectual fermentation spread not only in Paris but in London, Edinburgh, and throughout the continent. The "Enlightenment," the exchange of new and revolutionary ideas about personal freedom, representative forms of polity and society, was accompanied by an ever-increasing freedom of artistic creation. Although Voltaire was instrumental in communicating to the French the ideas of religious tolerance he had found in England, he was also intrigued by the work of several Restoration dramatists he encountered in London.

The most prominent English dramatist John Dryden (1631–1700) whose work will be discussed in more detail in the following chapters of this volume, was also the English dramatist who adapted some of the concerns of French neo-Classicism onto the London stage in his tragedies *Aureng-Zebe* (1676) or *All for Love, or the World Lost* (1678). Along with his poetry, translations and critical theories, Dryden was perhaps the most influential man of letters of the Restoration: he was England's first poet laureate and the author of poetry, theater and interestingly for our purposes, of critical treatises on "dramatic poetry." His treatise *Essay on Dramatic Poesie* (1668) was an attempt to define English dramatic production as independent of both the ancient dramatists and the dominant French model. In his most famous tragedies, however, the sway of France's insistence on rhymed verse and obedience to the Aristotelian dictates demonstrate his knowledge of and conformity to contemporary France's dramatic triumphs.

Dryden's influence on Voltaire has been the subject of debate among specialists of the period, but whether there was a direct inspiration or not it seems reasonably certain that Voltaire's stay in England and his positive impression of English society cannot have left him indifferent to a playwright who was being compared in influence and power to Shakespeare.

Voltaire became the spokesman for a progressive movement that clamored for the liberation of Europeans from what he and many other leading minds of the day considered outmoded forms of governmental and religious repression. Although a multi-talented satirist who used epic poetry, novellas, histories to flood European culture with his activist theories, it was the theater, and more specifically the tragic theater that was his most acclaimed form of public resistance.

Although it now strikes us that Voltaire's didactic tragedies are dramatically unconvincing, during the eighteenth century he was extolled as a "god" of the tragic theater, the equal to both Racine and Corneille. Voltaire's first theatrical success was his own version of *Oedipus Tyrannos* (1718) and this success continued unabated until his death (1778) the year of his return to Paris and his "apotheosis" as the supreme tragic writer of his age. Using "tragedy" he gave voice to his ideas of religious and political intolerance in such plays as *Zaïre* (1732) and *Le Fanatisme ou Mahomet le Prophet* (1736). While these plays were extremely popular in their time, they now appear to us too moralizing to have any real dramatic impact.

FIGURE 0.7: Engraving from 1834 featuring John Dryden (1631–1700). Photo by traveler1116/E+ Collection/Getty Images.

While Voltaire's theater enjoyed continued popularity, it became clear that a new type of drama was beginning to compete for the public's attention. One of Voltaire's contemporaries and sometime collaborator, Denis Diderot, author of philosophical novels, editor of the *Encylopédie*, art and theater critic, started publishing his own views on the new type of drama that was to gain the upper hand in the latter part of the century. According to Diderot what he saw as the decline of the theater of his day was due to the inadequacy of that theater to address contemporary concerns in a manner that would appeal to a modern theatergoing audience. As this audience was no longer concerned with purely aristocratic values, the modern theater should, according to Diderot, present dramas that responded to the lives of the common man with both a moral and a civil lesson. Diderot's "drame bourgeois" was meant as a remedy for a theater that had lost its way. What evolved from Diderot's theoretical writings on both the "actor" and the role of the theater was a break from what had become a sterile "académisme" that Diderot rightly saw as alienating to a contemporary audience. While Voltaire had written condemning the "barbarity" (and also the "sublimity") of Shakespeare, blaming him for his lack of civilized "taste," Diderot and his German contemporary G. Lessing in his *Hamburg Dramaturgy* of 1767–9, both argued for precisely the freedom from "taste" as it had been defined by the followers of the great French tradition of Corneille and Racine. Both, each in his own way, argued for a freer, more contemporary theater, a theater more responsive to the concerns of the new "enlightened" spectator. Each of these two theorists also wrote dramas that marked a decided departure in the history of the drama: Lessing's *Nathan the Wise* (1779) is perhaps his most well-known play outside of his native Germany, where nevertheless he is credited with reviving a living "national" theater, while Diderot's *Le Fils naturel, ou Les épreuves de la vertu* (1757) and *Le Père de Famille* (1758), known as bourgeois dramas, marked the beginnings of a new type of theater midway between tragedy and comedy, which in the nineteenth century would triumph on the stage as "melodrama."

It would be an understatement to say that the French Revolution changed many things, including it would appear the very notion of both "tragedy" and the "tragic." While the Revolution itself saw a proliferation of many "revolutionary" inspired tragedies, all of which sought to inspire proper feelings of democratic indignation about the abuses of the Old Regime and against any counter-revolutionary tendencies fueled by both native and foreign reactionary forces, the most radical revision in our conception of tragedy came not from France but from those foreign onlookers of the Revolution's terror.[20]

Recent scholarship has underlined the shift in our conception of tragedy in the philosophy and theory of German romanticism.[21] Joshua Billings, for instance, goes so far as to suggest that at the end of the eighteenth and beginning of the nineteenth century, German writers redefined what tragedy was to mean for the new age:

> Around 1800, tragedy's way of meaning underwent a major shift, with broad consequences for thought on literature and philosophy.... Through the eighteenth century, tragedy had been considered primarily in rhetorical terms (as a way of producing a certain emotional effect), but since 1800 it has more often been considered in speculative terms (as a way of making sense of the human world).[22]

All of the major thinkers in the German tradition, Goethe, Schiller, Hegel, the Schlegels, witnessing the turmoil of the French Revolution and the ensuing effects of the Napoleonic wars, turned back to the Greek tragedies of Aeschylus, Sophocles, and Euripides in their own attempts to both understand the underlying political and psychological forces at play in Greek tragedy and to apply their new understanding to their own attempts at writing for the stage. One of the major innovations brought about by German thinkers (especially Hegel's writing on tragedy) was a re-evaluation of Sophocles' *Antigone* which, with its moral and ethical considerations, was elevated to rival *Oedipus Tyrannos*, as the model tragedy for the new "citizen" of post-Revolutionary Europe. The French Revolution's "republican" values were being swept across the continent in the wake of Napoleon's armies, and with these new-found liberties, the individual citizen subject was to discover both the inner tragedy of his/her own destiny and the tragic fate of both nations and ideals.

# CHAPTER ONE

# Forms and Media

*The Evolution of French Tragedy in the Seventeenth and Eighteenth Centuries, from Scenic Cruelty to the Dramatic Poem*[1]

CHRISTIAN BIET

Let's begin with some simple observations on French theater and French tragedy during the early modern period:

- On the one hand, the theater and, subsequently tragedy, provided a sort of public spectacle in the city: a collective event, an assembly, whose many sessions were eagerly attended by an unruly and hierarchized audience.[2] Yet, on the other hand, tragedy was lauded as a literary text with long-standing traditions and aesthetics: those followed by Corneille, Racine, but also by the theorist Aubignac, then Voltaire and all of the historical tragedy of the eighteenth century.
- Although tragedy is often exalted as the pinnacle of literature, it nonetheless competes or merges with other established literary forms. Pastoral and tragi-comedy at the beginning and middle of the seventeenth century; or superseded by other nascent genres such as the lyric tragedy of the second half of the seventeenth century, or the sentimental comedy (*comédie larmoyante* by Nivelle de la Chaussée) and bourgeois drama (by Diderot or Beaumarchais) in the eighteenth.
- On the one hand, tragedy is considered part of the Epic: its fiction reveals the way in which passions, political and amorous conduct wreak havoc on kings and heroes. Yet, on the other hand, it also appeals to the emotions: eliciting *pathos* and entering into the religious quarrels wrangling over the notion of destiny. Tragedy must thus both look to the past and use its great canonical works and unique register to enact a "classical" tradition that will later be deemed "normative," "learned," or "scholarly," while also looking to the future, by inventing new scenic postures and engaging in more contemporary oratory and axiological practices.

It is amidst such contradictions that tragedy is born, evolves, and then transforms with great success throughout the seventeenth and eighteenth centuries. Later criticism has too often led us to believe that tragedy was at first trying to find itself, then discovered its identity, and then fell into a slow decline. This is because the evolution of the tragic genre fascinated thinkers of the eighteenth century. Indeed, this was the true era of tragedy in terms of how many people were familiar with the genre, with Voltaire leading the charge and enthralling his contemporaries. Voltaire's authority can be traced throughout all of the great minds of the time, with a large number of writers of tragedy inventing new dramatic forms, while tragedies more generally continued to comment on the world and on politics, in particular, through historical and mythological references. If tragedy seems to disappear as a genre under the rebuffs of the romanticists of the 1830s, it has not been all doom and gloom since the death of Racine. Tragedy has always questioned the world in which it was housed, attracted large audiences to the theater, provided a considerable number of texts and was more than simply a repetition of the great playwrights of the seventeenth century. Tragedy has proved time and time again that theater could be epic; that a spectacle could be both far-removed from the world and intrinsically linked to it, asserting a moral, political, and social function that excited the passions of the spectator to make them engaged both in the theatrical domain and in society more generally.

It is perhaps because the theater had moved towards a more dramatic aesthetic—projecting the viewer into the show, constructing a kind of ideal fourth wall and taking more of an interest in conflicts between characters rather than those in the outside world—that tragedy adapted itself to such ideas, before surpassing them completely. As for the term "tragic," while there is a tendency to equate it with the event of tragedy, we will see that in the context of French tragedy its definition is somewhat recalibrated: "tragic," or as it was widely accepted in the early modern period, refers more to the formal features of the play than to any central event. It is about finding a means of representing the actions of kings and heroes, examining the ways in which they can be performed, and exploring how these figures posed many of the salient questions within contemporary debates, all in a specific dramatic mode. And sometimes, albeit rarely, a destiny that is controlled by an already problematic metaphysics is also at stake.

So, let's ask ourselves: in what way is the tragedy we have described thus far, which marks a departure from the canon that has been defined by the dominant aesthetic and political perspectives, etched into the entire European production of the early modern period (crudely, between 1590 to 1790)? If this departure is rooted in a purely French domain, why does the genre of tragedy carry such influence even when it is being contested? How is it connected to a specific mode of writing, performing, and thinking that renders this type of theater deeply reflexive and constitutively critical?

What we can easily determine is that the genre of French tragedy was circulating around Europe during this period, systematically being performed, translated, analyzed, esteemed, and widely recognized as a figuration of the world through scenic art. The questions it raised, especially the political issues about the legitimacy of the sovereign, political machinations, or just power in general, as well as those related to the human passions, are disseminated around courts and cities from London to Berlin, Stockholm to Madrid. In addition to these tangible manifestations of the world, politics, questioning the role of the sovereign and exploring the passions, tragedy also established a much more significant legacy. Besides the emotions elicited by each session, it prompted *a sound social conscience and a diligent, civic practice of criticism as a reflective activity*. In fact, in the seventeenth and especially the eighteenth centuries, the practice of judgment and analysis (based on taste, fashion, and on the aesthetic and political criteria that either brought the audience together or divided them) sat alongside their shared social spectatorial practice (we go to the theater to be seen and to meet other citizens). From then on, the theater—and tragic theater, in particular—becomes a place of civic and critical freedom. It was a site of contradiction as much onstage as within a dramaturgical system, as much in front of the stage as beyond it, given the amount of opinions, writings, and the profuse circulation of critical commentary. This is perhaps one of the idiosyncrasies of European theatrical art: its capacity for judgments; for aesthetic appreciation; stylistic criticism of theatrical trends; and for the unabashed encouragement of debate both within the plot and among the audience.

## 1. TRAGEDY AND CRUELTY IN THE EARLY SEVENTEENTH CENTURY COMPARED TO NOW

Contemporary theater has become bloody, cruel even. It takes a keen interest in violence and its representation. For instance, among the main shows of the Avignon Festival in 2005 were *The History of Tears* (Jan Fabre), *Puur* (Wim Vandekeybus), and *Anathema* (Jacques Delcuvellerie), which intersect theater, dance, music, cinema, and the plastic arts, and which all placed the body, suffering, and violence center stage. In the autumn of 2005, we find similar figurations of violence were visible in the staging of Botho Strauss' *Rape* by Luc Bondy (at the Ateliers Berthier at the Odéon Théâtre), based on Shakespeare's *Titus Andronicus*, but which went one step further in its dramatization of the rape. This was a *Titus Andronicus* in the style of Deborah Warner (whose *Medea* also tackled the representation of violence) and Lukas Hemleb, which has seen several performances in France and England over the past few years and which is now an essential part of a Shakespearian corpus tackling scenic horror.

If classical theater (as it is understood in France and as it has been represented since the second half of the seventeenth century) has managed to put bloody crime into words, it does so at the expense of action itself. Yet, classical tragedy is derived from an erstwhile form of tragedy, which, from the end of the sixteenth century to the first thirty years of the seventeenth all across Europe, really did seize its spectators with a terrible, bloodcurdling portrayal of the most heinous crimes. Given that this article is concerned with classical tragedy, we must also devote a few pages to its original form, as this illuminates a great deal about how theater is represented today: a theater haunted by a violence it endlessly sought to dramatize.

Only when Italian tragedy managed to theorize horror as one of its constitutive components; when Elizabethan England started to perform and publish the works of Marlowe, Shakespeare, and John Ford; when Spain, in the *corrals* and in the streets, became acquainted with the passion plays, the *auto-sacramentales*, and the *comedias* of the Golden Age, most notably with Lope de Vega, Tirso de Molina, and Calderon; when the first Dutch tragedies appeared in Amsterdam, Utrecht, and The Hague and then, following the bloodshed of the sixteenth century, when the whole continent sought an outlet for such horror and terror, did French tragedy also begin to partake in this violent movement.

These European tragedies mark the rebirth of theater after the wars. When dramatized onstaged and mounted onto the theatrical scaffold of the city, the striking effects of these tragedies seem to spring out and captivate a wildly diverse audience, without us ever being able to really measure the impact. What is clear, however, is that this rowdy and heterogeneous audience would have had to have been struck, seduced, and stunned to remain attentive. The stupefaction of sensations does not seem to hinder or prevent reflection; rather, fear and thought, staggering and reflection, horror and analysis, and pathology and distance, all help the violent action of the actors to mingle with the audience's own participation.

> "SCAFFOLD—Be sure upon mounting it to utter some eloquent words before dying"
> —Gustave Flaubert, *Dictionary of Received Ideas*

At the very end of the sixteenth century and the very beginning of the seventeenth, a new type of theater was created in France, and it is from this that our modern theater takes its model. This scaffold theater has been largely effaced from our memory; it has now been forgotten, or at least neglected, eclipsed by the national shadow of a sacrosanct Classicism that is much closer to the theater of its Elizabethan and Spanish contemporaries. The tragedies of Alexandre Hardy, Nicolas Chrétien des Croix, and so many other anonymous Normans, are simply invisible from the pedestal of national glories. This is despite the fact that Corneille was extremely interested in this "nascent" tragedy, and who even lauds Hardy's *Scedase, or Hospitality Violated* (1624) at the beginning of his 1660 *Discourse on Tragedy and methods of treating it according to probability and necessity*. But it is not the fact that this tragedy was in its infancy, nor the false belief that its barbary would need taming in the classical era that was at stake. Rather, the issue was the infinitely creative birth of the spectacle itself, the pleasure of experiencing all of its new theatrical forms, and the legal casuistry and tensions that produce them, interrogating the very notion of representation in the problematic and composite place of the theater itself. This was a question, quite simply, of the birth of modernity.

While the publication of the French corpus from the end of the sixteenth century to the beginning of the seventeenth has only just appeared (for example in *Theatre of Cruelty and Bloody Stories in France*), and already seems to be attracting a number of artists hoping to stage these plays, Shakespeare, Marlowe, and Tourneur have dominated our theater for many years now.

There has thus long been a history of violence on the stage. Yet, in each era, playwrights have managed to ensure that the affective and intelligible merge; that is, whether in the text or onstage, striking, violent images arrest the viewer while still giving rise to reflection and judgment. So, how to go about representing the sheer horror and terror of tragedy? This is a topic that is often tackled in contemporary European theater and presents no great departure from the Elizabethan or French tragedies from the beginning of the seventeenth century. However, to stage a play such as Shakespeare's *The Lamentable Tragedy of Titus Andronicus* presupposes that there was some consideration of how to represent the torrents of blood and perform a steady accumulation of violent scenes onstage (rather than on screen), without falling foul of the risible excesses of the Grand Guignol.

I aim to show that the theater that is inspired by early seventeenth-century tragedy is nowhere near as settled or determined as we try to make out. Rather, I want to argue that it reflects many of the questions that are pertinent to contemporary spectators and European theaters today. Namely, the vital issue of how to represent things and actions, and how to broach the axiological reflections that this type of theater demands. Despite seeming more foreign to us than Corneille or Racine, I want to suggest that this type of spectacle, which is so often treated as crude and archaic by French criticism, and yet which by those of Spain, those of England, and those of Germany as the very jewels on the crown of their national theater, has a great deal to teach us, posing many more questions with much greater profundity than we tend to let on. Gradually, French criticism extricated itself from centuries of myopic, blissful respect for the myth of Classicism, to encounter Shakespeare and Marlowe, and a little later, Lope and Tirso, all the while continuing to neglect the rich potential of its own national repertoire. We must erase the unfortunate term "pre-classicism," and even "baroque" in the French sense of the word too, in order to properly observe this new art form that imagines, suggests, plays with its own freedom and diversity without being shackled by the constraints of Classicism that appear thereafter. Perhaps we must redefine the outcast term *seventeenth-century baroque* in the way that our European neighbors understood it, just as Walter Benjamin defined it, as an *extension* rather than a *confrontation* of Classicism.[3] Above all, we must not be complicit in an erroneous chronology that implies that a period of supreme beauty follows this one, and that these tragedies are simply the clumsy nascent stages, or the confused laboratory, for the real tragedy that will find its feet later on.

This dramatic moment of the first years or decades of "the advent of a new art," replete with a new audience, actually presents a social phenomenon and establishes new sites of sociability. The end of the reign of Henry IV, the regency of Marie de Medicis and the beginning of the reign of Louis XIII all testify to the vibrant revival of forms of representation that adversaries of the theater neither expected nor hoped to see being performed in the city, on real tennis courts, or on city bridges. New burgeoning forms of representation slowly turned into well-established genres that exploited their plasticity to imitate other artforms: speech, inspired by the church pulpit and the judicial bar; other performing arts, including ballets, *entrées*, and royal entertainments; and finally, more macabre realities, like the deadly scaffold.

## *Experimental theater and a theater of excess: The deadly scaffold*

These elements offer a valuable springboard from which to read and evaluate both Hardy's theater and the "irregular" tragedy of the turn of the seventeenth century. Historically speaking, these plays are inextricably linked to the end of the Wars of Religion and to the end of the reign of Henry IV. Accordingly, they share an aesthetic and dramatic tendency to explore possible socio-political transgressions, while self-reflexively questioning their impact on the viewer (and less frequently, on the reader) without any theatrical conventions yet established. Keenly aware that this allegedly "baroque" tragedy belongs both to a general aesthetic trend of affect (these "bloody" or "tragic" stories have a great deal to do with the tragedy of the time) and to a much broader European movement (English theater on the one hand and Spanish and German Counter Reformation theater on the other), I will seek to determine how this spectacular, transgressive, and bloody lack of realism is able to achieve the following. To define the possible role of a secularized sovereign. To envisage *extraordinary* social conduct. To dumbfound the audience via astonishing violence. To engross them in representations of different mechanisms of transgression (moral, political, aesthetic); all this while using the antagonisms of both plot and poetry to plant a seed of doubt about the nature of pacified world, about the mystical unity of the state that is often re-instated at the end of the play, about the way in which the family and the law (mal)function, but also about the way in which the sovereign (whether this be a king or some abstract transcendental figure of sovereignty) is truly or realistically legitimate, and even on which principles such validity is based.

However, in order to do this, we must carefully choose examples that are steeped in visual drama with a *striking effect* that will thrill the spectator of this new civic theater. Action thus paves the way for a sort of projective theater which assembles extraordinary

FIGURE 1.1: Engraved illustration of Henry IV (1553–1610). Engraving from *Great Men and Famous Women: A Series of Pen and Pencil Sketches*, by Charles F. Horne and published in 1894. Digitally restored. Photo by bauhaus1000/DigitalVision Vectors Collection/Getty Images.

facts, rapes, murders, battles, suicides, while offering blindingly, terrifying events that demand that the spectator reflects carefully on the problems dramatized onstage. Narrative facts are tied to a long chain of cause and effect, organized according to their desired emotional impact on the spectator and provoking such anguish in the audience that begets their critical judgment. These are not mercurial tendencies; rather, they respond to the realism or truth of the time. These plays do not simply pile up the worst crimes imaginable simply in order to represent excess; rather, they envision a discontinuous linearity, punctuated by poignant moments which open up a debate that will then be played out on scene. It is the epic and hyperbolic dramatization of terrestrial disorder that captures the audience's attention and leads them to comment on such catastrophe and thus consider what the world around them could do to mitigate it.

To render such calamity visible, these plays must take place in an extraordinary site. And in order that this site is itself privileged, and that we absolutely have to go and see it, there must also be other remarkable sites nearby. Thus, in re-used spaces, in real tennis courts, mead halls, entertaining spaces, sport-halls, or polyvalent fully furnished rooms, the audience finds themselves faced with a new artform they try to understand using the familiar dramatic conventions they already know. But in this respect, theater is itself a new art, or rather, a burgeoning artform that offers a new way of representing the world in a particular place, at a particular social moment (the time of the performance responds to a broader theatrical practice which exceeds the brief time of the fiction, since it is also a moment of sociability), fixed in a concrete space inside the city (even more than in the court).

The audience thus sits facing a riser, or scaffold, that has been installed up high. This is a familiar scenographic space, inspired by the scaffolds that were located in many of the public places at the time. Indeed, it would be wrong to skim over the lexical, dramatic, and aesthetic proximity of these two types of scaffolds; yet it is useless to draw on all of the seventeenth-century texts which defined the scaffold as the platform on which convicts, theatrical characters, plays, and religious ceremonies were *executed*. Rather, the scaffold is actually an elevated scenographic device designed to give the public a better view of the three sites it denotes: first, a place of torture; then an area of the stage; and then the ritual altar. In its original meaning, the torturer and his victim play their roles and, as Furetière puts it in his 1690 *Dictionnaire universel*, it becomes "the small theater set up in a public square, on which criminals are beaten and gentlemen beheaded."[4] In that sense, it is a space upon which a very real "tragedy" is played out (a word that is often found in such cases since "tragic" equated to a "bloody scene" at the time). Its third meaning comes from the place on which a sacred ceremony is carried out, a mystical liturgy that represents the mystery of transubstantiation: the sacred transformation of the host into the body, or *corpus*, of Christ, in other words, the qualitative transformation of bread into flesh. Between those two is located the stage, used both to carry out sacrifices and represent the transformation of the body of the actor into the entity of character. Because of this, for a long time the stage on which actors played was referred to as the "scaffold." In this way, the scaffold never lost its initial meaning: that of an elevated, easily observable place, a tribune or platform, and which, by its very existence, is distinguished from those who watch, and distinguishes the viewing area from the performance area or the place of sacrifice.

In the high art of capital punishment, the stage provides a singular spatio-temporal locus of death as a judicial, social, justified, and legitimized ceremony, and a ritual intended to dramatize legal punishment, and celebrate the passage of the repentant convict hoping for salvation *via* atonement and rehabilitation. Condemned by the world, confessing before death, pardoned by God (the objective of confession), and then cut off from life, this strict ritual offers the executed convict the possibility of eternal life. Right at the heart of this classical schema of fault-accusation-confession-pardon-rehabilitation is the great scene of death, which occupies both a social and religious place: here is where the "salvation technique" (as Max Weber theorized) comes into its own. However, we might remind ourselves of those arguments we made at the beginning of this chapter. That this ceremony loses its religious, even sacred, character in order to offer a mode of secular or political atonement without having to sacrifice any of its ritualistic qualities. This is the first step towards judicial and social capital punishment: towards the idea that only society is capable of punishing and making an example out of a guilty party; and that this manifestation of legitimate and legal vengeance offers rehabilitation from the very moment when the convict renounces everything that makes them a citizen. Of course, this is just the beginning insofar as the sacred ceremonial and ritualistic signs, and the entire procedure of salvation of the soul, all doggedly resist the secularization and political deployment of capital punishment. Once again, we can start to make out a transition, a sort of problematic and ambiguous threshold on which tragedy will come to an end.

And at the same time, this ritual, scenographic transition, at once social, judicial, and ceremonial, offers a very real elevated spectacle and a series of effects that serve the purpose of moral edification (punishment as a means of convincing, for example), the ennoblement of the condemned (who becomes a hero), the perverse gratification of those who take pleasure in the sight of blood and in the suffering of their fellowmen (Saint

Réal, in 1672 in *De l'usage de l'histoire*, is certainly not the first to note this),[5] and even the most grotesque humor. To quote Corneille, we see on this raised space the "undisguised face" ("À visage découvert") of crime.[6] In so doing, the *capital* punishment that takes place on the scaffold cannot be disentangled from the actor's performance in a tragedy, given how frequently the term is used in relation to the theater. And just as the performance area becomes the space of a sort of performance-sacrifice on a raised platform and in front of an audience, the theatrical space itself represents the same space observed in the same way, but on a stage whose stated purpose is to represent the world: a decaying and comical world for farce, a heroic world for tragedy. So much so that it is this very death—whose bloody, ceremonial actualization in a public place is at once sacred (the passage to the eternal life of the sinful culprit), social (the punishment of the culprit), and aesthetic (the pleasure from the sight of blood or from the sight of someone really dying)—that provides the foundational stakes of tragic theatrical representation mediated through the fiction and the bodies of the actors. This is where we find the transition towards modernity, from the sacred and social ceremony to an aesthetic, political performance.

## 2. *TIMOCRATE*: THE GREATEST BOX-OFFICE SUCCESS OF TRAGEDY

From 1640 onwards (beforehand, and in particular in the twenty years prior, it was the spectacle of cruelty that was holding court) the primary affects that the playwrights of tragedy strived to elicit in the audience were as follows: weeping; admiration for the passions and for the extraordinary attitudes of the heroes; and the pleasure of analyzing the contradictions within the play that directly mirrored those in society at large. In order to illustrate these affirmations and to understand the norms of tragedy for a seventeenth-century audience a little better, we will turn our attention here to the most successful play of the time: Thomas Corneille's *Timocrate* (1656). This tragedy was well-thumbed and poured over in all of the gentlemen's salons well before it was staged. It was sponsored by the benefactor Duke of Guise—a well-reputed theater enthusiast who enjoyed ostentatiously dramatizing the novels he would read with great fervor. Galvanized by the trend of *preciosité*, this tragedy was an immediate hit, to such an extent that even Louis XIV and his court went to the Marais to see it! Eighty performances were staged over the first season alone (1656–7). Given that most successful plays at the time had barely more than fifteen performances, *Iphigénie* had forty, *The Pretentious Young Ladies* had forty-four, and *The School for Wives* had forty during its first season, it is not hard to deny that the considerable success of this tragedy brought almost the entire future audience of the genre to the theater.

What was it all about? Primarily, the archetypal riddle of a disguise narrative, just as it was popularized by the Spanish *Comedia* or in the "great novels" of Mlle de Scudéry or in La Calprenède's *Cleopatra* (an episode of which serves as a blueprint for the type of plot we are talking about). In *Timocrate*, Cleomenes, an unattached hero, is introduced to the court of Argos, which is at war with the Cretans. He befriends the prince Nicander—a subject of the queen of Argos—and becomes both adviser of the queen and a lover (he is loved by her) of the princess Eriphilus. In opposition to his many rivals, he is a lover who is all the more illegitimate because he is neither Argan nor a prince. At the same time, the prince of Crete, Timocrates, uses his position of military strength to challenge Argos to an ultimatum: to choose either to embark on a war or to accept the conciliatory solution of a matrimonial compromise in which he will ask for Eriphilus' hand in marriage. The queen of Argos, who must avenge the death of her husband who Timocrates has killed, refuses and contests Cleomenes' arguments in favor of pursuing peace in the region, deciding instead to betroth her daughter to the victor able to seize the king of Crete. During a battle where Argos has the upper hand, Timocrates' lieutenant, Trasilus, is taken prisoner, after which Timocrates takes the helm and his troops finally triumph over the queen's army. Having been taken prisoner by the Cretans, Nicander, a valiant Argan warrior, is suddenly freed by Timocrates (who he has never met) and arrives onstage. He becomes keenly aware of the Cretan sovereign's grandeur and magnanimity. Cleomenes also joins the stage, having been presumed lost, and renews his oath before the queen, states that he has Timocrates in his power, and demands the just reward for his act: the hand of Eriphiles. Bound by her oath, and yet aware that she cannot allow a princess to marry a foreign adventurer, the queen finds herself hesitating but ultimately prioritizing her matrimonial promise. While everything could conclude here at the end of the third act, thus allowing us to solve the riddle, Corneille invents a new twist that puts Nicander, the rival prince, loyal friend, and generous lover, center stage. Indeed, it is he who doubts the legitimacy of Cleomenes' maneuver and thus he who has Timocrates' lieutenant interrogated. He realizes that the prisoner of this mercenary hero is an imposter, confronts Cleomenes and Trasilus until the truth outs, and the queen, clairvoyant at last, realizes that Cleomenes and Timocrates are one and the same person. There is still a political dimension of the fable that remains unresolved: Argos is not ready to accept a Cretan who besieged them to be their king. Once again, it is Nicander who disentangles the situation: he delivers the keys of the city to Timocrates, allowing the Cretan prince to enter into majesty and to reign instead of the queen—who is impotent to carry out her oath and exert her revenge—and, finally, to marry Eriphiles.

Love and history, poignancy and subterfuge, a monarchic figurehead and a chivalric attitude are all woven together through the twists and turns of the play, structured by a riddle that the spectator must decipher through the actions of each character. The play is thus ultimately a sort of game that doubles up as a love story at once novelistic and political, a game that ends well, since the play offers a denouement full of emotional and civic harmony after the political upheaval with which it begins.

Just like many other literary works of the time, *Timocrate* managed to neatly condense the multifarious possibilities of other fictions, while also exploring the cause and effect of romantic and political situations *via* a dramatic structure of riddle and disguise, which then evolved into sentimental and political harmony. In this quagmire of manifold possibilities, all of which elicited great *pathos* from the audience and indulged their desire to muse on the world of Greats, the plot is fundamentally based on a dramatic irony: that the characters are ignorant of their fate, while the audience is already privy to it from the initial stage directions ("Timocrates, King of Crete, disguised as Cleomenes"). The secret is to make the audience guess the "truth" of what they are witnessing, to play with the spectator by moving them, surprising them, and guiding them through the different behaviors of the hero and other characters so that they learn how to solve the riddle. In addition, the spectator must be led to contemplate the political stakes of establishing peace and this is achieved through the gentle intertwining of love, friendships, tenderness, and political calculation. We cannot reproach Nicander for having betrayed his country and freed Argos, since it is all in the interest of his friend, his loved one, and securing peace for his people. After having proved how the initial situation was caused by a universe in which the fathers were at war, the continuation of the plot proves that the offspring settle instead for peace and choose romantic trysts, gallant subterfuge, and tender honor over conflict. Through honest calculation, *pathos*, even tears if necessary, and strength, Nicander strives to build a peaceful world through the *entente cordiale* of the marriage agreement. It is thus not only a love plot, nor a tragic map of the land of tenderness, but an eroticized policy (a term which René Demoris uses to speak about novels of the time), and a way to role-play peace in the face of a half-century of unrest, quarrels, and conflict that was all too familiar to the spectator.

Thus, the use of politico-amorous terms, which are quite specific to the romantic, chivalric, and tragic universe, come into their own. To be a prisoner or rival and embark on a conquest means to locate oneself in two different camps: warfare and romance; conflating state with sentiment; public with private. An extraordinarily tender and quixotic love must triumph over archaic hatred, through the acceptance of compromise, play, and honest subterfuge. And after having been seized by fear, then moved to tears (as shown by archival testimonies of the reception of the play), all while playing the game of trying to solve the riddle of the play, the spectator was also able to relate politically to this fable. They started to recognize that civil and international wars must be rejected as part of the violence of past troubles (civil conflicts and incantations of all sorts, the Thirty Years' War, and the European terrors); that countries must strive to secure peace through marital unions (France and Spain, for example, were in full negotiations over the marriage of Louis and Maria Teresa); that warlike heroism, steeped in all of its post-rebel nostalgia, must give way to kings who understand the importance of being a talented general, a fervent lover, and a national hero capable of cleverly camouflaging themselves so that their noble cause triumphs.

In Cleomenes and Timocrates, the figures of the warrior price and the romantic sophist coalesce and develop as one. The amorous mercenary becomes king, and the king is thus able to love. It takes 2,009 lines, a litany of novelistic and dramatic techniques, the formal influence of the "great novel," historic and chivalric short stories, as well as the *comedia*, to overcome the hatred with which the play begins. It requires all of this to remind us that

FIGURE 1.2: Engraving from "The Miseries and Misfortunes of War." Scenes from the Thirty Years' War. Wood engraving after an etching by Jacques Callot (1592–1635), Lorraine engraver. Published in 1878. Photo by ZU_09/DigitalVision Vectors Collection/Getty Images.

deeds depend on the heroic generosity and the passionate love we see not just in the king, but also in these Cretan kings: even if they are liars, their untruths seek to keep the peace by rejecting a Machiavellian approach that is too trenchant (note how swiftly the dishonest adviser Cresphontes is removed from the scene for this kind of scheming behavior) and by forging an alliance with an aristocratic elite—the honest Nicander, capable of betraying Argos in order to bring about monarchic harmony. This is how the Regents, thwarted by their archaic decisions, make way for a new Princely couple.

Perhaps after this brief foray into a tragedy which achieved the greatest possible box-office success, we have a slightly better understanding of how French tragedy does not put forth a tragic perspective in the Nietzschean sense of the term. Rather, this sort of tragedy indulges in complex structural forms and deeply emotional and political questions capable of bringing the audience to tears even at the height of the narrative tension, while also inviting them to ruminate on the governmental and monarchic hurdles trying to be resolved. This tragedy evinces fear as much as it does admiration. In the distance that such a spectacle requires in order to fully glean its many layers of meaning—that is, the satisfaction derived from such a harmonious ending, and the recognition that over the course of the plot, the status quo was challenged and political low-blows were eschewed—we realize that only the honest moves and legitimate subterfuges of the princes (whose legitimacy is contingent on the outcome achieved) can save the state while also satisfying romantic impulses. Still, the idea of an antiquated chivalric love will struggle to survive as tragedy develops. Racine, for example, may promulgate it in characters like Britannicus among other tender heroes But he will soon start to intensify the role of the destructive passions and towards the end of his career in plays like *Athalie*, will even forgo love as a new driving force behind his dramaturgy.

## 3. TRAGEDY AS EPIC THEATER

What the eighteenth century retains from this state of affairs is the central idea that tragedy is able to lay bare the human passions, to expose political conduct, and to show man and state at their most vulnerable. Because tragedy explores such extraordinary moments and tackles such rare, conflicting behaviors, the spectator finds themselves in the position of judge. Because tragedy introduces distance without sacrificing emotion, because it avoids awe as a way of identifying with the characters (it is precisely because I am *not* Phèdre that I am touched, and why I am able to apprehend her dismay and thus understand the plot), that this dramatic form enables intellectual reflection. Resting on an opposition between disorder and an order which does not necessarily lead to ultimate harmony (as Corneille remarked in his 1660 speeches, that this is not "a rule of the art, but a usage we have fully embraced"), tragedy indulges in a well-reasoned, impassioned spectacle that is also rich in poetic rhetoric: as we read in the preface of *Britannicus*, "what might have escaped an audience, may be detected by readers." All of these factors combine to produce a theater of questions—those directed *at* the spectator or questions posed *on their behalf*—about the world, family, law, the state, and finally, human nature itself.

"Art is not a land of plenty," Brecht used to say. Rather, it is a means of dramatizing the contradictions of the world through complexity, paradoxical problems, *agons*, or debates, which lend the spectator-reader the experience of leaving the theater happy. This is both an emotional satisfaction—having been moved, then rejoicing, the spectator sometimes even feels relief in the final scene (as Corneille claimed)—and an intellectual pleasure, since the spectator goes away with more questions than answers to ponder. Such factors are behind my decision to label this type of theater "epic" rather than "dramatic": it does not overlook the emotions, but does set up a critical distance; it dramatizes contradictions rather than conflicts; it endeavors to discover national secrets and human passions by unveiling them through action and poetic discourse; it is founded on a unique gestural and rhetorical code; spatially, it addresses the spectator rather than other characters onstage (each actor generally facing the audience); it respects a dramatic form that is both malleable and yet sufficiently robust to embed some basic theatrical constraints; and above all, it proposes an overarching meaning, which more often than not comes together in the denouement, without overriding the various hermeutic intersections and opposing interpretations that are brought together throughout the plot. And it is this epic and tragic theater—in the way we have described these genres thus far—that will be systematically performed over the course of the eighteenth century. After which point, these aspects will be diminished and slightly modified to pave the way for a dramatic and moral way of reading that yields to the charms of psychology and the pleasures of identification.

Allow me to make a brief clarification: I am certainly not intending to suggest that Brechtian theory was inspired by seventeenth-century French tragedy, nor that that he had a grandiose idea of what this genre was, nor that the seventeenth century had read Brecht! Regardless of what Borges might have to say on the matter ... The author of *A Short Organum for the Theatre* only saw this so-called "classical" theater through a German lens, and through the criticism that emerged at the eighteenth century and throughout the eras that followed. In other words, he saw it via a national French canonization on the one hand, and a rigorous German condemnation on the other. Furthermore, what he was able to glean about this tragedy made him think that its nobility, its "tragic" quality and its "psychology" transformed it into a form that was much closer, if not identical, to the dramatic theater he staunchly opposed. However, what he was not able to see, or, rather, what he was not able to read at the time, was that this theater resonated with many of his own categories and theoretical positions. Except that a seventeenth-century audience was far less easily manipulated than a twentieth-century audience, being more naturally inclined towards diverse forms of behavior, feeling emotion, and distance, attending shows, and reading tragedies without self-consciously having to justify it. If contemporary playwrights really did appoint their spectators and readers to be the judges of the plot and of its many facets and truths, then they were not reacting against a form of dramatic theater; rather, they were simply partaking in a new theatrical movement at the turn of the century and indulging in the theater as a sociable space, which would continue right until the end of the "Ancien Régime," or early modern period. Thus, epic theater has none of the trappings of Brechtian self-consciousness, but it was fully aware of its role and the fact that the questions it raised, providing that they were well positioned in the play and had an emotional impact, were far more interesting than any possible answers.

## *The political premise of tragedy in the eighteenth century*

Let's pick tragedy up where we left off: tragedy of the operatic and religious sort that we see in Racine's *Athalie*. Finally, a spectacular tragedy that knew to avoid a love plot in order to capture the audience's interest! This is certainly the grounds on which Voltaire championed the play. Love is generally diminished in eighteenth-century tragedy to make the genre conform to a canonical idea of the spectacle. Love will have to be returned to the majestic world of opera, or because it is becoming more specialized, psychologized, privatized, and considered as profoundly intimate, will be brought back to figure in "tearful comedy" (*comédie larmoyante*) and later in bourgeois drama. Despite a thirst for spectacle, politics, and current affairs, tragedy is no stranger to affect and emotion; indeed, it is quite the opposite. However, the eighteenth century differentiates the tragic *plot* from sentimental intimacy by insisting on the fact that tragedy only ever emphasizes the most extraordinary of the passions. Of course, this is part of the strength and interest of tragedy: its eminently spectacular triumph, the rich diversity of its formal exploration, the energy that reflects the time; but it is also part of its limitation, insofar as the extraordinary becomes increasingly challenged by the growing importance of the domestic, the familial, or, rather, of the private sphere in general.

According to the critics, tragedy would thus decline after Racine, breathe its last breath with Voltaire, and then die out, exhausted, at the end of the eighteenth century. We are skipping over quite a lot of work just to make the seventeenth century, once again, the unparalleled zenith of classical tragedy. It is as though France lost something after the great authors of the "Century of Louis XIV" had died. Thus, eighteenth-century French tragedy is called "neo-classical tragedy" in a manner that suggests that it obediently imitates Classicism, scholastically and without any inventive genius of its own. However, if there is a style in art called "neo-classical," it is more an aesthetic or pictorial effect that refers to the very end of the eighteenth century when there was a great fondness for allusions to classical antiquity, Latin history and mythological fables following the belief that these were the only arts able to sublimely transcribe the world and the morals of the time, while the outside universe was giving way to the birth of a new era.

To challenge this vision of the history of tragedy, long underpinned by arguments that are far more political than literary in nature, we would need to consider tragedy in the eighteenth century as far more esteemed than in the seventeenth, to realize that it produced a greater number of plays, playwrights, and successful tragedies (seventy-two tragedies were created between 1715 and 1750 at the Comédie-Française), and we would have to appreciate that Voltaire was recognized by all of his contemporaries as much more of a tragic author than an essayist. Tragedy in the eighteenth century remains a noble genre par excellence, attracting far greater audiences than for comedies staged at the Comédie-Française. All writers would hope to begin their literary career by penning a tragedy, as is testified by the early Voltaire's masterstroke *Oedipus* in 1718.[7] Of course, the great reference points are still Corneille and Racine who have their devotees, their critics, and we tend to take sides with one or the other: those that admire *Le Cid*, *Horace*, *Polyeucte*, *Rodogune*, *Cinna*, or *Heraclius* (the play with the most performances); and those that laud *Andromache*, *Britannicus*, *Iphigenie*, *Berenice*, and *Athalie*. But even among their supporters, Corneille and Racine are still not immune to critical misgivings. The eighteenth century was all too familiar with the repertoire that preceded it and thus was unable to purely admire its predecessors. It claimed ownership of them. Indeed, Crebillon the elder (1674–1762), with his nine tragedies (from *Idomeneo* in 1705 to *Triumvirat* in 1754), hoped to arouse pity in his viewers through the use of horror and pompously proclaimed that "Corneille conquered the earth, Racine the Heavens, all that is left for me is Hell." Concurrently, the works of Houdar de la Motte, de Belloy, Ducis, Lemierre, and, among other great authors, Voltaire from *Oedipus* to *Irene* (1778), permeated a whole century. It is thus important to appreciate that the tragic genre survived well into the mid-nineteenth century (the first work of Honoré de Balzac, for example, is a tragedy: *Cromwell, a tragedy in five acts and in verse*, 1819). In the end, it became a

Cornelian and Racinien heritage that was always being referred to and renewed through staging, performance, or scenography; by political work on the text; or even, by drawing on affect and psychological analysis, which then catalyzed a change in aesthetic, reception, and interpretation.

Thus, Age of Enlightenment tragedy is both in keeping with an older, re-appropriated genre, and in line with a contemporary genre that is the most respected, well-read, and formally innovative both in terms of dramaturgy and staging. Even if the codes of tragedy have not really changed (despite Houdar de la Motte's attempts to replace the Alexandrine with prose), even if we leave its pompous rhythms and the cadences of its versification, even if we are conscious that tragedy might only ever reproduce the same dramatic situations as the French tragic poets by indulging in a constant play of intertextuality, even if it always insists on portraying the noble, tragic story of characters who are on the margins of common humanity, without always integrating love into that narrative, tragedy is nonetheless aware of the importance of progress in art and in life more generally. In this vein, the eighteenth century does produce its own innovative masterpieces, while paying homage to the archetypes that preceded it. At first, with Campistron, then Crebillon, tragedy tried to inscribe the horror of massacres, incest, and monstrosities of any kind through classical Alexandrines. The fashion was to evoke atavistic atrocities that were hardly ever witnessed in noble discourse. Then, tragedy diversified a little and turned the stage into a platform on which political, religious, or philosophical ideas could be discussed without censorship. Here, the importance of spectacle was vital, and plays would indulge in melodrama to emphasize poignant surprises and moving scenes. Through its attention to affect, to the pathos of horror, its intensification of actions through grandiose language, along with the evolution of scenographic techniques, tragedy moved towards much more hyperbolic spectacles that responded to the crowd and even teetered on opera. Other civilizations appear onstage, be they Peruvian, Chinese, or Arab, equipped with their own cultural tendencies, their relative autonomy and especially their costumes. In other eras, the zeitgeist tends towards the Middle Ages and the troubadours: the virtues of knights and Crusaders providing a point of nostalgic comparison for contemporary figures and ideas. The final trend is to fill the stage with pyres all set ablaze, with characters doing archery in 1786 to imitate the gestures of William Tell of Lemierre. Shakespeare was even misinterpreted, and weapons were put onstage to thrill those that love spectacle, as were ghosts (*Semiramis*) and even cannons (*Adélaïde du Gesclin*).

The tragic theater of the eighteenth century was a theater of ideas, even if these were not of the same level as the philosophical essay that comes later. Virtue is put center stage: heroic, domestic, familial, and civic towards the end of the century, virtue must triumph and serve as an example to the spectator. Yet, virtue was only ever refracted through politics, and as tragedy portrayed kings and heroes, it is only logical that these plays would explore political values. This was a double bind, however. Tainted by politics, the very possibility of virtue was brought into question. How can tragedy dramatize an epistemological reflection on the virtuous practice of kingship, without reproaching tyrannical behaviors and proposing new attitudes towards sovereignty? This is why maxims appear in full force throughout the discourse in order to clarify the political position of the author while edifying the spectator. The philosophical current of the time was growing in criticism towards the monarchy and tragedy followed suit: representing perverse and reproachable kings, and rebellious heroes who championed the freedom to confront or depose the sovereign (Saurin's *Spartacus* in 1760). Of course, the anti-philosophers were determined to defend the monarchy by using the very same weapons of tragedy (*The Siege of Calais*). Indeed, at the very heart of the Revolution and just after Varennes, Duprat of Touloubre, a counter-revolutionary in his aesthetics and his re-reading of the myth, attempts to transform Oedipus into a just king, who is sacrificed and ready to be exiled when he is summoned by his devoted followers to return to the head of the state (*Oedipus at Thebes*, 1791). At the same time, M.-J. Chénier and Ronsin advocate for the patriotic union of the people with the king, standing against the nobility and the clergy, only then to oust or condemn the monarchy in their next plays. At a time when patriotism offered a unanimously shared vision of hope for the future, the tragic playwrights took full advantage.

Clearly, tragedy was a malleable form able to tackle politics and propaganda. But it was also a privileged space in which to fight against religion. One of the most ubiquitous themes in tragedy is the condemnation of Christianity and its superstitions through classical forms of religion or exotic beliefs that provide a safe distance from which to levy criticism. In order to reproach Catholicism, Voltaire condemns the intolerance of followers of Islam (in *Mahomet*), and in *Zaïre* he demonstrated the cruelty of Christians towards a virtuous pair of Sudanese slaves, while even in *Oedipe* he accused paganism of having incited Jocasta to commit a crime. All manner of other religions were targeted, but it was the Catholic Church that suffered the greatest scorn: for example, Marie-Joseph Chénier, dramatizing the horrors of Saint-Barthelemy's massacre in *Charles IX*.

## *From tragic commitment to dramatic projection*

Such political engagement did not occur only in the name of reason and virtue, but also on behalf of sensibility and nature as the common denominators that subtend the ideas and plot of a tragedy. Emotion affirms human values and legitimizes virtue. Only by working with affect can a king be considered just and good; only by leaning on people's emotions is a hero able to fulfill their destiny and fight. Sensibility is a ubiquitous trope in the eighteenth century and especially in tragedy. It triumphs by drawing on *pathos* and continues to bring tears to the eyes of the spectator. The very foundational law of dramaturgy is to affect the audience through discourse and spectacle, to persuade and delight them, even at the risk of creating unrealistic situations or using a dazzling spectacle to shock, outrage, or frighten, as a cathartic, productive outpouring of emotions that allows the spectator to reach the ultimate good at the end.

If this dynamic form of tragedy is much more political than tragic, always inciting the spectator to think through the contradictions dramatized onstage, we might also note that it is becoming increasingly insistent and prescriptive in the way in which it asks the audience to engage in current affairs. It eschews the neutral distance of the tragedy of the previous century, eager instead to share quite divided opinions on morality, government, the place of the sovereign, and the role of law. The spectator-judge is still preserved, and with a great deal of play and irony by Voltaire, but they are gradually encouraged to take sides by authors who settle into the complacency of *pathos* and admiration: two decent values, albeit a little tiresome. Behind all the innovation, and behind the discovery of Shakespeare, sadly there is also the militant work of moral and political demonstrations and the movement from troubling and productive contradictions to the exhibition of "good" through the newly didactic role of theater. Indeed, tragedy is now transparent and militant, there to coerce the audience rather than help them to contemplate; it has lost its aesthetic core of distance, and now expresses itself with classic compunction on the hot topics of the time.

Alongside tragedy and fighting hard to maintain its status as an epic, theater was also inventing new genres in which the world of heroes and kings capitulated to the growing importance of the family, the bourgeoisie, and to those affective intimacies neglected by tragedy. Many people were asking the same question as Beaumarchais in his *Essay on the Serious Genre of Drama*: "What real interest can I take in the death of a tyrant from the Peloponnese? Or in the sacrifice of a young princess in Aulide?" This catalyzed a movement towards dramatizing the day-to-day onstage, depicting the conditions of daily life, of family, and seeing common affects rather than valiant heroes of the past (Louis Sébastien Mercier, *On the Theatre, or New Essay on Dramatic Art*, 1773). Theatrical innovation took place: rejecting the play of contradictions to embrace conflicts in order to make theater a space of the purely "dramatic." There is a tendency in theatrical art to separate the space of fiction from the social space of reception, the stage from the auditorium, and then to try to prolong the moments of perfect illusion, if not identification. This is the dream of those that advocate for dramatic theater—radically opposed as it might be to the tragedy of the seventeenth century and so consistent with the injunctions of theorists like Aubignac—who know full well that even when the auditorium is empty and the stage is dark (1759), that the theater will always be a site of exchanged glances.

With theatrical art on the one side, and the truly epic, layered, self-conscious, reflexive, and reflective tragedy of the seventeenth century on the other, whose key principle is contradiction and the importance of playing off different points of view from one another rather than focusing exclusively on the end and its harmony, a radically different form of theater also burst on to the scene: a *non-dramatic theater*, to borrow Goethe's distinction, that imposes the *necessity* of drama. Indeed, Goethe differentiated the epic poem which exposes "the event as perfectly past" from the dramatic poem which exposes the event as "perfectly present,"[8] to which Schiller, who relished this generic opposition and was very much in favor of German dramatic poetry, added:

> The dramatic action moves itself before me, around the epic I move, and it appears as it were to stand still. According to my opinion, there is much in this difference. If the event keeps itself in motion before me, I am strictly chained to the present, my fancy loses all freedom, there arises and continues an incessant unrest in me, I must always stick to the object, all looking back, all reflection is denied to me, because I obey a foreign power.[9]

Although Schiller's choice of the word "foreign" merits discussion, I would like to focus here on the immobility he explores. If I am able to move around epic action, it is because it creates sufficient distance and freedom to allow me to be inattentive or indifferent to what is being dramatized onstage, to what is "past," without yoking me to an affective, present reality that would cast me into the show itself. We have to approach the epic theater that Schiller is opposing here almost from the negative: this epic that does not immobilize the gaze, does not set its sight on one specific object, but demands that we start to circumnavigate the discontinuities of the play and look in the places that really make us think. In other words, I think that it is time to see seventeenth-century tragedy as something other than a homogenous entity that fixates on one singular meaning, something other than an obdurate desire to conform to Aristotelian tragedy and on the principle of a reversal of fortune and a cathartic conclusion. It is high time we saw seventeenth-century tragedy not through the eyes of Aubignac whose viewpoint has long prevailed throughout the history of the genre. We need to consider tragedy separately from the way in which it has been re-appropriated by the eighteenth century, in which it is first exalted and canonized through the repertoire, only to later be rejected and condemned. It is because of playwrights, dramatic theorists convinced of the legitimacy of the genre (which was read far more than it was seen onstage) and especially because of the literary modernity that privileged this projected fantasy, the effect of illusion, and the identification with the present, desperate to make the theater a catchy and morally instructive fiction, that drama and "the dramatic" have triumphed so long in tragedy. However, did they also triumph in the eyes of the spectator? It is perhaps because eighteenth-century tragedy did give in to the dramatic, to the necessity of projection, and, even with spectacular effects, to using *pathos* and adopting domestic themes that were infinitely more suited to spectator-identification, and, thus, for having rendered all of its bastard nobility and systems of contradiction inoperative, that this era of tragedy has all but been forgotten; just as seventeenth-century tragedy witnessed its own identity change simply because this new way of reading it *post-facto*.

Let's not be too swift to condemn tragedy for not knowing how to be tragic, or for having staged the death of ancient tyrants. Perhaps we should focus instead on the extent to which the whole spectacle of tragedy systematically deliberated and debated the antitheses and contradictions of things; how each scene counted in and of itself; and how tragedy is perceived by a riven, discordant, and multiple audience who witness what is onstage, perceive one another, and behold those that watch the fiction unfold. In the seventeenth century, theatergoers had a circular perspective on the complex site in which the fiction was being acted out and which actually refers to a fiction happening offstage. The viewer looks up, down, and all around them, observing other partners engaged in this act of seeing, in discussion, judge and gage.

> This urge to drive the spectator into a single-track dynamism whence he can look neither right nor left, up nor down, must be rejected from the standpoint of modern dramatic art . . . Complex seeing must be practiced. Though thinking *about* the flow of the play is more important than thinking *within* the flow of the play.[10]

Brecht is always believed to be so remote from seventeenth-century French theater. Indeed, he actively distanced himself from it; but, as we can see here, is he not paradoxically closer than the formidable, doctrinarian regulator and author of all the dramatic rulebooks, Aubignac?

This is a theater that is ordered but composite; allegedly fixed but really in constant evolution, or at least in transition; both a thoroughfare and the mechanism that enables that passing through; able to position spectator and reader as judges after having appealed to their emotions; a producer of contradiction and thus infinitely self-conscious as well as poignant. Seventeenth-century tragedy is both self-reflexive and highly problematic, insofar as it reveals a specific, spatial moment, while also enabling diverse, indeterminate, and individualized perspectives that transpire throughout each and every session. This is why the theater is an assembly of full (legal and aesthetical) *capacity*: it is observed at the same time as it observes; it taps into the infinite towards which it tends; it is entwined with the intellectual joy of understanding and evaluating the poetic discourse that constitutes it. And this is why this *conscious assembly* that houses the epic theater of the time, was fundamentally convivial, scarcely "tragic" at all, and, under no circumstances, could it be called "dramatic."

CHAPTER TWO

# Sites of Performance and Circulation

*Tragedy in the Repertory of Molière's Troupe and its Successors, 1659–89*

JAN CLARKE

## OBJECTIVE AND SOURCES

The years 1659 to 1689 were important in the history and development of tragedy.[1] Pierre Corneille returned to writing for the stage as they were beginning, and Racine's illustrious career began in 1664.[2] They have, however, been much studied, and my objective here is to throw new light on the performance and reception of tragedy by examining the part it played in the programming of three companies that succeeded one another: Molière's troupe, the Hôtel Guénégaud company, and the Comédie-Française. In 1659, the actor La Grange joined Molière's troupe, which had returned to Paris from the provinces the year before, and began to keep his celebrated *Registre*.[3] Molière had begun his career in Paris in the 1640s as a member of the Illustre Théâtre, which he founded with members of the Béjart family. When it failed, he left the capital and spent over a decade touring the provinces. Upon his return, he found three troupes operating in Paris: the Hôtel de Bourgogne and Marais companies, and an Italian *commedia dell'arte* troupe performing in a theater in the Petit-Bourbon palace. The king, Louis XIV, first ordered Molière to share the Petit-Bourbon with the Italians. Then, when that was demolished, both troupes moved to a theater in the Palais-Royal.[4]

When Molière died in February 1673, his troupe lost its leader, chief playwright, and principal actor. Moreover, its theater in the Palais-Royal was immediately allocated to the composer Jean-Baptiste Lully for his operas. It must have appeared that the company would not recover, and four actors left for the relative security of the Hôtel de Bourgogne. The remaining members of Molière's troupe succeeded, however, in taking over the Hôtel Guénégaud, where they were joined by actors from the Marais Theater, whose own company was dissolved.[5] This new troupe performed at the Guénégaud until 1680, when the Hôtel de Bourgogne was itself closed down and its actors transferred to the Guénégaud to form the Comédie-Française.[6]

La Grange's *Registre* is a personal summary of the "official" account books of the three companies to which he belonged, and which are the focus of our attention here, where details of plays performed, income, and expenditure were recorded. All those of

Molière's troupe have been lost except for three: La Thorillière's first and second account books (1663–4, 1664–5) and that of Hubert (1672–3).[7] The full set of Guénégaud account books is preserved in the archives of the Comédie-Française; they have never been reproduced in full, but I have analyzed them and published a summary.[8] The Comédie-Française also holds its own account books from 1680 onwards, and many have recently been made available online as part of the Comédie-Française Registers Project.[9] The account books of the Hôtel de Bourgogne and Marais companies have, however, disappeared, as have those of the Comédie-Italienne prior to its reestablishment in 1716. This is frustrating, since the Hôtel de Bourgogne was known as the home of tragedy. Scholars have, however, done much to establish the company's repertoire,[10] although obviously without the detail we have for Molière's troupe, the Guénégaud company, and the Comédie-Française.

## GENRE AND SPECIALIZATION

If the Hôtel de Bourgogne was known for tragedy, the Marais specialized in spectacular works known as machine plays, while the Italians offered improvised *commedia dell'arte* and Molière contributed comedy, farce, and, eventually, *comédie-ballet*. Machine plays and *comédie-ballet* (and indeed opera) were means by which companies sought to exploit the public's passion for spectacle. Many spectacular works were on tragic subjects and are described as *tragédie en machines*, *tragédie-ballet*, or *tragédie lyrique*. Inevitably, companies competed for a limited audience,[11] and while each troupe had its specialization, they all gave works across a range of genres and sought to emulate each other's successes, particularly where these involved music and spectacle. However, from 1672 onwards, Lully had a monopoly on stage music that was protected by the imposition of limits on the numbers of singers and musicians other companies could employ.[12] The troupes, though, also competed with regard to tragedy, as we will see.

## RHYTHM OF PERFORMANCES

Theatrical seasons ran from Easter to Easter with a pause of approximately three weeks in between. Companies did not perform every day; the most favored days were the "ordinary" days (Tuesday, Friday, and Sunday), with the remainder being known as the "extraordinary" days.[13] Chappuzeau in his *Théâtre français* of 1674 boasts of the number of "spectacles" available to the theatergoing public, which added up to more than 800 per year.[14] This seems few, though, in comparison with modern norms, and Molière's troupe never performed more than fourteen times in a month and frequently less or not at all, when called upon to entertain the king.[15]

At the Petit-Bourbon, Molière's troupe performed on the "extraordinary" days, switching to the "ordinary" days when the two troupes transferred to the Palais-Royal. When actors from Molière's troupe and the Marais came together at the Guénégaud, the Italians went with them, still performing on the "extraordinary days." However, when they were abroad or at court, the French performed every day, which became the norm at the Comédie-Française. This was possible primarily because the Italians had been sent (reluctantly) to the Hôtel de Bourgogne, but was also facilitated by the large size of the new company, which was able to perform simultaneously at court and in town, thereby eliminating the enforced breaks endured by Molière's troupe.

## THEATER DESIGN AND SOCIAL STRATIFICATION

The dominant model in seventeenth-century French theater design was the real tennis court or *jeu de paume*.[16] From the 1630s onwards, companies occupied these buildings by means of installations ranging from the temporary to the more-or-less permanent. The form was so fixed in the collective psyche that when companies moved into buildings that were not tennis courts, such as the Petit-Bourbon or the Palais-Royal, they constructed what were effectively tennis courts within them. Yet tennis courts did not make good theaters; they were long and thin, and people in the boxes had a better view of the public opposite than they did of the stage.[17] This was installed at one end of the rectangle with two rows of boxes with a gallery above around the remaining three sides. The center was left empty to form the *parterre* or standing area, which was exclusively the domain of male spectators, and a stepped area of seating known as the *amphithéâtre* occupied the far end, above or below the rear boxes. Privileged male spectators could occupy seats on the stage;[18] women were limited to the two rows of boxes and the gallery above.[19] There was also pronounced social stratification, with the aristocracy and upper bourgeoisie occupying the lower boxes and the seats onstage, while the third-row gallery was reserved primarily for servants.[20] The *parterre*, on the other hand, was socially mixed. It is often stated that the upper classes preferred tragedy,[21] and it might appear possible to test this by comparing sales for tragedy in the different areas of the house with those for other genres. There are, though, complicating factors, as we will see.

## PROGRAMMING—GENERAL CONSIDERATIONS

Companies gave either one or two plays in an evening. The main play would usually be a comedy, *comédie-ballet*, or tragedy, while the second play, sometimes referred to as a "petite pièce," would generally be either a comedy or a farce. Tragedies are, though, occasionally found in second position and, on two occasions, two tragedies were performed together.[22] Certain comedies by Molière, on the other hand, are found in both first and second position, sometimes during a single season.[23]

When new plays were introduced, they were usually given a run of continuous performances, and the length of this is one indicator of a play's success. Either the first play or the second could constitute the main attraction. When a main play was new, it was generally given alone during its first run, but might then be bolstered by the addition of old "petites pièces." Or when a new second play was given, it would be with series of "stock" main plays. This use of double bills, where either play could constitute the main draw, renders almost impossible any analysis of ticket sales by genre. For example, how can we know that when 205 people sat on the stage and in the first-row boxes at the opening night of the Comédie-Française in 1680, they were there to see Racine's *Phèdre* rather than Champmeslé's *Carosses d'Orléans*, which had been created at the Guénégaud just two weeks before?[24]

For roughly half our period, ticket prices for the cheaper seats were raised during the first run of new main plays (but not of new "petites pièces"), while prices for the more expensive areas (stage, first-row boxes, *amphithéâtre*) remained unchanged. These were known as performances "au double." From late 1676 onwards, prices for these expensive seats were lowered for regular performances, so that the public in them was also affected by the "double." The financial impact would, though, obviously have been less for them than for people in the cheaper areas. Indeed, the "double" seems to have been specifically designed to benefit more wealthy members of the audience by enabling them to see new works as a privileged elite.

Another factor affecting programme composition was the season, and Chappuzeau recounts how new plays were generally performed between All Saints Day and Easter, with "heroic plays" ("Pieces Heroiques") being preferred in winter and comedies in summer.[25] Indeed, he defines *répertoire* as "a list of old plays to sustain the theater during the heat of summer and the outings of autumn, so as not to be forced on the evening of every performance to decide in haste and tumult which play to announce." ("Une liste de vieilles pieces pour entretenir le Theâtre durant les chaleurs de l'Esté et les promenades de l'Automne, et n'estre pas obligez, tous les soirs qu'on represente de deliberer à la haste et en tumult de la piece qu'on dort announcer.")[26] This is, though, a simplification, since old plays were performed all year round. Indeed, across our period, on average 86 percent of plays performed in any given season were old.[27] It is, though, the case that only four tragedies were created between April and October, and for all but one of these there are obvious factors determining the choice of date.[28] Warfare was also a seasonal occupation and one reason for preferring winter to summer for new tragedies was that male members of the *noblesse d'épée* would have been away on campaign during the summer months, while other members of the aristocracy would have retired to their country estates. A company's repertoire of stock plays constituted, therefore, an important resource, and it aimed to select new plays that would be popular enough to enter the repertoire, thereby allowing it to capitalize on its investment. These new plays were usually only published once their initial run had ceased and, by custom, remained the property of the troupe that had produced them and were not performed by any other company during that time.

The total number of plays given per season varied hugely across our period, with the lowest figure being twelve in 1669–70 and the highest 105 in 1686–7.[29] On average, four new plays were created per season by Molière's troupe, falling to three at the Guénégaud, then rising to ten at the Comédie-Française, with the highest figure being thirteen in 1685–6. In only comparatively few seasons were no new tragedies given (1661–2, 1663–4, 1667–8, 1668–9, 1672–3), all of which were during the "Molière" phase. Thereafter, one or two new tragedies were given each season at the Guénégaud, and between two and five per season at the Comédie-Française.

When Molière's troupe returned to the capital, the numbers of tragedies and main plays in other genres in his company's repertoire were roughly equal, but as he came to specialize in his own works the proportion of tragedies fell. Indeed, his company performed no tragedies at all in 1669–70 and only one new tragedy (*Psyché*) in 1671–2. This same low level continued during the early years at the Guénégaud but rose rapidly towards the end of this phase for reasons we will discuss. Following the creation of the Comédie-Française, not only did the size of the repertoire increase exponentially, but so did the number of tragedies it contained. This is, though, hardly surprising, given that it now included the stock plays from the repertoire of the Hôtel de Bourgogne. These fluctuations appear most clearly when percentages are used to indicate the relation between tragedies and main plays in other genres (Graph 2.1), or the number of performances involving a tragedy (Graph 2.2).

The two peaks that appear in the second chart in particular relate to the productions of *Psyché* and *Circé* (see below). The increased presence of tragedy in terms of both repertoire and performances from 1679–80 onwards is similarly striking. Tragedy may only have equaled or exceeded main plays in other genres in two seasons for repertoire (1659–60, 1685–6) and three for performances (1675–6, 1683–4, and 1685–6), but it was significantly more prevalent at the Comédie-Française, where roughly half of all performances involved a tragedy, than it had been at either Palais-Royal or Guénégaud. This, then, nuances Sara Harvey's view that "from 1684–1685 onwards, comedy was on

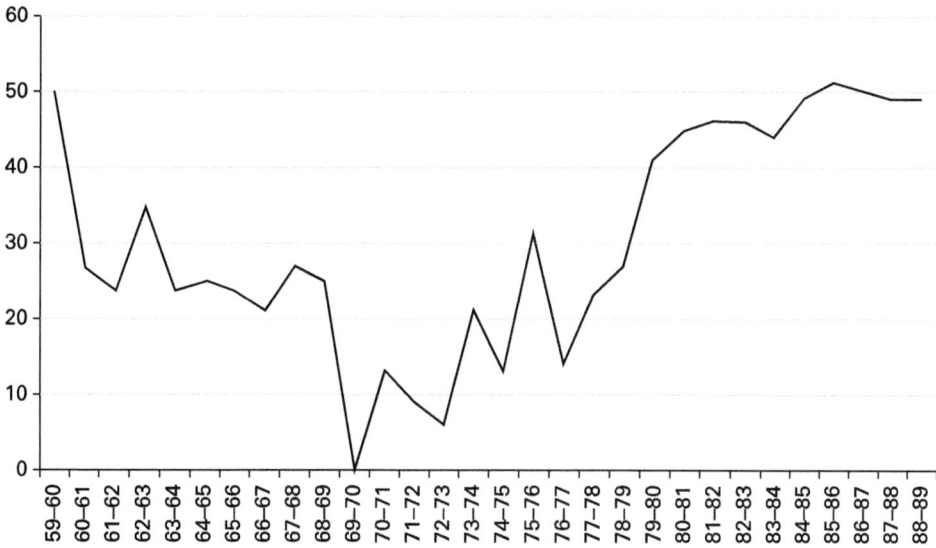

GRAPH 2.1: Percentage of "main plays" that were tragedies.

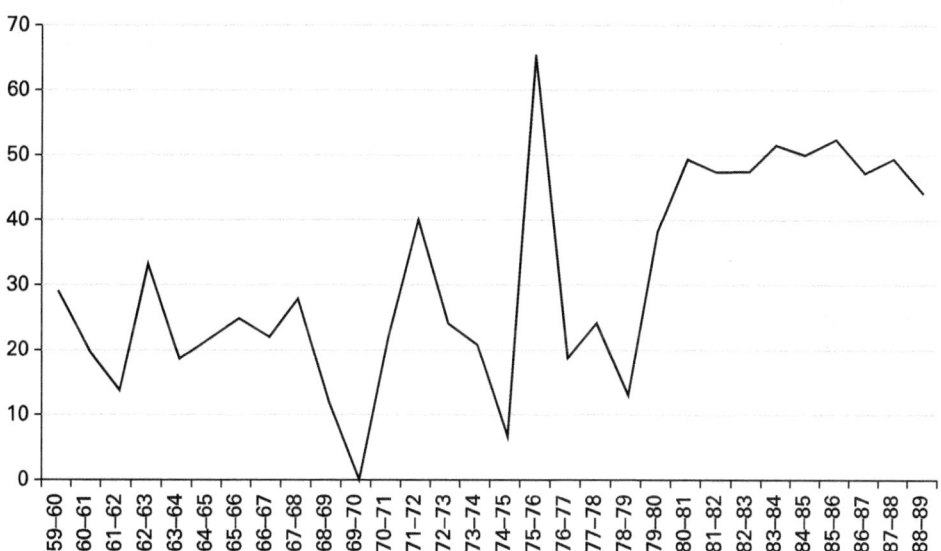

GRAPH 2.2: Percentage of performances that involved tragedies.

the rise from all points of view and this tendency was maintained up to the end of the century." ("À partir de 1684–1685, la comédie est en hausse à tous points de vue et cette tendance se maintien jusqu'à la fin du siècle.")[30] Interestingly, in 1712, the king, "having been informed that the actors are performing as few tragedies as possible," ordered them "to perform alternately a serious play and a comic one," thereby advocating a return to the practice of thirty years before.[31]

Stock plays were each given very few performances per season: frequently between three and five and sometimes only one. At first glance, this seems a colossal waste of effort—why bother to keep a play in the repertoire but only perform it once or twice a year? It also represents a remarkable feat of memory. During its last few seasons, the Guénégaud company regularly performed over fifty plays, and more than double that number became the norm at the Comédie-Française. This practice of giving very few performances of a large number of plays may, in fact, have been introduced specifically to aid their retention in the repertoire—enabling actors to refresh their memories by means of an occasional outing.[32] Nonetheless, it is extraordinary that the public would have had only one or two opportunities per season to see a much-loved elderly play. This might suggest that, with the exception of novelties, the public did not care what it saw, which De Visé explicitly states in his *Nouvelles nouvelles* when writing about the high proportion of old plays in the repertoire of Molière's troupe when newly returned to Paris: "people came through habit, without intending to listen to the play and without knowing what was being performed."[33] This returns us, though, to our initial question: if people did not care what they saw, why did troupes keep so many plays in their repertoires?

## MOLIÈRE'S TROUPE

As we have seen, Molière returned to Paris with a roughly equal number of tragedies and comedies in his baggage, and his troupe continued to perform a small number of tragedies both old and new in all seasons but 1669–70. Many of the former were by Pierre Corneille: *Héraclius*, *Rodogune*, *Cinna*, *La Mort de Pompée*, *Le Cid*, and *Horace* were all given in 1559–60, and *Nicomède* and *Sertorius* were added in later seasons.[34] Molière had frequented the Corneille brothers in Rouen immediately before returning to the capital,[35] and according to Georges Couton, wanted to become a Pierre Corneille specialist.[36] He performed *Nicomède* for the king at his Paris "try out," but his success there was more thanks to the farce that followed, which may be why it was not given in public until the following season.[37] Corneille returned to writing for the stage in 1659, but gave his new works elsewhere.[38] Nevertheless, Molière continued to perform the old ones he had in his repertoire. Other old tragedies performed by Molière's troupe during its first Paris seasons were *Mariane* and *La Mort de Crispe* by Tristan l'Hermite, *Scévole* and *Alcionée* by Du Ryer, and *Venceslas* by Rotrou. Certain of these works had probably previously been performed by the Illustre Théâtre in the 1640s, notably *Cinna*, *La Mort de Pompée*, *Horace*, *Le Cid*, *Scévole*, *Mariane*, and *La Mort de Crispe*.[39]

According to legend, Molière went onstage to follow his lover, Madeleine Béjart. She was a great tragic actress and a number of commentators have attributed the continuing presence of tragedy in the repertoire of Molière's troupe to her influence, sometimes in a somewhat misogynistic way. C.E.J. Caldicott, for example, claims that Molière's acting style and repertoire were determined by Madeleine and that his obligation to her threatened to divert him from his true vocation.[40] Virginia Scott, on the other hand, while agreeing that Madeleine's preference for tragedy may have been a factor, believes Molière shared the prevailing view as to the superiority of that genre. She also quotes lines from Le Boulanger de Chalussay's satire *Élomire hypocondre*,[41] describing how the public was dissatisfied with Molière's productions of *Héraclius*, *Rodogune*, *Cinna*, *Le Cid*, and *Pompée*, but considered his *Étourdi* a marvel.[42] This is, though, a comic simplification and Molière's troupe continued to perform tragedies (including those of Corneille) throughout the greater part of its Paris career, although they were performed less as Molière's own works came to dominate the repertoire.

FIGURE 2.1: Portrait of the French actor and playwright Jean Baptiste Poquelin, known by his stage name Molière (1622–73), as Julius Caesar in the play "La mort de Pompee" by Corneille. Painting by Nicolas Mignard (1606–68), c. 1657. 75 × 60 cm. Comédie-Française, Paris. Photo by Leemage/Corbis via Getty Images.

Another legend has Molière despising comedy and writing his "heroic comedy" ("comédie–héroique") *Dom Garcie de Navarre* (1661) as the "next best thing."[43] The outcome was disappointing, causing De Visé to comment in his *Nouvelles nouvelles* (1663) that it was not entertaining because it was a serious play and Molière had the lead role. He also attempts to explain both Molière's persistence and his success: "the esteem in which he was beginning to be held meant that people put up with him." ("l'estime que l'on commençait à avoir pour lui fut cause qu'on le souffrit.")[44] This view of the incapacity of Molière and his troupe in tragedy was widely held,[45] and he soon gave up performing in the genre himself.[46] Molière is known, of course, for having advocated a more "natural" acting style, which according to Sabine Chaouche was considered lacking in nobility and, therefore, unsuitable for tragedy.[47]

Molière was not, though, prepared to give the genre up. His troupe created two new tragedies in 1659–60: *Pylade et Oreste* by Coqueteau de la Clairière, given just three performances, and *Zénobie*, by Magnon, a previous supplier of the Illustre Théâtre, which did slightly better with seven. Both subsequently disappeared from the repertoire. In comparison, Molière's first new Parisian "petite pièce," *Les Précieuses ridicules*, was given thirty-three times that same season.[48] This conjunction was not lost on his contemporaries, and Thomas Corneille wrote to the abbé de Pure deploring the failure of Coqueteau's tragedy: "Everyone says they performed his play detestably; and the large number they had at their farce of the *Précieuses*, after having taken it off, shows clearly that they are only fit to sustain such trifles and that the strongest play would fail between their hands."[49]

In 1660–1, Molière revived an example from a more recent phase of his provincial activity. Gilbert's *Amours de Diane et d'Endimion*, created at the Hôtel de Bourgogne in 1657, had been performed by Molière's troupe in Rouen in 1658.[50] *Endimion* is a spectacle tragedy—a genre with which Molière's troupe and those that followed were to enjoy considerable success. It was performed eleven times then disappeared, but re-emerged at the Comédie-Française some twenty years later (1681–2), which might suggest it had remained in the repertoire of the Hôtel de Bourgogne throughout that time. The single new tragedy performed by Molière's company in 1660–1 was *Le Tyran d'Égypte*, also by Gilbert,[51] given eight performances plus four the following season. No new tragedies were given in 1661–2 (the season that saw the creation of *L'École des maris* and *Les Fâcheux*), but in 1662–3, Boyer's *Oropaste ou le faux Tonaxare* received a highly satisfactory fifteen performances, whereas De Prade's *Arsace roi des Parthes*, was given only six.

A more significant event this season was the addition to the repertoire of Pierre Corneille's *Sertorius*. This had been created at the Marais to great acclaim in February 1662, and Molière's troupe rushed to perform it, just as it had done for *Endimion*. As we have seen, works customarily belonged to the troupe that had created them until they were published. But Molière's troupe got in a little early, giving *Sertorius* for the first time on June 29, over a week before its publication. Mlle Des Oeillets, who had created the female lead at the Marais, moved to the Hôtel de Bourgogne at Easter 1662 and *Sertorius* went with her, meaning it was simultaneously in the repertoires of all three competing French companies.[52]

No new tragedies were given by Molière's troupe in 1663–4. The following season saw, though, the arrival of a fresh new talent with the creation by Molière's troupe of Racine's *Thébaïde*, which, according to Georges Forestier, had originally been intended for the Hôtel de Bourgogne.[53] Its summer creation (June 20, 1664) was due to Molière's need of a new play following the banning of *Tartuffe*, and Racine's impatience at having to wait for a winter slot at the Hôtel de Bourgogne.[54] The results were not outstanding—sixteen performances in 1663–4 plus four in 1665–6.

The Hôtel de Bourgogne got its revenge the following season. On December 4, 1665, Molière's troupe gave the premiere of Racine's *Alexandre*,[55] and public reaction was initially good. However, ten days later, the Hôtel de Bourgogne gave a private performance of Racine's tragedy at a festivity for the king and added it to its to own repertoire shortly afterwards, causing the takings at the Palais-Royal to drop off disastrously.[56] The troupe's reaction is described by La Grange:

> That same day the troupe was surprised when the same play *Alexandre* was performed on the stage of the Hôtel de Bourgogne [and] as the thing was done with the connivence of M. Racine who behaved so badly as to have given the play to the actors and had them learn it[,] the author's shares were divided and each actor had for his [or her] share 47 *livres*.[57]

("Ce mesme jour La troupe fust surprise que la mesme piece d'Allexandre fust jouée sur le Theatre de l'hostel de bourgogne comme la chose estoit faitte de complot avec M.' Racine qui en usoit si mal que d'avoIr donné et faIct aprendre la piece aux autres comedians lesd.s parts d'autheur furent partagés et chacun des douze acteurs eust pour sa part 47 livres.")

This perfidious behavior is usually attributed to Racine's dismay at the lack of ability displayed by Molière's actors. More recently, Georges Forestier has attributed it to a royal command.[58] Whatever the case, Molière and his troupe were outraged and no works by Racine were performed at the Palais-Royal during the remainder of Molière's lifetime. We must not, though, forget that Molière had done something similar with regard to *Sertorius* only a short time before.

Molière scored a significant retaliatory blow in 1666–7 when he finally succeeded in obtaining a new play by Pierre Corneille—*Attila*. Corneille's star was, though, on the wane, and his previous tragedy, *Agésilas*, had flopped at the Hôtel de Bourgogne the year before.[59] Unusually, Molière bought the play from Corneille for a fixed price of 2,000 *livres*.[60] According to Chappuzeau, the actors employed this method when they were not certain a play would be a success.[61] However, Forestier believes it was Corneille and not Molière who was taking care to ensure a definite return.[62] The initial reaction was favorable and Subligny wrote that the actors performed:

With all the strength and skill
Of which we previously thought capable
Only the inimitable Hôtel.
People are wrong to say everywhere
That serious acting is not their thing.[63]

("Avec toute la force et l'art
Dont on crût jusqu'ici capable
Le seul Hostel inimitable?
On a tort de dire en tous lieux
Que ce n'est point leur fait que le jeu sérieux").

Couton describes *Attila* as a failure, since it was given only eleven times in its first season.[64] Its first run was, though, interrupted by the Easter break and, taking the two halves together, gives a respectable figure of twenty. 1667–68 also saw the creation of a new tragedy, *Cléopâtre*, by one of the troupe's own members, La Thorillière, which was given eleven times.[65] Chappuzeau comments on the desirability for a company of having such "actor playwrights" ("comédiens poètes") among its ranks, since professional dramatists had a tendency to be high handed.[66] Molière's troupe was, of course, led by the greatest "actor playwright" of the age for comedy, but must have longed to be similarly independent in tragedy.

No tragedies whatsoever were performed by Molière's troupe in 1669–70. However, in 1670–1, he offered a second tragedy by Pierre Corneille: *Tite et Bérénice*, with Mlle Molière as the heroine, again paying an advance sum of 2,000 *livres*.[67] This was created on November 28, 1670, just a week after the Hôtel de Bourgogne had opened Racine's tragedy on the same subject.[68] Roger Duchêne describes this as an aggressive act on Molière's part, claiming he waited for the Hôtel to announce its play before bringing out his own. Duchêne is forced to admit though, that, contemporaries did not mention competition,[69] and Forestier's account of an accidental opposition, unlikely as it might seem, appears correct.[70]

As Forestier puts it, "someone had to lose" ("Il fallait un perdant"), and this was undoubtedly Corneille (and Molière).[71] The appearance of the Hôtel de Bourgogne's new star, Mlle Champmeslé, as Racine's tragic heroine obviously played a part,[72] but it did not help that Corneille's play was performed in weekly rotation with Molière's *Bourgeois gentilhomme*. Again, Couton presents this as a serious failure,[73] but *Tite et Bérénice* was given twenty-one times during the season. Corneille, however, was not content, writing ironically in 1676 with regard to an unexpected return to favor, that "finally *Bérénice* will find actors." ("Bérénice enfin trouvera des acteurs")[74] This is, though, as Sylvie Chevalley has pointed out, manifestly unfair,[75] and Armande Béjart followed her sister in sustaining a number of tragic roles in the repertoire, and was still appearing as Andromaque and Mariane in 1685.[76]

The following season, 1671–2, saw the creation of the most successful tragic play of this phase: *Psyché*. It is described on its title page as a "tragédie ballet" and, like *Endimion*, featured considerable spectacular content. *Psyché* was a collaborative effort: Pierre Corneille assisted Molière with the versification, while Quinault provided lyrics for the songs. First performed for Louis in the Salle des machines in the Tuileries Palace,[77] Molière had to renovate his Palais-Royal theater to give it in public.[78] The investment paid off, and *Psyché* was given an astonishing fifty-one performances in 1671–2, plus thirty-one more the following season.

The following chart (Graph 2.3) shows the number of performances per play for those tragedies given by Molière's troupe between 1659 and 1673.

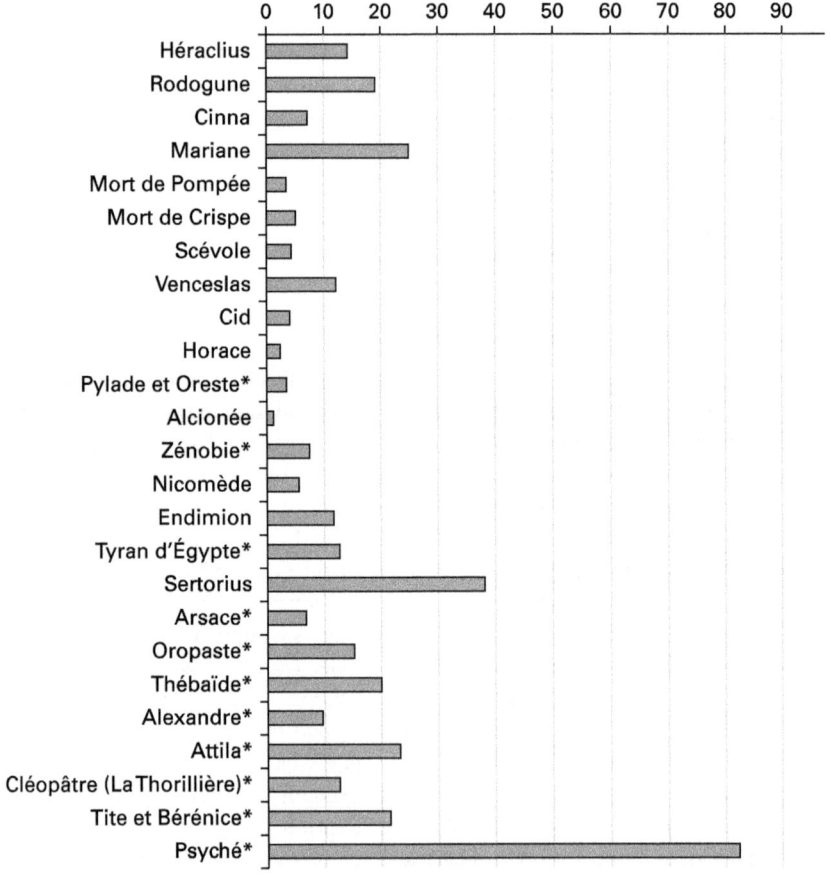

GRAPH 2.3: Total number of performances of individual tragedies given by Molière's troupe, 1659–60 to 1672–3. The plays are shown in performance order and premieres are indicated by an asterisk.

We see that *Psyché* was by far the most successful (eighty-two performances), followed by *Sertorius* on thirty-eight, and with *Mariane*, *La Thébaïde*, *Attila*, and *Tite et Bérénice* all achieving figures in the twenties.

## HÔTEL GUÉNÉGAUD

The Guénégaud company was formed in 1673 by the union of actors from Molière's troupe with others from the Marais, but Molière's former actors had the upper hand and their repertoire dominated.[79] The Marais actors had, though, one fairly recent tragedy that the new troupe was able to perform: Boursault's *Amours de Germanicus* (1672), which was given nine times in 1673–4 and twice in 1676–7, before re-emerging in another form. It also gave Montfleury's *Ambigu comique*, created at the Marais just before its closure. This strange play consists of a three-act tragedy on the subject of Dido, plus three "petites pièces" that serve as prologue and *intermèdes* and were sometimes performed seperately.[80] *L'Ambigu comique* became a staple of the Guénégaud repertoire, being given between one and five performances during every season between 1673–4 and 1678–9.[81]

The Guénégaud company gave a single new tragedy during its first season: *La Mort d'Achilles* by Thomas Corneille, which received nine performances before disappearing. This was a more significant event than this meager tally would suggest. As we have seen, Thomas had been hostile to Molière, writing that his troupe was fit only to perform "trifles" ("bagatelles"). The animosity was returned, with Molière satirizing the playwright (known as M. de l'Isle) in act I, scene 1 of *L'École des femmes*. However, following Molière's death, Thomas became, in effect, the Guénégaud's "house playwright" and, working in collaboration with De Visé, provided some of its greatest successes.

Indeed, in 1675–6, Thomas and De Visé furnished the Guénégaud with its greatest triumph in the form of *Circé*—described on the title page as a "tragedy decorated with machines, scene changes and music."[82] As such, *Circé* not only followed on from *Psyché*, but also capitalized on the expertise of the former members of the Marais team, who had enjoyed considerable success with machine plays by Pierre Corneille, Boyer, and De Visé.[83] The creation of *Circé* did not, though, proceed without incident: some members of the troupe opposed its production and were first excluded from the company then reintegrated, and preparations were long and costly.[84] As a result, it was only possible to give *Circé* nine times before Easter. However, as with *Attila*, performances continued after the break, and it was given a further sixty-eight times in 1676–7. Curiously, while other machine plays were revived at the Comédie-Française in the period we are considering, *Circé* was not among them and it had to wait until 1705, when Dancourt provided a new prologue and *divertissements*.

There may have been doubts as to the intentionality of the opposition of the two *Bérénices*, but 1675–6 saw the start of what Guy Boquet describes as the "war of the tragedies" ("guerre des tragédies")[85] whereby the Guénégaud gave plays specifically designed to oppose Hôtel de Bourgogne productions. During this season, it gave *Iphigénie* by Le Clerc and Coras, originally planned to compete with Racine's play, although ultimately there was no direct opposition; it received just seven performances. Pradon's *Phèdre et Hippolyte* of 1676–7 was more successful in opposition to Racine's *Phèdre*, with nineteen performances.[86] Racine did not take kindly to these attempts to undercut him; he delayed the production of the rival *Iphigénie* and attempted but failed to do the same for *Phèdre et Hippolyte*.[87] According to Pradon's preface, he even dissuaded the Guénégaud's leading actresses from taking on the main female role, which was ultimately played by the relatively unknown Mlle Guyot.[88] Racine retired from writing for the professional stage in 1677, but the "war" continued. In 1677–8, the Guénégaud company set Boyer's *Comte d'Essex* up against a tragedy of the same name by its own purveyor of spectacular entertainment, Thomas Corneille; it received just eight performances.

Other new tragedies performed between 1675–6 and 1678–9 were Abeille's *Coriolan*, given eighteen performances in 1675–6;[89] Pradon's *Électre*, given just eight times in 1677–8; and Boursault's *Princesse de Clèves*, which, according to its author, was a reworking of *Germanicus*, designed to capitalize on the success of Mme de Lafayette's novel,[90] but which was withdrawn after just two performances in 1678–9. Of these, only *Coriolan* and *Phèdre et Hippolyte* can be deemed to have been successes. At the same time, the company sought to increase its performance of tragedy more generally through the revival of old works, sometimes after a considerable interval: Tristan's *Mariane* (ten seasons), Du Ryer's *Scévole* (eighteen seasons), *Tite et Bérénice* (seven seasons).[91]

Three other tragedies revived at this time are of interest for not having previously been given by either Molière's troupe or the Guénégaud company. Pierre Corneille's *Médée*, performed three times in 1677–8, was created at the Marais in 1635,[92] and may have continued in the repertoire of that troupe. Quinault's *Astrate roi de Tyr* is more problematic, since it was created at the Hôtel de Bourgogne in 1664–5 and there is no record of it having been performed elsewhere in the intervening period.[93] Its revival for just two performances in 1678–9 would, though, suggest it had previously been given at the Marais and was still part of its repertoire. As for Pradon's *Tamerlan ou la mort de Bajazet*, given four times at the Guénégaud in 1677–8 and twice the following season, it had been created at the Hôtel de Bourgogne just two years earlier in 1675.[94] Its addition at this time suggests, then, the adoption of an aggressive production policy involving the rapid production of plays from a rival company's repertoire, as previously practiced by both Molière and Racine.

Things were to become more aggressive still for, during the break between the 1678–9 and 1679–80 seasons, the members of Guénégaud company persuaded Mlle Champmeslé, the leading tragic actress of the age, and her husband to leave the Hôtel de Bourgogne to join them. The inducements were considerable: the Champmeslé couple each received a full share in the company plus a bonus of 1,000 *livres* per annum over and above their shares. In recording this arrangement, La Grange notes neutrally that "we accorded them in addition to their shares 1000 [*livres*] per year" ("on leur a accordé outre leurs parts 1000 [livres]: par an"), but his later description of this sum as "Mlle Champmeslé['s] pension" ("Mlle Champmeslé pension 1000 [livres]") makes clear the intended beneficiary.[95] This move enabled the Guénégaud to add the masterworks of Racine to its repertoire as well as tragedies by other authors in which Mlle Champmeslé played the lead. Thus, in 1679–80, it gave Racine's *Andromaque*, *Bérénice*, *Bajazet*, *Mithridate*, *Phèdre*, and *Britannicus*; Thomas Corneille's *Ariane* and *Camma*; and Pradon's *Pyrame et Thisbé*.[96] Other revivals this season that may have been influenced by the arrival of Mlle Champmeslé were Pierre Corneille's *Le Cid* and *Cinna*, since these were both in the repertoire of the Hôtel de Bourgogne and had last been performed by Molière's troupe in 1659–60 and 1664–5 respectively.[97] More problematic is *Rodogune*, which was also revived in 1679–80 and was also in the repertoire of the Hôtel de Bourgogne,[98] but which had last been given by Molière's troupe more recently in 1668–69. Similarly, *Héraclius* and *Venceslas* were both revived at the Guénégaud during the first months of 1680–1 (before the creation of the Comédie-Française), having last been given by Molière's troupe in 1662–3 and 1668–9 respectively, but while the latter was also in the repertoire of the Hôtel de Bourgogne,[99]

FIGURE 2.2: French School. Portrait of Marie Desmares La Champmeslé (1642–98), actress, as Roxane. Paris, Comédie-Française. Photo by Christophel Fine Art/UIG via Getty Images.

there is no evidence to that effect for the former. Only one new tragedy was given in 1679–80: *Agamemnon*, attributed to Pader d'Assezan in the account books but later claimed by Boyer.[100] It did moderately well, being given fourteen performances in 1679–80, plus twelve the following season, and was the only one of the new tragedies given at the Guénégaud to become part of the repertoire of the Comédie-Française.

The poaching of Mlle Champmeslé was, undoubtedly, one of the defining moments in French theater history. The Guénégaud actors were able subsequently to combine their own Molière inheritance with the tragic repertoire from the Hôtel de Bourgogne and thereby establish the basis of what would become the French national canon. The Hôtel de Bourgogne was badly hit and, only sixteen months later, was closed down and its actors transferred to the Guénégaud to form the Comédie-Française. This union might have taken place earlier were it not for the animosity that existed between La Grange and La Thorillière—one of those actors who had left Molière's troupe after its leader's death.[101] An article published in *Le Mercure galant* well after the event, in September

1681, emphasizes the superiority of the Guénégaud in this merger, saying that it had "raised up" ("releva") the Hôtel de Bourgogne troupe.[102] However, the journal, then under the direction of De Visé and Thomas Corneille, was notoriously partial, and there is evidence that De Visé at least received payments for the publicity he supplied.

A document drawn up to calculate what was owed by the Hôtel de Bourgogne troupe to La Thorillière's widow provides precious information as to what that company performed between July 28 and August 18, 1680. It continued to give *Le Cid*, *Mithridate*, *Cinna*, *Andromaque*, and *Ariane*, which were, therefore, in the repertoires of both troupes.

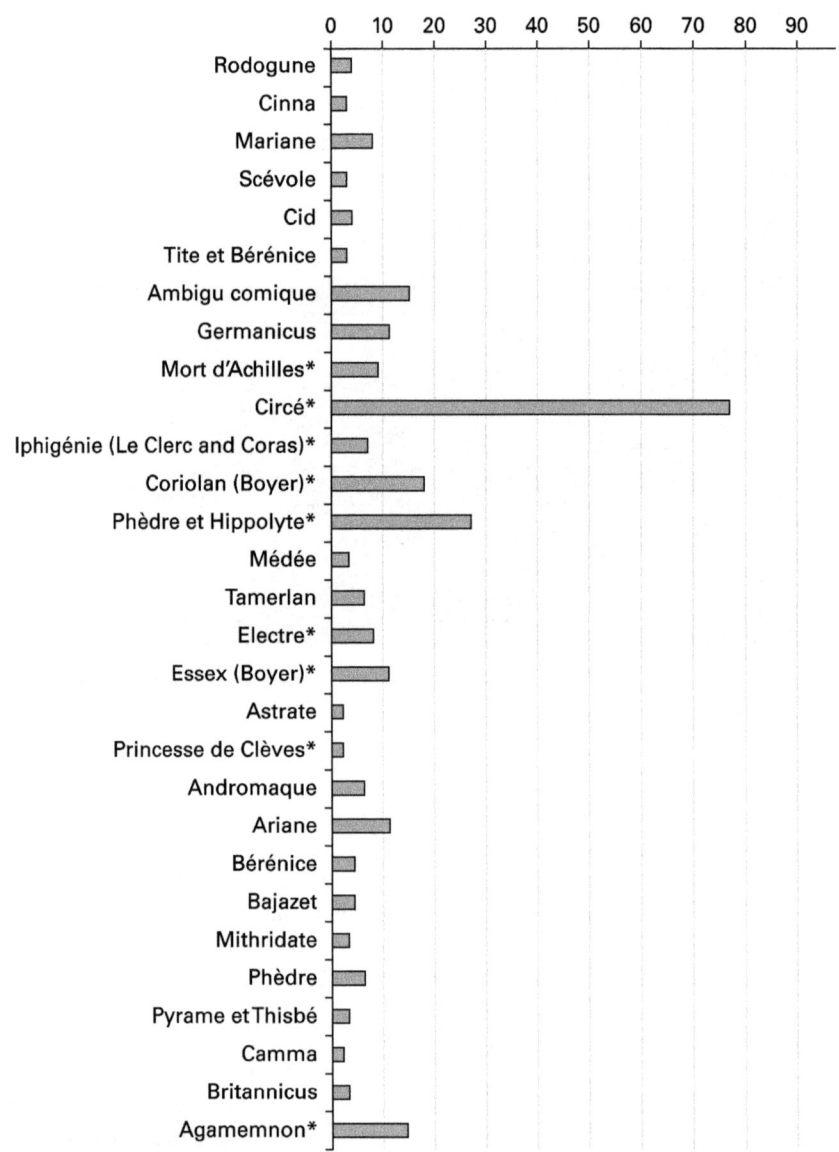

GRAPH 2.4: Total number of performances of individual tragedies given by the Guénégaud company, 1673–4 to 1679–80.

More surprisingly, it was also performing Molière's *Cocu imaginaire* and *Les Fâcheux*.[103] Mlle Champmeslé's roles had been taken over by Mlle Bellonde, who joined the company specifically for that purpose, following her successful reception at a private performance of *Ariane*. The *Mercure galant* account of her appearance in *Polyeucte* is, though, careful to underline what the Hôtel de Bourgogne had lost and the Guénégaud gained.[104]

The Comédie-Française was founded part way through the 1680–1 season, on August 25, 1680, with performances continuing uninterrupted. While it is possible to analyze the two halves of this season separately (as I have done in my previous studies), I here consider the 1680–1 season as a whole and include it in the Comédie-Française section so as to facilitate comparison across phases. It is at this point, then, that we can consider the relative success of those tragedies given at the Guénégaud. (See Graph 2.4.) Again, a spectacular tragedy, in this case *Circé*, was by far the most successful. The new tragedies, *Phèdre et Hippolyte*, *Coriolan*, and, to a lesser extent, *Agamemnon*, also did well, but the majority were undistinguished. As for the revivals, most were introduced too late to feature in any significant way and would only come into their own at the Comédie-Française. We should, though, note the continued popularity of *L'Ambigu comique*.

## COMÉDIE-FRANÇAISE

The proportion of tragedy in the repertoire increased exponentially during the Comédie-Française years, in terms both of the number of plays and performances. One contributing factor was an increase in the production of new tragedies, with varying degrees of success. In 1680–1, these were: La Tuilerie's *Soliman* (twelve performances plus four the following season then dropped), Fontenelle's *Aspar* (three performances then dropped), and La Chappelle's *Zaïde* (fifteen performances then dropped). This last disappearance is surprising, given that fifteen performances was a respectable figure; La Chappelle did, though, provide new tragedies for the troupe in subsequent seasons.

In 1681–2, the troupe created *Oreste* by Le Clerc and Boyer (three performances then dropped), La Tuillerie's *Hercule* (sixteen performances then given in repertory up to 1687–8), La Chappelle's *Cléopâtre* (twenty-two performances then given in repertory up to 1688–9),[105] Pradon's *Tarquin* (four performances then dropped), and Genest's *Zélonide* (seventeen performances then given in repertory apart from 1686–7). This was the greatest number of new tragedies ever to be given in a single season. The rate dropped off slightly in 1682–3, when the following were given: Boyer's *Artaxerce* (five performances then dropped), La Chappelle's *Téléphonte* (eleven performances plus one the following season), Campistron's *Virginie* (ten performances then one in each of the following two seasons), and La Tuillerie's *Nitocris* (five performances then dropped).

The number fell again to three in 1683–4: Boursault's *Marie Stuart* (seven performances plus three the following season), Genest's *Pénélope* (eight performances then given in repertory apart from 1686–7), and Campistron's *Arminius* (fourteen performances then given in repertory apart from 1687–8). This rate continued as the norm in the next two seasons. Thus, three new tragedies were given in 1684–5: Louvart's *Mort d'Alexandre* (four performances then dropped), La Chappelle's *Ajax* (sixteen performances then dropped), and Campistron's *Andronic* (twenty-one performances then given in repertory). In 1685–6, the troupe created: *Aristobule* by an anonymous author (three performances then dropped), Campistron's *Alcibiade* (twenty-nine performances then given in repertory), and *Antigone*, again attributed to Pader d'Assezan but claimed by Boyer (three performances plus six the following season).

In 1686–7, the number of new tragedies dropped to two: Campistron's *Phraate* (two performances plus one the following season) and *Géta* by Péchantré (sixteen performances plus fourteen the following season and five in 1688–9). It remained at this level in 1687–8: Dupy's *Varron* (seven performances then dropped) and Pradon's *Régulus* (twenty-eight performances plus ten the following season). Then, in the final season of our period, the number returned to three: *Annibal* by Riuperous (six performances), an anonymous *Coriolan* (three performances), and *Laodamie* by Catherine Bernard, the only female author of a tragedy in the thirty years we are considering (seventeen performances).

We see, then, that although the company tried hard to introduce new tragedies, the results were less than brilliant, with only ten plays achieving fifteen or more performances and few going on to form part of the repertoire. There was, though, as previously noted, an overall rise in the number of tragedies given, as the actors returned to their stock repertoire, reviving old favorites performed by Molière's troupe and the Guénégaud company in the past, a number of which had also been given at the Hôtel de Bourgogne and the majority of which were performed with regularity: *Héraclius, Rodogune, Cinna, Mariane, Venceslas, Le Cid, Horace, Nicomède, Sertorius, Andromaque, Ariane, Bérénice, Bajazet, Mithridate, Phèdre, Polyeucte* (given in nine seasons), *Pompée, Pyrame et Thisbé, Britannicus* (eight seasons), *Alexandre* (seven seasons), *Scévole, Agamemnon* (six seasons), *Attila* (four seasons), *La Thébaïde, Astrate* (three seasons). Other tragedies previously performed at the Hôtel de Bourgogne (but not by Molière or at the Guénégaud) similarly entered the repertoire: Racine's *Iphigénie*, Pierre Corneille's *Oedipe* (given in nine seasons), Pierre Corneille's *Othon* (seven seasons), Thomas Corneille's *Comte d'Essex* and *Stilicon* (four seasons), Quinault's *Bellérophon* (three seasons). While Pierre Corneille's *Agésilas* was given a single performance in 1683–4 and then dropped.

1681–2 also saw the introduction of a new strand in the company's production policy whereby it embarked on a series of revivals of spectacular works. The first of these was *Endimion*, given eight performances in 1681–2, plus three in 1685–6. Spectacular plays did not normally enter the repertoire due to their demanding technical requirements. It is, therefore, surprising to see *Endimion* being performed as a stock play at this time, perhaps suggesting its spectacular content had been reduced.[106] However, after this testing of the waters, the strategy was taken to a new level in 1682–3 with the revival of Pierre Corneille's machine tragedy, *Andromède*—a play that had been created by the Hôtel de Bourgogne in 1650, given by Molière's troupe in Lyon in 1653, and finally revived at the Marais two years later.[107]

More than *Endimion*, the revival of *Andromède* at the Comédie-Française is evidence of the company's commitment to spectacle. As we have seen, Molière's troupe and the Guénégaud company had enjoyed considerable success with *Psyché* and *Circé*, causing Lully to respond by having restrictions imposed on stage music. As a result, Thomas Corneille and De Visé's subsequent efforts had all been in the comic vein and enjoyed diminishing degrees of success,[108] culminating in the withdrawal after two performances of *La Pierre philosophale* in 1681.[109] *Andromède* represents, therefore, a return to the back catalogue as a source of spectacle, not so much as a money-saving exercise (the production cost as much if not more than for a comparable new work),[110] but in a search for "safe bets"—works whose popularity might as far as possible be guaranteed by past success. Where *Andromède* was concerned, the strategy paid off and it was given forty-five times in 1682–3, before disappearing once more. *Andromède* was followed in 1683–4 by Pierre Corneille's other great machine tragedy, *La Toison d'or* (created at the Marais in 1661), embellished with a new prologue by La Chappelle and given thirty-four times. Then it was the turn of *Psyché*, performed twenty-three times in 1684–5. Finally, in 1685–6, the company turned to De Visé, but his *Amours de Vénus et d'Adonis*, created at the Marais in 1670, was only able to hold its place for six performances, at which point the troupe appears to have temporarily abandoned machine tragedy.[111]

How to explain this falling off in the popularity of machine tragedy? According to La Fontaine, in his *Epistle to M. de Niert on opera*, this was primarily due to a change in public taste:

> First the surprising spectacle of the machines
> Dazzled the bourgeois who called it a miracle;
> But the second time he did not rush to see them;
> He preferred *Le Cid, Horace, Héraclius*.[112]

> ("Des machines d'abord le surprenant spectacle
> Eblouit le bourgeois, et fit crier miracle;
> Mais la seconde fois il ne s'y pressa plus;
> Il aima mieux *Le Cid, Horace, Héraclius*.")

These lines were, however, written shortly after the comparative failure of Lully's opera *Isis* in 1677 and do not account either for the efforts of the Comédie-Française to relaunch machine tragedy, or its steady decline in popularity from 1682–3 onwards.

Graphs 2.5a and 2.5b allow us to compare the total number of performances accorded to those tragedies performed at the Comédie-Française. We see, then, that this is the period when what we now consider the great classics of the French national canon came to dominate, with *Le Cid, Andromaque*, and *Phèdre* being given between fifty and sixty performances; *Cinna, Mithridate, Iphigénie*, and *Andromaque* between forty and fifty; and *Rodogune, Nicomède, Ariane, Bérénice, Bajazet*, and *Oedipe* between thirty and forty. Perhaps more surprising, though, is the comparative success of new works that have since been forgotten: La Chappelle's *Cléopâtre*, Campistron's *Andronic* and *Alcibiade*, Péchantré's *Géta*, and Pradon's *Régulus*. And we should also note the popularity of the company's first two machine tragedy revivals: *Andromède* and *La Toison d'or*.

Bringing all this information together, allows us to establish a league table (Graphs 2.6a–c) showing the relative popularity of all those tragedies performed by our three companies across these thirty years. Immediately apparent is the extent to which the spectacular works *Psyché* and *Circé* outstripped other tragic creations. We should also note the good showing of the revivals of *Andromède* and *La Toison d'or*. This is particularly remarkable in that, with the exception of *Psyché*, each of these enjoyed only one run (*Psyché*, it will be recalled, was initially performed across two seasons and then given a further revival). Of the other high performing plays, those by Racine had been created comparatively recently at the Hôtel de Bourgogne, as had Thomas Corneille's *Ariane*, but were well on their way to becoming "classics." It may also have been significant that Mlle Champmeslé was still starring.[113] Some of these successful tragedies were very old (*Mariane* had been created in 1636 and *Venceslas* in 1647), and although their high ranking might partially be explained by their having been performed across a long period, that they remained in the repertoires of these companies for so long itself attests to their continued popularity.

The last years of the seventeenth century are frequently seen as a period of decline, following the death of Molière and the retirements of Pierre Corneille and Racine,[114] with no playwrights of merit emerging to replace them.[115] It is, though, impossible to test this statistically, at least where tragedy is concerned, given the absence of information

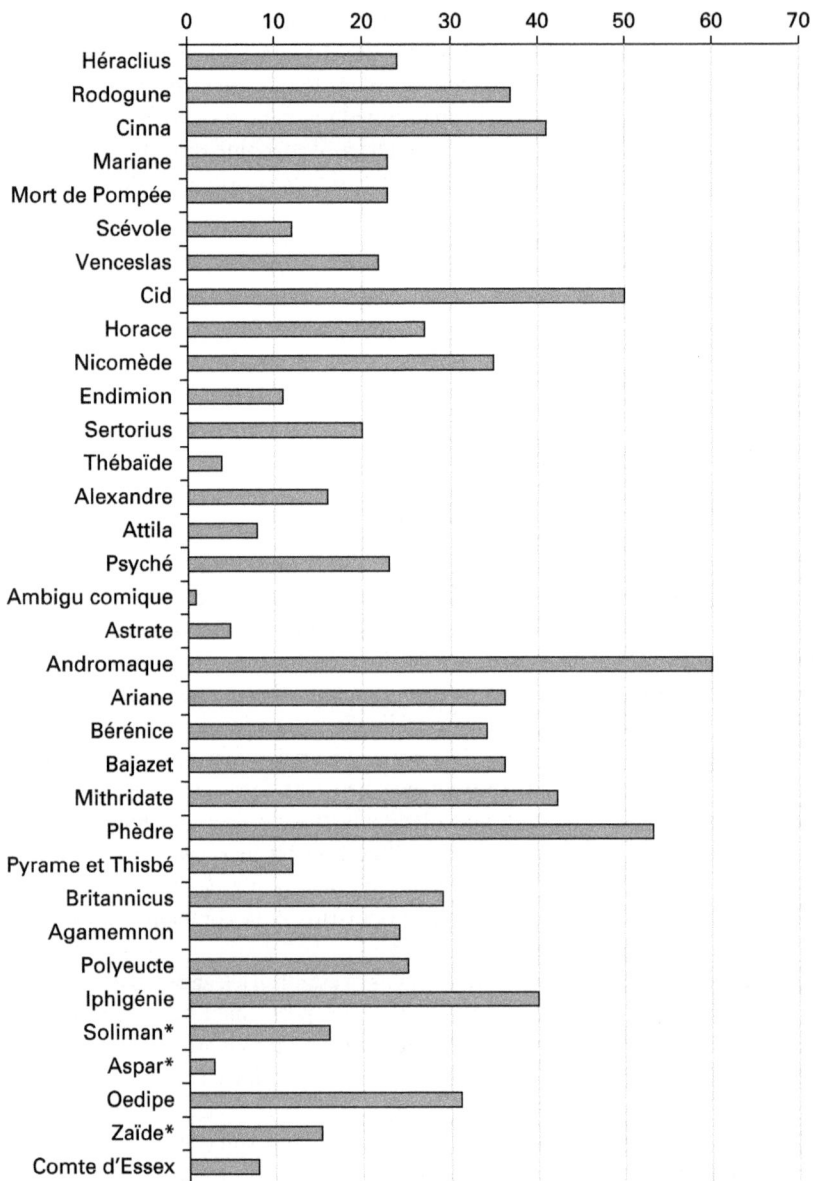

GRAPH 2.5a: Number of performances of individual tragedies given by the Hôtel Guénégaud company and at the Comédie-Française, 1680–1 to 1688–9 (part 1).

regarding audiences and takings at the Hôtel de Bourgogne. Who is to say, for example, that the initial runs of *Alcibiade* or *Andronic* were not more successful than those of *Andromaque* or *Phèdre*? Setting aside contemporary commentaries, which may well be biased, all we can say with certainty is that the former plays did not go on to become part of the canon whereas the latter did. It is, though, apparent as we scan our overall league

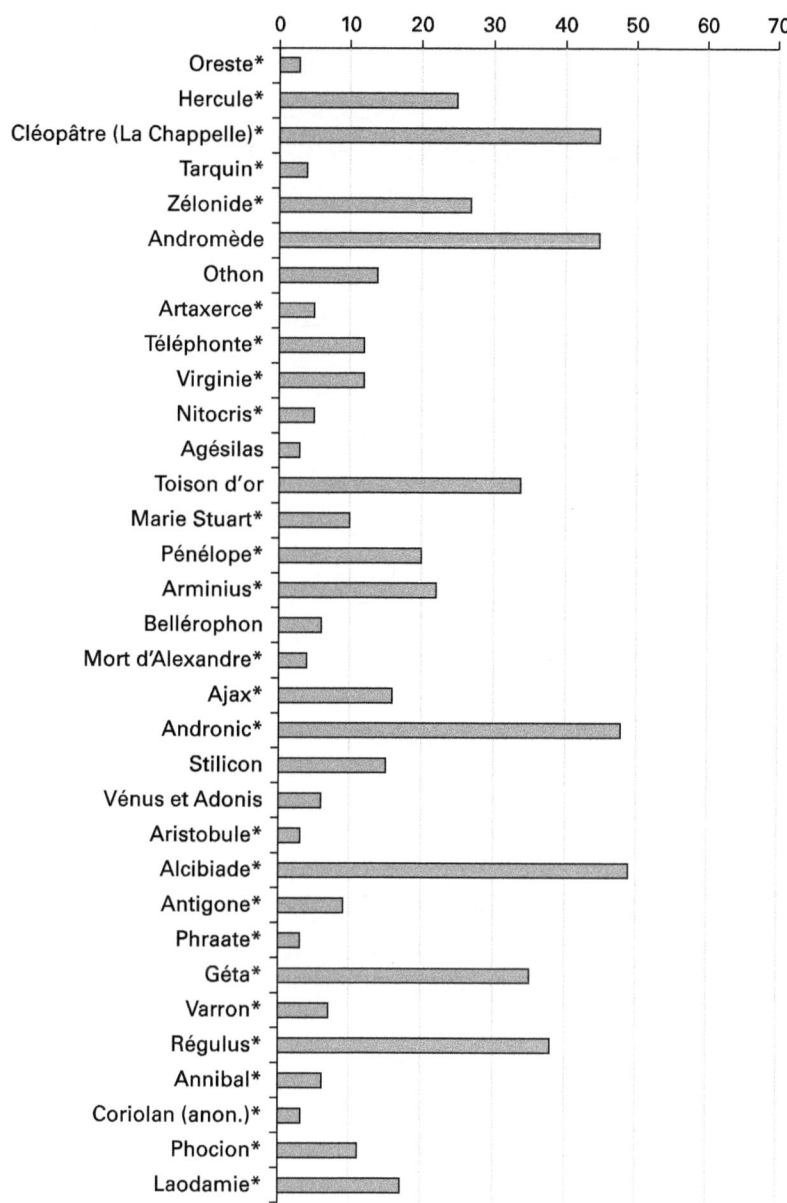

GRAPH 2.5b: Number of performances of individual tragedies given by the Hôtel Guénégaud company and at the Comédie-Française, 1680–1 to 1688–9 (part 2).

table that many tragedies created during this period performed poorly, even by the standards of the day, with 39 percent being accorded fewer than ten performances. Moreover, whereas during the Molière phase, four tragedies were performed in only one season (out of eleven), rising to five (out of nine) at the Guénégaud; at the Comédie-Française, this rose again to thirteen (out of twenty-nine).[116] It is indisputable, therefore,

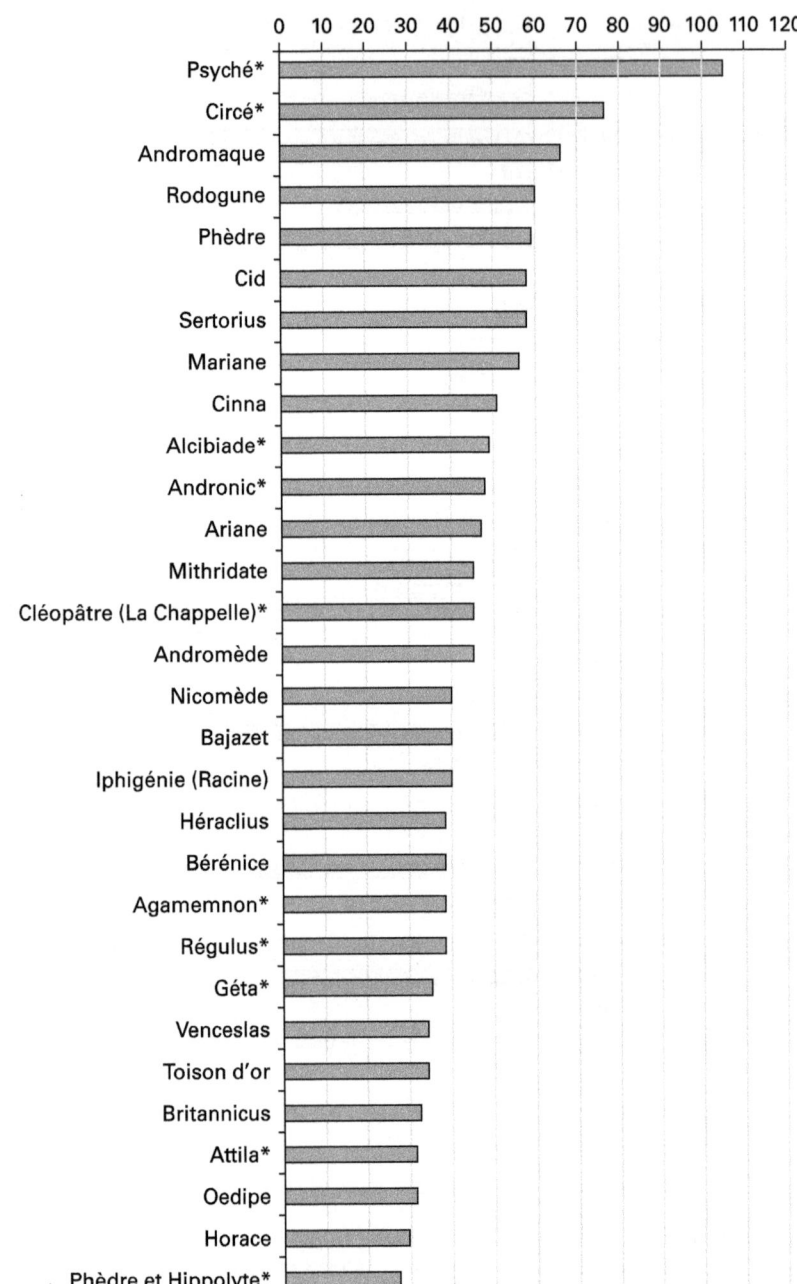

GRAPH 2.6a: League table of relative popularities (top third).

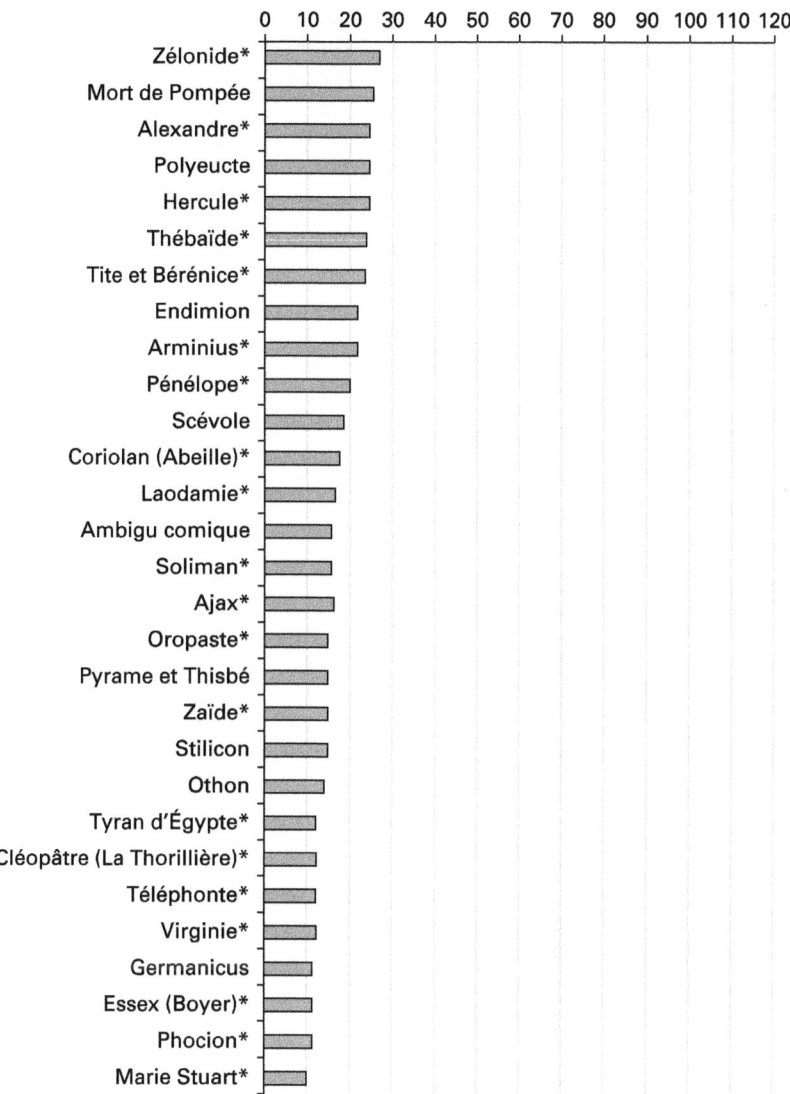

GRAPH 2.6b: League table of relative popularities (middle third).

that a high number of those tragedies selected for performance were failing to attract and retain audiences.[117] And when we consider the above figures as percentages (36 percent, 56 percent, and 48 percent respectively), we see that the Guénégaud, in fact, performed worst—perhaps understandably given that it was confronting the might of Racine at the Hôtel de Bourgogne. Little wonder, then, that it should have sought to triumph by other means via the suborning of Mlle Champmeslé.

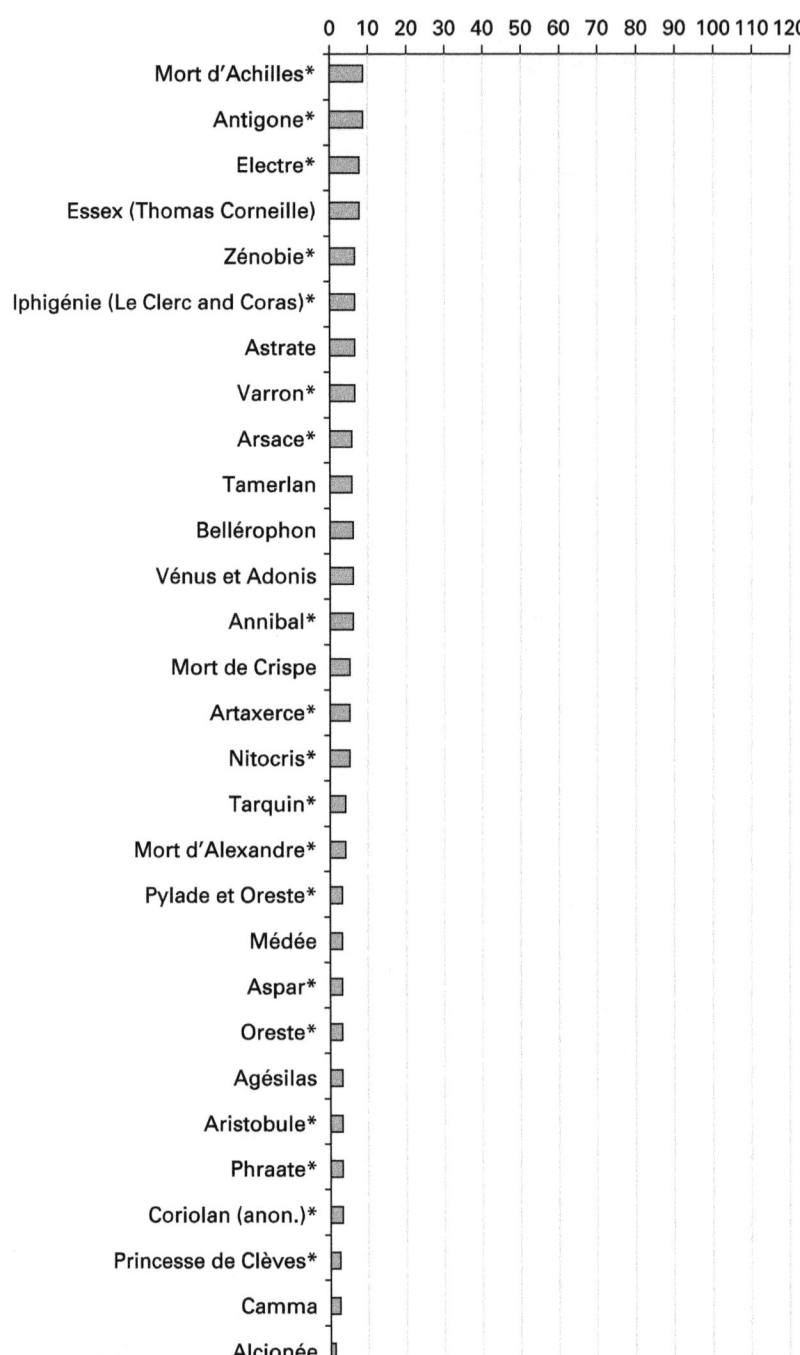

GRAPH 2.6c: League table of relative popularities (bottom third).

## TRAGEDIES PERFORMED AT COURT OR "EN VISITE"?

Thus far, I have described solely activity in the capital. However, these companies also gave private performances: for the king or for wealthy and usually aristocratic patrons. Many are recorded by La Grange, especially when they involved absence from Paris or the receipt of income. Others are not and can only be identified from other sources. Moreover, when La Grange does mention a court trip, he does not always state what plays were given. The accuracy of the recording of such trips increased considerably with the advent of the Comédie-Française. Even so, the figures I will give are necessarily approximate and can only serve to indicate general trends.

Of the 192 private performances I have identified Molière as having given at court and for other patrons, where plays are named only fifteen (8 percent) are tragedies: *Sertorius* three times, *La Thébaïde* three times, *Attila* twice, La Thorillière's *Cléopâtre* once, *Psyché* six times. This is scarcely surprising given that he and his company were celebrated primarily for comedy. Royal favor appears to have been personal to Molière and, following his death, the Guénégaud company appeared far less frequently at court, despite petitioning to be allowed to do so. Indeed, only eight private performances are recorded, of which three (38 percent) were of tragedies: *La Mort d'Achille* at Saint-Germain-en-Laye in 1674, and, in 1679, following the transfer of Mlle Champmeslé, Racine's *Phèdre* for the Spanish Ambassador and *Mithridate* for Colbert.[118]

This was not because the king had given up theater, for the Hôtel de Bourgogne performed at court much more frequently, with Pierre Corneille being a particular favorite. Thus, it is noted in the *Nouveau Mercure galant* (from January to March 1677) à propos of *Isis* that "The beauties of this opera did not cause the king and all the court to forget the inimitable tragedies of M. de Corneille the elder, which were performed at Versailles last autumn."[119] In the verses Corneille addressed to the king on that occasion, he boasts of Louis having "resuscitated" him in the face of challenges from younger rivals, and mentions recent performances of *Cinna, Pompée, Horace, Sertorius, Oedipe*, and *Rodogune*.[120] And in October 1677, the *Mercure galant* published a list of twenty-five plays performed at Fontainebleau by the Hôtel de Bourgogne that included *Iphigénie, Mariane, Pompée, Mithridate, Horace, Bajazet, Phèdre, Oedipe, Venceslas, Cinna*, and *Nicomède*.[121] Pierre Corneille was also resurgent in town; in March 1678, *Le Mercure galant* noted that his plays continued to be revived and that *Polyeucte* had recently been performed "with an extraordinary crowd and acclamations."[122] And on September 19, 1679, the new Queen of Spain attended a performance of *Sertorius* on the eve of her departure for her new country: "Thus it was with a play by the great Corneille that she enjoyed for the last time this entertainment in France."[123]

The Comédie-Française appeared at court with far greater regularity than the Guénégaud company, not least because its increased size meant it was able to split and simultaneously entertain both king and Parisian public. I have identified 406 performances between 1680 and 1689, 275 (68 percent) of which were of tragedies. Interestingly, an article in *Le Mercure galant* of September 1681 suggests that following the fusion the two component companies were still seen as separate entities when it came to performances at court:

> The actors who occupied the Hôtel de Bourgogne before the union of the two troupes have been chosen to entertain the king first. While they were at Fontainebleau, they performed many plays by M. de Corneille the elder and M. Racine, with a new tragedy entitled *Oreste*.[124]

("Les Acteurs qui occupoient l'Hôtel de Bourgogne avant la jonction des deux Troupes, ont esté choisis pour divertir le Roy les premiers. Pendant qu'ils ont esté à Fontainebleau, lis ont representé beaucoup de Piéces de Mr de Corneille l'aîné & de Mr Racine, avec une Tragédie nouvelle, appellée Oreste.")

The merger had, however, taken place over a year before and these were not the first works to be given at court. Moreover, tragic and comic works were never performed in isolation, as is clear from an article describing performances organized by the King's brother at Saint-Cloud: "*Zaïde Princesse de Grenade* and *Les Prétieuses ridicules* were performed. ... There were balls or plays every day. Apart from the two I have just mentioned, *Iphigénie* by M. Racine ... was performed with *La Comtesse d'Escarbagnas* by the late Molière; *Dom Bertrand de Cigarral* by M. de Corneille the younger; and *Les Usuriers* by the Italians."[125] And the popularity of older tragedies with the court is further attested to by an article reporting on another series of entertainments at Saint-Cloud that included *Nicomède*, *Oedipe*, *Polyeucte*, *Venceslas*, *Britannicus*, and *Phèdre*.[126]

Of the sixty-six tragedies given by the Comédie-Française in this period, only sixteen were not given at court. Four of these were spectacular works, whose technical requirements would not have allowed them to be transported (*Endimion*, *Psyché*, *Andromède*, *La Toison d'or*, *L'Amour de Vénus et d'Adonis*). Of the remainder, seven were new plays (*Aspar*, *Tarquin*, *Nitocris*, *Marie Stuart*, *Mort d'Alexandre*, *Annibal*, *Coriolan*), none of which had been given more than seven times in town. However, *Oreste*, *Artaxerce*, *Aristobule*, *Antigone*, and *Phraate* all fared just as badly in town if not worse, and that did not prevent them from being seen at court. The remaining three plays that were not performed at court were *L'Ambigu comique*, *Astrate* and *Agésilas*; and while the neglect of the former two is understandable, it is an indication of the unpopularity of Pierre Corneille's tragedy to find it on this list.

The fifty-one tragedies that were performed privately were not, however, treated equally (see Graphs 2.7a and 2.7b). We see that the great "classic" tragedies by Pierre Corneille and Racine were much more in demand for private performances than were the majority of new plays, although *Alcibiade*, *Andronic*, and *Cléopâtre* again did remarkably well. The presence of one play on this list must, however, be singled out, for Pierre Corneille's *Tite et Bérénice* was performed at court in 1682–3 without, to my knowledge, having previously been given at the Comédie-Française. On February 9, 1683, the Comédie-Française gave a performance at Versailles of a work identified in the account book as "Bérénice,"[127] which commentators have generally identified as Racine's work.[128] However, letters preserved in the Comédie-Française archives, not only reveal it to have been Pierre Corneille's *Tite et Bérénice*, but also attest to the Dauphin's determination to see it. On January 18, 1683, Duché, who was responsible for liaison between the company and the Gentlemen of the Bedchamber who organized court entertainments, wrote to La Grange instructing him to replace Corneille's *Tite et Bérénice* at the top of the list of plays to be performed there with *Pyrame et Thisbé*, *Attila*, *Agésilas*, and *Sophonisbe*.[129] He wrote later the same day, saying that the reason for this postponement was to allow the troupe time to prepare. The performance was next programmed for January 21, by order of the Dauphin, but was delayed yet again, finally taking place on February 9.[130] And it is no doubt this performance that explains the inclusion of "*Bérénice* by M. Corneille" ("Berenice de mr Corneille") in the list of scenic requirements known as the *Mémoire de Mahelot*, where it is specified unhelpfully that the "stage is a palace" ("Theatre est un palais").[131]

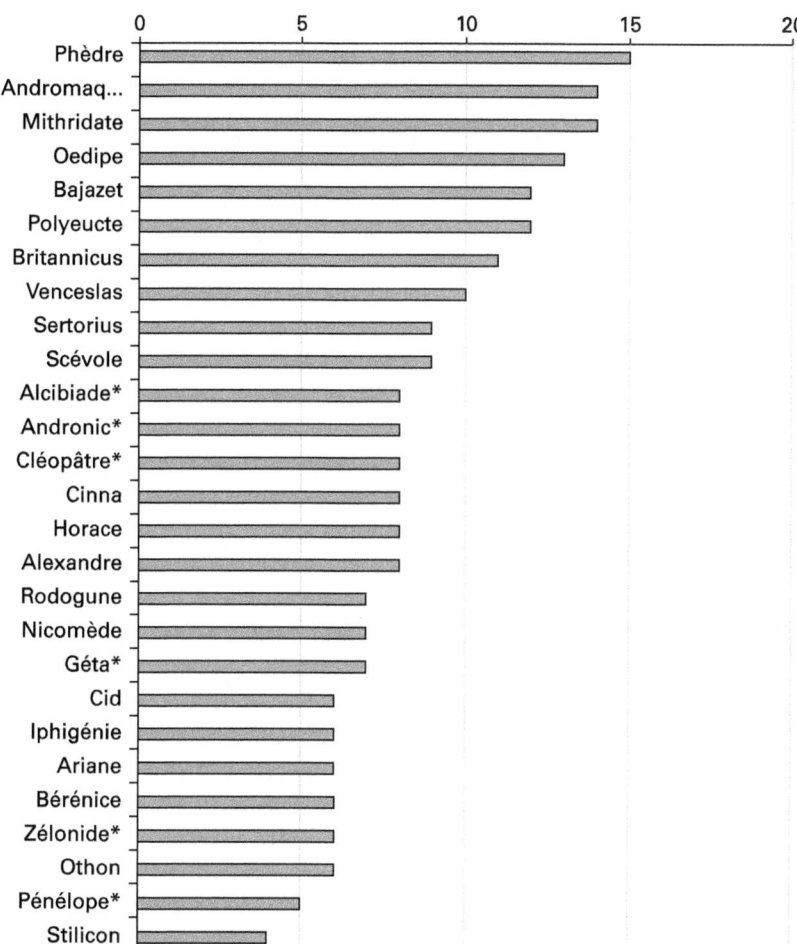

GRAPH 2.7a: League table of tragedies performed privately, 1680–1 to 1688–9 (top half).

## CONCLUSION

I have long been convinced of the necessity of studying not just those new works given in any one season or by any one company, but also how companies put their programmes together day by day, week by week, season by season. In this regard, the Comédie-Française Registers project is a major advance, but only begins in 1680. The Comédie-Française was, though, very much a product of what had gone before in terms of the repertoires and administrative practices of the four companies (Hôtel de Bourgogne, Marais, Molière, Hôtel Guénégaud) that contributed to it directly or indirectly. All four of these had performed tragedies, to a greater or lesser extent and with a greater or lesser degree of success. A study of the repertoires of the three companies for which we have the most complete records and which succeeded each other chronologically enables us to see how tragedy played a major role in subtly different ways in the activity of each of them: from Molière, with his passion for Pierre Corneille, via the Hôtel Guénégaud and its "war of the tragedies" ("guerre des tragédies") to the establishment of the tragic canon

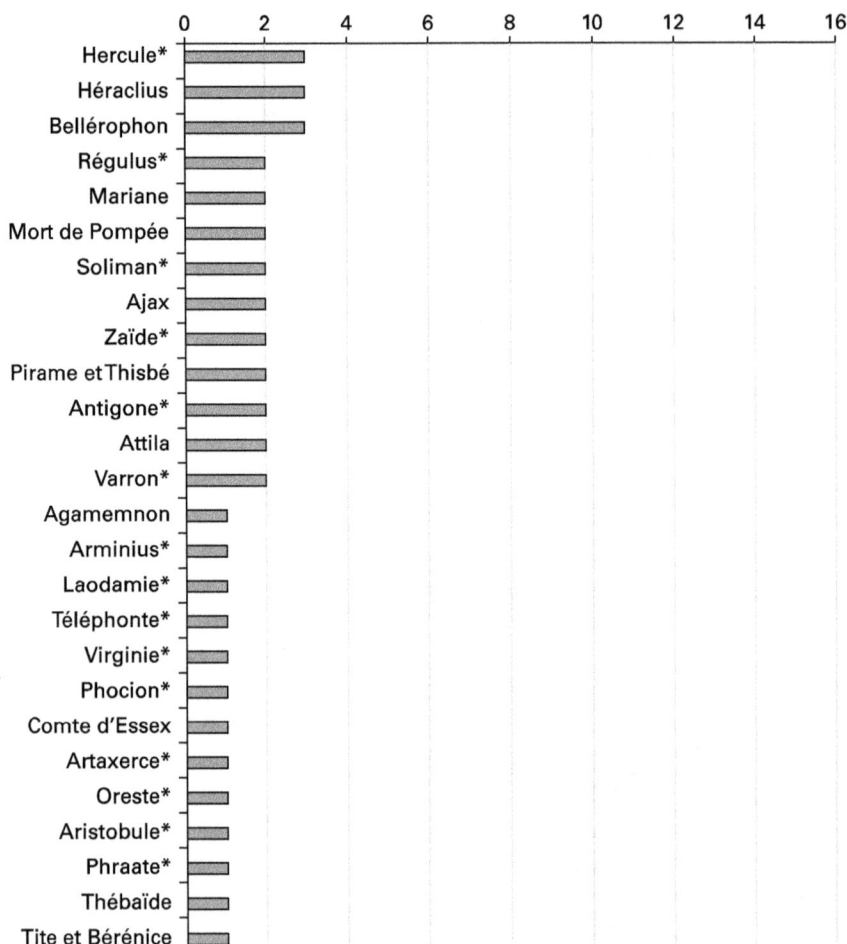

GRAPH 2.7b: League table of tragedies performed privately, 1680–1 to 1688–9 (bottom half).

at the Comédie-Française. Of course, any such study necessarily comes to a somewhat abrupt conclusion and this is no exception. Not only did plays introduced in the last of the seasons considered here continue on (however briefly) in the repertoire of the Comédie-Française (*Laodamie* for example), but policies were maintained or evolved over time (as with the revival of *Circé* in 1705). It is also important to remember that our views as theater historians are influenced by the work of those scholars (and practitioners) who have preceded us, and Sara Harvey rightly points to the "drastic selection" ("tri drastique") effected in the nineteenth century with regard to the national repertoire.[132] I hope, therefore, to have also reminded readers that the diversity of tragic output was greater in this period than is often supposed and to have drawn their attention to some tragic triumphs of the age that have since been largely forgotten.

# CHAPTER THREE

# Communities of Production and Consumption

SYLVAINE GUYOT AND CLOTILDE THOURET

The period from 1660–1800 witnessed an increasing professionalization of artistic producers, an expansion of the public sphere of cultural consumption, the emergence of a market-dependent theater still partly structured by political power, and the growth of transnational artistic exchanges along with a drive to establish national canons. This multifaceted movement ushered in new relationships between stage, state power, and market, between playwrights and performers, and between theatergoers, practitioners, and the definition of socio-aesthetic value. Tragedy—as a genre, a repertoire, and an event—was part of this evolving theatrical culture, which developed progressively as a cohesive yet highly competitive and polemical community of in(ter)dependent agents. Focusing on Paris and London, the most influential cities in the production and mediation of performing arts culture in seventeenth- and eighteenth-century Europe, this chapter will consider four intersecting contexts and their corresponding influences on the production and consumption of tragedy: the monopoly of official urban theaters, the unprecedented elevation of the status of actors and actresses, the growing affirmation of playwrights, and the rise to power of an increasingly diverse theater audience.

## THE TRAGIC REPERTOIRE: THEATER INSTITUTIONS AND COMMERCIALIZATION

Contrary to what the scholarly discourse has tended to assert, tragedy did not fade from European stages during the Old Regime. Right up to the end of the eighteenth century, national theatrical institutions continued to accord tragedy a place that, while hardly dominant and even rather diminished, remained nonetheless central to their repertoire. Tragedy continued to be an economic resource for the managers of official theaters (it attracted a steady audience), a form of socio-aesthetic capital (it was prized by celebrity players, literary critics, and foreign visitors) and a political stake (it was perceived as a site of national significance).

The system of monopolies established by the state in seventeenth-century England and France (in 1660 and 1680 respectively) resulted in the development of theatrical management based on profit-seeking, on the one hand because it accentuated commercial competition between official theaters as well as between official and unofficial theaters, and on the other hand because in conferring a certain autonomy on troupes, it made them dependent upon box-office gain. Within this context of commercialization, the programming of tragedies involved an economic logic: secure existing parts of the market by reviving old favorites while adapting to evolutions in taste by promoting novelty. But the constitution of a tragic repertoire also involved logics of consecration (of classical authors) and legitimation (of new productions), and therefore the creation of a canon that engaged a cultural politics. In this respect, privileged theaters combined multiple functions, as custodians of national patrimony, sites of institutionalization of recent plays, and spaces of innovation. Of course, the Comédie-Française and London's patent theaters were not the only places of diffusion for tragedy: it was also performed in royal residences, society theaters, regional theaters, other European courts, and in the colonies.[1] On all these other stages, however, it occupied a relatively smaller place than it did in the official city theaters of Paris and London, which played a decisive role in the definition of the tragic canon.

Who *did* compose the repertoire? In October 1680, a royal decree founded the Comédie-Française, uniting the Guénégaud troupe, a fusion of the troupes of Molière and the Marais in 1673, with the Hôtel de Bourgogne. The troupe was granted a monopoly over non-musical, French-language performances, and thus over the playing of spoken tragedy, at court and in Paris. On January 5, 1681, an act of union made the twenty-seven members of the newly fashioned company into a "society" defined by collective participation in artistic management, shared profits and losses, and communal financial responsibility. As the actor Lekain put it, "the Revenue" from ticket sales and thus the commercial potential of programmed plays became the actors' priority.[2] In one sense, programming came down to their initiative: they gathered every fortnight to establish the programme for the coming weeks and to decide to accept, reject, or request edits to new plays submitted to them. In another sense, however, it fell under the control of the First Gentlemen of the King's Bedchamber, who could interfere with any aspects of the theater's operation. Their regulations included such impositions as the alternation between tragedies and comedies as well as censorship, entrusted to the Lieutenant-General of Police in 1706: in 1731, for instance, Voltaire's *Samson* was banned as his *Mahomet* will be ten years later. During the French Revolution, censorship was suspended under the decree on "the liberty of theaters" of 1791, but it was restored in 1793. Tragedies that staged Old Regime values were prohibited or expurgated: titles of nobility were stricken from *Phèdre* and *Britannicus*, and even the patriotic *Mort de César* by Voltaire was modified, with the addition of a final chorus that justifies regicide.

The situation was somewhat different in England, though it relied on the same principles of monopoly and censorship. With the Restoration of the monarchy, patents issued in 1662 and 1663 established the basic structure of a shared monopoly, reinforced in 1737 by the Licensing Act. Apart from brief periods of lax enforcement, Drury Lane and Covent Garden were the only two troupes in London with the right to give public performances of legitimate drama. As they possessed only minimal royal financial support, companies could be sold in whole or in part to outside investors. Though servants of the king, actors were first and foremost salaried employees, working for the financial benefit of investors. However, financial as well as artistic management often came down to actor-managers, like Colley Cibber or David Garrick at Drury Lane. Throughout this period, censorship from the office of the Lord Chamberlain put a direct stranglehold on the London stage programming. In 1680, when, after the initial denial of a license for Nahum Tate's allegedly "antimonarchical" adaptation of *Richard II*, Drury Lane manager Thomas Killigrew tried to go forward with the show by changing the character names and the title to *The Sicilian Usurper*, the Lord Chamberlain closed the theater for ten days. With the passage of the Licensing Act of 1737, which toughened the censorship regulations, many tragedies with political resonance or heretical opinions were denied licenses, with the consequence of a swift reduction of new plays and an increased presence of Shakespeare in the repertoire.

What place did tragedy occupy in the repertoire between 1650 and 1800? A typical evening of theater comprised, at the Comédie-Française, a main play (tragedy or high comedy) and a short play, and in the patent theaters, a mainpiece and an afterpiece (a short comedy, a farce, or a pantomime), with a curtain-raiser as well as vocal, musical, or choreographed interludes. It is thus within a heteroclite ensemble that the serious genre stayed on the programme throughout the period.

Let us consider the Parisian case.[3] If we limit ourselves only to those plays labeled "tragedy," it appears that between 1680 and 1793, the Comédie-Française programmed 13,686 evenings that contained a tragedy (counting 474 performances of the *Cid* but not the seventy-three evenings with a bourgeois tragedy, the 141 with a tragi-comedy and the thirty with a heroic, patriotic, or historical drama)—which makes up approximately 40 percent of a total of 34,363 evenings. Racine leads the pack (2,522 evenings), followed with a tie between Corneille (1,961) and Voltaire (1,951), then Thomas Corneille (586), Campistron (577) and Crébillon père (523). Over the period from 1740–93, however, Voltaire carries the day by a large margin, with 1,701 evenings, compared to 892 and 513 respectively for Racine and Corneille, whose performance numbers decreased by half from 1740. The commercial success of Voltaire was enormous; in the 1770s, *Tancrède*, *Alzire*, and *Mahomet* figured among the six most lucrative plays.[4] Tragedy never failed to bring in audiences and, between 1720 and 1789, evenings with a tragedy brought in more (1,635 *livres*) than those without (1,169 *livres*). Moreover, the Comédie-Française owed 60 percent of its most profitable evenings to the tragic genre: of the 1,235 days exceeding 3,000 *livres* in revenue, 759 included a tragedy—with the top sellers being Voltaire (220 evenings), Racine and Corneille (62 evenings each), Pierre-Laurent de Belloy (52), Antoine-Marin Lemierre (31), and Jean-François Ducis (30). Inversely, tragic evenings were less likely to flop: of the 9,718 evenings with takings less than 400 *livres*, only 20 percent included a tragedy. Evidence of the symbolic prestige enjoyed by the genre, the theatrical season most often closed, before Easter, with a tragedy. At the beginning of the century, these were most often religious tragedies: *Polyeucte* brought in more than 6,000 *livres* of revenue on March 16, 1720 and April 1, 1724, exceptional for the decade. From the 1740s, following the secularization of the repertoire, successful tragedies took precedence: *Zaïre* closed the season on April 10, 1734, only two years after its premiere, then again in 1735, 1743, and 1744. Programming patterns also reveal competition between spoken and musical tragedy. Tragedies were most often performed on Mondays, Wednesdays, and Saturdays, which were off days for the Royal Academy of Music, eliminating the need for the Parisian public to choose between opera and theater.

As for the relationship between neoclassical tragedies and tragic novelties, evidence reports a clear decline for seventeenth-century plays in the last decades of the Enlightenment century. While around 1770 Lekain still deemed older plays to be as likely to succeed as Voltaire's greatest hits—"the less lavish repertoire plays such as *Britannicus*, *Mahomet*, *Mérope* and *Cinna* sell seats, these precious resources must always be kept around in case of a lull"[5]—taste seems to have changed two decades later: "the Theater is empty when we perform the masterpieces of Molière, Corneille and Racine."[6] Between 1740 and 1790, 1,922 evenings included a seventeenth-century tragedy, some 31 percent of tragic programming. Never absent from a season, Corneille and Racine stand out as the two canonical authors, even if their programming became very irregular after 1745. Of

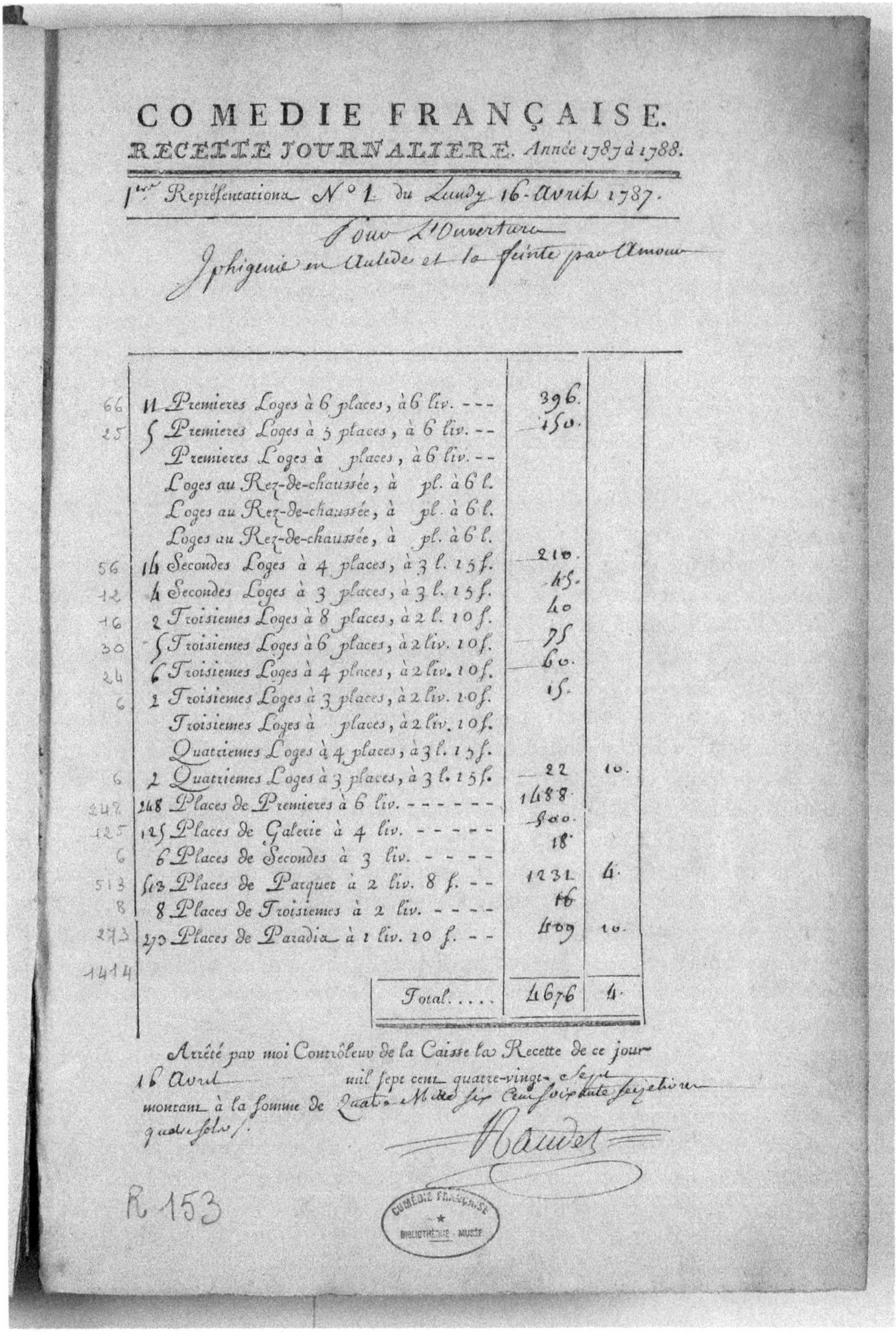
COMEDIE FRANÇAISE.

RECETTE JOURNALIERE. Année 1787 à 1788.

1ère Représentation. N° 1. du Lundy 16 Avril 1787.

Pour L'Ouverture

Iphigenie en Aulide et la feinte par l'Amour

| | | | |
|---|---|---|---|
| 66 | 11 Premieres Loges à 6 places, à 6 liv. | 396. | |
| 25 | 5 Premieres Loges à 5 places, à 6 liv. | 150. | |
| | Premieres Loges à places, à 6 liv. | | |
| | Loges au Rez-de-chaussée, à pl. à 6 l. | | |
| | Loges au Rez-de-chaussée, à pl. à 6 l. | | |
| | Loges au Rez-de-chaussée, à pl. à 6 l. | | |
| 56 | 14 Secondes Loges à 4 places, à 3 l. 15 f. | 210. | |
| 12 | 4 Secondes Loges à 3 places, à 3 l. 15 f. | 45. | |
| 16 | 2 Troisiemes Loges à 8 places, à 2 l. 10 f. | 40 | |
| 30 | 5 Troisiemes Loges à 6 places, à 2 liv. 10 f. | 75 | |
| 24 | 6 Troisiemes Loges à 4 places, à 2 liv. 10 f. | 60. | |
| 6 | 2 Troisiemes Loges à 3 places, à 2 liv. 10 f. | 15. | |
| | Troisiemes Loges à places, à 2 liv. 10 f. | | |
| | Quatriemes Loges à 4 places, à 3 l. 15 f. | | |
| 6 | 2 Quatriemes Loges à 3 places, à 3 l. 15 f. | 22 | 10. |
| 248 | 248 Places de Premieres à 6 liv. | 1488. | |
| 125 | 125 Places de Galerie à 4 liv. | 500. | |
| 6 | 6 Places de Secondes à 3 liv. | 18 | |
| 513 | 513 Places de Parquet à 2 liv. 8 f. | 1231. | 4. |
| 8 | 8 Places de Troisiemes à 2 liv. | 16 | |
| 273 | 273 Places de Paradis à 1 liv. 10 f. | 409 | 10. |
| 1414 | | | |
| | Total.... | 4676 | 4. |

Arrêté par moi Contrôleur de la Caisse la Recette de ce jour 16 Avril mil sept cent quatre-vingt sept montant à la somme de Quatre Mille six Cent soixante seize livres quatre sols.

Haudet



FIGURE 3.1: Comédie-Française Registers, Monday, April 16, 1787. 1787–8 Season Opening, *Iphigénie en Aulide* by Racine, followed by *La Feinte de l'amour* by Claude-Joseph Dorat. Bibliothèque-Musée de la Comédie-Française. © Comédie-Française.

Corneille's work, only eleven tragedies survived, led by the "tetralogy" (*Le Cid*, 144 performances; *Cinna*, 103; *Horace*, 51; *Polyeucte*, 74), but including also *Rodogune* (137) and *Héraclius* (86). The Racinian corpus lost its earliest plays (*La Thébaïde* was performed for the last time in 1722–3 and *Alexandre* in 1704–5) as well as *Esther* (long banned from public performance, its revival without music flopped in 1721). Proof of Racine's status as an institution, *Phèdre* played the opening of the Tuileries in 1770 and *Athalie* that of the Odéon in 1782; between 1680 and 1740, the Comédiens-Français staged forty-seven "Racine evenings," for which one of his tragedies was coupled with *Les Plaideurs*.

For the eight other seventeenth-century playwrights whose works were performed in the eighteenth century, the selection reduced most often to a single play, and many disappeared after 1750: by Thomas Corneille, *Le Comte d'Essex* (131 performances) and *Ariane* (104), *Médée* by Longepierre (112), *Manlius Capitolinus* by La Fosse (52), *Vanceslas* by Rotrou (38), *Pénélope* by Genest (38), *Andronic* by Campistron (16), *Astrate* by Quinault (6), and *Scévole* by du Ryer (5). Various factors can explain such choices. For example, *Le Comte d'Essex* and *Ariane* were Thomas Corneille's tragedies that had immediate success when they premiered and which were subsequently published as a pair: the Comédie-Française seems to have taken into account the stage success and editorial strategies of the seventeenth century. But the presence of the *Comte d'Essex* on the bill can also be attributed to the prestige given to its title role by actors. The programming of neoclassical plays also echoed the judgment of critics. La Harpe, for instance, deemed only two seventeenth-century tragedies, besides those of Racine and Corneille, to be worthwhile, *Venceslas* by Rotrou and *Manlius Capitolinus* by La Fosse, and these were the only plays by those authors to be performed, even intermittently, up to the Revolution.

While priority went to new works in the second half of the eighteenth century, the Revolution disrupted this trend. Both the conservative Théâtre de la Nation and the patriotic Théâtre de la République privileged revivals, especially comedic ones, to such an extent that new works occupied less than one-tenth of the programming, and tragedy less than one-quarter.[7] On August 2, 1793, the government required the Théâtre Français to give thrice-weekly performances of republican tragedies with characters such as Brutus, William Tell, and Caius Gracchus, a decision that favored plays by Voltaire, Antoine-Marin Lemierre, and Marie-Joseph Chénier. During the Revolutionary years, Voltaire predominated largely, while the neoclassical repertory tended to be limited to Racine's works, of which only *Phèdre* and *Britannicus* counted more than ten performances. A patrimonial canon was thereby established, one which Napoleonic politics would soon reinforce.[8]

While the Comédie-Française's programming responded above all to commercial imperatives, it also manifested the institution's hybrid political position. Anti-Philosophe successes (like *Le Siège de Calais* by Pierre-Laurent de Belloy) figured on the bill at the same time as Voltaire took his place as a consecrated author central to the repertoire.[9] This double positioning came fully into play in 1789 when the troupe splits between the "Red squadron," grouped around Talma, and the "Blacks," led by Naudet.

In England, patent theaters followed somewhat conservative repertoire patterns, which can be explained by both a form of self-monitoring in a censorship context and the lack of competition resulting from their duopoly.[10] From 1660, the proportion of comedies, pantomimes, and musical shows was far larger than that of serious genres, a tendency that increased over the course of the eighteenth century. Tragedy was included, between 1700–28, in 2,361 performances out of a total of 11,837 (20 percent) and, between 1747–76, in 3,802 performances out of 24,870 (15 percent).[11] Revivals predominated by far over new works, and adaptations were numerous. After the Licensing Act of 1737, only three to six new works were programmed per season, often with little success. Recent plays with political overtones were rarely revived, with the exception of Otway's *Venice Preserv'd* (1682) which remained in the repertoire until the end of the eighteenth century. From 1660, Shakespeare dominated the mainpiece repertoire (along with, to a lesser extent, Jonson, Beaumont, and Fletcher). Adaptations made frequent concessions to contemporary taste (*King Lear* received a happy ending in Tate's version), and some strayed so far from the original text that, accompanied by ballets and music, they became almost semi-operas. Between 1730 and 1780, an average of fifteen Shakespeare plays were performed per season, which amounts to one-sixth of all evenings.[12] These evenings brought in more than the average, although when Shakespearean tragedy was coupled with a successful pantomime, such as those by John Rich, revenues climbed even higher.[13] Due to the dominance of Shakespeare, none of the tragic playwrights of the eighteenth century, with the exception of actor-managers like Cibber and Garrick, succeeded in making a complete living from their works.[14]

Thus, between 1650 and 1800, as new tragedies diversified in form and appeared regularly on programmes without becoming permanent fixtures (except for Voltaire in the French case), the repertoire of tragic "classics" narrowed and set. Previously, critical attention had tended to focus on the dramatic text; now, public interest concentrated as much if not more on the performers, who took on unprecedented importance in the cultural sphere of the Enlightenment era.

## THE TRAGIC PLAYER AS SOCIAL ACTOR: EVOLUTIONS AND PARADOXES

Over the period of 1650–1800, critical attention underwent a major shift. Now, the practice acting was considered alongside the poetics of dramatic texts. In France, during regional tours, the names of stars such as Lekain and Mlle Clairon appeared on publicity posters, while in London, monuments went up in the Poets' Corner, next to the statue of Shakespeare, to Hannah Pritchard (in 1772) and David Garrick (in 1797). Raised to the status of a theoretical object, the figure of the actor took center stage in burgeoning texts that recognized acting as an art form. Considered an essential vector for the emotions, actors' performance became a definitive criterion in the evaluation of a play. Valued for preserving the memory of great authors as well as for renewing theatrical aesthetics, actors were perceived as cultural mediators. As both economic agents and public figures, they participated fully in the new urban culture. Tragic acting played a decisive role in this institution of the actor, which reached its full expression at the end of the Old Regime. Paradoxically, even while tragedy as genre diminished in public interest, and the actor's moral and legal statuses remained precarious, the figures of tragic actors and actresses commanded increasing cultural fascination. To play a tragic lead was often a fulcrum point in an actor's career. It was an instrument of social mobility and a means of gaining cultural capital.

Early modern innovations in acting practice mostly centered on tragic performance. Although in the mid-eighteenth century Lekain declared that "there is almost nothing left" of the "old tradition," the change in acting style was less a revolution per se than a progressive transition from the declamatory model, based on rhetorical conventions privileging the voice (Figure 3.2), to an interpretative model, relying on emotional expression and full body engagement.[15] This reform in acting took place through disparate changes made by a handful

FIGURE 3.2: Antoine Watteau, *Les Comédiens-Français*, c. 1720. Oil on canvas, 57.2 × 73 cm. Metropolitan Museum of Art, New York City.

of daring performers. Each decade had its own champions of change: in the late seventeenth century, La Champmeslé in Paris and Thomas Betterton in England distinguished themselves by their natural embodiment of codes of eloquence; from the 1720s to 1730s, Michel Baron and Adrienne Lecouvreur set diction on a path toward simplicity; from the 1740s to 1750s, the great Voltairian actors Mlle Dumesnil, Henri Lekain, and Mlle Clairon contributed to the liberation of gesture, while David Garrick's expressive acting, a triumph in the Shakespearean repertoire, became a European model (Figure 3.3); at the end of the century, François-Joseph Talma in France and Sarah Siddons across the Channel were both celebrated for their marriage of statuesque style and passionate fervor. Some were limited to tragic roles (like Siddons, whom Reynolds depicted as a "Tragic Muse"), while others succeeded across genres (such as Garrick, portrayed as "between Tragedy and Comedy"). This movement owes much to European exchanges. Although the French model dominated until the middle of the eighteenth century, the gold standard migrated in the 1780s first toward England and then toward Germany, both of which were less marked by the legacy of Aristotle. For tragedians of the Enlightenment, the task was to combine English expressivity and French *bienséance*, both of which could potentially undermine tragic nobility by falling into their respective traps of banal prosaicism or excessive emphasis.[16]

Given the definition of tragedy as the realm of passions, the principal transformation in acting involved the naturalization of their expression. The declamatory model, structured by oratory rules of moderation and decorum, dominated the seventeenth

FIGURE 3.3: William Hogarth, *David Garrick as Richard III*, c. 1745. Oil on canvas, 190.5 × 250.8 cm. Walker Art Gallery, Liverpool. Wikimedia Commons/Google Art Project.

century. The tragedian had to adapt his diction, gesture, and facial expression to the meaning of his speech, according to a coded semiotics borrowed from physiognomy, painting, and rhetoric.[17] From the 1660s, the artificiality of tragedians drew more frequent ridicule, as in Molière's parody of the grandiloquent Montfleury in *Versailles Impromptu* in 1663. Under the influence of sensualism, as well as a challenge to the hierarchy of genres, tragic acting in the eighteenth century evolved toward a more life-like interpretation, in which bodily mobility and speed variation prevailed. In a move unprecedented for 1750s France, Garrick told Parisian salons that he played King Lear by imitating a father desperate at having caused his child's death. Far from constituting a consensual criterion, however, the notion of "naturalness" remained an unstable category: in 1763, Garrick deemed the acting of Mlle Dumesnil, who was celebrated for her spontaneous impulses, artificial.[18] Moreover, this tendency toward the natural must not occlude the diversity of styles that coexisted throughout the period (the enthusiasm of Mlle Dumesnil versus the coldness of Mlle Clairon) or over the career of a single performer (like Siddons, whose passionate acting became sculptural).

Second evolution: tragic acting became increasingly visual, under the double influence of comedy and the pictorial model, with stage movement gaining in expansiveness as seats were removed from the stage. Most obviously exemplified by Garrick, and later Talma, the accomplished tragic actor could make himself understood to an audience that did not speak his language. Pantomime, inherited from Elizabethan theater and Italian commedia, and celebrated as a return to the original acting of Antiquity, arrived in France, where its fortune manifested in two short-lived, but revelatory, endeavors: in 1714, two dancers from the Opéra performed a wordless version of Act IV of *Horace* and in 1769, Saint-Foix's adaptation of *Iphigénie* at the Comédie-Française ended with a sacrifice tableau. Suitable for ensemble compositions as well as solos, this "tableau aesthetic"[19] gave rise to unexpected actor inventions: Mlle Dumesnil surprised her audience by running across the stage in *Mérope* (1743); Lekain made the audience tremble in *Sémiramis* (1748) when he emerged from Ninus' tomb with bloodstained arms and quaking body; Pritchard put down the candle to rub Lady Macbeth's hands off (1748), an innovation reprised by Siddons.[20] Detaching itself from the illustrative function to which the rhetorical model had confined it, tragic gesture tended to define itself as a flash that creates a rupture, marks its audience, reverberates in the press, and thereby inscribes its performer as legend and model.

Third evolution: driven by an increasing concern for historical accuracy, tragedians progressively rejected the costume and make-up traditions of the seventeenth century—tonnelets, powdered wigs and feathered three-cornered hats for men, and large side hoops and courtly dresses for women, whether playing Roman dignitaries or Oriental slaves. Here again, there was hardly a clean break: in 1775, in *Pygmalion*, Mlle Raucourt wore a modern hoop skirt to play opposite Larive, himself in a classical toga (Figure 3.4).

FIGURE 3.4: *Théâtre Français, Mr Talma dans Brutus*, engraved by Adrien Godefroy, 19.8 × 14.7 cm. Galerie théâtrale ou Collection des portraits en pied des principaux acteurs des trois premiers théâtres de la capitale, Paris, Bance aîné, n.d. gallica.bnf.fr/Bibliothèque nationale de France.

As with gesture, this evolution can be attributed to a few tragedian reformers: Mlle Clairon was the first to appear without formal dress in *Didon* by Lefranc de Pompignan in 1745–6; in 1790, Talma, playing Proculus in Voltaire's *Brutus*, scandalized audiences by appearing bare-armed in a linen Roman toga. Painters and scholars served as reference points in this historicizing reform: Talma consulted his friend Jacques-Louis David and drew inspiration from research published by Levacher de Charnois as well as the work of antique dealer Aubin-Louis Millin.[21]

These transformations allowed for the emergence of individualized acting, based on the particular expression of the performer rather than on a universal typology of the passions. Actors also played an increasingly active role in theatrical creation. First, it was common for them to modify the text of tragedies: in 1765, *Adélaïde Du Guesclin* was republished in a version "corrected" by Lekain, whose name even replaced that of Voltaire; in 1772, Garrick cut the gravediggers' scene from *Hamlet*. Second, they had their say about generic evolutions: Sedaine attributed the failure of prose tragedy to Lekain's refusal to "prostitute his talent for the sake of prose."[22] Third, they drove the recognition of acting as a formalizable technique. Acting manuals were mostly the work of practitioners, as were the first pedagogical projects: Charles Macklin put an apprentice system into place, while François Molé developed the principles for a Royal School of Declamation that opened in 1786 (but closed in 1789) and taught language, dance, history, and geography, according to the new ideal of an *actor doctus*.

Actors' autonomy remained nevertheless circumscribed by a network of multiple dependencies. First of all with regard to the playwrights who formed couples with their favorite actors: Racine with La Champmeslé, for whom he demonstrated gestures and intonations; Voltaire with Mlle Clairon and Lekain, whom he rehearsed at Ferney or to whom he sent instructions by letter, reminding them that the text "belongs" to him.[23] Dependence, as well, with regard to the audience's expectations, as emblematized by Mlle Dumesnil who "courted the parterre."[24] Dependence, also, with respect to other actors: in 1721, Baron performed a silent sequence in *Mithridate*, but he never did so again because one of his fellow actors judged it a "false note."[25] Dependence, finally, with respect to the commercial demands of institutions: when, in 1765, Mlle Clairon, Lekain, Brizard, and Molé attempted to protest the dubious morality of one of their colleagues by refusing to perform the successful *Siège de Calais*, they were imprisoned for several days at For-l'Évêque.

The heightened social visibility enjoyed by performing artists, and tragedians in particular, makes them key figures of the celebrity culture that emerged during the Old Regime.[26] In 1742–3, the presence of Garrick doubled revenues, which passed from an average of £55 on the fifty-nine evenings where he did not perform, to £118 for the seventy-eight performances in which he figured.[27] In the 1760s, "fans" of Mlle Clairon showed up at each of her performances and interrupted her lines with their applause.[28] As Joseph Roach has noted, the *persona* of the first tragic stars was a composite of *stigmata* and *charismata*, which added up to the singularity of genius.[29] La Champmeslé with her ill-proportioned face, Betterton with his short arms and thick legs, Lecouvreur with her shrill voice, Lekain with his ruddy face, Garrick with his short stature, Siddons with her stoutness, all of them were nonetheless adored for their acting, understood as a total effect that transcends appearance.

The most famous tragic actors epitomize what Chris Rojek refers to as "achieved celebrity."[30] Agents of their own celebrity, they undertook a conscious self-refashioning, multiplying the by-products of fame made available through the developing urban media culture. They commissioned portraits by prominent painters, who immortalized them in their emblematic roles: while in Paris in 1764, Garrick had himself sent prints of portraits by Reynolds, Benjamin Wilson, and Joseph Zoffany who depicted him as Lear and Hamlet; 130 Wedgewood chess sets on which Siddons figured as the queen were sold between 1785 and 1795 (Figure 3.5). Acting treatises formed another site for the diffusion of notoriety. Mainly based on an empirical approach, they took stars as their examples, participating in the European circulation of references: in 1769, under the title *Garrick ou les Acteurs anglois*, the Italian Michel Sticotti loosely translated into French the 1755 version of John Hill's English treatise, *The Actor*, which was itself a translation, coupled with examples from the London stage, of the French *Comédien* by Pierre Rémond de Sainte-Albine (1747); between 1770 and 1777, Diderot wrote, in response to the work of Sticotti, his *Paradoxe du Comédien*, in which he uses Baron, Clairon, Molé, Lekain, and Garrick as case studies. The actors themselves took stances in the theoretical field through autobiographical writing: in 1798, twenty years after retiring, Mlle Dumesnil, apostle of passionate acting, published her memoires, *In response to the Memoires of Hippolyte Clairon*, which defended the opposing ideal of rational acting.

Oppositions were not merely theoretical. Palpable tensions during performances, plots to have rivals fired, competition for the distribution of roles ... small in number, this community of theatrical celebrities was torn apart by rivalries. During a performance of Nathaniel Lee's popular tragedy *The Rival Queens* in 1677, Peg Woffington literally stabbed George Anne Bellamy onstage.[31] Theaters sometimes used this competition for

FIGURE 3.5: *Sarah Siddons as Lady Macbeth*, by Staffordshire Pottery. Ceramic earthenware. Attingham Park, Shropshire. © National Trust/Catriona Hughes.

commercial ends, creating opportunities to test different acting styles against one another: in 1745, when Covent Garden revived *King John* with Quin in the title role, Drury Lane put on the same play, in a version closer to Shakespeare, with Garrick.[32]

Actor's celebrity went beyond the domain of theater. Integrated into high society culture, famous actors kept company with aristocrats and intellectuals. Regularly hosted by the maréchal de Richelieu and the duchesse de Gramont, Mlle Clairon enjoyed the support of major philosophers, while Garrick made a splash in European salons, notably those of the Helvétius couple, Madame Geoffrin, Baron d'Holbach, and the Duke of Parma. Theatrical stars also launched fashions: such was the case of the famous "Garrick cut," a small wig with five curls on each side, or of Pritchard's Warehouse at Covent Garden, where the actress sold costumes and fashionable clothes for society events. The emerging press played a central role in the image formation of performing artists. For actresses in particular, public celebrity ended in an overexposure of private life, sometimes for defamatory purposes, sometimes in the name of publicity. In the *Mémoires secrets pour servir à l'histoire de la République des Lettres*, Mlle Clairon and Mlle Raucourt received as much mention for their performances as for their private escapades, the former for her supposed nymphomania, the latter for her Sapphic liaisons.

The social glory of actors clashed with the precarity of their religious and civil status. Eighteenth-century culture continued to associate actresses with prostitutes. As actors were still excommunicated, the corpse of Adrienne Lecouvreur was likely thrown into a public ditch in 1730. And in 1761, when Mlle Clairon tried to use her influence in defense of actors' civil rights and incited the lawyer François-Charles Huerne de La Mothe to write a pamphlet in favor of the "civilization of actors," the work was condemned to be burned. While actors received greater recognition in England and Germany, in France it was not until the 1790s that they underwent moral rehabilitation.

Nevertheless, celebrity produced spectacular social ascendances and professionalization. Salaries increased, particularly for prominent tragic actors. Judith Milhous estimates that in 1795–6, Joseph Philip Kemble and Siddons earned six times what Betterton earned in 1703, and according to Claude Alasseur, although they dropped between 1720 and 1750, the salaries of the Comédiens-Français tripled over the course of a century, to reach an average of 25,000 *livres* per year in 1793 (equal to the salary of the Director of Ponts et Chaussées).[33] This access to financial autonomy was remarkable for actresses, who acquired an unprecedented independence in the social history of women. In London, several came into property, borrowed, invested, and became associates in theatrical management. While women remained less well paid than men, some could compete with eminent actors (in 1799–1800, Siddons made as much in an evening as Kemble made in a week) or negotiate their salaries as legitimate professionals (Mlle Clairon demanded 10,000 *livres* for a second trip to the court of Vienna, not counting travel costs).[34] The income gap between artists of renown and others was nonetheless enormous and deepened throughout the eighteenth century: in London in 1789–90, upper-scale actors could earn as much as 200 times as the lowliest performer.[35] Tragic stars had diverse means of supplementing their incomes. Many actresses were supported by influential benefactors. In London, the practice of benefit nights emerged, where ticket sales went to those actors who were well known enough to bring in audiences: Pritchard earned between a third and a half of her annual income from benefit nights. Moreover, in the "culture of mobility" that characterized European society of the Old Regime, players began to capitalize on their prestige through regional tours.[36] Lekain performed in twenty-nine regional cities, where he earned up to 6,000 *livres* in ten days, or the equivalent of one year's salary for a local actor. Stars also circulated in the emerging European cultural market, in a context of artistic emulation between royal courts.[37] Lekain performed periodically in half a dozen cities throughout Europe and, in 1763, Garrick embarked on a "Grand Tour" of two years. In France, this touring practice met with reluctance on the part of the King's Gentlemen, who complained of profit losses, and when in 1756, Lekain traveled to the court of Bayreuth without permission, he was imprisoned for three weeks, this episode indicating once again the limits of an actor's freedom as well as the growing tension between institutional interests and individual trajectories.

## TRAGIC AUTHORSHIP: BETWEEN CONSTRAINTS, LEGITIMACY, AND VISIBILITY

The constitution of the first literary field coincided with the promotion of dramatic arts and the institutionalization of theater.[38] The playwright, who had been writer-for-hire at the start of the seventeenth century, became an established author (Corneille and Racine), then a celebrity (Voltaire) and, finally, a recognized literary professional with the creation of the Society of Dramatic Authors in July 1777, on the initiative of Beaumarchais. The first laws covering literary and artistic property, in 1791 and 1793, reinforced this new playwright's status.

Such a linear progression tends to occlude the diversity of situations and trajectories, as well as the dynamic contradictions at work in the literary field. Playwrights at the turn of the eighteenth century built their careers by playing at once upon literary institutions (Academies), their ties with the elite (patronage, clientelism, etc.) and the commercial market for literature. As Gregory Brown has shown, "status and identity in Enlightenment literary life arose from the language, institutions, and practices inherited from the seventeenth century more than it anticipated new forms in the nineteenth and twentieth centuries."[39] Tragic practice is particularly revelatory of the situation of the playwright since writing tragedy played a decisive role in achieving the status of man of letters and in acquiring visibility in the public sphere.

The history of author remuneration is one of a power play between playwright and theater company. While the troupes maintained a dominant position, the overall power dynamic evolved to the advantage of the playwright, and often in favor of tragic authors. In the early seventeenth century, the poet was attached by contract to a troupe that owned the rights to his works. Richelieu's initiatives and the institution of dramatic art changed the game as it became possible for a tragedian to combine identities as both troupe author and court poet, and to unite symbolic recognition by the elites with public success.[40] A playwright could then add commercial revenues to gifts from protectors, or even obtain posts and offices that ensured financial stability. A new threshold was crossed in 1653 when Quinault, whose gallant tragedies met with great success, convinced the theater to pay him a percentage of ticket sales. Yet purely commercial revenue did not suffice, and playwrights had to find protectors and patrons. Racine received aid from Colbert, to whom he dedicates *Bérénice*. At the pinnacle of his career as tragic author at thirty-five years of age, his copyright revenue represented less than a third of his income: it amounted to 2,000 *livres*, while his position as Treasurer of France brought in 2,400, his royal pension 1,500, and various other placements 700.[41]

After the creation of the Comédie-Française, the situation changed: as the Comédiens-Français were the only ones to perform elevated genres, they regained the power they had lost due to rivalry between troupes. The playwright received a percentage of ticket sales only during the first uninterrupted series of performances, and then only if overall revenue exceeded a certain amount. The programming was often arranged such that the first series did not run for long. In the second half of the eighteenth century, due to a general growth of theatrical enterprises on the one hand, and the decrease in individual patronages on the other, authorial claims toughened, with several of them dragging the Comédie-Française into legal proceedings (Lonvay, Mercier, Palissot). Indeed, it was to put an end to the ceaseless conflicts that the Duc de Duras, First Gentleman responsible for overseeing the Comédie-Française, asked Beaumarchais to bring together "several of the most moderate and honest (*honnêtes*)" writers. From these meetings, the Society of Dramatic Authors was born. United against the actors, the playwrights demanded higher pay and detailed accounts to verify the amounts they were allocated by the troupe as well as to exert control over their texts (for example, the right to publish a play if it was not performed within two years of its acceptance by the troupe). In fact, the playwrights' aim was more to obtain public markers of association with the Comédie-Française, which could identify them as *gens de lettres*, than to assert their rights in economic terms, which would have shown a level of greed incompatible with the *ethos* of the man of letters.[42] Still, without going so far as to upset the balance of power, the foundation of the Society of Dramatic Authors moved in the direction of greater autonomy and promotion of the author.

To succeed in the Belles Lettres and take maximum advantage of this upgrade in the status of author, writing and producing tragedies appeared to be a judicious choice. The high genre did indeed allow for the aspiring man of letters to activate what Viala calls the "multiple alliance," which united renown given by a wider public (the people) and the elite audience (the court), recognition and legitimacy conferred by institutions, and the construction of a social network that provides access to protectors and patrons.[43] This was especially true for authors who adopted the "strategy of success," like Racine and Voltaire, in a context where the Comédie-Française found itself at the confluence of different dynamics that structure the literary field.[44]

From 1680, the Comédie-Française became almost an obligatory site of passage for those looking to achieve man of letters status: as a royal theater, it gave access to the restricted network of urban elites; as a commercial theater, it brought together a heterogeneous audience. Under the reign of Louis XV, royal patronage and court performances diminished; as a consequence, the King's Players controlled a playwright's access to revenue and prestige. Moreover, the influence of the Comédie-Française's programming was also national and even European. The social profiles of playwrights for the royal theater confirm this decisive role.[45] At the start of the reign of Louis XVI, they came for the most part from social backgrounds lower than those of other writers, and much lower than those of Academy members. Close to half of them came from bourgeois families, belonging to administrative, judicial, or financial milieus, and a little less than a third had a name with an aristocratic particle.

François-Marie Arouet's career is emblematic of tragedy's strategic role in social ascent. Son of a notary, Arouet studied at the Jesuit school Louis-le-Grand in Paris, where he gained a solid classical and dramatic education and socialized with economic elites. However, Arouet lacked well-placed connections and sufficient social status to obtain the recognition that make an author. To launch his career, he presented a work at the Comédie-Française, *Œdipe*, whose subject and dramaturgy paid homage to classical models, was an instant success: the play was performed thirty-two times in 1718. The young author then published the play with a dedication to the Regent himself and an introductory text that allowed him to dialogue with his great ancestors, Sophocles and

FIGURE 3.6: *Mlle Clairon couronne Voltaire sur la scène française*, engraved by Nicolas Dupin, after Claude-Louis Desrais. Gravure à l'eau-forte et taille douce, 20 × 26.5 cm. Bibliothèque nationale de France.

Corneille. This respect for norms, mixed with boldness and success, earned him recognition as a man of letters; indeed, it was from then on that Arouet took the name Voltaire, sign that he had achieved a new identity. A second tragedy (*Hérode et Mariamne*, 1725) and his new social connections granted him access to the entourage of the king. Voltaire's trajectory as court poet took a detour when he offended the chevalier de Rohan and chose to exile himself to England. On his return to France, the construction of his poetic authority would pass once again through tragedy, and therefore through the Comédie-Française, with *Brutus*, followed by other successes (*Zaïre*, *Mérope*, *Sémiramis*, *Tancrède*, etc.) that appealed to the era's taste for tears. Voltaire's plays made him into a new Racine in the eyes of his contemporaries and occupied, as we have seen, a dominant place in the royal theatrical repertoire. It is in fact at the performance of his tragedy of *Irène* that he was crowned a poet in 1778 (Figure 3.6).

In a literary space still largely structured by the norms, values, and institutions of the seventeenth century, tragedy remained the royal road for a playwright. By contrast, Mercier, who believed in the new genre of "drama" and sought foremost to secure the approval of a popular audience, took the most difficult path. He failed to have his plays performed at the Comédie-Française and was therefore constrained merely to publish his works. Significantly, a pejorative noun, "dramaturge," was coined for Mercier, which stripped him a priori of the authority and status of man of letters.

The status of the English playwright underwent a similar evolution.[46] While before the civil war, the author of a play was rarely identified by a large public and had minimal control over his texts, the second half of the seventeenth century saw the emergence of the playwright as a legitimate figure, with his own identity, dignity, and visibility. This resulted from institutional changes as well as an evolution in publication practices. Because of the distribution of the repertoire between the two companies founded in 1660, Davenant's company had to produce new works and adaptations, creating demand for playwrights on the one hand, and generating competition between the two theaters on the other as those new performances proved successful. Playwrights were awarded the net profits of the third night (and later in the century and the eighteenth century, the sixth and ninth nights). The theater thus became the most lucrative literary vocation—even though risks were higher for playwrights than for actors.[47] Moreover, the exclusive rights held by companies over their repertoire of plays encouraged the publication of texts. As playwrights acquired at this time the unrestricted right to publish their scripts, they found in publishing not only a new source of supplemental income but also a site of properly authorial existence. Two differences between France and England are nonetheless worth mentioning. First, tragedy carried a weaker legitimizing force for an English playwright than it did for a French one. In addition, while few women practiced tragic writing in France, they were much more numerous in England.[48]

The social and economic promotion of the playwright corresponded to his-or her-increased visibility in the public sphere. There were three modalities to this authorial presence, which over time came to resemble a type of stardom. The first was the publication of plays. Paratexts constructed the tragic poet *ethos*, through the publication of patronage relationships and explanation of his (or her) relations to Antiquity, to scholars, and/or to audiences. Thus, Dryden defined the "heroick play" as an imitation of the epic poem in his preface to the first part of *The Conquest of Granada* (1671). The publication of collected works (in *folio*) was an even more significant gesture. When Corneille published in 1660 his *Théâtre* in three volumes, he accompanied each volume with a *Discours* and each play with an *Examen*. Theoretical reflection thereby bolstered poetic authority and claimed a legitimacy superior to that of scholars through arguments based on playwriting experience. Further, the *folio edition* was a means of presenting one's works as the product of a singular authorial figure, a cohesive ensemble; it also forefronted, through its format, the quality of its printing, and through the paratextual materials, its author's civility, which could controvert the association of theater with immorality.[49]

A second form of authorial visibility concerned authors' involvement in the numerous quarrels which punctuated the Age of Enlightenment. These quarrels were one of the forms of exchange and elaboration of ideas constituting an alternative arena for authors. They offered an ideal opportunity to make oneself known: this was in part what pushed Racine to write his *Lettre à l'auteur des Hérésies imaginaires et des deux Visionnaires*, in response to Nicole who had called the poets "public poisoners" ("empoisonneurs publics").[50] To relaunch a quarrel could be the means to launch a play: in his nationalist and patriotic tragedy, De Belloy stigmatized so-called "citizens of the world" and picked up Palissot's attack against the Philosophes; the play thus echoed the debates between Philosophes and anti-Philosophes that had animated the French stage sometime prior.[51]

A third practice, finally, demonstrated the particularization of the figure of the author: the ceremony of premieres, which was established with the premiere of Voltaire's *Mérope* in 1743. The playwright was summoned by the audience at the end of the play, and had to appear onstage to receive "the judgment of the parterre."[52] This new ritual received ample commentary in the press and in letters, showing a symbolic exchange between playwright and audience: the first acquired the status of public figure, the second recognition of the legitimacy of its judgment, and both of them benefited from a recalibration in their favors of the balance of power between the different authorities at play within theatrical protocol.

## TRAGIC AUDIENCES: NEW PRACTICES, NEW POWER

It is difficult to identify any specific audience for tragedy or define what would have been the social characteristics of a tragic audience member. In the royal theaters, programmes combined tragedy and comedy in a single evening. Moreover, the gap in seating prices certainly indicated a social disparity between the audience of privileged theater and that of the boulevard theaters, but the diversity of spectators and their ordinary practices means that audience attitudes cannot be analyzed according to socio-economic criteria.[53] Knowledge concerning the privileged theaters nevertheless allows us to pinpoint the composition of audiences who attended tragedies and identify their practices, some of which extended beyond the space of the theater into the streets, the cafés and in print.[54] Besides the growth in number and social diversity of spectators, three aspects characterize tragical spectatorship during the Age of Enlightenment: the affirmation of the power of audiences; the inflection of taste in favor of pathos; the birth and development of specialized criticism.

In this period of theatermania, the number of spectators continued to grow as the seating capacity of theaters increased and numerous patent theaters opened in provincial cities. Drury Lane could accommodate 1,268 spectators in 1747, 2,206 in 1762, and 3,611 in 1791. A Theatre Royal opened in Bath in 1750; in Norwich in 1758; in Glasgow in 1764; and in Manchester in 1774. The seating capacity of the Comédie-Française in the successive houses occupied by the troupe increased continuously: 900 seats at the Hôtel Guénégaud in the 1680s, 1,000 seats and another forty-odd boxes in the theater at rue des Fossés Saint-Germain from 1689 to 1770, to around 1,750 seats in the salle des Machines at the Tuileries between 1770 and 1782, then to close to 2,000 at the Théâtre de l'Odéon from 1782 to 1793.

In the second half of the seventeenth century, the court audience continued to be a significant one for tragedy. But by the turn of the eighteenth century, the heart of theatrical life was situated essentially in the city, and in Paris in particular. While the Comédie-Française was less accessible to the lowest classes, its audience remained relatively diverse. However, the spatial arrangement of spectators within the theater indicated a sociological difference. On the stage until 1759, benches sat nobles, officers, and gentlemen of fashion. Gentlewomen for their part could sit at the front of the first boxes. The affluent audience occupied the amphitheater; bourgeois and merchants took the second boxes and the least fortunate spectators, young men, and working girls found themselves in the upper balcony. The majority of the audience (61 percent during the first half of the century) occupied the pit, exclusively male and socially mixed as it comprised officers, lawyers, financiers, employers, artisans, apprentices, and students (Figure 3.7). The truly popular audiences (shopkeepers, colliers, etc.) could, for their part, attend the free performances given on the occasion of national events and on Sundays, until the Revolution opened the doors of the theater to them.

FIGURE 3.7: *Représentation d'une salle de spectacle avec des acteurs en scène*, drawn by Pierre-Alexandre Wille, 1767. *Recueil. Collection Michel Hennin. Estampes relatives à l'Histoire de France*, T. 106, Vol. 1. gallica.bnf.fr/Bibliothèque nationale de France.

Contrary to what has been thought, the patent theaters of the Restoration were not reserved for aristocrats or privileged people but welcomed a great variety of people. This audience was not, however, representative of London's population: tickets prices were generally beyond the means of the working class, and performance times were hardly compatible with the working day of journeymen and laborers. With a decrease in royal subsidies and an economic transformation, the social composition of audiences did however evolve during this period; the mercantile bourgeoisie became more present and more influential, and the petty traders and merchants gradually replaced the exporters and financiers, in their role as patrons. In the country, patrons issued from the gentry and the aristocracy maintained their effective power and assumed the right to select their chosen play from the company's stock book; the Liverpool slave merchants succeeded in having Southerne's *Oronooko* taken off the bill. The new covered theaters of the Restoration entailed a new distribution of the audience, which remained relatively stable over the period. The pit, with its backless benches, was the place of sexual and social mixing; it brought together gentlemen, bourgeois, apprentices and prostitutes (Figure 3.8). Elsewhere, the social hierarchy reasserted its rights: the more aristocratic, fashionable and

FIGURE 3.8: *The Pit Door at the Theatre Royal, Drury Lane*, 1784, print by Carington Bowles, after Robert Dighton. Hand-colored mezzotint, 35 × 24.9 cm. The British Museum, London. © Trustees of the British Museum.

affluent patrons sat in the boxes, tradesmen and their wives in the middle gallery, and servants, footmen, and sailors in the upper gallery.

An evening at the theater was a social event. This was obviously already the case in the Elizabethan era and in early seventeenth-century France, but the phenomenon intensified in the eighteenth century. Many new theaters were free-standing buildings, surrounded by shops beneath its colonnades, with a large vestibule at the entrance and cafés inside. There, the audience performed for itself, as well as during the performance, since it was impossible to obtain complete darkness. In order to be seen and heard, one took a place in the boxes and on the stage, while that remained possible, from 1685 to 1762. Going to the theater was, for Samuel Pepys, a social practice of the same sort as going to the café or the club: during a performance, Pepys would eavesdrop on a conversation, have an interesting passage of the newspaper read aloud to him, or chat with others.[55] As for the *parterre* in Paris, according to police archives, engravings, newspapers, and novels, it was a highly turbulent and eroticized space, where heterosexual as well as homosexual desires manifested, sometimes aggressively.[56]

A site of festivity and gathering, the theater was a space where audience members put on a show as a constructed collective, which could imagine itself a reflection of society or even of the nation. But far from uniting theatergoers in a harmonious, ideal, and illusory unit, the theater was at times traversed by tensions and conflicts that renewed, sometimes in different terms, the dynamics at work within the social fabric. Thus, the society spectacle of the first boxes served as a means for aristocrats to show off their distinction. At the Comédie-Française, aristocrats found themselves progressively edged out of the stalls by the bourgeoisie. In London, footmen who accompanied their masters received free entry and frequently fueled disorder in the upper balcony. The Licensing Act of 1737 did away with this arrangement; the footmen violently opposed the ban and, as the result of threats and riots, recovered "their" gallery—at least for a time, as it will be removed again by Garrick in 1759.[57]

The theatrical space was moreover a site of negotiations in the balance of power between audiences and practitioners. Audiences at professional theaters had never been passive; dissipated and noisy, they had always expressed their reactions in tangible and audible manifestations. But in the Enlightenment era, the porosity between stage and house intensified, the very idea of audience as a receptive body was established, and this audience asserted itself as an agent in the theatrical ceremony.[58] This occurred in part through the writings of playwrights themselves, who assigned the pleasure of the audience as the first supreme end of tragedy. In France this discourse served in the Quarrel of the Ancients and the Moderns, the latter claiming the right to judge by reason and taste, and not by the authority of ancient models. More generally, a whole group of writings on the theater gave a new place to the audience was acknowledged as a judge, but also as the beneficiary of a theater conceived as a public service, a site of moral education and of diffusion of reason. Tragedy gave occasion to reflect on the form taken by the collective of spectators: often described as an entity wholly seized by a single emotion, the audience tended, from the end of the seventeenth century, to be conceived as a community that brought together individuals (or groups) with potentially differentiated reactions.[59] Architects envisioned their theaters as a meeting place for the whole of society, and historians and theoreticians constructed the theater audience as representative of the nation.[60] From this perspective, Revolutionary discourse may appear as a culmination: school of all virtues, the theater would educate the new citizens and be the place where the nation became aware of itself; tragedy, the noble genre that favored political subjects, would be the primary instrument for this lay liturgy.

The audience's new power and role had more than a discursive existence. Communication with actors was encouraged in England by the architectural layout, thanks to the proscenium that placed them in the middle of the theatrical space. Audience members expressed their displeasure by throwing fruits and vegetables, hissing and catcalling, or even leaping up onto the stage. A dialogue with companies also took forms that, while less aggressive and more positive, were just as visible. Certain actors carried a reputation for throwing audiences into terror, such as Thomas Betterton in the closet scene in *Hamlet*; pathetic spectacles drew tears and highly theatricalized reactions from both women and men. But the audience was not always a united group; tensions appeared, and the communities of consumption formed and dissolved according to individual performances and the evolution of taste. At the moment of its publication, the author of *Hecuba* justified the failure of his play in the preface (1726): "It was not heard. A Rout of vandals in the galleries, intimidated the young actresses, disturbed the audience, and prevented all attention."[61] Associations of spectators began to appear such as the Mohocks in the early eighteenth century or the "Shakespeare ladies."[62]

At the Comédie-Française, the power of the audience was above all that of the pit, which had more control over performances in the eighteenth century than at any other time in history. Audience demand drove the institution of the premiere ceremony; it enabled or hindered the creation and maintenance of new plays; finally, it claimed the right to interrupt any performance and demand a different work from the repertoire. Mirabeau père tells of an uprising from the pit against a performance of *Britannicus* in order to have *Tartuffe*; only the intervention of a duchess finally curbed the conflict between audience and actors. The role of the pit was a subject of debate. When Voltaire, in the preface to *Sémiramis*, equated the uproar of the pit to popular sedition, incompatible with high culture, Condillac and Diderot saw in this same uproar a disposition favorable to the intellectual and emotional intensity of the theatrical experience. When in 1777, Jean-François de la Harpe suggested putting seating in the pit for the purposes of discipline,[63] Marmontel wrote against it in the "Parterre" article of the *Encyclopédie*: for Marmontel, the groundlings' taste, certainly less refined, was less pretentious and more reliable; standing, the audience was more vigorous and therefore more fair and accurate.[64] Beyond the oppositions, a single premise appears: the audience, and the pit audience in particular, was recognized as a legitimate body of judgment. Still, during the end of the period, attempts to impose order on the theatrical event became sharper and political power sought to limit as much as possible the spontaneous manifestations of an audience who had gained in the theater a space of expression.[65]

During the Revolution, tragedy brought about another form of political coalescence among its audience, with spectator practice at times corresponding to political engagements. As early as 1788, *Charles IX* by Chénier gave rise to a campaign against censorship stronger than any seen before, and throughout the whole period, the pit of the Comédie-Française became a site of protests or oppositions between factions. There were also moments of communion such as a performance of *Brutus* on November 13, 1793, where republican fervor found expression in songs and dances before the performance, applause during the speeches in favor of the republic, and silence when characters spoke in favor of royalty.[66]

Over the long period considered here, however, tragedy was more often associated with other collective affects. The end of the seventeenth century saw a resurgence of a taste for the macabre and horror, in particular in England where certain tragedies tried to stoke fears of a Catholic insurrection, such as the plays of Nathaniel Lee (*The Massacre of Paris*). But it was above all a sentimental vogue that took hold of audiences. From the second half of the seventeenth century, gallant tragedies on the French stage and the Restoration "she-tragedies" demonstrated this pathetic turn. In 1696, Gildon, in *The Life and characters of the English Dramatick Poets*, considered tears to be the "true end of Tragedy." Through critical texts and tragic performances, a theatrical experience characterized by empathic availability and adherence rather than by distance found its elaboration, which was marker of the sociological evolution of an audience more susceptible to bourgeois values. The development of pathos was particularly felt in France, where tears become a token of the success of a tragedy and a touchstone of the moral significance of the tragic spectacle.[67] In the second half of the century, two genres, the domestic drama and the melodrama, claimed their rights over the tears of the audience, even though tragedy still retained its throne.

Finally, over the course of the enlightenment period, the reception of tragedy gained a new modality, specialized criticism, and a new space, the periodical press. A type of specific discourse on theater, born of the immediate experience of its reception, had already begun to develop in the latter half of the seventeenth century. This burgeoning criticism could be found in paratexts, gazettes, memoires, letters, and accounts of performance, but also in novels, stories, poems, etc. This criticism then developed in the press; in biweeklies, weeklies, and monthlies such as *The Tatler* (1709–11) and *The Spectator* (1711–12). In the second half of the eighteenth century, periodicals proliferated, and criticism specialized even further. In the *British Journal, Grub Street Journal*, and the *Theatrical Review*, journalists covered current events, acting styles, actors' debuts, new plays, etc. In France, the evolution was much the same. Performances were first evoked in the general press, and current events in the *Almanachs, Annales, Calendriers des spectacles*. Then a specialized press emerged: in 1752, the *Tablettes dramatiques* by Mouhy appear, and starting in 1770, the *Journal des théâtres* written by Le Fuel de Méricourt and then Grimod de la Reynière. At the same time, the first theater histories, written by Beauchamps or the Parfaict brothers, became bestsellers. The critics' power of influence remained modest due to the fact that publication frequency was low, and plays failed or succeeded before articles appeared; it was very acutely felt, however, in the long-term career of a play and its regional distribution. More generally, the development of criticism was indicative of an ever more numerous audience, or rather *audiences*, with increasingly diversified practices, and not limited to those physically present in theaters of the capitals.

So functioned a community of theatrical creation, characterized by collaborations between producers, receptors, and managers, transnational and interdisciplinary circulations of models and artists, the trajectories of brilliant careers, as well as by hierarchies, rivalries, disparities, and forceful power plays. From 1650 to 1800, tragedy, though performed less and less, remained the object of constant political investment—from early modern court celebrations to the Revolutionary decade—while being ascribed an increasing cultural value, which secured its place in the formation of national canons or the evolution of its artists' socio-economic status demonstrates. Consequently, the tragic genre crystallized a reflection on the type of community that theater could produce: affective or reflective, fusional or individualized, national or European, conservative or critical. In 1789, detractors accused Chénier's Charles IX of "bringing about a dire change in the character of the Parisian people,"[68] whileie in 1792 critics of Ducis's bloody Othello lamented, inversely, in its success "the influence that the revolution has wrought upon our stage."[69] This indicates that tragedy was, at the end of the eighteenth century, deemed a prismatic mediation, equally endowed with sociocultural agency and seen as a reflection of the political world.

# CHAPTER FOUR

# Philosophy and Social Theory

*From Political Tragedies to Tragic Politics*

JONATHAN STRAUSS

To appreciate the interdependence between tragedy and the State during the Baroque and Enlightenment periods, let us, as Leibniz liked to say, *reculer pour mieux sauter*—that is, back up to get a running start, the better to leap into our subject. Let us, then, return to the origin, since from the first tragedy was political. Its birth was not just contemporary but conjoined to the emergence of the polis in fifth-century Athens, and it was political in both its context and its content. The stagings of those fifth-century tragedies took place under the shadow of the Acropolis and created a reciprocal flow between the city and its theatrical self-representation. The annual festival of Dionysos, at which the plays were first shown, combined dramatic contests with ritualized expressions of state power, including the delivery of tribute money from subjugated cities and islands. In that setting, issues of state passed back and forth between the stage and city leaders. Sophocles, for instance, incorporated principles of Pericles' building policies into his *Antigone*, while Demosthenes quoted Creon's speech about the polis from the same play in one of his orations.[1] As Christian Meier has put it, "[t]he institution of tragedy . . . represents the remarkable process of the developing city putting its developing structures of thought at risk and under scrutiny in the public arena of a civic festival. It is in this that we can locate the role of tragedy in the 'politicization of the citizen.'"[2]

What was under scrutiny, in this public context, were images of the city and the citizen, since the content of these plays engaged the very essence of the polis itself. As Jean-Pierre Vernant has argued, tragedies arose out of a need to resolve a rift in the social structure that resulted out of the transition from a collective experience based on myth to one grounded in laws: "The tragic turning point," he wrote, "occurs when a gap develops at the heart of the social experience. It is wide enough for the oppositions between legal and political thought on the one hand and the mythical and heroic traditions on the other to stand out quite clearly. Yet it is narrow enough for the conflict in values still to be a painful one and for the clash to continue to take place."[3] The rise of the polis, of a social order premised on the conjunction between state and laws, thus entailed the rejection of an earlier community organized around out-sized personalities and their family lines. This new set of values, as Vernant calls them, was thus the laws themselves, and their legitimacy was not self-evident, since they conflicted with other standards of behavior that had been expected, and enforced, under the more archaic order that the polis replaced. In this sense, the tragic moment, the moment in and from which tragedy emerges, is the moment in which justice itself must be justified. The stories those first tragedies told were not only about guilt and punishment; they were about justice itself, about justice and the state, or the justice *of* the state. For its origin was not clean; a certain guilt was attached to its very legality.

The oldest of the tragic trilogies that have come down to us more or less intact, Aeschylus' *Oresteia*, expresses these concerns with a disarming directness. The cycle concerns a cascading series of retributions for an ugly succession of familial crimes, including adultery, murder, and matricide, that ends in a courtroom trial, presided over by Athena herself, to judge Orestes for killing his mother. But this court is unique: it is invented for the purpose, and in it, the prosecutors—the Erinyes or avenging Furies— agree not only to stop punishing Orestes, but also to surrender their powers in general, withdrawing instead into the netherworld, where they will be honored in memory by the citizens of the new city and granted the title of Eumenides, or the good-natured ones. Aeschylus thus portrays the Furies of the archaic order relinquishing their authority in exchange for an "eu" or euphemism. In short, they traded their own system of justice for a name, their real violence for a symbol.

In identifying the order of justice that went before and by representing its willing acquiescence to the new laws of the city, the *Eumenides* both specifies and expunges two forms of guilt: Orestes' and the city's, for the Furies accepted the trial in principle and agreed in advance to honor its verdict. As a result, a matricide is forgiven, and the vengeful female deities withdraw into the underworld, while the defense attorney (Apollo, the god of light) and the judge (Athena, born without a mother) prevail. The male law thus represses the female and familial. And so, Athens, the polis as such, arises, in this telling, constitutionally haunted by an original sin—and an original, contradictory value system— that never entirely disappear.

Tragedies are saturated in and blossom from an inexplicable guilt that demands an infinite atonement. The ancient ones repeatedly depict crimes whose criminality depends on a perspective whose own legitimacy is open to question, such as in *Iphigenia at Aulis*, that are involuntary, as in Sophocles' *Philoctetes*, or that make no sense, as Oedipus argues about his own guilt in *Oedipus at Colonus*.[4] And in this respect, these plays stage and restage, in different forms, scenarios involving insoluble or arguably unjust guilt, thereby revealing a (divine) justice that is itself potentially guilty.[5]

To the extent, then, that the tragedies represented the city, the work that representation performed was not so much to define the structures and coherence of the political body it portrayed as to legitimize them. In this sense, the tragic polis was characterized by a fundamental concern about its own right to exist, about the rightness of its existence, which is to say the legitimacy of its laws. Tragedy in its original and originary form was, as I have said, a justification of the justice of the political state, and the circularity of this formulation is important, since it captures the paradoxical structure of tragedy itself as a political programme—the dynamic symmetry of its groundlessness and the effort to remediate that groundlessness. It does not, therefore, simply legislate for those entities that it comprises, but instead submits itself as a whole to the principle and rule of law. In its original and originary form, the tragic State is defined by its concern not with the question "what am I?" but "am I just?" The tyrant who asks, "how can I rule?" is not tragic, while the one who asks, "do I have the right to rule?" may well be. And since the justice of the State is grounded either in itself or in something else (and is therefore not just in its own terms), the answer to the constitutive question of the tragic State is either circular or negative. The tragic State is therefore characterized both by a structural failure of legitimacy and the interminable effort either to remediate or dissimulate it. In this sense, the tragic State—the polis as it emerged in fifth-century Athens and any other subsequent one that is organized by the question of its legitimacy—is structured as the deferral of the discovery of its own original guilt.

Now, tragedies represent general or abstract ideas of the State through individual persons or heroes. The hero symbolizes or otherwise encodes the paradox of the State's legitimacy, and this is why his guilt almost inevitably appears inexplicable and excessive: inexplicable because misplaced, infinite, because the hero cannot atone for the guilt of another.[6] René Girard observed that the tragic hero functioned as a scapegoat or *pharmakos* for collective guilt and that in this capacity he embodied the ritual transformation of real violence into its "symbolization."[7] In Girard's analysis, there is no actual misdeed that the scapegoat expiates. I would contend, on the contrary, that we can, in fact, identify a systematic and unspeakable crime for which the tragic hero is endlessly sacrificed: the violent illegitimacy of the city and its laws themselves.

Heidegger wrote of the beginnings of history as Sophocles represents them in *Antigone*, "the genuineness and greatness of historical knowing lie in understanding the character of this inception as a mystery."[8] For political history, that original mystery would be a double-bind: the interdependent need and impossibility for the State to establish its legitimacy according to its own terms. The tragic State is the one that tries to remediate that primordial illegitimacy or to dissimulate it. We say, in structural terms, that such a State is tragic because it *assumes* a guilt that is at once alien and constitutional to it. It is also tragic in affective terms, because the task it has set itself is both intolerable and interminable.

The origin of tragedy thus occurs *as* a tragedy of origins, anchored in the expiation of an inexpiable guilt—the injustice of justice itself, the impossibility of justice to justify itself in its own terms. Tragedy fills in the missing page of the origin of the just State as a crime of violence and momentarily palliates it not through justice but through catharsis or emotion. Since the palliation of this guilt occurs on another level than its source, it never actual actually resolves the underlying problem, whence the need to repeat, endlessly, the tragic act. This compulsive repetition expressed itself materially in the groups of tragedies—at least nine—produced annually at the Athenian Dionysia for more than a hundred years, and cumulatively, over time, both in the seemingly undying restagings of the small remnants of the original tragic repertoire and in the resilience of the genre itself.

And so, we can identify four principal characteristics of tragedy in relation to politics: first, it endlessly attempts, but fails to legitimize the State itself; second, that need to justify expresses an original political guilt; third, that guilt is personalized in the figure of the hero; and fourth, it is gendered as a male violence against an original, feminine force.

Some two thousand years after the first staging of the *Oresteia*, tragedy reasserted itself as a political ideology in Europe, and I will concentrate, in the period from the mid-seventeenth century to the end of the eighteenth, on one country in particular—France—because it experienced the most significant political events of the time, because it produced the most important tragedies in its repertoire during this period, and because the impact of both its politics and theater extended far beyond its borders. It is true that England was wracked by revolution and regicide in the middle of the seventeenth century, but the revolution ended, and monarchy was restored by 1660. The most influential tragedies in the language—by Shakespeare, Marlowe, Kyd, Middleton, and Webster—date from a brilliant flowering that ended a few decades earlier. Politically, Spain was relatively calm, and although one of its golden-age poets, Pedro Calderón de la Barca, continued to write tragedies until late in the seventeenth century, they were dramas of individual honor rather than reflections on the political State. The Treaty of Westphalia in 1648 brought an end to the Thirty Years' War and created an extended period of general stability among the German-speaking countries, whose authors produced tragedies with little lasting impact, although they would later find a defender in Walter Benjamin.[9] Italy was largely a battleground for internal and foreign interests, and tragedy played a relatively minor role in its literature of the seventeenth and eighteenth centuries.

The political history of France in this period is, however, bookended by two seismic events—on the one hand, the hard-won concentration of power in the sole person of the king accompanied by the rise of an absolutist State dependent on elaborate protocols of self-representation and, on the other, the Revolution, which brought an end to the monarchy, ushered in a democratic republic, condemned representation, and institutionalized a politics of absolute impersonality. While the first of these, the rise of Louis XIV (Figure 4.1), may have felt specific to France at the time, it subsequently served as a model for absolutist monarchies throughout modern Europe. The Revolution, however, cast its monstrous shadow—or light, depending on the viewpoint—across the

FIGURE 4.1: Illustration of Louis XIV of France. Photo by Nastastic/DigitalVision Vectors Collection/Getty Images.

Europe of its time. In England, Wordsworth would recall the "hope and joy" that it instilled in all those around him, writing in the *Prelude*: "Bliss was it in that dawn to be alive, / But to be young was very heaven!" Immanuel Kant, in Germany, would consider not so much the Revolution itself as the "mode of thinking" of peoples interested but not directly involved in it as proof of the "moral tendency of the human race" toward progress and improvement. "Owing to its universality," he wrote, "this mode of thinking demonstrates a character of the human race at large and all at once; owing to its disinterestedness, a moral character of humanity, at least in its predisposition, a character which not only permits people to hope for progress toward the better, but is already itself progress in so far as its capacity is sufficient for the present."[10] Universal concern about the Revolution, concern for the Revolution *as* a universal issue, was in itself, for Kant, human progress and, therefore, the promise of the Enlightenment kept.

As various writers have observed, the classical period was, despite its name, a turbulent time, wracked by upheavals in the State and society, and its tragic plays returned repeatedly to concerns about the origins of the State and, indeed, of its legitimacy. When Louis XIV acceded to the throne in 1643, at age four, France had been embroiled for some eight years in a multi-front war against Spain that would last until 1659. From 1648 to 1653, during the Regency, the period when Louis' mother ruled in his name, the country was roiled by internecine wars, collectively known as *La Fronde*, that arose in reaction to a progressive centralization of power under Henri IV and Louis XIII at the beginning of the century and pitted first the parliaments and then the nobility against royal authority—nominally Louis', but effectively that of his chief minister, Cardinal Mazarin. The king's party emerged victorious, but the struggle seems to have determined Louis to consolidate his authority and contributed, in this sense, to the rise of the absolute State under his rule. When Mazarin died in 1661, the king himself took full charge of the country, refusing to appoint a chief minister and declaring that all acts should be signed only under his express orders. As the king himself put it before his assembled ministers the day after Mazarin's death: "I want to govern on my own."[11] And as Louis moved to enact this programme—placing his overly ambitious minister of finances, Nicolas Fouquet, in prison, then taking his team of architects, landscapers, and decorators with him to Versailles, where he moved the court so that the nobles would have to live under his close, personal surveillance—he also set in place an elaborate policy of self-representation, a semiotics of power wherein virtually everything that came into contact with him—from pageants, to the appointments of his palaces, to the gardens that surrounded them, to public executions—became symbols both of his person and his absolute rule. They were, as Jean-Marie Apostolidès has pungently phrased it, "ideology made concrete."[12] With the exception of corporal punishment, in all of these cases, physical and military forces were sublimated into a symbolic register that expressed varying degrees of favor (i.e., position in relation to the king) and, in that respect, the individual subject's incorporation into the body politic. Even a gesture as seemingly simple and anodyne as reading a contemporary guidebook to Versailles, as Claire Goldstein has argued, amounted to situating oneself in precise subordination to the sovereign.[13]

Tragedy numbered among these forms of royal representation, for, as one of the leading playwrights of seventeenth-century France, Pierre Corneille, observed, it is "an imitation."[14] And it was, more specifically, an imitation or representation of the monarch, for while Corneille described politics as a sort of "embroidery" that an author might choose to include or not within a dramatic poem, he also argued that it was not sufficient that the characters in a tragedy be illustrious. The genre's "dignity demands," he wrote, "some high interest of State, or some passion more noble and masculine than love, such as ambition or vengeance. . . . I will go further. Even if there be high matters of State in a Poem, and that the care a Royal person must have for his glory muzzle his passion, as in *Don Sanche*, but he find in it some peril of his life or of the loss of his States or of banishment, I do not think that it may take a name above that of Comedy."[15] And so, tragedy, in Corneille's description, is by essence the personification of the State in the moment of its peril. He speaks here too of the "dignity" of tragedy, and indeed it seems to have played a privileged role in the ubiquitous proliferation of the semiotics of royal power that accompanied the advent of absolutist monarchy in France. As Hélène E. Bilis has written, "[s]eventeenth-century France witnessed the concurrent rise of absolutist politics and tragedy's establishment as the preeminent literary genre."[16] In defense of this claim, she charts the "'complete reversal' from the genre's unpopularity in 1628" to its systematic codification and triumph in the following decade.[17]

Tragedies, during the seventeenth century, were not just about the State, however, they were more specifically, as the above passage from Corneille suggests, about the State in moments of disruption or upheaval. John Lyons has developed this idea in his own readings of the French playwrights of the seventeenth century, arguing that the tragedies of the period developed in a reciprocally constructive relation with their cultural, social, and political context, so that the stage and the State not only affirmed and critiqued but, more important, invented each other.[18] These tragedies, according to Lyons, consistently represented the replacement of one political system with another, and in this sense, can be considered origin stories. As he writes:

> Each tragedy . . . concerns the disappearance of one political entity and the emergence of another that, in a sense, takes its place. In each instance, however, the very idea of one thing "taking the place" of another is an impossibility that generates a tragic structure, the always retrospective perception of origins. Moreover, this group of plays, read in sequence, forms an account of the origin of France, a matter of intense historical, juridical, and political interest in the sixteenth and seventeenth centuries.[19]

The reason that it should be impossible for one thing to take the place of another is, in Lyons' account, a little unclear, but he seems to mean that the transition between two political systems will inevitably produce social elements that can no longer fit as comfortably into the collective body as they had before, resulting in fissures and conflicts as those atavistic elements struggle to find a place within a new world, adapt to it by reinventing themselves, reject it, or disappear. The replacement of one political system with another will, by this thinking, inevitably produce an *agon logon*, that conflict of incompatible discourses that was central to classical Greek understandings of tragic drama.[20] This disruptive, inherently conflictual origin of the State is, according to Lyons, only perceptible in retrospect because "the distinction between 'periods' is a matter of political or erudite decision of later generations."[21] While it is hard to argue, as we shall see, that the members of the *Assemblé constituente* of 1789 or the *représentants* who demanded and voted for the death of Louis XVI in 1792 and 1793 were unable to perceive their engagement in the creation of a new State, Lyons' observation about the retrospective nature of origins generally holds true for the tragedies of seventeenth-century France.

Corneille's 1637 wildly successful tragi-comedy, *Le Cid* (Figure 4.2), offers an especially clear example of Lyons' point. The play marked a turning point in the history of French tragedy by establishing the popularity and aesthetic pre-eminence of the genre, even while provoking a scandal that ultimately had to be adjudicated by the newly

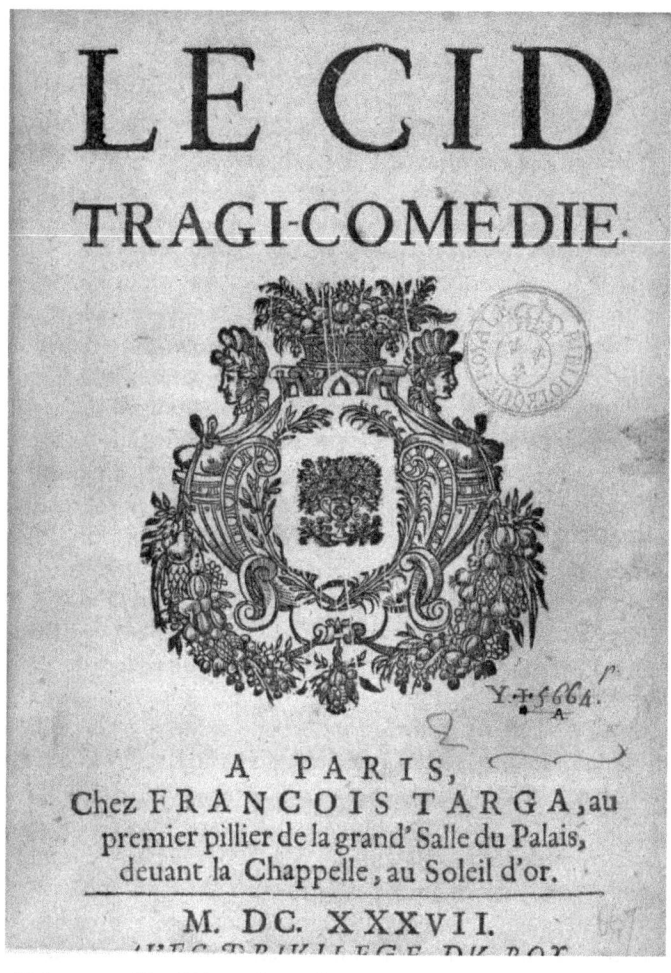

FIGURE 4.2: Title page of *Le Cid*, performed in Paris in 1637. Wikimedia Commons.

established *Académie française*. Although it enumerated the play's formal errors in respect to the recently codified rules of French tragic drama, the trial nonetheless validated the play as a whole and sanctioned its popular success. In many ways, the plot captures the political climate that surrounded its creation, even before that climate expressed itself in open action, since the play foreshadows the events of *La Fronde*. The action is based on historical events from eleventh-century Spain and depicts the tumultuous love story between Rodrigue, who will subsequently win, through feats of arms, the honorific title of *Le Cid*, and his lover Chimène, whose father Rodrigue has killed in a duel meant to salvage his own father's honor. Chimène, duped by the king into believing that Rodrigue has been killed, reveals her true feelings for him in an outpouring of grief. Torn between her love for Rodrigue and her duty to her father's memory, she finally submits, at the end, to the king's command to marry Rodrigue. "When a king commands," she acknowledges, "one must obey him." ("Quand un roi commande, on doit lui obéir.")[22] This more intimate story condenses a larger societal context: the conflict between an older political order based on the rights of individual nobles and an emergent system premised on their submission to the central authority of the king. In accepting the hand of her father's killer, Chimène at once violates the feudal codes that had previously governed her family and acquiesces to a new, incompatible set of values. As such, according to Lyons, the play represented a new "concept of justice" at arms against an older one.[23] I think it is important to recognize, however, that at its end the play offers only a deferred reconciliation and resolution to its central conflict, since Chimène merely agrees to but does not actually marry Rodrigue—before that consummation, he must first leave and lead the royal armies into war. As the king says to Chimène at the close of the play's final scene: "Time has often legitimized / What at first seemed impossible but as a crime / ... Take a year, if you wish, to dry your tears" ("Le temps assez souvent a rendu légitime / Ce qui semblait d'abord ne se pouvoir sans crime / ... Prends un an, si tu veux, pour essuyer tes larmes").[24] Time itself, he asserts, can redeem a crime, and he puts a specific term—one year—to the amount needed, but Rodrigue himself senses that the task is longer, indeed infinite, for he is ready to undertake and achieve *everything* to atone for his guilt. "If it can finally wash away my crime," he tells Chimène, "I shall dare undertake everything, and then complete it all." ("Si mon crime par là se peut enfin laver, / J'ose tout entreprendre, et puis tout achever.")[25] In this sense, the atonement for the original sin, for the sin of origination, that his murderous act embodies, is endlessly deferred, in part because its redemption is infinite and in part because it is not included in the play itself. That endless postponement suggests the infinite nature, too, of the guilt to be expiated, which is the structural impasse of justice that lies in the origins of both tragic States and dramas.

A comparison with the *Eumenides* is revealing, since both it and *Le Cid* forgive the murder of a parent, involve the replacement of one system of justice by another, and entail the submission of familial values, personified by female characters, to the values of the State, which are embodied by male ones. But Chimène, unlike the Erinyes, agrees not to an abstract principle of justice but instead to the will of the king, which, in turn, expresses her own erotic desire. In this context, Mitchell Greenberg's approach to classical French drama and its psychosexual relations to power sheds an important light on their underlying libidinal structures. For Greenberg, classical theater represents the subjugation of individual desire to a more general law embodied in the sovereign prince.[26] This more general law, however, comprises a "dichotomization of the sexes," and this "splitting that is shown to be 'natural' is nevertheless presented as antagonistic: the paternal and maternal poles of this sexual opposition are opposed in hierarchical ordering that implies and enforces the repression of a certain excess coded as 'feminine.'"[27] The recurrent repression of the female or feminine that seems to accompany originary acts of legislation in the tragic tradition, as evidenced in the *Eumenides* and *Le Cid*, would find its cause, according to this psychoanalytic approach, in the submission to the symbolic order itself.

The other dominant French tragedian of the seventeenth century, Jean Racine, was born two years after the première of *Le Cid*. His dramas are often less explicitly political than Corneille's and even his sense of time, as John Lyons has observed, differs from that of his older rival, since Corneille's plots tended to draw on actual historical events, and thus suggested a linear flow in which unique incidents succeeded each other, while Racine's concentrated more on mythical figures, whose archetypal status created a cyclical temporality in which certain characters and situations constantly repeat themselves.[28] If Racine's plays thus lend themselves less readily than Corneille's to Lyons' historical analysis, in which seventeenth-century dramas represent concerns about the origins of the French nation, their mythical nature conforms quite easily to interpretations, such as

Greenberg's, that are based on more permanent, and indeed recurrent, psychosexual structures. Powerful and frightening women fill Racine's plays. His most famous and enduring character, Phaedra, the daughter of the queen who spawned the minotaur in a frenzy of bestial eroticism, is herself a terrifying maternal figure, whose uncontrolled incestuous desire for her stepson sows disorder and death in her princely family. Phaedra finds echoes in other women that populate Racine's dramas, such as the eponymous heroine in *Athalie* or Agrippina, Nero's mother, in *Britannicus*.

At once more dissimulated, more abstract, and purer, the origin story that these plays recount represents the advent of male symbolic law and the concomitant eclipsing, or repression, of an earlier maternal order that now, retrospectively, appears monstrous, horrifying, and incomprehensible. To the extent that the new psychosexual order is also a law—a legislation of libidinal relations as a way to organize desires and social interactions on their most basic levels—it embodies a form of justice, one based on the splitting of the sexes and the submission of maternal or otherwise (retrospectively) inchoate libido to the dominance of paternal figures. This advent or origin would thus entail the conflict between two systems for making sense of the world, which Greenberg loosely identifies with Jacques Lacan's imaginary and symbolic registers, and the subordination of the former to the latter.[29] This incompatibility and the refusal of the now archaic order simply to submit to its replacement would constitute the *agon logon* of patriarchal and princely rule in Racine's tragedies. Absolutism, in this reading, would be troubled by the recurrent anxiety about a return of the repressed, where the repressed takes shape in the powerful maternal figures that people contemporary tragedies. More than a simple return of the repressed, however, they would figure the persistence of its claim to legitimacy and justice, the undying guilt at the basis of the symbolic order. And because that guilt *is* undying, because it inheres to the structure of the symbolic law itself *as* a repression, the circular, mythical time that Lyons' describes in Racine's tragedies is entirely appropriate, since it captures the inescapability of the origin. In this sense, the ritual temporality of Racine's tragic universe functions as an equivalent to the deferred marriage at the end of Corneille's *Le Cid*, which offered the promise of a comedy always still to come.

We can find an elegant example of the conjunction between psychosexual drives and anxiety over the legitimacy of the State itself in Racine's *Britannicus*. Although the play's characters are members of the Roman Empire's ruling family, the plot seems to revolve around questions of love and sexual desire rather than politics—that is, until the very end, where, in a prismatic shift of perspective, we discover that they are the same story. In her final lines, Nero's mother, Agrippina, observes that were her son to take his life, "He would do himself justice." ("Il se ferait justice.")[30] Four verses later, the play itself closes on the word "crimes." Agrippina, the ravening mother, the restless Erinys, judges the embodiment of the State, and her use of the reflexive verb (*se faire justice*) captures the circular structure inherent in the paradox of justice itself: were the State to do itself justice, it would destroy itself. And the audience is left amid the echoes of one word: "crimes."

It has long been argued that individuals' sense of self varies according to their cultural context, or, as Jacques Brunschwig has put it, "[t]he relation to oneself (l'être pour soi) has its own history."[31] Heidegger contended, for instance, that "[a]mong the Greeks there were no personalities yet."[32] Perhaps the most important result of subordinating the State to the symbolic law of sexual desire was the transformation of the people into subjects in a modern sense of the word. For Greenberg, the subordination of luxuriant individual desire to a stricter and more general law entails its structuring in compliance with the Oedipal complex and therefore also constitutes the process by which that individual becomes a subject, which is to say a figure related to others within a cohesive and coherent symbolic system.[33] Within the semiotics of absolutist royal power, as described above, the subject was defined not only by its compliance to the law of desire, but more specifically by its situation in relation to the person and will of the king. Moreover, thanks to its recent, metaphysical systematization in Descartes' *Discours de la méthode* of 1637 and *Meditationes de prima philosophia* of 1641, the modern subject was also understood to be both self-aware and the lynchpin or fulcrum for systematic certainty in a world obscured by misperceptions and doubts.[34] Part of the newness of this subject, then, was that it was visible as such, rather than functioning simply as the imperceptible background upon which life and the world displayed themselves; paradoxically, it was thus both the world and a point within it. Or as Descartes' contemporary, Blaise Pascal, wrote: "By its extension, the universe encompasses and swallows me; by my thought, I encompass it." ("Par l'espace, l'univers me comprend et m'engloutit; par la pensée, je le comprends.")[35] This self-aware subject, this subject *of* self-awareness, subject both in the sense of what lies beneath, subtends, or undergirds the world and in the sense of the one who submits to a master, found representation, along with its inherent structural paradoxes, in seventeenth-century tragedies. As Greenberg writes, "[s]ubjectivity in Racine floats upon the fantasies of its own impossibility: either that pre-Œdipal multiplicity that has been repressed, destroyed, in order precisely for the subject to be; or that subject as an already gendered, but therefore guilty, being, trapped in a familial dialectic that condemns the subject to its own end."[36] I would argue, therefore, that these plays stage the mythic origin not only of the absolutist State, but also of the modern, symbolic subject that colluded with it, a subject marked by the guilty repression of a previous order of meaning and haunted by the structural impossibility of satisfactorily atoning for it. As we shall see, this figure will return with a newfound tragic force under the Revolution—indeed it will become the hero of modern politics.

Within the semiotics of royal power, even the person of the king himself is a function of the symbolic system rather than an autonomous, positive entity; he is, in this sense, abstract. In his dying breath, Louis XIV is reported to have recognized this fact, stating to his assembled gentlemen, "I am leaving, but the State will remain forever." ("Je m'en vais, mais l'État demeurera toujours.")[37] The state itself, in this depiction, would thus seem to exist as separate and distinct from the specific individual who embodies the monarch at any particular moment. Still, the fact that Louis felt the need to assert this separation suggests that it was not self-evident or universally accepted, even among his subjects. The monarch may, then, have been a symbolic function, but that function was, in some sense, personalized, so that the king enjoyed a double ontological status as accident and essence—what Ernst Kantorowicz, in his detailed readings of Elizabethan and Jacobean legal codes, has called his two bodies.[38] For this reason, I would have to disagree with Greenberg, who argues that "Louis, making a spectacle of himself, finally eclipses that 'self,' scatters it in its own representation, disperses it in its own disappearance."[39] On the contrary, the specification of the monarchical function, of the sovereign prince in the person of the king will constitute, as we shall see, one of the key points that distinguish the *ancien régime* from the democratic republic that would replace it under the Revolution.

Concern about the legitimacy of justice itself was not simply an invention of the tragic poets of the age, but resonated more widely through society, so that in this regard the theater seems to have expressed broader contemporary anxieties, even if they dated back to ancient Athens. The issue vexed Pascal, who wrote among the fragments that were later collected as *Les Pensées*:

> Custom creates the whole of equity, for the simple reason that it is accepted; this is the mystical foundation of its authority; whoever carries it back to first principles destroys it. . . . The art of opposition and of revolution is to unsettle established customs, sounding them even to their source, to point out their want of authority and justice. We must, it is said, get back to the natural and fundamental laws of the State, which an unjust custom has abolished. It is a game certain to result in the loss of all; nothing will be just according to these scales.
>
> (La coutume fait toute l'équité, par cette seule raison qu'elle est reçue; c'est le fondement mystique de son autorité. . . . L'art de fronder, bouleverser les États, est d'ébranler les coutumes établies, en sondant jusque dans leur source, pour marquer leur défaut d'autorité et de justice. Il faut, dit-on, recourir aux lois fondamentales et primitives de l'État, qu'une coutume injuste a abolies. C'est un jeu sûr pour tout perdre; rien ne sera juste à cette balance.)[40]

This is a particularly lucid expression of the inherent injustice of justice itself, for it captures the paradoxical temporality that creates the impression of legitimacy. Justice is justified, is made equitable, only retrospectively, through the slow constancy with which a people accepts it, and, in this sense, it becomes just over time, as the king in *Le Cid* had argued. Pascal describes the basis of the law's legitimacy as "mystical" or, in French, "mystique"—and it would seem to be so for at least three reasons. First, because it is a mystification: we accept the law since we think it is just, but in fact it is just because we accept it, and this misperception is necessary. Second, because it is mysterious: we must not question or know it, lest we destroy it. And third, because it is mythical or, in French, "mythique": due to its retrospective nature, the legitimacy of the law, the justice of justice itself, exists, like Racine's tragedies, in the circular time of myth. Now, Pascal does not use the word "origin" itself, but he speaks of foundations, which sounds very similar, and then says that anyone who tries to return to first principles would destroy the legitimacy of the law. What he seems to be saying is that the best we can hope for is that laws be effectively, rather than absolutely legitimate, and that we can legitimize them if we abandon the attempt to understand their origin or, more precisely, if we subscribe to the mystification that their origin *must* have been just because we accept them. We must, then, submit to these laws of custom, even if they are unjust. In this passage, Pascal describes an eminently tragic political State, for it is structured around the original and originary double-bind of its own justice: it seeks to be equitable, but, according to its own terms and desires, it can never succeed, and so must deceive itself, placing its trust in a mythical construction. And yet, precisely because it is so lucid, Pascal's description *itself* is strangely disabused. It may be pessimistic, and it may be wrong, but it is not blind to its own artifice and does not, consequently, displace its injustice onto a crime for which the social order itself, or its figurative replacement, must endlessly atone.

Pascal's pessimism fell out of favor in the following century, which, in direct contradiction to his assertion that a return to "natural and fundamental laws . . . is a game certain to result in the loss of all," elaborated and endorsed a legal system premised on just such natural laws. Drawing on Isaac Newton's ability to abstract constant physical laws from the apparent vagaries of the material world, and his ability to express those laws through the language of mathematics, eighteenth-century thinkers strove to apply the same principles to the moral and social spheres. "The Enlightenment," Ernst Cassirer wrote, "constructs its ideal according to the model and pattern of contemporary natural science" and then added, "the goal and basic presupposition of Newtonian research is universal order and law in the material world."[41] The laws of nature, as exposed by Newton and others, are universal and therefore not subject to the local variations that Pascal had observed among human customs. They are, moreover, uniquely intelligible to human beings, which means that human beings enjoy a unique relation to the intelligibility of nature as expressed in the regularity and universality of its laws—human beings are, in other words, somehow *similar* to those laws, and the locus of that similarity is the faculty of reason itself, for it is through reason that the laws of nature are legible. What distinguished the human subject from other animals, in an Enlightenment perspective, is therefore not thinking itself or as such, which had seemed to be the case for both Descartes and Pascal, but instead reason. "I first observe something that it seems to me both the good and the evil man accept," reads Denis Diderot's entry on *droit natural* or natural law in the *Encyclopédie*, "which is that one must reason in all things, since man is not merely an animal, but an animal that reasons."[42] If natural laws are universal, and if human beings can perceive them through reason, that means first that those laws are, by definition, reasonable and second that human beings can participate in their universality by acting reasonably.

Diderot extrapolated the legal consequences of human beings' unique rationality in the following terms: "*natural law* admits only what is in conformity with true reason and equity . . . . The precepts of *natural law* . . . are the purest source and the base for the greatest part of public and private law."[43] For Enlightenment theories of natural law, such as Diderot's, reason itself is the legislator. These theories would be put in practice during the Revolution. The young revolutionary Louis-Antoine-Léon Saint-Just, one of the leading members of the dreaded Committee of Public Safety and a principal architect of the Terror, wrote that "laws are the natural relations between things . . . . Nature is the first of all legal systems (*droits*) and is for all time, whereas general conventions are only legitimate for a single day."[44] Human law, as Saint-Just put it, "takes the place of nature and speaks for her and for everyone. Whoever attempts to corrupt or violate it shall be driven from the State."[45]

In defiance of Pascal's lucid pessimism, Enlightenment theorists and politicians would seem to have resolved the apparent impasse inherent in any attempt to establish the equity and legitimacy of justice itself, thereby repairing the tragic structure of the State. I would argue, however, that this was not the case, but to see why we will need to draw back and consider the theatrical, political, and theoretical contexts of the period. What stands out when we do so is a general repudiation of representation in all its forms—theatrical, political, and symbolic—in favor of immediacy and presence. And as the value of representation changed, so did the locus of tragedy within society. Under the Revolution, the sacrificial victim to the constitutive injustice of the State shifted from the realm of theatrical representation to the actual individual as such; the subject *of* expiation became, now, the subject *as* expiation.

Theater, as has often been remarked, flourished during the Revolution. The Le Chapelier law, passed on June 14, 1791 abolished guilds throughout France, allowing any citizen to practice professions that had previously been restricted to the members of accredited associations. Among these professions was the stage. "French men, women, and children," write Emmet Kennedy and Marie-Laurence Netter, "went to the fifty newly-opened theaters in droves during the 1790s. Compared with the monopoly exercised by the three privileged theaters of the Old Regime, this multiplication of stages provided undreamed-of possibilities for entertaining the Parisian masses."[46] Despite the intervention of the Committee of Public Safety, which attempted to promote "heroic republican tragedy" through prescriptions and subventions, tragedy as a genre mostly languished during the period.[47] The public, as Netter observes, directed its favor elsewhere. "The supremacy of comedies over all other genres," she writes, "is clearly demonstrated by the number of comedic performances. ... Among the fifty most performed plays during the Revolutionary decade, there are thirty-two comedies."[48] Or as Kennedy grimly summarizes the situation: "While tragedy was the touted Jacobin genre, it did not fare particularly well."[49] Still, it *was* officially sanctioned and promoted. The most performed tragedy during the Revolution was probably Voltaire's *Brutus*, which was based on a historical anecdote about heroic self-sacrifice in the founding of the Roman Republic, while the most successful tragedian was Marie-Joseph Chénier (Figure 4.3).[50] Honoré Mirabeau, one of the early leaders of the Revolution, recommended Chénier's *Charles IX* as one of three tragedies to be performed for the first Festival of the Federation—the annual commemoration of the storming of the Bastille—while his *Caïus Gracchus* was one of three tragedies recommended by the Committee of Public Safety during their campaign to promote republican and revolutionary values in the theater.[51] Despite these endorsements, however, Kennedy describes the cumulative run of *Caïus Gracchus* as "close to the least-performed plays."[52]

In certain key respects, Chénier's plays bear a profound similarity to the tragedies of the *ancien régime* and indeed to those of fifth-century Athens. First, they take as their heroes noble personages who are elevated to mythic status, as if in conformity to Corneille's precepts. Second, as if to demonstrate the Erinyes' endless resentment, they are stalked by terrifying maternal figures. In *Charles IX*, Catherine de Médicis leads her

FIGURE 4.3: Portrait of Marie-Joseph Chénier (1764–1811). Photo by Photo12/UIG/ Getty Images.

son into an irredeemable crime by convincing him to approve the betrayal and slaughter of Protestants under his rule—or, as one of the characters observes, "slaking his thirst for blood-soaked pleasures in deep draughts, Charles seeks his duty in his mother's eyes." ("Charles goûte à longs traits un plaisir sanguinaire, / Et cherche son devoir dans les yeux de sa mère.")[53] Similarly, in *Caïus Gracchus*, the eponymous hero submits to the demands of his mother, who urges him to redeem their family's honor and avenge his dead brother—"make the Senate pay for the tears I've wept" ("Fais payer au sénat les pleurs que j'ai verses") she begs—ultimately driving Caïus to suicide to avoid civil unrest.[54] Third, and most important, Chénier's tragedies raise the question of justice itself. One of the principal characters in *Charles IX* urges the king to rebuff the murderous machinations of his mother: "reign by yourself," he recommends, "that under just laws the people may breathe free at long last." ("Régnez par vous-même. . . . Que sous de justes lois le peuple enfin respire")[55] It is, in short, the justice of the laws themselves that is at issue in the drama, and although it is not the hand of fate that drives the king into error, but that of his mother and his own moral weakness, there is an infinite guilt that attaches to his person, a guilt whose irredeemable character suggests a structural anxiety about justice itself, though displaced onto a particular individual. Charles himself will be the sacrificial victim who must expiate an endless sin, although not with his death, but through his regret and the exemplary status of his crime. "I am no longer a king," he cries out at the play's end; "I am a murderer. . . . I have betrayed the nation, and honor, and the laws: In striking me, heaven offers an example to kings." ("Je ne suis plus un roi; je suis un assassin. . . . J'ai trahi la patrie, et l'honneur, et les lois: / Le ciel en me frappant donne un exemple aux rois.")[56] The case is more direct in *Caïus Gracchus*, where the hero is repeatedly identified with laws themselves, as if he as an individual had disappeared into their abstraction. Speaking of the patrician senators who have wronged both his family and the plebs, Caïus observes that "these tyrants of the world, accustomed to blood, are not alarmed by a lictor's death; they are afraid of my laws" ("Ces tyrans de la terre, au sang accoutumés, / Du meurtre d'un licteur ne sont pas alarmés; / Ils le sont de mes lois")[57] and later, speaking again of the senators, claims, "Rome knows how deep is the hatred my heart should harbor for them, but it is with the law that I want to punish them." ("Rome sait à quel point mon cœur doit les haïr,/Mais c'est avec la loi que je veux les punir.")[58] Indeed, as another character remarks, Caïus' whole family is known for "sacred and just laws that throughout the entire world have laid the foundations of liberty." ("Des lois saintes et justes, / Qui dans le monde entier fondaient la liberté.")[59] The hero is guilty, in short, of not being guilty. Or rather, of creating and defending just laws. Now, if Caïus personifies the justice of law, as he seems to do, his self-immolation would represent the law turning against, condemning, and punishing itself—and the justice of the law would thus consist in its self-sacrifice.

If the tragic dramas of the Revolution cleaved neatly, for the most part, to the ethos and aesthetics of their predecessors, there are two elements in *Caïus Gracchus* that hint at the tectonic shifts that were occurring beneath and through them. First, Caïus as an individual seems to disappear into his personification of the law, as if he were less a person than a principle, so that the expiation of his guilt—his self-sacrifice *to* the laws—precedes his actual death. Second, the enemies of the state are the senators, who style themselves its representatives but have usurped the rights of those they are meant to serve.[60] The action and political message of the play thus hinge on an anxiety about the dangers of representative government, the risk that the representation can gain autonomy, act in its own self-interest, and, as a result, inflict damage on the represented.

Based on Kant's observations about the French Revolution, which attributed the moral and philosophical importance of the event not to its protagonists themselves, but to the disinterested interest of what he called "spectator" nations ("die Denkungsart der Zuschauer"), it would seem that contemporaries viewed the Revolution as a form of spectacle, and some have made this argument, most notably Marie-Hélène Huet, who has written that the revolutionaries viewed themselves as actors and their endeavors as theatrical performances.[61] To illustrate her point, Huet quotes the outburst by Georges Danton, the first president of the Committee of Public Safety, during Louis XVI's trial for treason; Danton, exasperated by a long digression concerning Jean-Louis Laya's revolutionary comedy, *L'Ami des lois* (The Friend of the Laws), lashed out at his fellow members of the Convention: "A comedy indeed! The matter before us is the tragedy you owe the nations; the thing at issue is the head of a tyrant which we are going to sever with the axe of the laws."[62] The idea of political theater, or theater as politics, that Huet elaborates in her analyses of the Revolution is not, however, entirely intuitive, since it requires the active participation of the audience and its essence lay not in the message it conveyed but in the conveyance or communication itself. Discussing public executions during the Revolution, she writes:

> revolutionary justice was inscribed in a system of communication, rather than a system of values, and . . . the spectacle death offered the spectator was a message the exchange of which constituted the law. With this in mind, it is interesting to note that the main actor, the guilty party, was sacrificed, in every sense, for the benefit of the audience, the public. That the legislators of '91 seemed more concerned with the readability of the message than with its content was also in the order of revolutionary justice.[63]

If the king's execution is a necessary tragedy, one that France owed to all nations, according to Danton, Huet's subsequent analysis of revolutionary executions in general argues that they are tragedies of justice itself, in which the message or content of the spectacle is less important than the event itself, especially its form. I will return, in a moment, to the role of what Huet calls the "main actor," or the sacrificial victim in this system of justice, but first I want to pause for a moment on Huet's observations about the "readability" or transparency of revolutionary justice, since it is crucial to understanding the displacement of the victim of tragedy from the stage to the scaffold, from the theater in a more limited sense to theater in a radically—indeed, revolutionarily—broader sense.

Rousseau had railed against the deleterious effects of theater on the moral and civic life of citizens in his 1758 *Letter to d'Alembert*, where he placed justice foremost among human responsibilities and described the potential guilt that accompanies that responsibility, thus framing the relation between theater and State in terms of justice and guilt.[64] He rejected the theater as antithetical to the State, or at least the State as it should be, since theater excites the passions, while only reason can purge them. He thereby understood the State as a rational entity and the theater a spectacle of the passions.[65] The State that embraces theater, Rousseau warned, would succumb to it. "It is by its mania for theater that Athens perished," he wrote, "and its disasters justified only too well the sorrow that Solon felt at Thespis' first performances (*représentations*)."[66] Still, Rousseau did not reject performances as such—on the contrary, he saw them as vital to the civic order in a republic, a crucial means to join together the population through "the gentle bonds of pleasure and joy."[67] "But what," he asked, "will be the object of these spectacles? What will be shown in them? Nothing, if you like (*Rien, si l'on veut*). . . . Or better yet, let the spectators be the spectacle; make them the actors themselves; let each one see and love himself in the others that all may be more closely united as a result."⁶⁸ What matters, then, is not the content or message that it conveys, as Huet had argued about the public executions under the Revolution, but the event of the festival itself. To the extent that they represent anything, the civic festivals so necessary to a republic are spectacles of *nothing* (*rien*). This can be taken in two senses: first, that the spectacles Rousseau promotes reject representation in favor of presentation and, second, that they do represent something, but that the thing they represent is, paradoxically, nothingness. These two interpretations are not incompatible and both, I would argue, are operative in the tragic politics of the Revolution.

Rousseau's repudiation of theater was but one expression of a broader distrust of representation that characterized revolutionary political theory in general, a distrust whose pervasiveness was attested to by seemingly unrelated details of public policy and debate. Faced with an inflationary crisis caused by the issuance of paper money or *assignats* against the value of property the State had seized from the Church, for example, Saint-Just attempted to theorize the dangers inherent in such symbolic systems. "It is a principle most obviously true (*juste*)," he wrote, "that signs, in a State, must not exceed the value and quantity of what they represent. If money (*l'argent*) is represented by paper and there is more paper than money, the money will disappear, and if the quantity of things that the paper represents should happen to diminish, one will then have neither money nor things."⁶⁹ Saint-Just was discussing a specific form of representation (the word *signe* was a synonym for *assignat*), but his concerns had a larger semiotic reach (*signe* also meant "sign" in general), such that a State, according to his reasoning, has a just and vested interest in policing the relation between sign and referent. The representation must not, according to him, gain autonomy in relation to what it represents. No secondary market for *assignats* must be allowed; no tolerance for independent symbolic systems. And the response that he mandated if things should go awry, as was the case in the inflationary crisis, was to burn the sign.⁷⁰

Susan Maslan has argued that this distrust of representation extended to representative democracy itself, to the point that the people who filled the theaters and streets felt an almost constitutional distrust of their elected officials. "The relation between representative and direct democracy," she writes, "was an urgent problem during the Revolution and has remained one of the central topoi of revolutionary historiography. ... There was, however, a strong and widespread sense among ordinary people that to cede power to representatives was, at least in part, to lose what had been so recently gained. To lend others their newly won authority was to submit themselves to new masters. When the people elect representatives, as Rousseau had warned, they become 'nothing.'"⁷¹ This was the concern that the hero of Chénier's *Caïus Gracchus* had repeatedly expressed about the senators in Rome—that they had subverted their role as "représentans" of the public will to their own, independent interests. And if the elected members of the Convention, such as Saint-Just and Robespierre, were similarly expressions or signs of the French people, then any deviation between them and the people should, by Saint-Just's reasoning about independent signs, lead to their immolation. That, of course, is what happened to both Robespierre and Saint-Just on the tenth of Thermidor, year II of the Revolution, when they were both guillotined, along with their associates, in what is now the place de la Concorde.

Revolutionary theory and practice thus feared and rejected the autonomy of representation, moving the site of political identity away from semiotic systems toward actual persons. Consequently, if the Revolution as political event was in some sense tragic, its most important protagonists and structures will not be found in its theatrical productions, but among the citizens themselves. Maslan has argued that the revolutionary rejection of representation created an ideology of "presence," which would suggest that the public constitutive of the new republic would consist in real, embodied people understood in their actual specificity, but not every individual or aspect of an individual is a citizen.[72] Consequently, the citizen is a role that one plays, and that role, I would argue, is tragic, since in it an individual must expiate an endless guilt for which she or he is not individually responsible.

When, in mid-1791, Louis XVI effectively abrogated the new constitution by denouncing the Revolution and attempting to flee the country, the newly established republic found itself suddenly and strangely stateless, since the king had withdrawn a pillar of its legitimacy. As Robespierre would observe during Louis' trial,

> [i]t is a blatant contradiction to suppose that the constitution could preside over this new order of things. That would mean that it could outlive itself. What laws replace it? The laws of nature and that law that forms the very basis of society: the welfare of the people (*le salut du peuple*). . . . But the people! What law are they to follow if not justice and reason, seconded by their almighty force?[73]

France, according to Robespierre, had been cast into a moment when laws, justice, and the State itself were shaken by doubt and their foundations broken. It was a moment, in short, when the State must invent itself, and to do so it must return to a basic principle, that of the people's welfare. But the argument here is unnerving: on the one hand justice—or the basic law of society—depends on the people, while, on the other, the people find that law by following justice and reason. Unless it exists independently from society, justice would thus seem both to precede and to derive from the people. It is therefore circular, groundless, unjustified, and, in this sense, guilty.

The "people" was thus a name for the mystification of justice itself, the veil drawn over the circularity of its legitimation, the mask for its original inequity and guilt. The question arises, what or who is the people that Robespierre identifies with the legitimacy of the State? We know from this passage that the people are both rational and just, while other moments from the trial suggest to what an extent it is an abstraction rather than a presence. On November 13, for instance, Saint-Just addressed the Convention in the following words: "You will never see me place my personal will against the will of all. I shall want what the French people, or the majority of its representatives, wants. But since my personal will is a portion of the law that has yet to be made, I shall openly explain what I mean."[74] The law is still to be made, it is a justice still to come, and the person that can speak in its name is only the one who absents himself from his individuality to identify, instead, with the people. He is divided, for he is both a "personal will" and "the will of all," and those two aspects of his identity are not the same, since they can come into conflict; when they do, he will, he promises, submit to the common will. He will *want* what the people wants, thus submitting and structuring his desire itself to a collective abstraction—and it *is* an abstraction because it is an entity that exists only in the rejection of the particular *as* such. "The man who listens only to his individual will," Diderot had written, "is the enemy of the human race."[75] Robespierre decried "the abjection of the individual self."[76] The citizen, in short, was the repudiation of the person.

The Revolution set this ideology of impersonality into literally terrifying practice, as no less a figure than Hegel observed shortly after. He saw the guillotine itself as a concrete manifestation of this policy, for its functioning, he argued, separates a person from their essence, so that in bowing his or her head to its blade, the individual becomes a citizen. In his analysis of the Revolution, he wrote:

> The sole work and deed of universal freedom is therefore *death*, a death too which has no inner significance or filling, for what is negated is the empty point of the absolutely free self. It is thus the coldest and meanest of all deaths, with no more significance than cutting off a head of cabbage or swallowing a mouthful of water.[77]

This death is meaningless in the sense of being redundant or superfluous, because, Hegel argued, the person who is subjected to it has already disappeared as an individual, abstracted into the impersonality of the State in its theorization as universal freedom. Universal freedom is, in other words, freedom from the non-universal or the individual, and the work of the State, during the Revolution, thus comes to a point—or a head—in its violence against the aspects of a person that remain alien to the State in its abstraction, which is to say, against the individuality of the individual. In other words, the work of the State is the death of the individual. And, as Hegel observed, it did not matter if the individual was actually guilty of anything in order to be found guilty and sacrificed.[78] That guilt came always from somewhere other than the person who paid for it.

In his *Poetics*, Aristotle described tragedy as inspiring pity and terror. In their attempt to create a new civic order, a new State, and a new politics, the revolutionaries seem to have foregone the pity and cleaved to the terror. They also destroyed the separation between audience and actors. The citizen that the Revolution both demanded and created was abstract and impersonal, caught in the circular logic that governed the origins of revolutionary justice and forced to expiate, *as* an individual, an endless crime which he or she did not individually commit. During the Terror, the tragic hero—that is, the victim of the infinite and displaced guilt of society itself—was everyone individually.

But this subject was not unique to the French Revolution, although it may have become particularly and painfully visible there. Enlightenment figures, especially Kant, as Gabriela Basterra has argued, generally understood subjectivity in relation to a new definition of the law. According to this new paradigm, the autonomous subject—that is, the subject that forms the basis of liberal democracy—arises through its submission to the law in principle. Since this submission to the law is in principle, the particular expression that law may take and whether or not the subject obeys it are immaterial.[79] This is what it means to be a citizen of a liberal democracy, and since the law to which the subject submits, in order to become a modern legal subject, is entirely formal, it is also infinite, which means that the citizen subject can never satisfy its demands. Or, to put it another way, since the principle of law is without content, since it comprises no specific laws, one is never sure of not having violated it. Consequently, the modern subject is originally or, as Basterra likes to put it, primordially guilty. The modern democratic subject thus emerges from a paradox of justice itself, from the formal structure of original guilt that results from a change in the principles of law itself and their relation to the individual. It is specifically tragic, Basterra argues, because of its underlying paradox: the modern subject tries to assert its freedom through the principle of autonomy—that is, through the freedom of individual action—even as it submits to the alterity of the law, and in this way replicates the free submission to the principle of fate, the "self-denying creativity," that defined, for her, the earliest tragedies.[80] I would describe this subject as tragic for a different reason, however. It is tragic because it conforms to the structure of original guilt that arises with the very principle of justice itself. The will to be just is never, in itself, just, and that injustice demands an expiation. To the extent that we define individuality as

Kantian autonomy, what seems to be specific to the Enlightenment and its aftermath is that the guilty party is the individual subject as such.

And so, the tragic politics, the political tragedy, of this long period was a tale of two cities, of Paris and Versailles. Under the semiotic system of seventeenth-century French absolutist monarchy, the organizing principle of the State came to be personified in the king, whose relative position—and therefore identity—found expression in a complex system of representations, among which tragedies played a pre-eminent role. They, or their ill-fated heroes, assumed the infinite and painful task of legitimizing the new social order that the monarch embodied. As Hippolyte-Jules Pilet de La Mesnardière put it in his 1639 *Poétique*, tragedies should "establish the throne of justice upon the stage (*établir sur le théâtre le trône de la justice*)."[81] Under the Revolution, however, representation itself was discredited and rejected, so that, in theory at least, the law found its embodiment elsewhere. That elsewhere was the citizen themselves, and so the burden of expiation now fell not to mythic figures on the stage, but to actual individuals in the streets, assemblies, and other public spaces. The individual paid off the infinite and constitutional guilt of being a citizen. And to the extent that we are still citizens of Enlightenment liberal democracies, we too are still tragic.

# CHAPTER FIVE

# Religion, Ritual and Myth

JULIETTE CHERBULIEZ AND CHRISTOPHER SEMK

## INTRODUCTION

Around 1738, the famous actor Luigi "Lélio" Riccoboni wrote his own cultural history of European theater. Explicitly addressing the long-standing problem of how theater might perfect itself while respecting "religion, reason, and good taste," Riccoboni started with the twelfth century and worked from culture to culture, from the Italian and through the Spanish before addressing the histories of Northern Europe: France, England, Holland, and Germany.[1] This story sounds familiar: from mystery plays of the fifteenth century to the ever-popular farces and burlesques of his eighteenth century, it should trace theater's evolution away from the sacred toward the secular. Even today, accounts exploring the connection between religion and theater in the premodern period would emphasize such a progressive history. From performance's sacred roots in Passion plays, we too might follow the gradual secularization of theater over the centuries. Yet Riccoboni's perspective is rather that religion is not merely a historical root of theater. It thoroughly permeates theater's institutions, its practices, cultural specificities, and traditions. A minor anecdote from his history serves to complicate most versions of theater's relationship to religion, as well as to ritual, and myth—both of those of Antiquity and those of tragedy itself.

In a footnote to his discussion of Paris' first permanent theater, the Hôtel de Bourgogne, Riccoboni remarks on the fate of a stone block affixed over the entrance, marking it as that of its troupe, the Confrérie de la Passion. This escutcheon, carved in relief upon the block, included the confrères' thoroughly medieval device: The cross with instruments of the Passion. It was paradoxically under the sign of these marks of Christ that the theater troupe adhered to the royal ordonnance to "play only profane, licit, and honest subjects, and to present no sacred Mysteries." During decades of renovations to the Hôtel de Bourgogne, this "antique monument" was repeatedly in danger of being damaged, and so Riccoboni recounts the great efforts he made attempting to preserve it, including a futile call for help to the architect in charge of the project. Finally, in 1732, Riccoboni obtained permission to safeguard the block at home until he could have "the satisfaction of seeing it put back in place, and so to serve to Posterity of proof and witness of Theater's origin in France."[2]

Despite Riccoboni's refusal to give any religious significance to the stone, saving the bas-relief grants it a relic-like quality, a memento of the sacred space of the Hôtel de Bourgogne as theater. Just as an eighteenth-century Italian practitioner of *commedia dell'arte* might fetishize a representation of the instruments of Christ's passion and the deep history of theater with which it is imbued, in this chapter we excavate the religious and sacred dimensions of tragedy in France and Europe more generally, in the second half of the seventeenth century and the eighteenth century. Although our trajectory remains roughly chronological, we aim to trouble the neat narrative of progressive (in both senses of the word) disenchantment in early modernity. We will show how tragedy remained invested in ritual and religion, despite cultural pressures that appeared to effect a move of increased secularization.

Ultimately, throughout Europe the secularization of theater was not just gradual but also only partial. Even as it developed its own rituals and mytho-histories, tragedy remained intertwined with Christian practices and performances. Whether alongside the seventeenth century's responses to ecclesiastical critiques striving to protect the pious and preserve religion by ostensibly banishing it from the stage, or the eighteenth century's increased rejection of the sacred warrant of tragedy, we trace also the persistence of the mythological, the divine, the ritualized, and the religious in tragedy.

The French case is a remarkable example of this investment, unique perhaps in Europe. Generally, European tragic repertoires drew on the Renaissance assessments of Aristotelian notions of form and decorum for legitimacy, and on a capacious body of history, including "fable" (or mythology) for its dramatic subjects. Protestant and Catholic scholars alike wrote treatises on poetics, rhetoric, and tragedy that were read across confessional and national lines. The commentary on Aristotle's *Poetices libri septem* (1561) by J.C. Scaliger (1484–1558), published posthumously in Leiden and Lyon, has perhaps the strongest legacy. Poetic treatises by Lodovico Castelvetro (1505–71) and Catholic bishop Antonio Minturno (1500–74) appeared in England and France, while works by the Dutch Protestant theologian Gerardus Vossius (Gerrit Janszoon Vos, 1577–1649) and playwright Daniel Heinsius (1580–1655) circulated in England, France, and Germany.[3]

By the 1650s, however, the structures of cultural authority in Catholic countries came to have a particular impact on theater. Like Italy and Spain, France's Catholicism, which during the Counter Reformation upheld the long-standing split between Church and civil authority, paradoxically also reaffirmed the humanist lay authority over taste. It thus facilitated the defense of a vibrant theater culture. The very debates which Church authorities exposed, the tensions between sovereign powers and religious moralists: all of these made possible in Catholic countries a lively theater with a public whose tastes mattered to dramaturges and performers.[4]

The story of tragedy in the "Age of Enlightenment" is usually considered to be a chapter in the longer narrative of progressive "disenchantment" that characterizes secular modernity. Yet this tidy narrative of tragedy's ever-decreasing investment in religion overlooks the actual historical relationship between the two. French tragedy, both religious and profane, borrowing from Italian traditions and exported across Europe, was influenced very early on by its Catholic culture. Yet pagan myth—from Oedipus to Orpheus, from Apollo to Aries, equally permeated all variations of tragedy, from the machine play, the tragi-comédie, lyric tragedy, to the "tragédie pastorale."

For Christian Delmas, the use of mythology as a source of spectacle, starting with Corneille's spectacular Ovidian machine-play *Andromède* (1650) through Racine's *Phèdre* (1677), makes visible one of tragedy's principle subjects: the "above and beyond the real," whether treated as a special effect through which gods fly, or a metaphysical question through which the human relation to a seemingly irretrievable communion with the divine is interrogated.[5] Greek and Roman mythology infused the tragic stage with the same order of questions that authorized borrowings from Biblical and other religious histories. By the 1650s, French tragedy was inflected as much by the religious concerns that sought to constrain or exploit it as it was by its deep roots in the dramas of Antiquity.

In a climate that was politically disposed to theater as a powerful cultural arm of the monarchy, early modern theorists of tragedy advanced a utilitarian vision of the theater as a wholly secular enterprise. They did so precisely in response to and with deference to, first, pre-existing relations between religion and theater, and second, to religious criticism of the stage. The result was the cultivation of new dramatic rituals that eventually competed with those of the church.

## "THEATER IS NO LONGER ANYTHING BUT ENTERTAINMENT"

François Hédelin, abbé d'Aubignac (1604–76), was among the theater's most ardent reformers and defenders in seventeenth-century France. Author of several plays himself, he undertook the composition of a practical manual for the proper construction of a dramatic poem. The *Pratique du théâtre*, written in the 1640s but not published until 1657, is an apt starting point for a critical examination of how religion, ritual, and myth shaped tragedy at the dawn of the Enlightenment. The "pratique" of the title signals d'Aubignac's concern with the present moment of theater and all of theater's constituencies: playwrights, actors, and spectators.

D'Aubignac's theater is strictly Aristotelian, abiding by the dual imperatives of verisimilitude and decorum as well as the three unities of time, place, and action. Its purpose is both pleasure and edification, or more precisely an edifying pleasure. Such a pragmatic agenda fostered a theory of theater's social utility. D'Aubignac argues for the public benefit of the theater on the grounds that a well-regulated theater occupies the public in times of peace, distracts them in times of war, and above all offers them a form of "honest entertainment." Emancipating theater from religion, reform-minded writers like d'Aubignac not only advanced a new dramatic theory of rational, moral theater; they also developed a strategy for responding to religiously motivated antitheatrical sentiment. The theater and the church could be considered two distinct entities, ideally playing complementary but not competing roles in instructing the public.

There was another consequence to this emancipation, however, beyond its impact on the moral life of the public and the authority of the Church. The autonomy granted to theater also seemed to outline something of a sacred purview for dramatic art itself. D'Aubignac seems to allude to this possibility in a particularly ambiguous assertion, when he says that theater "no longer has a share in sacred things and cannot tolerate this mixture without desecration."[6] But what is desecrated? Sacred things? Or the theater? Through such ambiguity, d'Aubignac allows that religious subjects may in fact threaten the secular stage, which, open to desecration, has become a sacred thing in itself. By distinguishing between the reasonable, secular tragedy of modernity and the ritual theater of the ancient world, defenders of the stage like d'Aubignac sought to address long-standing religious opposition. If Church Fathers fulminated against the stage, it was because the spectacles they targeted were pagan aberrations worthy of condemnation. Modern tragedy, on the other hand, was purged of immorality. Guided by the rule of reason, conditioned by verisimilitude and decorum, neoclassical tragedy was, when properly executed, above reproach.

The result of this was twofold. Although the Catholic Reformation favored the creation of religious drama in Italy (*sacre rappresentazioni* and Rospigliosi's religious operas), Spain (*autos sacramentales*), and France (*tragédies chrétiennes*), the theorization of neoclassical tragedy in France tended to exclude religious subjects. In Germany, however, sacred dramas were widely practiced, especially through the performance of Jesuit drama in public theaters.[7] In France, a desire to establish a non-heretical theater resulted in a re-examination of tragedy's historical foundations. In one of the few reflections on history in the *Pratique*, d'Aubignac acknowledges tragedy's ritual origins, writing that it "was, at its founding, only a pagan hymn."[8] Paradoxically, then, readers of the *Pratique* could justify their love of theater by appreciating its pagan, which was to say false, origins. "True" religion had no place on a stage dedicated to entertainment.

At a time when Cardinal Richelieu's political programme had also begun to institutionalize theater, d'Aubignac too envisioned royal intervention sanctioning the secular vocation of the French stage, imagining "that the king issue a declaration that theater performances are no longer an act of religion and idolatry, as in the past, but only a public entertainment."[9] The proclamation never happened, and while the state remained embroiled in the debate about the theater, its perspective also shifted. With the succession of Cardinal Jules Mazarin (1602–61) as Chief Minister, anti-theater moralists had a new political landscape which may have strengthened their position.[10]

## THE SECULAR RITUALS OF THEATER

Moralists had been right; theater was beginning to compete adeptly with religious practice. It did so by achieving much of the rituality that Church practice demanded, both inserting itself into and shaping everyday life, especially in Paris. Theater historians have long established the relationship between the spectacle and communion of theater with that of religion; the culture of theater increasingly shared structural elements with Church rituals and other mechanisms of order. As a consequence of moral and poetic debates seeking to legitimize tragic performance, theater created new rituals and temporalities proper to tragedy and its audience. The codification of regulations relating to what kinds of plays could be performed, when, and how often, created a new rhythm to Parisian lives that overlapped with and complemented, but also superseded the Church calendar. This rhythm was increasingly standardized over the course of the century. For example, in the first part of the century, contracts relating to the Hôtel de Bourgogne's troupe ended by Mardi gras or *mi-carême* (mid-Lent), allowing them to leave Paris in the spring to go on tour in the provinces, only returning between October or late December.[11] By the time Samuel Chappuzeau wrote *Le théâtre françois* (1674), the season had two established periods: winter (October–Lent), and the less important summer season, with troupes abstaining on religious holidays. Even in provincial cities without established troupes, the theater season revolved around religious festival periods.[12]

Over the course of the century the rhythm of performances also achieved greater regularity, with three performances a week becoming the mid-century norm—Tuesdays, Fridays, and Sundays, Friday being the best day to introduce new works—a routine that respected such other significant city routines as post, market, and sermon days.[13] Also over the course of the century, and as theater became more popular, Parisian troupes each developed its own schedule; since the first weeks of its founding in 1680, the Comédie-Française generally performed daily. This regularity introduced another specificity: extraordinary and ordinary days, with the extraordinary being reserved for new performances or reprises of celebrated works. Performance times themselves, confined to the afternoons before dark, adapted to the seasons as well.

Theater thus became an institution with its own rhythms and rituals, integrated into the life of Parisians. While it has long been commonplace to think of theater, especially tragedy, as the culture of the elite, theater historians have established that throughout the seventeenth and eighteenth centuries, spectatorship was economically and socially diverse, with ticket sales—and seating—at many price levels. Just like church, the whole social body could be represented in the theater: the faithful and the occasional. And, just like church, attendees did not go only for the performance, but for the benefits of community and the prestige of being seen.

Alongside these moves toward the imbrication of the theater into Parisian lives, theater culture was also succeeding in institutionalizing and codifying what a tragedy was. Particular normative concepts emerged from an engagement with Aristotelian concepts of tragedy. The French version of the three unities of time, place, and action not only created guidelines for what was acceptable theater, but also established a set of constraints which could offer a kind of moral and dramaturgical choreography for tragedy. The tragic thus came to have its own liturgy, in the word's original sense: it came to be a public ceremony with a prescribed form.

Theater's liturgy is intimately connected to church: not simply because of the analogous disposition of sacred and dramatic spaces (the shape of the church and the shape of the theater, for example), nor because of the spectacular quality of dramatic or ecclesiastical ritual (vestments, candles, images, and so on). Tragedy resembles liturgy because it is above all an "action," performed by a living human being whose words and gestures repeat and above all restore the actions of another (Christ/the character), before an assembly of participants. Consider the performative dimensions of D'Aubignac's famous assertion that onstage to speak is to act ("Parler, c'est Agir").[14] That the word is efficacious is as much a ritual or sacred axiom as it is a dramatic one. After all, it is the "words of institution" (*hoc est enim corpus meum*), echoing those of Christ, that guarantee the transformation of bread and wine into the eucharistic emblems.

## RELIGIOUS ANTITHEATRICAL POLEMIC

Despite—or because of—reformers' efforts, moralists were right: the theater posed a danger. We can see this danger on two levels. The first is in the simple clash of liturgical times: how can it be anything but heretical to attend two rites, sometimes even in one day? As the Carmelite and royal preacher Léon de Saint-Jean lamented, "Ah, how I loathe those profane Souls ... who take communion in the morning, and after dinner return to their passions, their gambling, to the Theater."[15] The habits of the theater undid the practices of the church, or at least exposed their ephemeral potential.

Perhaps related to this charge was a more serious one: that of the effectiveness of theatrical feigning. In his antitheatrical *Maximes et réflexions sur la comédie* (1694), Jacques-Bénigne Bossuet (1627–1704) ironically appears to agree with d'Aubignac. Stage heroes and passions, brought forth by actors, move the spectator more forcefully than a mere painting or even the printed text. "How much more are we touched by theater's expressions, where all seems real, where it is not lifeless gestures and dry colors that act, but living personages."[16] The performative status of theater, more than any other art, could rival the real effects of the Church.

The secular theater, where all *seems* real, comes to embody the antithesis of the church, where all *is* real. As a perversion of the truth, the theater advances a diabolical agenda. While playwrights and pro-theatrical writers argued that tragedy had become a secular enterprise, religious adversaries of the stage held that tragedy retained something of its pagan origins and consequently had no place in Christendom. Across Europe, both

Catholic and Protestant writers denounced the stage as a place of lies, vice, and waste. Religious writers appealed to the authority and continued validity of ecclesiastical tradition, countering the relativism of dramatic reformers who argued that the modern stage was a world apart from the pagan spectacles condemned in patristic literature. In the eyes of antitheatrical writers, tragedy's purportedly secular character did little to weaken its spiritually devastating impact. It did not matter that seventeenth-century tragedy was no longer a literal "shrine to Venus," as Tertullian had described the illicit passions that animated characters and so stirred spectators.[17] Arousing the passions in this way was, in the words of the Prince of Conti, contrary to the entire goal of the Christian religion, which is to "calm them, demolish and destroy them as much as possible in this life."[18] For religious antitheatrical writers, tragedy produced the very same illicit passions it represented. Spectators would exit the theater contaminated by the spectacle, becoming themselves unwitting agents of contagion. It is for this reason that Pierre Nicole famously denounced playwrights as "poisoners of the public."[19]

The situation was not uniform across Europe. Lutheran moralists railed against the dangers of theater in similar terms to Protestants elsewhere, while Catholic German tragedies of the seventeenth century were at once bloody, spectacular, morbid, and nevertheless religious. In certain corners, for part of the seventeenth century, both traditions developed a tragic repertoire side by side. Breslau, capital of the biconfessional state of Silesia, was a remarkable center for a whole range of religious tragedies: Gryphius' foundational martyr play *Catharina von Georgian* (1650) and subsequent martyr plays pit tyranny against the innocence of a victim; anti-Hapsburg allegory in favor of a republican Silesia. Daniel Caspar Lohenstein wrote no fewer than six religious tragedies between 1653 and 1680, using Gryphius as a model and drawing on Church and Ancient texts for contemporary political interpretation.[20] At the other extreme, and in a very different political-religious context, in England, the Puritan-led Parliament succeeded in closing all theaters in 1642 and they would not reopen until the Restoration in 1660.

Despite the acerbic tone of their discourse, French antitheatrical polemicists did not advocate the closure of France's theaters. Instead, they encouraged their readers to convert—to turn away from the stage and from the public life it entailed toward a private life of reflection, repentance, and prayer. Christianity and tragedy's incompatibility led these critics to fiercely denounce attempts to purify or Christianize the stage, so they reserved their harshest condemnation for so-called *tragédie chrétienne* (Christian tragedy). A monstrous marriage of piety and peccancy, the dramatic adaptation of Christian subjects did nothing to change the nature of the stage; it did, however, alter the character of its subjects. As Nicole pointed out, because a playwright needs to fill seats, he must please his audience, and nothing is as unlikely to please as a cold lesson in temperance or humility. It follows that the playwright must portray saints as he would his historical or pagan heroes: full of pride, eloquent, and subject to passionate extremes. Better, then, to focus on history and myth and leave the saints to the church.

# MYTH AS THE HISTORY OF THE PRESENT

After 1660, the vast majority of tragedies created in France treated ancient history or mythology, with a slim group of exceptions drawing from more recent and more local European events. Despite the prominence of pagan gods, displays of sacrifice, immoral family alliances, and threats of supernatural and monstrous beings, Greco-Latin subjects could offer a guarantee of "vraisemblance" through the warrant of pure tradition. As

FIGURE 5.1: Set design for Act 2 of Pierre Corneille's *Andromède*, as first performed on February 1, 1650 by the Troupe Royale at the Petit-Bourbon in Paris. Wikimedia Commons.

Corneille said, the subject of Andromède "is a fiction that Antiquity received; as it has been transmitted to us, no one is offended to see it in theaters."[21] Filtered through the tradition of Renaissance humanist interpretation, Greco-Latin history had been vulgarized and integrated into students' lessons, court pageants, and near-common knowledge.[22]

Their elaborations in Renaissance humanist natural science and art stripped these subjects of any precise temporality: neither that of the past nor, by allegory or analogy, of the contemporary moment. If tragedy's temporality is always a combination of the past made present, of history interrupting itself to pause for a moment before the catastrophe, the mythology of Greek history that dominates Racine and other French tragedians' work in the latter half of the seventeenth century is not so much an inquiry into either the mysteries of origins or the strength of divine power. Phèdre's oft-cited, oft-mocked one-line origin story, "daughter of Minos and of Phasiphaë," suggests rather that it is the collision of two forces, of the darkness of judgment that is also prosaic and human, with the light of the sun, a brightness that is also monstrous and calamitous in its reach.

It is perhaps because of this collision that we can also see a pure rationalization of myth in tragedy: deities appear embodied only in tragi-comedies and lyric forms. Racine's *Iphigénie* offers an account of the goddess Diana only third-hand: Ulysse transmits the testimony of a soldier who saw her come down from the heavens. The hand of Diana appearing onstage only as hearsay, the sense of the sacred can be captured by the playwright even as he remains agnostic about the precise causes for human downfall. Thus, Racine's invention of the jealous Eriphile who eventually suicides, which removed the morally dubious and "invraisemblable" potential of a human sacrifice, also dramaturgically precludes the high priest Calchas using a "profane hand" to wield his knife and kill. The possibility that human agents are fully responsible for their fate remains, even in a world of unnaturally stalled winds and sacrificial altars. Likewise, the myriad monsters in *Phèdre*—that legacy of deviant love of Phasiphaë for the Minotaur or the sea monster conjured up after Thésée's call to Poseidon for help in avenging his honor—are offstage, temporally or geographically removed. Yet so are gods: in his famous "Théramène's tale," Hippolyte's tutor reports having not witnessed, but heard from someone else, the appearance of a god holding a trident.[23] Was Hippolyte killed by Poseidon's sea monster? Or did he fall from his own overweening pride, tangled by the reins of horses he could not master?

The very same period in French culture also saw an engagement with mythology that was utterly contrary to such rationalization. The use of mythology in the creation of King Louis XIV's royal system at Versailles is well-documented.[24] In contrast to the obfuscation of the divine in Racinian tragedy, the full corporeality and actuality of Apollo, Mars, Mercury, Jupiter, Diana, and Venus, suggest the extrahuman dimensions of the king. Whether the programme itself found coherence or achieved the status of successful propaganda does not mitigate the significance of a mythological programme that contrasted so intensely with a parallel system on the stage.

## RETURN TO RITUAL

In the final years of Louis XIV's reign, some playwrights and critics began advocating a return to ancient tragedy that would not distract from Christianity. By and large, this involved revisiting the place of erotic love in tragedy. For these reformers, impassioned and unchaste love ought to be portrayed as detrimental to the lovers or replaced altogether with chaste love and selfless virtue. In 1675 Racine's *Iphigénie* downplayed love's role, prompting the abbé Pierre de Villiers (1648–1728) to consider it a model of virtuous tragedy. For Villiers, "Tragedy is a painting of civic life which was invented for the regulation of the passions."[25] Yet the erotic component had become so commonplace that it threatened to undermine tragedy's ostensibly civilizing mission. The relatively marginal place of erotic love in *Iphigénie*, coupled with its success both at Versailles and in Paris, demonstrated that love was an unnecessary embellishment: "Iphigénie's great success has disabused the public of the mistaken belief that a tragedy cannot hold up without violent love." In *Phèdre* (1677), Racine's last secular tragedy, unchaste love has disastrous consequences, which the playwright celebrated in his preface as a restoration of tragedy to its ancient vocation as a "school of virtue." The horror inspired by Phèdre's criminal desire for her stepson offers a powerful antidote to any contagion that her love might inspire.

What is perhaps most surprising about the late seventeenth-century call for the *tragédie sans amour* (tragedy without love) is the voice of religious advocates for reform. Bossuet allegedly approved of the absence of unchaste love and the eponymous heroine's marital fidelity in Charles-Claude Genest's *Pénélope* (1684), an anecdote speaking to the desire to create a moral tragedy that even the most virulent antitheatrical writers would applaud. When Genest, who was also an abbé, published his tragedy in 1703, he affirmed that his intention was to banish illicit love from the tragedy.

The *tragédie sans amour* was not only an attempt to bring tragedy in line with Christian morality; from a strictly literary point of view it was also considered a return to the principles and practices of ancient tragedy. As François Fénelon (1651–1714) wrote in his posthumously published *Lettre à l'Académie française*, "Among the Greeks, tragedy was entirely independent of profane love." ("Chez les Grecs, la tragédie était entièrement independente de l'amour profane.")[26] Fénelon was, like fellow prelate Bossuet, no fan of the contemporary stage. Yet he envisioned poetic reforms that would purge the stage of its modern excesses and restore its antique austerity. With characters' passions out of the way, the spectators' own hearts and bodies could be touched more directly: "Such a spectacle . . . would not be applauded; but it would be gripping: it would elicit tears; it would not let a spectator breathe. . . . It would contribute most usefully to the design of the best laws and it would not alarm even the purest religion." ("Un tel spectacle . . . ne serait point applaudi; mais il saisirait, il ferait répandre des larmes, il ne laisserait pas respirer. . . . Il entrerait fort utilement dans le dessein des meilleures lois; la religion même la plus pure n'en serait point alarmée.")[27] However idealized, this vision reveals a shift in ecclesiastical thinking about tragedy: a real return to ancient myth and ritual might even achieve a new form of tragedy in which the absence of erotic love inspires something new.

Less ecclesiastically oriented writers agreed; Saint-Évremond (1613–1703) concludes his essay on tragedy with a call for the admiration of virtuous characters: "Above all else, what must be sought in Tragedy is the good expression of a noble character, which excites within us a tender admiration. In this kind of admiration there is some mental joy; it raises one's courage and touches the soul." ("C'est ce qui doit être recherché dans la tragédie, devant toutes choses, une grandeur bien exprimée, qui excite en nous une tendre admiration. Il y a dans cette sorte d'admiration quelque chose pour l'esprit; le courage y est élevé, l'âme y est touchée.")[28] The "ravissement" of the tragic stage could satisfy both religious and non-religious imperatives.

## A CHRISTIAN THEATER AT THE TWILIGHT OF LOUIS XIV: NEW TEMPORALITIES, OLD MYTHOLOGIES

Traditional modern histories of Louis XIV's later years suggest an increasingly austere religiosity. Such accounts generally include the shifting culture and aesthetics at Versailles, where mythology and spectacle gave way increasingly to prayer and retreat. Thus the 1672 construction of the Chapel abutted the grotto of Thétis, where Molière's *Malade Imaginaire* was performed during the three-day celebration of Louis XIV's 1674 victory at Franche-Comté, becomes a metaphor for the emerging importance of religious practice, whose power is confirmed by the eventual destruction of the grotto to make way for the North Wing and its renovated Chapel in 1684.[29] The celebration of Racine's *Phèdre* as at once the summa and the swan song of the French tragic form is another mark of transition: the so-called beginning of tragedy's end. It has been commonly assumed that Racine himself abandoned the theater after *Phèdre* to better conform to his own Christian beliefs. Literary historians, however, suggest that Racine likely chose not prayer but the pension and prestige of the Royal Historiographer over dramaturgy; so too the role of tragedy in Louis XIV's later years is complex and multifaceted.

Nothing more suggests this complexity than Racine's own pendant plays, *Esther* (1689) and *Athalie* (1691). Commissioned by Mme de Maintenon to be performed by her young charges at the Maison de Saint-Cyr, the royal school for impoverished noble girls, Racine's last tragedies were not just biblical in subject matter, they came from little-known Old Testament stories. Both stories were also reinvigorations of the tragic form as well.

Their particularity answered one significant concern voiced repeatedly by moralists. If Christianity's "terrible mysteries" cannot be poetically enlivened without blasphemy, as Boileau wrote in his *Art poétique*, the Old Testament offered playwrights plenty of material for developing a new religious tragedy that did not expose Christianity directly to the scandalous stage. Yet *Athalie*'s particular success, its first public performance in 1716, and its enduring place in literary history tend to overstate this tragedy's singularity while ignoring its exemplarity. *Athalie* was indeed a Christian tragedy performed amid many others, some which used Old Testament stories, others which referred to the Gospels, and still others referring to post-biblical accounts of Christian martyrs.

Racine's Old Testament plays were a departure from his earlier works, but for nearly two centuries, Christian plays offering moral lessons for players and audience alike, were part of students' training all over Europe. Honing students' oratorical skills, plays encouraging students to spread the faith of the Counter Reformation dominated especially Jesuit colleges.[30] Because so many of these plays, designed for production, were never printed and do not survive in manuscript, some estimates put the number written at nearly one hundred thousand in German-speaking areas.[31] Jesuit school theater had a profound impact on dramatic production throughout Europe, through and even beyond the temporary suspension of the Order in 1773. In Italy, the Jesuit colleges were a hub for dramatic production. German schools wrote them for plays by Benci, Tucci, or Joseph Simons, whose tragedies were performed at the English College in Rome.[32] Lutheran schoolteacher Christian Weise (1642–1708) alone wrote fifty-five biblical or historical tragedies. School plays inspired a range of dramas even in France that hewed more closely to biblical stories than to contemporary concepts of drama, such as Le Gras' *Discours tragique* which versified primarily John and included violence onstage.[33]

Many of these plays had a life beyond schools; Claude Boyer's *Judith* was performed at the Comédie-Française in 1695, as were the plays of Duché and abbé Genest.[34] Venel's *Jephté ou la Mort de Seïla*, composed sometime after 1672 and published in 1676, showcases the piety of the ruler Jephté who must sacrifice his dutifully willing daughter; the analogy to Louis XIV is made through a description of the crossing of the river Jordan which is compared to the famous French military passage over the Rhine; tragedy here is a structure for the affirmation of sovereign triumph. This despite the play's central conflict, in which Seïla's death affirms God's will over that of the sovereign.[35] With the printed version of this play replete with detailed stage and set directions, it is presumed to have been part of the duc de Savoie's repertory at Dijon in 1677, suggesting that religious plays had integrated themselves into a variety of repertoires.[36]

Vehicles for a didactic form of theater, Christian dramas of the late seventeenth century also offer another order of hermeneutics in which typological readings of the Old Testament announced and confirmed the advent of Christ, while reaffirming the political order of the day. Tragedy lent itself particularly well to this interpretative strategy, where the time of the Old and New Testaments became one with the present moment. Witnesses to the first revival of *Athalie*, performed in the young King's chambers at the Tuileries, were moved to tears when they saw in the orphan Joas, the last scion of the House of David, whose survival was the only hope for the Messiah's birth, resurrection and return, an anticipation of the young Louis XV, then about the same age.[37]

Another source of morally sound histories were post-biblical histories, especially saints' lives. Jean Galbert de Campistron (1656–1713) wrote at least eighteen plays of diverse genres, including lyric tragedies, comedies, and idylls. His ten tragedies also range in subject matter, including *Adrien*, which premiered at the Comédie-Française in early

1690, and features secret pagan conversions to Christianity. Lancaster speculates from the timing, that *Adrien* might have replaced Racine's *Esther* whose *privilège* prohibited public performances.[38] Regardless, it indicates a public interest in religious plays.

Quite obviously, Church histories and saints' lives made for subject matter that assuaged moralists and yet allowed for the kind of edifying "admiration" which appealed to dramaturges and critics beyond the Church. David-Augustin de Brueys (1640–1723) based his *Gabinie* (1699) on the neo-Latin tragedy *Susanna* (1653), by the Jesuit Adrien Jourdain. Brueys was a Protestant theologian who was famously converted by Bossuet around 1681. Treating the same period of Roman persecution of Christians as *Adrien*, the tragedy's subject is Saint Susanna, rechristened a more "noble" Gabinie. In his preface, Brueys explicitly widens the scope of his project beyond the martyrdom of a single saint to include the expansion of Christianity, "which establishes itself miraculously without any human help." Accordingly, the tragedy depicts the discovery of Gabinie's Christianity, that of her father, and the progressive conversion of Diocletian's men.

Written for a lay audience, the reception of these plays was multivalent, and the religious conflicts that continued to dominate Europe at the time resonated for their audiences. In France, plays celebrating the triumph of Christianity over paganism could be read in response to Louis XIV's suppression of Protestantism. Following the Edict of Fontainebleau in 1685 stripping Protestants of their rights, Louis was hailed by fervent Catholics as a "new Constantine."[39]

On the other hand, the persecution of a minority faith at the hands of a powerful political establishment could lend itself equally well to readings sympathetic to the Protestant cause. When Mme du Noyer saw *Gabinie*, "I found many connections to the way Protestants were treated that I returned to our lodgings deeply saddened. Mr du Noyer noticed and begged me to no longer attend this Play."[40] The preface to Amsterdam's 1700 printing of Bruey's play proposes it as a Huguenot defense, implying in the author's own conversion a feint.[41]

## A THEATER OF ADMIRATION

Broad brushstrokes paint eighteenth-century tragedy in Europe as increasingly emptied of its religious and sacred dimensions. Moralists of the seventeenth century discussed the extent to which tragic form, structure, and performance should be shaped for the betterment of society, while such early Enlightenment quarrels as the "querelle des vers" (quarrel of the stanzas) of the 1730s did nothing of the sort. These critical debates seemed utterly devoid of moral, let alone Christian, impulses, and instead aimed purely at issues of form. But the real difference between seventeenth- and eighteenth-century tragedies was not their drive toward secularization, but how they expected audiences to be transformed.

Saint-Évremond's call to develop an intrinsically human tragedy proved immediately frustrating yet ultimately prescient. To attempt to find the human and the great in tragedies that resorted to neither banal passions nor the supernatural was to attempt a revolt against classical theater entirely. In a moment of fomented aesthetic (and so political) rebellion against an older order, what might constitute at once the "tragic" and the "human?" For students of Enlightenment literature, it is astonishing to read tragedies from the early decades of the eighteenth century, filled with precisely the bloody, violent elements that had been banished from the neoclassical stage. Among the many tragedies of Prosper Jolyot de Crébillon (1674–1762) offering a secularized interpretation of the power of tragedy, the summa, *Atrée et Thyeste* (1707), tracks the revenge of Atrée upon his brother Thyeste, culminating in Atrée's proposing a solemn vow of reconciliation over a ceremonial cup, which holds in fact the blood of Thyeste's son Plisthène. In this scene, blood is both the liquid substance that spills and stains, as well as the blood-ties of family: Thyeste to both his sacrificed son and murderous, vengeful brother.

Significantly, Enlightenment dramaturges abandoned a moralizing position: tragedy no longer could persuade didactically. Abbé Jean-Baptiste Dubos, Fontenelle, and d'Aguesseau all question theater's role in the social not through its utility, but through its pleasure. Catharsis was never guaranteed; reasonable spectators could instead attend to the illusion of others' misfortunes without being themselves tormented. Thus emerged a tragedy that moved its audience to experience a bare horror, with no moral apparatus or framework to direct the audience.

Some critics advanced for tragedy what d'Aguesseau called "jouissance de la vérité": a moment of happiness in the face of truth.[42] Tragedy's ideal spectator experiences something not unlike the ravishing experience of the sublime: a sacred terror. Yet, pleasure did not always manifest itself so clearly among audiences. Fifty years later, one writer recalled Crébillon's own memory of *Atrée et Thyeste*'s opening night, "The audience was appalled, and it left without applauding or whistling at the end of the play." Arguably, Crébillon offered the first great revolt against neoclassical theater through the horror of the "cup of blood": an object torn from a pagan sacrifice scene, whose power was in its concentration of all tragedy's horror, with none of its compassion.[43]

For every moment in Enlightenment society where critics and dramaturges strove to reform theater so as to break the grip of the religious over it, the potential sacred dimensions of the "serious genre" returned by other means. *Atrée et Thyste* represented one interpretation of Aristotelian values that broke decidedly with the Christian tradition elaborated since the sixteenth century but retained the sacred horror of Attic tragedy. And while other forms emerged that could rival the social function of tragedy—the *drame bourgeois* most prominently in France—the importance of this particular genre remains, in part because of its ties to the more cosmic, foundational, divine, and historical structures of the social.

## THE RE-ENCHANTMENT OF TRAGIC SPECTACLE: VOLTAIRE AND THE USES OF RELIGION IN ENLIGHTENMENT CRITIQUE

While Enlightenment Europe generally witnessed an interrogation of the relationship among state, faith, and public spectacle, the tragic stage never truly lost its religion. The French stage performed critiques against the collusion of aristocratic, monarchical, patriarchal, and religious forces that dampened the exercise of reason and restrained the individual's freedom of conscience. Familiar myths and biblical episodes were thus as examples of intolerance, cruelty, and oppression. Voltaire, today recognized as a champion of Enlightenment philosophy, was then appreciated for his remarkable tragic output, and his investment in public debates about the nature of the tragic. His dramatic writings, theoretical engagements, and political quarrels attest to the sustained presence of religion and myth on the Enlightenment tragic stage.

Hailed as a new Racine, Voltaire left a lasting impression with his first tragedy, *Oedipe* (1718), an immediate success with a run of forty-five nights. *Oedipe* introduced the public to a rising playwright and announced eighteenth-century tragedy's critical engagement with religion. By the 1720s, the same tragedies that could be interpreted along confessional lines just decades earlier were instead imbued with overt critiques of Catholicism: its abuses of power, to be sure, but also major doctrines, such as *Oedipe*'s critique of predestination.[44] But, as among the first volley of shots in *philosophes*' assault on the Church, *Oedipe* can also be read as a wholesale attack on organized religion as politically abusive. By transforming Thebes into a city under the spell of a high priest who exploits popular belief to his own ends, Voltaire replaces the role of the seer Tiresias with that of the charlatan. As Jocasta bitterly notes, the priestly class derives its power from a benighted people: "Our priests are not what an empty people think; / Our naïveté is what makes all their knowledge." ("Nos prêtres ne sont pas ce qu'un vain peuple pense, Notre crédulité fait toute leur science.")[45]

Freedom not from religion but from fanaticism characterizes *Zaïre* (1732) and the controversial *Mahomet, ou le fanatisme* (1743). The eponymous Christian heroine of the first play has been raised Muslim. Zaïre convinces her captor that the world's three largest monotheistic religions are fundamentally the same and on this basis advocates a cessation of Christian–Muslim hostilities. Zaïre's death, due not to fanaticism but jealousy, allows Voltaire to fold a critique of religious fanaticism into a more general moral lesson about

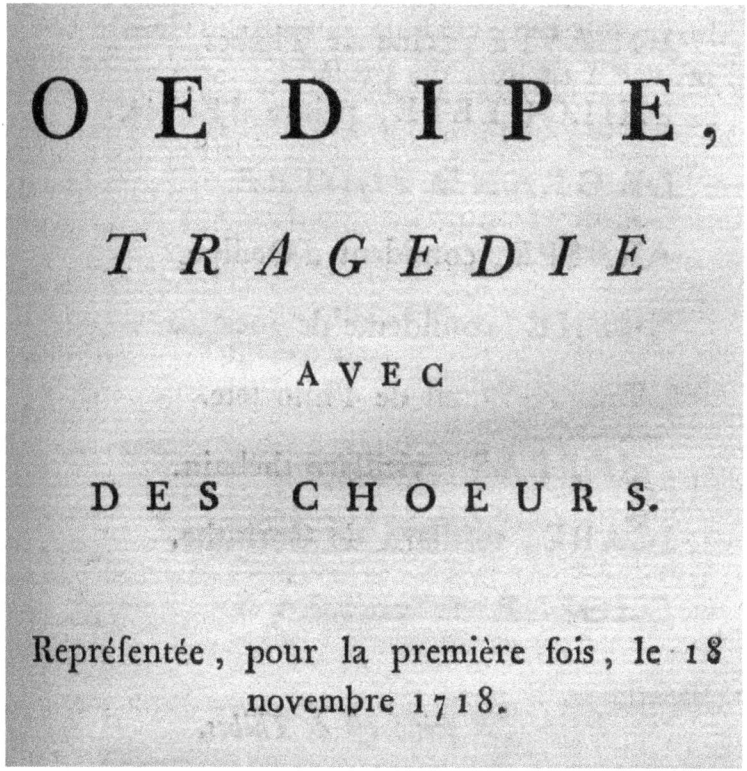

FIGURE 5.2: Title page of *Oedipe*, performed for the first time on November 18, 1718. From 1785 complete edition of works by L'Imprimerie de la Societe Litteraire-Typographique. Photo by Culture Club/Hulton Archive/Getty Images.

the dangers of rigid thinking.[46] If such an approach to religious intolerance was too subtle, *Mahomet* makes explicit the fatal consequences of fanaticism. In this tragedy, Muhammad appears as a cruel and scheming fanatic who has his critics killed, and Islam a religion that offers nothing more than "a new god to the blind universe," another false religion that serves to subjugate individual will and reason. It is likely that Voltaire was aiming more at Christianity than Islam; in 1742 the Parlement of Paris prohibited further performances, no doubt because the veil concealing the author's indictment of the contemporary church was all too thin. This did not stop antireligious theatrical production; Voltaire's only biblical tragedy, *Saül* (1762) displays the many crimes of Saul's divinely appointed successor David.

Voltaire's dramatic production thus seems to confirm the story of the gradual secularization of Enlightenment tragedy. His theoretical and critical engagements offer a more complex picture. Along with other critics, Voltaire railed against the sobriety and restraint of neoclassical theater. Repeatedly, he advocated for a new tragedy that would be visually and materially spectacular, and thus convey "great pathos."[47] Tragedy from the previous century could not do what tragedy was supposed to do, because of the material conditions of its performance. Even *Athalie*, which Voltaire considered one of the best tragedies for the quality of its verse, was not successful because of spectators seated onstage, the construction of the theater, and the poverty of the set design. Voltaire and his contemporaries saw the theater itself as a part of the experience, and increasingly advocated for a space designed for spectators in mind.[48]

Tragic conventions—its liturgy—evolved to support the new form of tragedy that will permeate civic discourse and practices, with new rituals and spaces. 1759 saw the elimination of onstage seating, which for many helped materialize the earliest form of the fourth wall, which Denis Diderot had told actors to imagine "a grand wall that separates you from the pit; play as though the curtain does not rise."[49] With the construction of the Comédie-Française's Odéon theater in 1782, the standing pit was made to sit: the *parterre* now had benches which compelled spectators to attend to the stage. Accompanied by the increasing pressure to enforce a "silent" audience, compelled to react at prescribed times, these audience-oriented reforms had the effect of creating a secular temple to public engagement.[50]

It should be no surprise, then, that this secular tragedy found its own deity-cum-high-priest in Voltaire, whose last tragedy *Irène* (1778) is remembered less for its action than for the conditions its performance created for the immortalization of its dramaturge. Voltaire returned from an unofficial exile in Ferney to attend a performance. Eighty-three years old, he was frail and well enough to attend only the sixth performance, where a crowd of two thousand waited to greet him. Seated in a front box and crowned with a laurel, he was applauded for twenty minutes, and again at nearly every line until the end of the play. In a display of something like Enlightenment idolatry, his bust was carried onto the stage to be crowned with flowers, and to which was recited an ode.[51] Voltaire was thus immortalized in his very own presence, a living icon to the sacred space of theater.

It is perhaps because of this very reconfiguration, indebted to the ritualistic and religious foundations of tragedy, that theater assumed the central role as locus for open political debate: its ability to make of contemporary, even living people, objects of veneration and sources of deep pathos.

## OTHER ENLIGHTENMENTS, OTHER SECULARITIES

These same issues, and even some of the same plays, could result in a very different set of debates with a shift in cultural and political landscape. Enlightenment philosophy in Germany was much less radical than in France; so too were the divisions theorists of tragedy created, especially as they intersected with matters of politics and religion. Gotthold Ephraim Lessing's ideas of tragedy also evolved away from both a mystified, religious tragedy and toward the "bürgerliches Trauerspiel" akin to the French bourgeois drama and exemplified by his *Miss Sara Simpson* (1755). In Lessing's theory of tragic pity, "emotion itself becomes an agent of Enlightenment": the continuous cultivation of pity throughout a tragedy reinforces the rational work of moral judgment.[52] As the position of French tragedy continued to exert influence across Europe, Lessing's theories evolved to stake claims against not only the classicism of Corneille and Racine, but also against his contemporary Voltaire.

Yet Lessing's own *Nathan der Weise* (Nathan The Wise, 1779) takes up some of the very same ideas as Voltaire's work on tolerance. Set in late twelfth-century Jerusalem, this "dramatic poem" stages through the interrelated travails and pasts of a Jew, a Muslim, and a Christian, an exploration of religious pluralism and relativism. Unlike *Mahomet*, however, *Nathan der Weise* undoes the basic tenets of the heroic tragedy by exposing the possibility not of divine mystery but of secular humanism as the source of both harmony among men, but also of religious wisdom. The Church prohibited performances of *Nathan der Weise* until after Lessing's death.

A year after the first public performance of *Nathan der Weise* at Berlin's Döbblinsches Theater, Friedrich Schiller opened a new chapter in German Enlightenment tragedy that in certain regards re-enchanted tragedy and the stage. In his public lecture *Theater Considered as a Moral Institution* (1784), Schiller reconnected religion, tragedy, and the state, while maintaining the language of sympathy that characterized eighteenth-century notions of spectator engagement:

> Whoever first observed that *religion* is the mightiest pillar of the state, and that laws themselves lose their power once religion is removed, has perhaps given us—without knowing or intending it—our best defense of the theater on behalf of its noblest side. . . . Consider now, how religion and law are strengthened as they enter into alliance with the theater, . . . where Providence solves its riddles, untangles its knows before his eyes; where the human heart confesses its subtlest stirrings while tortured on the rack of passion; where all masks fall away, the makeup is removed, and truth sits in judgment, incorruptible as Rhadamanthus.[53]

Schiller's argument that "[t]he jurisdiction of the stage begins where the domain of secular law leaves off" perhaps lays the ground for his student Friedrich Schelling's highly secular, individualistic analysis of tragedy in which free will predominates.[54] In his own works, however, Schiller himself advocated for almost a return to a mythical tragic form, using verse in his own tragedies (*Don Carlos*, 1787; *Mary Stuart*, 1803) and advocating for the renewed adoption of the chorus in his preface to *Die Braut von Messina* (1800).

The eighteenth-century Russian stage inherited the neoclassical tragedy of France, albeit demonstrating more flexibility with dramatic conventions. By and large, Russian tragedy was not explicitly religious, but rather nationalist in inspiration. Native myths and legends supplied Alexander Sumarokov (1717–77) with ready material to create a distinctly Russian expression of neoclassical tragedy. Notable exceptions include some of

Mikhail Kheraskov's plays, such as *Plamine* (1765), which recounts a young woman's conversion to Christianity and ultimate refuge in a convent, and *The Idolaters, or Gorislava* (1782).[55] Unlike the French context, in which Enlightenment tragedy contested monarchical, paternal, and ecclesiastical authority, Catherine's Russia favored a tragedy that sought instead a reconciliation between Enlightenment ideals and established authority.[56] Bolstering this reconciliation is the Eastern Orthodox doctrine of *theosis* (deification), according to which human beings can participate in divine nature. This in part explains the prominent place of Christ Pantocrator, rather than the Crucifixion, in Orthodox churches. It also explains how Russian playwrights could celebrate the full expression of an individual's agency and happiness while reaffirming a providential worldview in which all things are divinely ordained.

## TRAGIC POLEMICS—THEATER AND SOCIAL TRAGEDY, BELIEF AND TOLERANCE

In France, it is easy to read the fate of tragedy in the eighteenth century as entirely linked to the emergence of the secular society that the Revolution would confirm. In this way, the emergence of the bourgeois drama, as a new form of domestic and catastrophe-oriented theater, seemed to replace tragedy nearly entirely. Tragedy became a mode of political engagement with secular time, including history and the everyday. It did so as part of the response to the Affaire Calas (1761–2), a major cause for Voltaire, whose *Traité sur la tolerance* (1763) exposed the political machinations that prejudiciously condemned the Protestant Jean Calas to torture and execution for the murder of his son, rumored to have intended conversion to Catholicism. Multiple theatrical versions explored the controversy's martyr-like elements. The preface to Fenouillet de Falbaire's *Honnête Criminel* opposes religious fanaticism, "the shadows of barbarism," to Enlightenment. In distinction to plays featuring non-Christian religions, the stand-in for barbarism here is French. Printed in 1767, *L'Honnête Criminel* was not played publicly until 1790. The same year, Jean-Louis Laya took up the same subject in *Jean Calas* as did Auguste-Jacques Lemierre d'Argy in his *Calas, ou, Le fanatisme*. A year later, Chénier's *Jean Calas, ou l'école des juges* appeared. Billed as tragedy or drama, such dramatized causes célèbres staged Calas as the new Hippolytus, Oedipus, or Iphigenia. Unlike these mainstays of tragedy, however, Calas was portrayed as an innocent victim: heir to martyrs and not the sons of great houses.

On the eve of the Revolution, tragedy was a site of political engagement and protest. Censors blocked Marie-Joseph Chénier's *Charles IX*, which dramatized the St. Bartholomew's Day Massacre of 1572, for nearly two years because of its politically and religiously sensitive subject. Subtitled *l'Ecole des rois*, and written likely in the mid-1780s, its monarch is weak, susceptible to the corrupting influence of his mother Catherine de' Medici and the Cardinal of Guise. Like Molière's mordant comedy *Tartuffe* over a century before it, *Charles IX* aroused the ire of the clergy (who allegedly worked to have it suppressed) for one specific reason: its representation of a man of the cloth onstage. This exhibit of ecclesiastical vestment as theatrical costume also incriminated the Cardinal—not as a political actor, but as a religious one, thereby clearly signaling the church's role in Charles IX's oppressive treatment of the Huguenots.[57]

The debates between the play's supporters and its detractors sustained the public's interest, and the events of 1789 gave Chénier's notion of tragedy a role itself in the national drama. Finally performed on November 4, 1789, *Charles IX* was an immediate and controversial success. Rebaptized a *tragédie patriotique* by the author, *Charles IX* championed what Chénier would later call "the only universal religion"—*la patrie*. With equality its creed and magistrates its priests, this universal religion, Chénier optimistically imagined, would unite human beings in a common brotherhood, transcending sectarian division born of dogmatism and superstition.

## CONCLUSION: SACRED HEROES FOR A SECULAR REVOLUTION

The Revolution's tragedy, then, needed no Aristotelian "great families," only corrupt authorities and a renewed set of civic values. Accordingly, as clergy lost their hold on political decision-makers in the Revolutionary period, they appeared more frequently onstage in so-called anticlerical "convent dramas." Chénier's *Fénelon, ou les religieuses de Cambrai* (1793) adapts the conventions of convent drama to the tragic stage, while creating an unlikely hero for the Revolution. Astonishingly, Chénier mines France's recent history to see in François de Salignac de la Mothe-Fénelon, seventeenth-century archbishop and tutor to Louis XIV's grandchildren, a champion of tolerance and universal harmony. Fénelon rescues a girl forced to take vows, reuniting her with her father and wrongfully imprisoned mother. While some of its first spectators considered the play a *drame*, the author insisted that its sad and majestic tone, its characters' dignity, and, above all, its ability to make the audience cry, made it a *tragédie*.[58]

In line with other eighteenth-century receptions of Fénelon's work, Chénier's reinterpretation largely forgets Fénelon's aristocratic origins and his Christianity in order to transform him into "model of spotless virtue," a precursor to the Enlightenment.[59] This explains both the apparent incongruity of a late seventeenth-century archbishop appearing on the planks of the anticlerical Théâtre de la République and how, in 1791, Fénelon almost made it into the Panthéon alongside Rousseau and Voltaire.

Chénier's *Fénelon* constructs an alternative national mythology, recasting an *ancien régime* prelate as the harbinger of a new "universal religion" that would find its dramatic expression in the patriotic tragedies of the Revolution. Tragedy, as a public yet elevated dramatic form, provided a stage for the presentation of these myths to a wide audience. It furthermore guaranteed their literary fortune at home and abroad: *Fénelon* was soon translated into English, Dutch, and Italian, seeming to confirm Chénier's intuition that theater was the organ of a new "religion" that ideally transcended old sectarian divisions as well as new national ones. Thus, even as the Revolution proposed to form new citizens, freed from the shackles of superstition and religious obscurantism, tragedy retained something of its sacred origins, finding new tragic heroes in the vestments of the past.

# CHAPTER SIX

# Politics of City and Nation

*A Short History of Scaffold Tragedy c. 1650–1800: How a Classic Trope Salvaged the Spectacle of Punishment in the Age of Sympathy*

JULIE STONE PETERS

In his celebratory account of the 1736 *auto-de-fé* held in the "Theatre" built for it in Lima's Plaza Grande, the Peruvian Inquisition official Pedro José Bermúdez de la Torre y Solier describes the *auto* as a scene performed "with tragic figures."[1] After a "solemn" procession through the streets of Lima, the twenty-seven prisoners (wearing cone-shaped caps of shame and penitential garments) made their way toward the stage. Among them was a woman, the courtesan Ana de Castro, condemned "judaizer," whom "death ministers" led forth on a donkey while a priest explained: the scene was an allegory of *desengaño*, the revelation of worldly illusion and its vanity.[2] For here was a woman who had once had "rich gentlemen" at her command, now wearing the *coroza* and *sanbenito*, being led to the flames, where all would see her burning in a likeness of hellfire. Bermúdez rejoices that so many pious citizens—more than ten thousand—were able to witness this tragic scene which, portraying the terrors of hell, also served to manifest the work of the "demonstrative Actor of true representations"[3] (i.e., God). For (as a gloss on an earlier *auto-de-fé* in Lima explained), *autos* represent God's punishment of "the apostasy of Adam and Eve in the theatre of Paradise," but they also represent that later tragedy, the Passion, in which His sacrifice offered redemption to the penitent.[4]

## INTRODUCTION

This essay looks at the meaning of the word "tragedy" in judicial executions c. 1650–1800, in an attempt to illuminate both the history of punishment and the history of tragedy. My focus here is not theatrical performances or literary texts but the use of the term "tragedy" to characterize contemporary events. People used the word during this period to describe a variety of real-world happenings (as we do): wars, political upheaval, natural catastrophes, deadly epidemics, and more. But outside of theater, the word appears most frequently—across Europe, and in a variety of languages—in descriptions of crimes and punishments.

Scholars have long noted the early modern commonplace that cast public executions as "tragedies" staged in "theatres" (arising in conjunction with the proliferation of dedicated theaters across Europe). Crime-and-punishment narratives with titles identifying them as "tragic" such as François de Rosset's immensely popular *Tragic Histories of Our Time* (1614–1721) secured the identification of execution spectacles with tragedies, whether in the guise of learned legal treatises, romanticized tales, news reports, or cheap ballads.[5] The trope—in its most paradigmatic form—evoked tragedy's central generic features: both tragic plays and executions were serious and had unhappy endings, usually the premature death of the protagonist. But it also evoked shared performance conditions: executions and stage tragedies (unlike political tragedies or natural disasters) were intentional, concretely realized, localized practices, with clearly marked beginnings and ends, performed for large groups of spectators in the space of a few hours. Crime-and-execution narratives cast as "tragic" thus often specifically referenced theater as an institution: the *Great Theatre of Tragic Blood and Murder Histories* (1670), for instance (Simon de Vries' Dutch edition of Rosset), shows an architecturally framed stage with perspective scenery.[6] As the 1736 Lima *auto* suggests, "tragedy" was not just a legal *concept* during the period, but a legal *practice*: a way of staging events that realized tragedy.

The essential character of the tragic scaffold paradigm—the trope and its associations—remained remarkably consistent across the early modern period (indeed, well into the nineteenth century). The period *c.* 1650–1800 is bookended by the revolutionary trials and executions of Charles I in 1649 and of Louis XVI and Marie Antoinette in 1793. Royalists routinely cast Charles' trial and execution as a "horrid Tragedy," a "Bloody Tragedy of all Tragedies," and Charles as the "*Royal Actor*," "adorn[ing]" "[t]he *Tragick Scaffold*."[7] Almost 150 years later, people spoke of Louis and Marie Antoinette in nearly the same terms: Louis was "the hero of this bloody tragedy," Marie Antoinette a "heroine" whose "sufferings" were greater than any invented by "tragic poet[s]."[8] Popular engravings titled "tragic end of Louis XVI," "tragic end of the Queen," circulated.[9] But, while retaining its basic features, the paradigm grew more volatile in the eighteenth century, registering uncertainties about the meaning and purpose of punishment. Perhaps the most significant change was the virtual disappearance, by the end of the eighteenth century, of the trope's evocation of God's just vengeance against "Barbarous and Execrable" sinners whose crimes had brought them to the "bloody" scaffold.[10] By the end of the century, the word "tragic" had lost its power to damn, and become dedicated solely to expressing pity for suffering without blame (as references to real-world "tragedies" still do today).

Changes in the tragic paradigm accompanied radical transformations in attitudes toward and practices of punishment during the period: the growth of a genteel view that one ought not to take satisfaction in watching the violent punishment of malefactors (a view dominant by mid-century); the virtual disappearance, by the end of the eighteenth century, of such spectacularly brutal public punishments as live breaking at the wheel, drawing and quartering, and burning at the stake; and the multiplication of "non-sanguinary," non-capital sentences (primarily imprisonment, transportation, and hard labor).[11]

In the conventional historiography (which has persisted under the long shadow of Foucault), these changes signaled the disappearance of the early modern regime of theatrical public punishment and the appearance, in its place, of a modern regime of largely invisible, insidious discipline carried out not in public but behind prison walls—the regime that is still with us today. As I attempt to demonstrate (here and elsewhere), this still-influential historiography does not merely mischaracterize the cause of these changes, or offer an overly sanitized rendering of the nineteenth-century prison (as many scholars have argued). Its central claim—that in the eighteenth century, support for spectacular public punishment foundered and, by century's end, the early modern regime of theatrical public punishment had virtually come to an end—is mistaken.

First, throughout the eighteenth century, most people (even the most forward-thinking) continued to believe that dramatic public punishments were necessary to deterrence. Second, while critiques of penal spectacle emerged during this period, so did the first extended defenses and the richest body of thought on the necessity, utility, and effects of penal spectacle. Third, far from shedding its theatricality in the eighteenth century, punishment became in some ways more theatrical than ever, partly in an attempt to replace real pain with a spectacle of simulated pain. Fourth (as others have pointed out), far from disappearing, the routine administration of violent public punishment went marching on in Europe and its colonies, with an astonishing ability to survive humanitarian critique until well into the twentieth century (if not longer). While I do not elaborate on all of these claims here, they are the foundation for my central arguments in this essay: first, that the tragic scaffold trope became key to the debates about spectacle that were at the heart of both penal theory and practice during the period; second, that philosophical explorations of why we enjoy watching the suffering of others (in both tragedies and punishments) reshaped the trope's figural significance; and, third, that it was the concept of tragedy that helped salvage the spectacle of punishment in the age of sympathy.

## 1. THE CLASSIC TRAGIC SCAFFOLD PARADIGM

The 1657 frontispiece to John Reynolds' *The Triumphs of Gods Revenge Against the Crying and Execrable Sinne of . . . Murther: With His . . . Severe Punishment Thereof, in Thirty Several Tragical Histories* (Figure 6.1) shows God taking his revenge by hanging malefactors, breaking them at the wheel, beheading them, and burning them at the stake.[12] The figure of Justice presides over the scene, flanked by avenging angels with swords and shields, while God commands, "*Fiat Iustitia*" ("let justice be done"). The judicial drama is a revenge play: executions are a form of worldly vengeance that represent the "Triumphs of Gods Revenge." The title of a 1661 update, *Blood for Blood or Murthers Revenged, in Thirty Tragical Histories*, invokes the biblical basis for the tragic penal theory it represents, Genesis 9:6: "Who so sheddeth mans blood, by man shall his blood be shed: for in the image of God made he man."[13] Execution is God's revenge in part because murder is a crime against God. As the apprentice Nathaniel Butler (who had murdered a fellow apprentice) declared from the scaffold in 1657, "I have destroyed the Image of God in *John Knight*."[14] What makes these histories "Tragical" is not the tragic fate of the murder victims: the frontispiece shows six murderers but only one victim (and that one only by way of representing murderers in the act). Nor is it the nobility of their protagonists: among the murderers are servants, apothecaries, a miller, a chambermaid, an "Italian mountebank."[15] (Ignoring the mandates of tragic theory, crime-and-execution literature commonly identified stories of the low-born as "tragedies.") What makes them "Tragical" is the fact that they feature "Crying and Execrable" sinners who engage in bloody and cruel deeds "Willfull[y]" and with "Premeditat[ion]," and ultimately come to a violent end.[16]

The central function of the word "tragedy" in such accounts is the expression of collective condemnation, as their titles suggest, for instance Reynolds', or the German *Tragic or Sorrowful Histories of Criminal Penalties and Horrible Deaths of Sinners [Who] Deny God, Blaspheme, Practice Magic, Curse* (and so on) (1598), or Rosset's *Tragic Histories of . . . the Gruesome and Lamentable Deaths of Various Persons [Executed]*

FIGURE 6.1: John Reynolds' *The Triumphs of Gods Revenge Against the Crying and Execrable Sinne of (Wilful and Premeditated) Murther* (London, 1657). RB 138039, The Huntington Library, San Marino, California.

*Because of Their Ambitions, Dissolute Love Affairs, Thefts, Rapine* (etc.).[17] The "tragedy" lies not in the fate of the victims (indeed, sometimes the only victim is God), but in the criminal's deeds and "Horrible" end on the scaffold. While "lamentable," the malefactor's demise is also deeply satisfying, for it represents the victory not only of the state over the criminal but of God over the devil. Such tragedies may be "mournfull," "wofull," and "pitiful," but mourning, woe, and even pity are less subjective emotional terms than objective ethical terms, designating the appropriate attitude of (collective) moral condemnation.[18]

The damned were not, of course, the only kind of early modern scaffold protagonist. One might (somewhat reductively) identify two other types: the innocent and the redeemed. Scaffold performance was a key factor in determining which of these the spectators saw. The condemned were clearly aware of how much such performances shaped the public view of their fate (and perhaps that fate itself). In his highly metatheatrical scaffold speech, John Gerard—an ensign brought to London's Tower Hill in 1654 for conspiring to overthrow Cromwell—reveals his understanding of the significance of this final performance:

> As this kind of spectacle is no new entertainment to your eyes, . . . [s]o is it no strange thing to me to be made such a spectacle; for I have been bred upon the Theater of death, and have learned that part so well, . . . as to perform it pretty handsomly, both as becomes a Gentleman and a Christian.[19]

Upon arriving at the scaffold, he had demonstrated the courage that "becomes a Gentleman" (somewhat hyperbolically), "leap[ing] upon . . . that Tragical Stage, . . . skip[ping] up the steps to it," and, with a "cheerful smile," addressing the executioner, "*Welcome honest friend*," "desiring to see his Ax," kissing it with the declaration "*This will doe the Deed I warrant it*," calling for the block, "viewing it (as with delight)," laying himself on it and "almost play[ing] with it."[20]

Gerard followed this demonstration of fearlessness-writ-large with a display of piety befitting a "Christian." While innocent of the charges, he said, he was nevertheless "a miserable sinner," but "confident by the merits of Christ Jesus, that my sins are pardoned, and my salvation is at hand," he "heartily forgave" his accusers and the executioner and commended his soul to Jesus: "O Lamb of God that takes away the sins of the world, . . . Lord Jesus receive my soul."[21] He then

> bow'd himself to the stroak of death, with as much Christian meeknes and noble courage mix'd together, as I believe was ever seen in any that had bled upon that Altar. And [the] Spectators, did seem to understand and acknowledge [this]: beholding his fatal blow with an universal sadness and silence.[22]

Spectators may have experienced Gerard's scaffold performance as especially exemplary because of its contrast with another execution on Tower Hill that day: that of the Portuguese ambassador's brother, Don Pantaleon de Sá, who, visiting London, had ended up in a drunken brawl and had the misfortune to murder an Englishman. Accompanied by his confessor (as a witness reported),

> the Portugal Ambassadors brother was guarded up to the Scaffold, being extreamly dejected in spirit, and in a mourning Gown, where he endeavoured (by way of speech) to plead innocency; and then by his Interpreter to impute the chief Cause of the Riot and Murder to the English, . . . by the way of excuse.[23]

When Pantaleon's "head was severed from his shoulders," the spectators

> gave a great and generall shout, as applauding the Justice of the *Portugals* death; but pittying and bewailing the untimely fall of [Gerard], so brave and magnanimous a spirit, as did (through all the clouds of death) shine gloriously in this unfortunate Gentleman.[24]

For spectators, Pantaleon's shameful performance (fearful and "extreamly dejected," requiring guards to keep him from struggling, blame-shifting rather than confessing and forgiving, accompanied by a *Catholic priest*) confirmed not only his impiety and want of nobility but also his guilt and certain damnation, and thus warranted applause at "the Justice of [his] death." Gerard's performance of "Christian meekness and noble courage mix'd together" demonstrated his certain salvation, and thus warranted reverent silence and "universal sadness."[25] Indeed, viewing the "comely posture of [Gerard's] passion" (the author moralizes) may "dry up a friendly tear, . . . and still a murmuring groan."[26] For "[w]hy should I grieve that death, [or] dishonour that bloud with feeble tears, which was shed so like the holy Martyrs?"[27] Like those first tragedies (the Fall and the Passion), the execution of the innocent is merely part of God's providential plan, announcing salvation in the world to come. As if confirming Gerard's salvation, spectators later saw a miracle: for "Mr. Gerards hands when he was in the Coffin, were seen to move, and lift up the Lid thereof," in preparation for his resurrection.[28]

The execution of the damned displayed the righteous punishment of evildoers. The execution of those who turned out to be innocent could still produce deterrent fear while displaying pious resignation to God's will and the promise of salvation. But, because God loved a repentant sinner more than one who had never sinned, the execution of the redeemed was best of all, demonstrating the wages of crime while modeling pious repentance. The execution of Angelique Carlier Tiquet—condemned in 1699 for the attempted murder of her husband (in part so she could be with her lover)—offers a classic example. "Everyone knows that she tried to murder her husband," wrote Joseph Sevin, Comte de Quincy.[29] Tiquet's actions were "very criminal and very detestable," he explains. Her execution served as an "example" of where "young people's violent passions" lead.[30] (Without such "scene[s]," comments Nicolas Gueudeville dryly, spouses "would often have their throats cut in the name of Venus."[31])

However, her beauty and a brilliant scaffold performance of repentance, followed by a "tragic death,"[32] redeemed her in the eyes of the public. "I was in one of the Windows," wrote the journalist Anne-Marguerite Du Noyer, "and saw poor Madam *Tiquet* arrive at the Place, . . . all in white."[33] Because of the torrential rain, she had to remain in the cart,

> having the Materials of her Death before her Eyes. [W]hen she ascended the Scaffold, she reach'd out her Hand to the Executioner to help her, and giving it to him, carry'd it to her Mouth, that she might not seem to want civility. [N]ever was more Firmness and Constancy seen.[34]

This tragic performance was transparent—she performed as if in "a famous theatre" observed Gueudeville—but all the more successful for its transparency.[35] "When she was upon the Scaffold," writes Du Noyer, "one would have thought she had studied her Part, she kissing the Block, and observing all the Ceremony, as if she had only been going to act a Play."[36] Performing "as if [in] a Play" demonstrated not dissimulation but fearlessness and piety: an ability to treat the worldly event as unreal because she had already given herself to Christ.

If "it was her Destiny that she should be an Example," as Du Noyer writes, that destiny was simultaneously tragic and heroic for (writes Du Noyer, quoting the Curé of Saint Sulpice) she died "like a Christian heroine."[37] For the Abbé François Gastaud (who published an *Oraison funèbre* for Tiquet just after her death), her execution offered a theatrical lesson that was at once Christian, penal, and tragic. "Come, Ministers of the Lord," he intones, "come see a spectacle that will appear to you altogether new, and see it in all its brilliance": conversion, as Saint Augustine described it, performed before the "whole world, gathered to be witness to her sad Catastrophe."[38] "[S]ee with what air of Religion she lifts her veil, and drinks deeply the shame and ignominy from the most humiliating of all chalices."[39] See her freed from worldly illusions (*détrompée*), rising to "heroic fortitude" and "greatness of soul."[40] Her heroic death transforms the scaffold: a "theatre of shame for all the others," it has become a theater "of glory for her."[41] That "a life so little worthy of praise" ended "in a death so heroic" is a sign of "admirable providence."[42] "Immortal Judge," Gastaud prays "turn your eyes away from her criminal blood, turn them only on the blood of Jesus Christ, with which [hers] is mixed."[43] "[Y]ou oh my God," he cries "will you not receive with an odor of sweetness the sacrifice that she makes you of her life [?]"[44]

## 2. CHALLENGING THE CLASSIC TRAGIC SCAFFOLD PARADIGM

One could find this tragic scaffold paradigm relatively unchanged in some execution accounts in the second half of the eighteenth century. In the diary he kept between 1738 and 1780, Pierre Barthès, a Latin tutor in Toulouse and torture-and-execution fan, regularly uses the word "tragedy" to describe—without sympathy (indeed, with chilling sangfroid)—the execution of justly punished malefactors. 1763: "ordinary scene of military tragedies, two young male deserters, were condemned to have their heads broken" (a death sentence Barthès appears to approve).[45] 1762: "Three gentlemen, brothers, decapitated":

> Before beginning this tragic scene, the brothers asked forgiveness of each other; ... [T]he older was the first decapitated, [his head] was removed with one blow [except for] the skin at his throat which the executioner sawed, and [his head was] thrown on the ground.

Barthès' conclusion: "the executioner trained with new knives [so] it went well."[46] 1754: an "attractive" girl hanged for murder and theft. A tragic "heroine of our day" because she had served as a soldier. But she

> crowned so much glory with a shameful end, which proves that divine justice loses none of her rights, as Phaedrus says in his fables. ... Sooner or later, the guilty party is punished for his crime.[47]

However, while people like Barthès continued to use the trope in traditional ways, others had begun to question its meaning and implications. In his 1733 dramatization of the second part of *Don Quixote*, António José da Silva, a Portuguese playwright whom the Inquisition later executed for "judaizing," offers a savage critique of the comparison of so-called "justice" with tragedy. A bailiff asks Sancho Panza: "why did they make Justice out to have covered eyes, a sword in one hand and a scale in the other[?]" Sancho explains:

Know first, that this thing of Justice is merely a painted thing and that such a woman does not exist. [But] it was necessary to have this figure in the World to frighten people, like the boogeyman for children, [so] they painted up a woman and dressed her for tragedy, because all justice ends in tragedy.[48]

Painted and dressed up as the figure of Tragedy, sword raised (as in the frontispiece for Reynolds' *Triumphs*), Justice-as-Tragedy appears as a goddess: terrifying but magnificent. But she is a theatrical fraud, her glamor serving as a cover for the atrocities that the Justice system perpetrates. Underneath her gorgeous drapery and the blindfold representing impartiality is something quite different:

> They blindfolded her because they say she was cross-eyed and that she traded one eye for the other. And since Justice is supposed to be straight, they quickly covered her eyes to prevent people from seeing this defect.[49]

If we were to see Justice for what she is—not painted up and dressed as Tragedy but as a cross-eyed, crooked bogeyman—instead of being cowed into submission, we might resist her dominion.

In his *Enquiry into the Causes of the Frequent Executions at Tyburn* (1725), Bernard Mandeville offers a different though equally satiric portrait of judicial "tragedy."[50] For Mandeville, the problem is not (as for Silva) that Tragic Justice is a fraud, but that she was once glorious but has now tragically fallen on hard times. In a scene that anticipates William Hogarth's representation of the boorish crowd in "The Idle 'Prentice Executed at Tyburn" (1747) (Figure 6.2), Mandeville describes execution day, which begins with "howling in one Place, scolding and quarrelling in another, ... loud Laughter in a third, ... Seas of Beer ... swill'd, [with] never-ceasing Outcries for more, [the condemned] drinking madly, or uttering the vilest Ribaldry."[51] As the procession makes its way from Newgate to Tyburn, it is

> one continued Fair, for Whores and Rogues of the meaner Sort, ... Trollops, all in Rags, ... drink[ing] as they go; ... the Cart stop[ping] for that Purpose three or four, and sometimes half a dozen Times, ... always encreas[ing] the Numbers about the Criminals.[52]

As the condemned, surrounded by this swelling crowd, nears the gallows, the "Scene of Confusion" grows worse:

> terrible Blows ... are struck, [Heads] are broke, ... Pieces of swingeing Sticks, and Blood ... fly about, [Men] are knock'd down and trampled upon, ... whilst the Dissonance of Voices, and the Variety of Outcries ... make such a Discord not to be parallel'd.[53]

At last, "[t]he Ordinary and Executioner, having performed their different Duties, with small Ceremony," mercifully, "[t]he Tragedy [is] ended."[54]

In Mandeville's mock-heroic portrait of execution "Tragedy," the old "really tragical" ritual of repentance, fortitude before death, and reconciliation to divine will before a crowd of awed spectators has degenerated into a "Scene of Confusion."[55] All that remains of this ritual is the performance of specious courage—specious because the condemned is in fact blind drunk. Drunkenness gives him (male in Mandeville's account) the courage to "bi[d] Defiance to Heaven," and the crowd goes wild, cheering him as one who "dies like a Man" when "in reality" (writes Mandeville), he "goes off most like a Brute."[56] Even "the

FIGURE 6.2: William Hogarth, *The Idle 'Prentice Executed at Tyburn* (1747). Graphic Arts Collection, Department of Rare Books and Special Collections, Princeton University Library.

best dispos'd Spectator" seldom can pick out anything that is edifying or moving.[57] In fact, executions "are examplary [sic] the wrong Way, and encourage where they should deter."[58]

> [They] harden the Profligates that behold them, and confirm to them, by ocular Demonstration, what they [say] in viler Language, (low, as it is, permit me to mention it,) *That there is nothing in being hang'd, but awry Neck, and a wet pair of Breeches.*[59]

True Tragic Justice would present an altogether different scene. There, "either Silence, or a sober Sadness, [w]ould prevail, ... grave and serious."[60] Everyone would be singing psalms.[61] Such "decent Solemnity" would make penal tragedy properly "awful."[62] It would strike "Terror" into the beholders,[63] and impress its seriousness upon all concerned: "the condemn'd themselves" ("whose grand Affair it is to prepare themselves for another World"); "their Companions" ("who should be deterred"); and "the rest of the Spectators" ("who should be struck with the Awfulness of the Solemnity").[64] To "render these Tragedies more solemn," Mandeville proposes a simple change: keep the condemned in solitary confinement and on a bread-and-water diet until execution day.[65] When the day comes, "[he] should be drawn forth from his dark and solitary Dungeon" and placed in the "ignominious Cart."[66] "[H]is Spirits [no longer] buoy'd up by inebriating Liquors," he would feel all the terror of the moment.[67] His "restless Posture, the Distortion of his Features, and the continual wringing of his Hands" would "disclose his Woe within, and the utmost depth of Sorrow."[68]

> When we should hear his shrill Cries and sad Complaints interrupted with bitter Sobs and anxious Groans, and now and then, at sudden Starts, see Floods of Tears gushing from his distracted Eyes, how thoroughly would [this] Evidenc[e] convince us of the Pangs, the amazing Horror, and unspeakable Agonies of his excruciated Soul![69]

The "Spectacle would be awful": "[f]ew Profligates would be able to stand the Shock of Sounds and Actions so really tragical." And so, wending their way toward Tyburn, the "Licentious Rabble of both Sexes," would "drop off, and dwindle away by Degrees."[70]

We might view Mandeville's proposal for an execution ritual performed with a new sobriety and "decent Solemnity" as a manifestation of the bourgeois "civilizing process" that (some argue) led eventually to the "repression" of public executions.[71] His proposal certainly envisions a gentrification of the ritual ("Spectators of a better Sort"[72] are to replace "Whores and Rogues"[73]). Except that what he envisions is hardly the polite propriety of bourgeois civility. In Mandeville's ideal execution scene, the "Features" of the condemned are "Distort[ed]," their limbs shake, they wring their hands and utter "shrill Cries and sad Complaints," "bitter Sobs and anxious Groans," and "Floods of Tears gus[h] from [their] distracted Eyes." This "awful" "Spectacle" "strike[s] the Hearts of the Beholders," who are hardly better off than the condemned: they "sicken at such a Sight," they can barely "stand the Shock of Sounds and Actions so really tragical."[74]

Far from condemning penal spectacle in itself, Mandeville advocates the amplification of penal spectacle: he wants dramatically *bigger*, more *extreme* embodied emotion (gushing eyes, shaking limbs, shrill cries). Indeed, he scorns the idea that criminals might be executed in private, treating it as a kind of Swiftian "Modest Proposal"—"If no Remedy can be found for these Evils, it would be better that Malefactors should be put to Death in private"—an obviously ludicrous idea, a satiric rendering merely meant to highlight the desperate need for a new and improved execution spectacle.[75] Like most of his contemporaries, Mandeville views spectacle as in fact essential to fulfilling the principal function of executions: "For it is not the Death of those poor Souls that is chiefly aim'd at in Executions, but the Terror we would have it strike in others of the same loose Principles."[76] Without the spectacle of terror, executions would merely entail "sporting away the Lives of the indigent Vulgar."[77] Their public deaths—which prevent others from committing crimes—are unfortunate but necessary "Sacrifices" in the name of "publick Safety."[78] If only the authorities would put his reforms into effect, he writes "[i]t is not to be express'd, what lasting and useful Impressions such Shews would make."[79]

The extreme performance of suffering in Mandeville's "really tragical" execution ritual might appear to demand pity for the suffering condemned. But he wants the spectators to feel not pity but terror: the "Spectacle [must] be awful" enough to "strike the Hearts of the Beholders" with fear and trembling, not tenderness.[80] In fact, far from reducing the shame or suffering of the condemned, Mandeville seeks to increase it in order to intensify its emotional impact on the spectators (another unfortunate but necessary "Sacrific[e]" in the name of "publick Safety"). Watching "the Pangs, the amazing Horror, and unspeakable Agonies of [the criminal's] excruciated Soul," the spectators are to feel "the Horrors" of their own "accusing Conscience, and the Abyss of Misery" into which they may be plunged by "eternal Vengeance."[81] As in the *Triumphs* frontispiece, scaffold "Tragedy" (as it should be) entails not sympathy for victims or the condemned, but a vision of God's vengeance.

Bermúdez, apologist for the Lima *auto-de-fé* with which I began, might appear to inhabit an ideological and juridical universe altogether different from Mandeville's. But Bermúdez and Mandeville share many assumptions: for both, for instance, the execution "tragedy" must produce terror in the spectators, at once furthering "publick Safety" and displaying it. The "spectacle of the punishment frighten[s]" the spectators, writes Bermúdez, but it at the same time represents their protection from fatal heresy.[82]

In fact, Bermúdez—in the far reaches of the Counter Reformation Iberian empire—seems more aware of the nascent Enlightenment critique of public executions than the ostensibly enlightened Mandeville. Mandeville feels it unnecessary to defend scaffold spectacle (he merely seeks to reform it). And nowhere does he express discomfort with the spectators' enjoyment of a good execution (however foul he may find the drunken crowd). Bermúdez, on the other hand, seems to feel that his *auto* is in need of defense: from critics, for instance, who might view spectators as callous entertainment-seekers or sadists *avant-la-lettre*. The "universal anticipation" that news of the *auto* aroused, he writes,

> was not the result of common curiosity (natural and proper as that might be), but in fact an active inclination, [an expression] of the unwavering faith of this city, which fervently longs to see errors opposed to the Christian religion corrected.

True, citizens from far and wide could not wait for the day to come, fought for the best viewing places, and rejoiced when the executioner threw Castro onto the pyre. But they did not attend out of a mere desire for entertainment, and they were certainly not "guilty of enjoying another's pain": in fact, "the sight of the . . . chastisement distressed them." But they longed to participate in this collective act of faith. And they felt joy because they experienced in the *auto* their "blessed liberation from danger."

In a further attempt to justify the spectators' enthusiasm for the spectacle, Bermúdez offers an extended analogy: the spectator was, he writes, like a person "who spies, in the stillness of the port, the lopped off masts that are the ill-fated wreckage of the next shipwreck in the raging sea," and "quietly envision[s]" the "horror of the gulf's wrath." It is in the course of this analogy that he addresses the problem of pity. Not only do the *auto*'s spectators not "enjo[y] another's pain": in fact, gazing into the "horror of the gulf's wrath," they feel "pity for the carnage." But, while pity may be admirable, it does not "sto[p] the blood from flowing," nor should it. (Here he abandons the shipwreck metaphor.) This is because blood is in fact necessary to state security. The spectators know this. And so their "most tender sigh of compassion" does not turn into protest, but instead "diffuses itself as a breath of security." The individual sigh of pity becomes a collective sigh of relief: I feel for her, but thank God we are safe from her (and, implicitly: better her than me).

We might read this insistence on pity but simultaneous resistance to its potentially transformative consequences as a battle between Enlightenment feelings and counter-Enlightenment ideology. Bermúdez wants his spectators to offer "joyous praise and grateful ovations" for the destruction of heretics, but he also wants them to be compassionate. He wants them to experience the *auto* with joy, but he worries about the seemliness of spectator pleasure. This worry about seemliness appears in the passage that follows, in which he explains that his written account may be "full of shadows," a mere "reflection" of the *auto*, but reading it might be better than attending an *auto*. For the text "clothe[s] the Theatrical Representation with greater propriety." If the text "clothe[s]" the event "with greater propriety," there must be some impropriety in attending the *auto* itself. But in what does the impropriety lie? Clearly partly in the fact that, "[w]hen the fire first blew off [the beautiful judaizer's] clothes, her white body was seen."[83] But perhaps also partly in the now shameful indecency of "common curiosity" and spectatorial bloodlust, all too visible in the cheering crowd. That is, perhaps it lies in exposing the sadistic underside of the pleasure of tragedy.

## 3. SALVAGING THE SPECTACLE OF PUNISHMENT IN THE AGE OF SYMPATHY

Bermúdez' defensiveness raises two of the oldest questions in tragic theory: why do people enjoy watching the suffering of others; and should they? Those questions received renewed attention in late seventeenth- and eighteenth-century aesthetic and moral theory. There, scaffold spectatorship and stage tragedy—often examined in conjunction—served as touchstones for understanding why people take pleasure in watching the pain of others. Where the tragic scaffold trope drew on an implicit relationship between executions and tragedy, tragic and moral theory explored that relationship explicitly, most commonly drawing a parallel between the two and trying to understand their shared psychology.

In his influential *Passions of the Soul* (1649), Descartes had argued that the passions arose from agitation of the animal spirits. This argument (supplemented by Hobbes' insistence on the importance of motion and desire) provided the basis for a revolutionary theory of tragic pleasure that was to dominate tragic theory in the century to come. However, later seventeenth-century theorists effectively reversed Descartes' neo-stoic values. Descartes viewed most passions as dangerous and in need of mastery. As he wrote in a letter to Princess Elisabeth of Bohemia in 1645, it was true that, when the greatest of souls exposed themselves to tragedy, "this making trial of their strength [was] pleasant to them."[84] However, "constantly watching performances of tragedies, with death in every act, and dwelling all the time on stories of sadness and pity," excites the imagination of the weak and endangers the health.[85] Descartes' disciples, on the other hand, recommended *reveling* in the agitation of the passions, attending tragedies (for instance) for the exquisite pleasure of shaking up one's animal spirits. In tragedy, writes René Rapin in his *Reflections on Aristotle's Treatise of Poesie* (1674), "nothing ought to be idle, but all in agitation. [A]ll ought to be in trouble, and no calm to appear, till the *action* be ended by the *Catastrophe*."[86]

If, for Descartes, testing one's resistance to dangerous passions by exposing oneself to tragedy could be pleasurable, eighteenth-century theorists had a different explanation of why we take pleasure in viewing tragedy. The "agitation, in which our passions keep us," explained the Abbé Jean-Baptiste Du Bos in his influential *Critical Reflections on Poetry, Painting, and Music* (1719),

> is of so brisk a nature, that any other situation is languid and heavy, when compared to this motion. Thus we are led by instinct, in pursuit of objects capable of exciting our passions, notwithstanding those objects make impressions on us, which are frequently attended with nights and days of pain and calamity.[87]

The natural pleasure of agitating the passions also explained why "crowds of people flock to one of the most frightful spectacles, that human nature can behold, that is, the public execution of a man upon a scaffold, where he undergoes the most exquisite torments inflicted by the law."

> That natural emotion, which rises, as it were, mechanically within us, upon seeing our fellow creatures in any great misfortune or danger, hath no other attractive, but that of being a passion, the motions whereof rouse and occupy the soul.[88]

This explained the pleasure of watching tragedies and executions, but it had the unfortunate defect of being fundamentally amoral. Two eighteenth-century theorists—Anthony Ashley Cooper, Third Earl of Shaftesbury and Francis Hutcheson—were instrumental in producing theories that could explain not only the *pleasure* produced by tragedy's agitation of the passions but the *moral utility* of that pleasure. They did so by arguing that what drove people to such spectacles was not the pleasure of comparing their own happiness to another's suffering (as Lucretius and his seventeenth-century interpreters had claimed) but a fundamental ethical instinct. The "Horrour" that both "Sufferers" and "Spectators" feel at public executions, argued Shaftesbury in "An Inquiry Concerning Virtue and Merit" (1711), arises not from fear but from a shared abhorrence of the "Odiousness of th[e] Crime."[89] The "Efficacy" of executions similarly comes not "from the Fear ... which they raise" but from their ability to "awake[n] and excit[e]" the "natural Esteem of *Virtue*, and Detestation of *Villany*."[90] As "publick Expressions of the ... Hatred of Mankind" for vice, and collective affirmations of esteem for virtue, executions inspire not fear of the state but a renewed commitment to collective rectitude.[91] In this they are like tragedies, or at least tragedies as they ought to be.

In "An Inquiry Concerning the Original of Our Ideas of Virtue or Moral Good" (1725), Hutcheson developed Du Bos' and Shaftesbury's ideas about our attraction to the spectacle of suffering. For Hutcheson, as for Shaftesbury, we have "practical Dispositions to *Virtue* implanted in our *Nature*" and an "Instinct to Benevolence."[92] The reason we are drawn to scenes of suffering is in fact precisely such instinctive compassion. For the desire to *relieve* suffering hurries people, "by a *natural, kind Instinct*, to see Objects of *Compassion*," he explains, "as in the Instance of *publick Executions*. This same Principle leads men to *Tragedys*."[93] Children demonstrate this instinct: at executions, as "soon as they observe the evidences of Distress, or Pain in the *Malefactor*, they are apt to condemn this necessary Method of Self-defence in the *State*," experiencing a "*Compassion* ... too strong for their *Reason*."[94] As adults, however, they recognize that punishment of evil is necessary to virtue, so their moral sense leads them ultimately to approve scenes of merited suffering. He elaborated a few years later in his *Essay on the Nature and Conduct of the Passions and Affections* (1728):

> [A] *compassionate Temper* may rashly imagine ... the *Execution of a Criminal*, to be cruel and inhuman: but by *reasoning* may discover the *superior Good* arising from [it] in the whole; and then the same *moral Sense* may determine the Observer to approve [it].[95]

Executions are no longer theologically justified public revenge, but instead (like the best tragedies) pleasurable opportunities for exercising our instinct for compassion.

Hutcheson's basic stance—our compassion makes us feel executions to be "cruel and inhuman" but we recognize them as necessary—represents the view that was to remain dominant throughout the century. The feeling that executions were "cruel and inhuman" did nothing to reduce their number: in fact, the number of executions increased exponentially in the eighteenth century, along with the size of execution crowds.[96] However, the expanding discourse of sympathy did help change practices of punishment. Even in the late seventeenth century, many of those overseeing punishments had begun to feel uncomfortable with the calculated infliction of excruciating pain on people who, however guilty, were helpless to resist. At the same time, most people still felt that a display of public torture was necessary to deterrence. The solution—which satisfied both humanitarian and penal-deterrent impulses—was to fake certain tortures (such as the cutting out of the malefactor's tongue), or to covertly execute the condemned before subjecting them to the prescribed tortures.[97]

The penal torture of corpses was, of course, not new. In fact, it had long been a means of intensifying shame and foreclosing the possibility of salvation (many thought that if your body was destroyed, there would be nothing to resurrect on Judgment Day).[98] What was new was that corpse torture was no longer aimed primarily at the malefactor but at the spectator, as part of an official attempt to substitute a theater of pain for the real thing. In 1749, the Prussian Cabinet observed that the object of punishment was "not to torment the criminal but rather to make a frightful example of him." It ordered that henceforth "the criminal should be strangled by the hangman before being broken with the wheel, but secretly, and without it coming to the special attention of the assembled spectators."[99] Maria Theresa, Holy Roman Archduchess (and mother of Marie Antoinette), similarly told the Brussels magistrates in 1776 that they should always practice secret strangling before proceeding with torture because "[h]umanitarianism requires that we refrain from excessively prolonging the pain of those condemned to death," but the penal system must not "lesse[n] the awe of such punishments in the eyes of the public" for that would "encourage crime."[100] With notable exceptions, this practice became nearly universal over the course of the century. Told in 1803 that he was to be hanged, drawn, and quartered, Edward Despard supposedly cried out, "Ha, ha! what nonsensical mummery is this?"[101] Everyone knew that the execution's staging of excruciating pain would be merely an illusion, for the condemned would in fact already be dead. But, as in the theater, illusion could be powerful.

Other reforms similarly aimed at augmenting rather than reducing spectacle. In England in the 1750s, for instance, the legislature decided that, to intensify public shame, bourgeois felons would no longer ride to Tyburn in coaches but in open carts like common felons.[102] In 1775, the reformer Jonas Hanway argued that officials should aim not for intensified shame but enhanced grandeur and formality. Since common spectators were "awed by their senses, and ... exterior pomp and solemnity," executions should be "rendered [yet] *more* awful to the spectator."[103] To achieve this, the state should do away with carts and provide black mourning coaches attended by "*footmen* ... clothed in black" for all classes of felons.[104] "Every thing that can contribute to the solemnity of the procession ... should be considered as obligations" and "performed with the same external awe."[105] This solemn and awe-inspiring procession would lead not to the open crossroads at Tyburn but to a dedicated building "in form of a stage," where officials could more carefully orchestrate the scene of death.[106]

In the late eighteenth century, many jurisdictions moved their scaffolds from public crossroads or hills to the center of the city, a change that scholars tend to view as a sign of the imminent disappearance of penal spectacle. But those instigating this change seem interested not in limiting visibility but in *transferring* visibility: shifting criminological attention from highways to the center of the city, and controlling expanding crowds by replacing the older ambulatory and unbounded procession-and-execution with a spectacle staged in a fixed-perspective, carefully controlled urban theater (Figure 6.3).[107] In fact, two officials responsible for moving the gallows from Tyburn to the square in front of the Old Bailey Courthouse and Newgate Prison, sheriffs Barnard Turner and Thomas Skinner, explained in 1784 that the defect of the traditional procession was not excess visibility but a "most shocking and disgraceful ... Want of Ceremony."[108] This want of ceremony led spectators to "becom[e] indifferent to the Spectacle,"[109] watching it "with as little Terror or Concern as the Conclusion of a public Entertainment."[110]

> At most, when they view the Meaness of the Apparatus, a dirty Cart and ragged Harness surrounded by a sordid Assemblage of the lowest among the vulgar, their Sentiments are more inclined to Ridicule than Pity.[111]

The new location "add[s] to the Solemnity of public Executions" and thereby combats spectator indifference not by reducing spectacle but by increasing it.[112]

> [N]ow, instead of carting the Criminals through the Streets to Tyburn, the Sentence of Death is executed in the Front of Newgate, where upwards of five Thousand Persons may easily assemble.[113]

To heighten the drama, a "Scaffold, hung with black" encloses the platform, creating a somber *mise en scène*. "The Criminals are not exposed to View till they mount the fatal Stage."[114] A "funeral Bell" tolls from beginning to end.[115] The spectators "fix [their] whole Attention upon this Scene of awful Ceremony, [and] feel, with becoming Dread, the Pain of Disobedience and the Terror of Example."[116]

Through such intensified spectacle, people like Turner and Skinner sought not merely to generate greater "Dread" and "Terror," but also to create more humane spectators. Turner and Skinner's rhetoric suggests that not only is "Pity" (rather than "Ridicule") the sentiment most appropriate for execution spectators: generating pity is one of the central *aims* of execution spectacle.[117] Pity might make one close one's eyes, or avoid executions altogether. But the pleasures of pity (which could produce a gratifying sense of one's own benevolence) could also be a prime motive for attending executions. In a famous passage in Edmund Burke's *Enquiry into the Origin of Our Ideas of the Sublime and Beautiful* (1757)—in which he argues that spectators inevitably prefer real executions to even "the most sublime and affecting [stage] tragedy"—his contrast between stage and scaffold tragedy obscures an assumption about what they share: both offer audiences, above all, an experience of sympathy.[118]

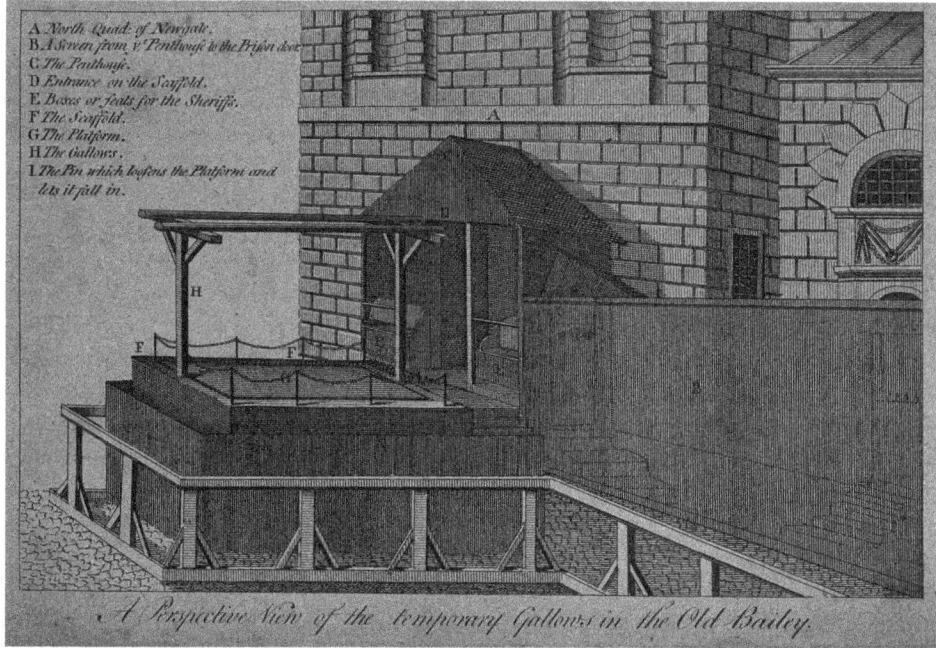

FIGURE 6.3: New gallows stage in front of the Old Bailey Courthouse and Newgate Prison (c. 1783). Wellcome Collection.

The superabundance of copiously weeping spectators in late eighteenth-century execution accounts (and the rarity of applause for the punishment) suggests the extent to which the cult of sympathy had transformed behavioral norms for scaffold spectatorship: at Tyburn, a condemned man's "Scene of parting with his Wife and youngest Child, about Five Months Old, was so extremely affecting as to force Tears from almost every Spectator";[119] another "was a tragical scene, . . . which melted the hearts and moistened the cheeks . . . of the throng of spectators";[120] in another, "deeply affected with the solemnity of the scene, [the spectators] were weeping witnesses of [the Malefactors'] departure from this world to meet the Eternal Judge of mankind";[121] in another,

> [j]ust as he was turned off, there was an universal silence; tears flowed from many eyes, but from one quarter there was . . . a general groan, that was deplorably affecting; and a mournful shriek . . . that pierced the hearts of those who heard it.[122]

In these descriptions, there is no retribution, no exchange of blood for blood.[123] And malefactors are (as one account describes it) surrounded by "a prodigious Number of sympathizing Beholders."[124]

Such sympathy did not, however, indicate waning support for the spectacle of punishment. On the contrary, with a few notable exceptions, almost everyone—including some of the leading figures of the Enlightenment—felt that some kind of deterrent spectacle was "necessary to public security."[125] This may be less surprising early in the century in figures like Shaftesbury, Mandeville, or Hutcheson, or in regime-apologists like Bermúdez or Barthès. But it is perhaps more surprising in Cesare Beccaria, author of the seminal treatise on humanitarian penal reform: the immensely influential *On Crimes and Punishments* (1764). Beccaria's vehement opposition to torture and the death penalty makes it easy to miss the fact that, far from arguing for the abolition of penal spectacle, he argues for its necessity, urging states to stage a perpetual and ongoing penal spectacle (though of a new kind).

The problem with current execution practices, for Beccaria, is that the "gibbet" and "wheel" fail to offer "the salutary fear that the law claims to inspire."[126] For the spectators are "spared almost all of [the punishment's] pain" and can imagine their own deaths only "in the hazy distance."[127] The "horror of the final tragedy"—a "frenz[ied]" and "terrible but fleeting spectacle of . . . death," "the affair of a moment"—"pass[es]" without leaving an impression.[128] Unfazed, the thief or murderer (whom Beccaria imagines as a male robber-baron-cum-*philosophe*) realizes that the day of "suffering and repentance" may come. But "that time will be brief, and, in return for a day of torment, I shall have many years of liberty and pleasure." Then "religion appears" to his mind, "and presenting him with the prospect of an easy repentance and a near certainty of eternal bliss, greatly diminishes the horror of the final tragedy."[129] In fact, the "sight of [the] barbarous and useless torments" that the state "devise[s] and carrie[s] out in cold blood . . . harde[n]" the spectators rather than "correct[ing]" them.[130] At best, such scenes are a mere "entertainment for the majority," "a diverting show for a fanatical crowd," "more [a] spectacle than a punishment."[131] The problem with this kind of tragic spectacle is not that it cruelly exposes the condemned to the heartless crowd. It is that it is too *short*, offering (as for Mandeville) too little display of suffering and terror.

Beccaria makes it clear throughout his treatise that—however failed the old tragic ritual—spectacle is essential to punishment, and to social order more generally. Like Mandeville, he insists that the target of punishment is not primarily "the criminal" but "those who witness" it.[132] It is for this reason that punishments must be "public": the first and foremost of the six features that he identifies as essential to a just penal system.¹³³ Publicity here is not mere transparency: the regime must stage "some sort of external show to win over the ignorant populace."¹³⁴ This "external show" has two goals: garnering popular support for the regime (with the crowd as cheering squad); and deterring crime. "Neither eloquence nor declamations nor even the most sublime truths" can dissuade the potential criminal. This is because what motivates crime are "emotions aroused by the vivid impressions of immediately present objects," emotions so strong that reason cannot overcome them.¹³⁵ The state can succeed in counteracting such emotions only with its own "tangible motives" (*motivi sensibili*)—motives with "a direct impact on the senses"— in the form of a spectacle showing the wages of crime.¹³⁶ Only such an "external show" can produce emotions sufficient to "dissuade the despotic spirit of each man from plunging the laws of society back into the original chaos."¹³⁷

Here, Beccaria combines Cartesian-inflected empiricism with Hobbesian social theory to explain the importance of penal spectacle to deterrence. The "vivid impressions" of "immediately present [external] objects" produce equally "strong impressions" in the soul, in the form of "individual passions."¹³⁸ Our naturally "despotic spirit" urges us to pursue these passions, which threaten to "plung[e] the laws of society back into the original chaos." However, whereas for Hobbes only the iron-fisted state can keep society from reverting to the violent state of nature, for Beccaria only penal spectacle, acting on the passions through its "direct impact on the senses," has this power.

As it happens, Beccaria has a particular form of non-capital, non-sanguinary penal spectacle to propose, well-suited (he explains) to producing such "vivid impressions": the ongoing display of convicts at hard labor.

> The most powerful restraint against crime is not the terrible . . . spectacle of a villain's death, but the faint and prolonged example of a man who, deprived of his liberty, has become a beast of burden, repaying the society he has offended with his labors.

Such a spectacle will serve far better than execution as a deterrent:

> [T]he man who sees before his eyes the prospect of . . . a lifetime of penal servitude and suffering, exposed to the sight of his fellow citizens, . . . will make a salutary comparison between all this . . . and the [brief] enjoy[ment of] th[e] fruits [of his crimes]. The constant example of those whom he actually sees [at hard labor] makes a much stronger impression on him than the spectacle of [sanguinary] punishment.¹³⁹

The display of hard labor will produce maximal terror with minimal cruelty (less messily than public corpse torture). For spectators will "substitute their own [more delicate] sensibility for the calloused soul of the wretch," and imagine such servitude as torture worse than death, whereas the convict will find "consolations unknown . . . to the spectators."¹⁴⁰ No blood, no dramatic violence, no climax, no catharsis, not ultimately (in Beccaria's view) tragic: just the ongoing spectacle of daily suffering to demonstrate the wages of crime.

In the notes he made on Beccaria in 1771, Diderot comments approvingly on this passage. "[H]ard and cruel slavery," "a state in which despair does not end [the convict's] ills, but begins them," is "preferable to the death penalty . . . because the example is more effective." He proposes that the regime make the example still more effective by providing the slave-driving guards "with chains and whips." The sight of "chains and whips" would exploit our natural "physical repugnance" for torturers and executioners: the "punishment [they] inflict on the culprit will be no less just" and the "spectacle of suffering" much

FIGURE 6.4: Proposed scene of highwaymen at hard labor. *The Malefactor's Register* (1779). *49–1509, Houghton Library, Harvard University.

stronger.[141] An illustration in *The Malefactor's Register* for 1779 represents its own (rather more picturesque and less terrifying) "New Plan" for such a scene: "the punishment of Highwaymen, by Hard Labour on the Roads" (Figure 6.4).[142]

Beccaria, Diderot, and *The Malefactor's Register* were not alone in envisioning less violent, less "tragic," but equally spectacular alternatives to traditional executions. Elsewhere, I have described Bentham's version of the Panopticon as he actually envisioned it in the 1790s: not hidden from the public (as Foucault describes it), but a public place filled wall-to-wall with spectators, providing an "affecting prospect" of prisoners "detained in durance" and other "picturesque" scenes, "not less interesting and affecting" than the sights spectators regularly saw in the asylum.[143] Responding to an imaginary interlocutor who charges that such a prison would "be a sort of perpetual pillory," where prisoners would be at first distressed but soon "harden[ed]" by being "thus exhibited," Bentham reiterates the central eighteenth-century justifications for penal spectacle: only public punishment can deter others from crime, demonstrate the citizens' safety from criminals, and publicly expiate the crime.[144] Shame is a key factor in deterrence and expiation, he explains. But if his interlocutor objects to shaming, "nothing can be simpler than the remedy": the prisoners can wear masks.

> Guilt will thus be pilloried in the abstract.... With regard to the sufferer, the sting of shame will be sheathed, and with regard to the spectators, the salutary impression, instead of being weakened, will be heightened.... The scene of devotion ... will be decorated by ... a masquerade, [but] not a gay and dangerous, but a serious, affecting, and instructive one.[145]

This serious, affecting, and instructive penal masquerade will, in fact, have more in common with the "Spanish [a]uto-da-fe" than with the (insufficiently decorative) English execution:

> [The Inquisition] must at least be allowed to have had some knowledge of *stage effect*. Unjust [and barbarous] as was their penal system, the skill they displayed in making the most of it in point of impression, their solemn processions, their emblematic dresses, their terrific scenery, deserve rather to be admired and imitated than condemned.[146]

Anticipating the charge that such penal theatricality would be not "serious, affecting, and instructive" but ludicrous, Bentham asks, "what is the objection [to the *auto-de-fé*]? That the spectacle is light or ludicrous? No: but rather that it is too serious and too horrible."[147] The Panopticon is not to be "light," "ludicrous," or callously "gay" (like English executions): it is not to be comedy. But nor will it be "too serious and too horrible": it is not to be the "Bloody" and "Barbarous" tragedies of the past. Instead, like sentimental drama or the French *drame*, it will be "serious" but "picturesque" and "affecting": serious, that is, but not ultimately tragic.

## CONCLUSION

George Steiner famously claimed that the Enlightenment belief in progress and human perfectibility announced the "death of tragedy": "Rousseauism closes the doors of hell.... The destiny of Lear cannot be resolved by the establishment of adequate homes for the aged."[148] One might be tempted to view the shift from execution tragedy to penitentiary *drame* (in fact realized in many nineteenth-century prisons) as announcing the "death of tragedy" in the judicial sphere. But the view that tragedy died with Rousseau is not really sustainable (even if one defines tragedy extremely narrowly), not least because it ignores the ongoing importance of the word to aesthetics, law, and culture more broadly. People continued to identify executions as "tragedies" in the nineteenth century, however much "melodrama, [b]ombast, blue lights and penny tragedies" seemed to have debased tragic experience.[149]

In an apocryphal letter from Louis XVI to his brother in May 1792, the fictional Louis writes: "They tell me that we are at the brink of ... a tragedy, whose denouement will be the fall of the monarchy, and my death."[150] As the real Louis mounted the scaffold, his confessor told him that the humiliating binding of his hands offered yet another "resemblance between your Majesty and [our] Saviour."[151] In the aftermath, prints showing the scene bore the title "Tragic End of Louis XVI" (in French, English, and German), quoting Louis' supposed last words: "I have never desired anything but the happiness of my people, and my last wishes are that Heaven pardon them for my death."[152] Another print represents the sequence of events leading to his execution in six medallions,

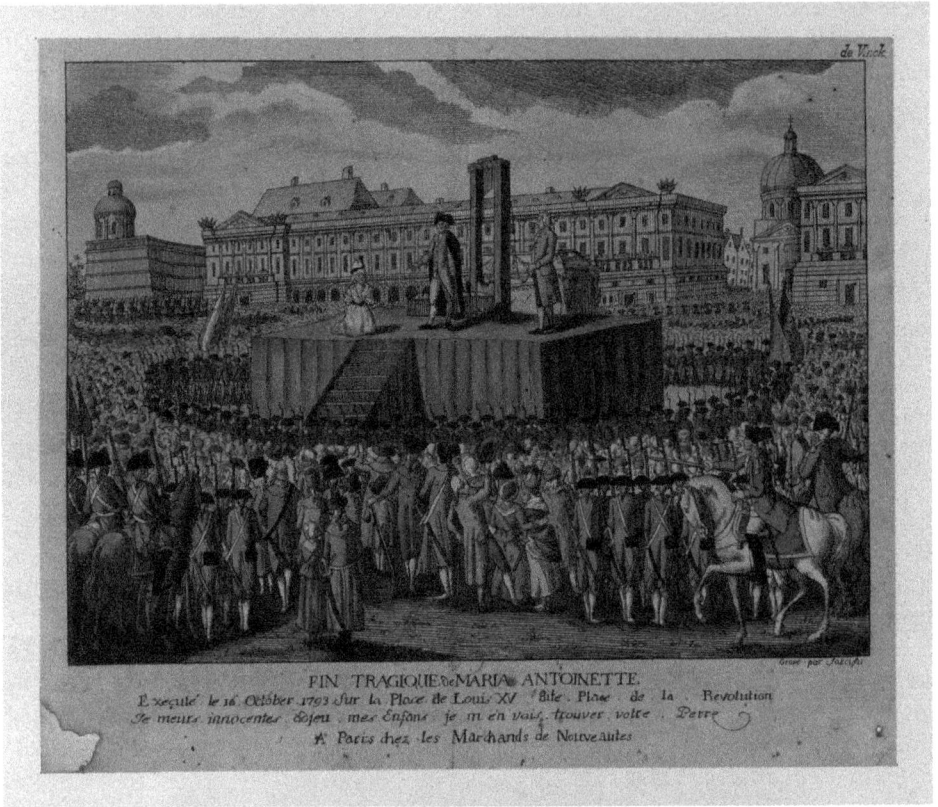

FIGURE 6.5: *The Tragic End of Marie Antoinette*: "I die innocent. Adieu my Children. I go to find your Father" (Paris, 1793). Bibliothèque nationale de France, De Vinck, 5493.

the last one showing "Louis XVI, his apotheosis," with his confessor's exhortation, "ascend to heaven son of S:Louis," recalling images of the apotheosis of Charles I almost 150 years earlier. In October of 1793, new prints appeared: *The Tragic End of Marie Antoinette*: "I die innocent. Adieu my Children. I go to find your Father" (Figure 6.5).

The image of Marie Antoinette's "Tragic End" offers one version of tragedy in the last decade of the century. The quote that accompanies the image, with its stress on the heartrending wresting of a mother from her children, evokes a transfer from the theological to the domestic: notably, she will ascend not to *the* Father but to "your Father." In this touching tableau (recalling those of the *drame*), the focus is the pathos of the domestic scene, not horror or social disorder (the crowd is orderly, the executioners remarkably genteel). An anonymous critic, writing in 1793, describes "the tragedy" in France with a similar genteel pathos: portraying it is, "indeed, a tragic pleasure; but in that class the most refined sensations are comprised."[153] Here, tragedy is no longer "Barbarous and Execrable" deeds but, on the whole, the "pleasure[s]" of "refined sensations."

There were, of course, other versions of tragedy *c.*1793, for instance in prints labeled "Tragic End of Marie Antoinette" showing the executioner brandishing her severed head. But many still held onto the idealized vision. Genuine tragedy did not produce horror. A reviewer of *The Martyrdom of Marie-Antoinette, Tragédie* protested in 1800: "there is no subject less tragic; ... it is neither terror nor pity that it inspires, it is horror, it is hopelessness, ... it is stifled cries of impotent rage."[154] If tragedy produced terror and admiration, these were actually just forms of pity, as Lessing had argued in 1756. "Tragedy raises no other passion in the spectator than pity," which is, in fact, its only purpose: "to increase sympathy ... for the miserable everywhere" and teach us to "adopt their woes as our own." Since those "who pit[y] most" are the most "benevolent" and "virtuous," watching tragedy is, in itself, an exercise in virtue.[155]

In his *Enquiry into the Effects of Public Punishments upon Criminals* (1787), Benjamin Rush offered a trenchant critique of such views, indicting what he termed "abortive sympathy."[156] "[D]istress of all kinds, when *seen*, produces sympathy, and a disposition to relieve it." "This sympathy in generous minds, is not lessened by the distress being the offspring of crimes," for crimes (we know) often spring from "extreme poverty" or "the loss or negligence of parents in early life." However, "as the distress which the criminals suffer, is the effect of a law of the state, which cannot be resisted, the sympathy of the spectator is rendered abortive, and returns empty to the bosom in which it was awakened."[157] Repeated experiences of "abortive sympathy" decrease our capacity to act.

> The principle of sympathy, after being often opposed by the law of the state, which forbids it to relieve the distress it commiserates, will cease to act altogether; and, from this defect of action, and the habit arising from it, will soon lose its place in the human breast.[158]

Over time, watching executions "extirpat[es]" our capacity for both action and feeling.

Aesthetic tragedy (he argued a few months later) produces a similar "abortive sympathy,"[159] a view he continued to reiterate. In his *Medical ... Observations, upon the Diseases of the Mind* (1812), for instance, he explained: "nervous diseases increase ... in proportion to the fondness of ... citizens for seeing tragedies."[160] Madness was common in England because "its inhabitants prefe[r] tragedy to comedy."[161]

> The *real* emotions excited by these exhibitions of *imaginary* distress are never accompanied with an effort to relieve it, by which means there is an accumulation and reflux of sensation in the mind, that cannot fail of affecting the nerves and brain, and thereby ... predispose to, or induce madness.[162]

However fanciful we may find Rush's Cartesian account of the link between tragedy and madness, his indictment of the culture of tragic-sympathy-as-virtue has a distinct contemporary resonance. It not only presages the Brechtian critique of empathetic identification-and-catharsis. It suggests the potentially negative consequences of divesting the word "tragedy" of its critical and retributive functions, leaving it to function almost solely as an expression of sympathy (as it does today). When we mourn natural or political disasters as tragedies, or a penal system that "sport[s] away the Lives of the indigent" (to quote Mandeville), we are often expressing a feeling of helplessness accompanied by political paralysis. At the same time, in deploring the tragedy, it is easy to substitute compassion for action, basking in collective consensus (whose pleasures in large measure compensate for shame at one's failure to act). Having expressed our humanitarian views, we are done.

In *Modern Tragedy*, written largely as a refutation of Steiner, Raymond Williams argues that tragedy need not be considered an expression of the futility of human struggle. Central to his argument is the idea that, if "[w]e have to recognize ... suffering in a close and immediate experience," we also have to "follow the ... action" that produced it.[163]

> Tragedy . . . is born in pity and terror: in the perception of a radical disorder in which the humanity of some men is denied. . . . It is born in the actual suffering of real men thus exposed, and in all the consequences of this suffering: degeneration, brutalisation, fear, hatred, envy. It is born in an experience of evil made the more intolerable by the conviction that it is not inevitable, but is the result of particular actions and choices.[164]

Tragic evil—not absolute, its source sometimes hard to locate—is nevertheless something against which one can take arms. Steiner is wrong, Williams argues, in claiming that revolution is antitragic: it is in fact tragic in both its "origins" and its "action," a response to "disorder that cannot but move and involve."[165] This action "is not against gods or inanimate things, . . . not against mere institutions and social forms, but against other men."[166] Although vengeance and retributive punishment may be dangerous, and we know that any attempt to take action has "the probability of secondary and unforeseen disorder," it is nevertheless necessary to hold people responsible.[167] Simply recognizing suffering is far easier. And yet, Williams argues, we must overcome abortive sympathy if we are to begin to fight those daily real-world "traged[ies] born in pity and terror, . . . born in the actual suffering of real men thus exposed, and in all the consequences of this suffering."[168]

# CHAPTER SEVEN

# Society and Family

*Tragedy and the Family*

JOHN D. LYONS

European tragedy was flourishing in the 1650s, but by the end of the eighteenth century, "tragedy" as an explicitly designated category of dramatic and literary production had all but disappeared. However, a new generic designation emerged as a successor form specifically to represent both fraught interactions concerning the family and the status of the family within society. It is the task of this chapter to trace this important change with respect to the representation of the family and of society in the serious dramatic genre. We will begin by recalling the role assigned to the family within the historically-attested poetics of tragedy—and thus necessary making some observations about the structure of society that is both explicit and implicit in those poetic doctrines. We can then consider important examples of dramatic tragedies (that is, plays specifically designated by their creators as "tragedies") written and performed in the period that stretches roughly from Pierre Corneille's *Nicomède* (1651), John Dryden's *The Indian Emperour* (1665), and Jean Racine's *Andromaque* (1667) to Schiller's *Die Räuber* (*The Robbers*, 1777). Thereafter we will need to make some account of the virtual disappearance of dramatic texts specifically labeled "tragedy" and to consider theatrical works performed and published as "drama," "dramatic poem," or sometimes even "comedy." What changes in the conceptions of the family and of society can account for the emergence of important serious plays whose authors energetically refused the term "tragedy," as did Friedrich Schiller for his *The Robbers* (1781) and *Don Carlos* (1787)?

## THE FAMILY AS CENTER OF THE TRAGIC PLOT

In the canon of tragedy that consists of ancient Greek and Roman works and then of texts in a number of European languages beginning in the fifteenth century, violent conflict between family members is usually the center of the action. From the earliest discussions of tragedy in antiquity, the family had been central to the action and the emotion of this literary and dramatic category. Plato, objecting to the dangerous weakening of civic virtue through the influence of the tragic poets (among whom he counted Aristotle) used the example of a father grieving for his dead son to show how easily will and reason could be subverted by sympathy for the unfortunate. At the beginning of book III of *The Republic*, the philosopher condemns the emotions provoked by the death of a friend or child, emotions that are indulged at length in tragedies but that should be repressed in a proper city:

> the good man will not consider death terrible to any other good man who is his comrade, . . . and for this reason the loss of a son or brother, or the deprivation of fortune, is to him of all men least terrible.[1]

The sight of such shameless emotional indulgence is dangerous for society because it is contagious and spreads outward from the infected family towards society through the medium of dramatic and literary art:

> But we have not yet brought forward the heaviest count in our accusations: the power which poetry has of harming even the good (and there are very few who are not harmed). . . . The best of us, as I conceive, when we listen to a passage of Homer, or one of the tragedians, in which he represents some pitiful hero who is drawling out his sorrows in a long oration, or weeping, and smiting his breast—the best of us, you know delight in giving way to sympathy. . . . This feeling which is kept under control in our own calamities is satisfied and delighted by the poets . . . because the sorrow is another's; and the spectator fancies that there can be no disgrace to himself in praising and pitying.[2]

As Elizabeth Belfiore writes, "The desire to weep at the theatre is treated in this dialogue as . . . an anti-rational desire. Even a temporary indulgence in tragic pity and fear has a permanent deleterious effect on the soul, although it does not lead directly to any action."[3]

When Aristotle replied in his *Poetics* to Plato's anti-poetic doctrines he appropriated and emphasized the crucial role that the family plays both in the tragedy as plot and in the genesis and modeling of those emotions that for him defined tragedy, fear, and pity. He notes that actions productive of fear and pity "must involve dealings between those who are bonded by kinship or friendship; or between enemies; or between those who are neither." The philosopher goes on to argue that "what must be sought are cases where suffering befalls bonded relations—when brother kills brother (or is about to . . .), son kills father, mother kills son, or son kills mother."[4] This lesson was taken to heart by early modern dramatists, whether they learned it from some of the multiple editions and commentaries of the *Poetics* or from the same source that Aristotle had used, direct observation of the plots of the Greek tragedians and Seneca. To condense the traditional emotional core of the tragic story, we can say that tragedy happens when kin and friends, rather than enemies, physically attack one another.

While the family was centrally important in the Greco-Roman tradition, the pertinence of larger social issues varies considerably in the period with which we are concerned. Indeed, this variability offers a useful comparative standard for the shifts in what playwrights offered and what audiences sought during the period 1650 to 1800. While it is true that the principal characters of most of the plays in the seventeenth and early eighteenth centuries were kings, queens, princes, princesses, and generals, towards the end of the eighteenth century such pre-eminent political and social standing was no longer required of protagonists. But even when the main characters were rulers, the relation between the action of the play and the political situation varies widely.

Pierre Corneille, for instance, considered it essential that a tragedy show the impact of the characters' actions on the state. In his *Three Discourses on the Dramatic Poem* (1660) he argued that a plot involving kings or princes, no matter the outcome, did not qualify as a "tragedy" unless it concerned "some great interest of state, or some passion more noble and male than love, such as ambition or vengeance." ("Sa dignité demande quelque grand intérêt d'Etat, ou quelque passion plus noble et plus mâle que l'amour, telles que sont l'ambition ou la vengeance.")[5] It is possible, of course, that private individuals of modest rank might seek bloody revenge, but in Corneille's practice family struggles were always intertwined with political considerations and often had decisive impact on the state. Though Corneille's dominance as a playwright was diminishing at mid-century, his *Nicomède* (1651) illustrates this tight binding of the family with the political situation. Briefly, Nicomède, the first son of Prusias, king of Bithynia, is a powerful and successful military commander, though his father, under the influence of a second wife, prefers Nicomède's younger half-brother Attale, who has been raised at Rome as part of a treaty of alliance with the Republic. The king plots to kill Nicomède, who is a strongly anti-Roman voice, and leave the throne to Attale (Figure 7.1). As this plan is unfolding, with the assistance of the Roman ambassador, Nicomède is released from captivity by persons unknown, the king and ambassador flee, the people favor Nicomède, and the wicked stepmother seems about to meet her unhappy end. In the event, Nicomède proves to be magnanimous and forgiving, and—in perhaps the greatest surprise—it becomes known that his half-brother, far from being the passive tool of his mother and of Rome, was responsible for saving Nicomède. Corneille's play displays the inseparability of family conflict, political values, and socio-political outcome. At the center of the protagonist's motivation seems to be Nicomède's nationalistic and aristocratic disdain for Rome, along with the inter-generational conflict of a strong son and weak father, while in the background there is a much less emphasized amorous rivalry between the two half-brothers. The most important deep structure of the tragedy comes from the conflict between a weak father and a strong son, a conflict in which Rome is identified with the weak father while Nicomède has chosen an elective father ideal in Hannibal, Rome's opponent.

*Nicomède* is a tragedy with a "happy ending," a type of play that many twentieth-century critics have found suspect and even rejected. Indeed, the history of tragedy studies is filled with articles denying "tragic" status to some of the most important texts that were historically performed and published as "tragedies." Let us not impose a more restrictive standard than Corneille's but note instead a consistent tendency on his part to craft works in which the character of the protagonist is heroic and exemplary. Casting off the stealthy, conspiratorial, and subservient model of his father Prusias, Nicomède chooses to act in a noble, frank, enlightened way (with *générosité*, to use Corneille's term for such virtue). The son triumphs peacefully over the father and thus exerts a charisma that not only wins the prize of marriage with the Armenian queen Laodice but pulls into his orbit the half-brother who had been groomed as an agent of Rome. It is always risky to generalize about the body of work of a dramatist as prolific as Corneille, but *Nicomède* offers a glimpse of two tendencies in tragedies as varied as *Le Cid* (1637) and *Rodogune* (1647): first, the intensity and vividness of the main figure (his or her character) is a primary goal in Corneille's dramatic practice; second, children are almost always morally superior to parents. In *Nicomède* we find both of these qualities. The son crushes the father, not by killing him, but by the even more devastating gesture of not-killing him, of granting him defeated survival.

In John Dryden's *Aureng-Zebe* (1675) a fairly similar plot is inflected in such a way as to make conflict over a political principle—should one favor subservience to Rome

FIGURE 7.1: Frontispiece to the 1660 edition of *Nicomède*, assumed to be a depiction of the king's plot to behead Nicomède to placate his subjects. Photo published in 1935. Wikimedia Commons.

or militant nationalism—recede into the background of entirely domestic intrigue (Figure 7.2). *Aureng-Zebe* shows a family in which all members are set homicidally against one another. Set in Mogul India, the play is loosely based on events within the family of Shah Jahan (1592–1666), who was succeeded by his son Aurang-Zebe. The characters pursue two categories of desire: political and sexual. Three of the principal male characters of the play wish to be emperor of India: the elderly reigning emperor himself, and his sons Aurang-Zebe and Morat (as well as two other sons not seen on stage). These three, plus a fourth male character, Arimant, are in love with a captive Kashmir queen, Indamora. The emperor's wife also wishes to seize power, at various times on behalf of Morat, her son, for herself, and for Aurang-Zebe, with whom she is in love. To state it more simply, there is the couple of what could be called the universal attractors (Indamora and Aurang-Zebe) around whom swarm those who wish to break up that couple to obtain power and amorous possession.

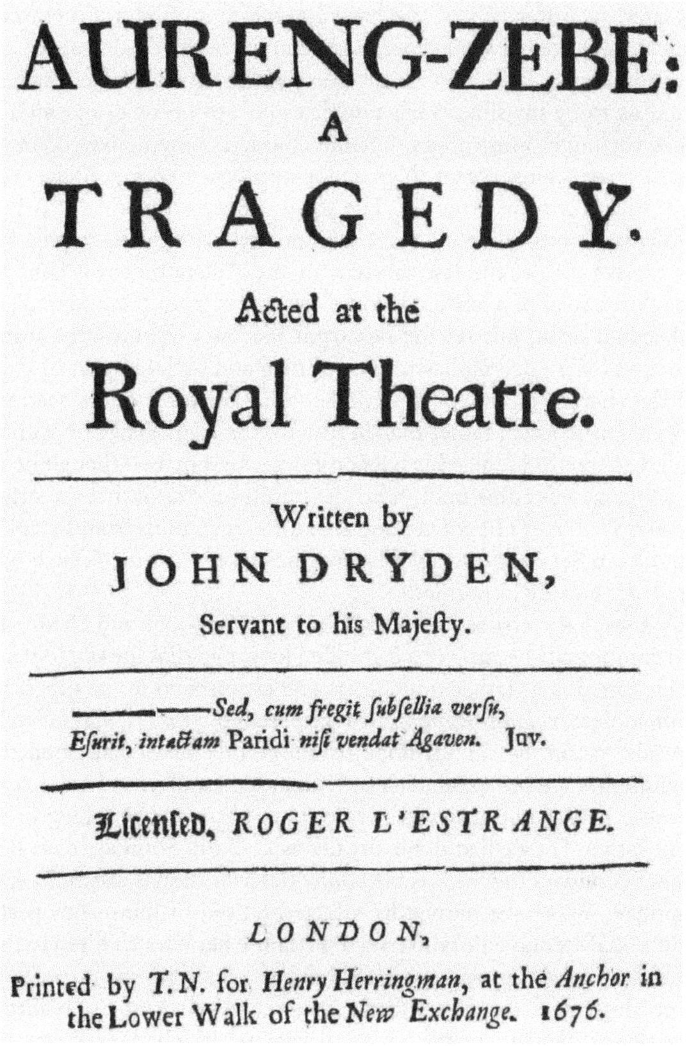

> # AURENG-ZEBE:
> ## A
> # TRAGEDY.
> ### Acted at the
> # Royal Theatre.
>
> Written by
> **JOHN DRYDEN,**
> Servant to his Majesty.
>
> ———*Sed, cum fregit subsellia versu,*
> *Esurit, intactam Paridi nisi vendat Agaven.* Juv.
>
> Licensed, ROGER L'ESTRANGE.
>
> *LONDON,*
> Printed by T. N. for *Henry Herringman*, at the *Anchor* in
> the Lower Walk of the *New Exchange.* 1676.

FIGURE 7.2: Title page of the first edition of *Aureng-Zebe*. Page 29 of *Aureng-Zebe, a tragedy; and Book II of The chase, a poem by William Somervile [sic] Edited with biographical memoirs and notes by Kenneth Deighton*. Hathi Trust Digital Library, original from Cornell University Library.

The similarity to *Nicomède* is immediately apparent, and this is hardly surprising given Dryden's great attentiveness to contemporary French tragedy and poetics. However, there is no political *principle* at stake, as there is in Corneille's play, nor is there an external political power foregrounded, as is Rome in *Nicomède*. Power and sex are desired for their own sake within what looks like the complete meltdown of family structure. Father and sons are competing for possession of the same woman; the mother-queen, unlike in *Nicomède*, is eager to sacrifice her son's aspirations in the hope of marrying Aureng-Zebe. Dryden's use of what could be called plot modules from ancient and early modern tragedy (and comedy) is so complex that some readers, beginning with Samuel Johnson, have considered *Aureng-Zebe* to be satirical.[6]

Two years later, Jean Racine's *Phèdre* gave a much more highly structured version of the entanglement of desire between generations, but in this work, one of the most revered of the tragic canon, the social and political aspects of the conflicts have receded so far into the background as to be invisible. Such ramifications are present, and an attentive and analytical spectator might grasp them, but the characters themselves seem to attach so little importance to anything except their family concerns that a political reading of the play would constitute critical virtuosity. The story concerns the king of Athens, Thésée, his son Hippolyte, his second wife Phèdre (Hippolyte's apparently hostile stepmother), and Thésée's captive Aricie, the last survivor of the Pallantide royal family of Athens, which was the bitter rival of Thésée. It would seem that from these ingredients a highly political work could arise, but Racine has from the outset shifted the location of the action in such a way as to de-emphasize the political and social impact of the characters' concerns. All the characters, except for Thésée (who has for months been mysteriously missing), are living in Troezen, rather than in Athens, the equivalent of a country vacation, where Hippolyte is free to indulge his passion for racing horses—though he does not do this, because a change has come upon him.[7] It is useful to recall that the original title of Racine's play was *Phèdre et Hippolyte*, and this difference both from Euripides' tragedy *Hippolytus* and from Seneca's tragedy *Phaedra* does better suit the French play in which these characters are equally important.

In parallel scenes in the first act, we learn that both Hippolyte and Phèdre are suffering physically and emotionally because of a forbidden love, and that the key to the prohibition is Thésée, in his function as father in one case and as husband in the other. Hippolyte is in the throes of adolescence, suffering in two interrelated ways. He has fallen in love with the captive Aricie, whom he cannot hope to marry (his father had condemned her to perpetual virginity in order to extinguish the Pallantide family), and he also feels himself unworthy because he has not achieved heroic status through the killing of robbers and monsters as his father Thésée had done already as a youth. Soon after we hear Phèdre's confession to her confidant that her visible bodily deterioration is caused by her concealed love for Hippolyte. While she outwardly affected hatred of him—thus performing the role of the traditional second wife who tries to promote her own children to the detriment of the older children by a previous wife—she has been suffering from a deep erotic attraction. The shift from the city, Athens, and the absence of the paternal-conjugal-political authority of Thésée, creates a kind of vacuum in which everyone can focus on personal turmoil.

In Hippolyte's case that turmoil appears quickly—to his mentor Théramène and surely to the audience—to be the plain and inexorable result of adolescence. The ordinariness of this experience is one example of the aspect of Racine's tragedies that has led numerous critics to see them as melodramas, as concerning banal events, even if those events take place in the lives of legendary personages. It certainly is easier for an ordinary member of the audience, whether in the seventeenth century or in the twenty-first century, to identify with a young man or woman forbidden to date a specific, highly attractive person. Hippolyte and Aricie are thus in the same situation as Romeo and Juliet, and the universal staying power of Shakespeare's play is impressive. Racine, like Shakespeare, has thus made his characters much more available, much closer to ordinary spectators, than Corneille's. Even if the protagonists of *Le Cid*—Chimène and Rodrigue—find their love thwarted by the quarrel between their fathers, how many of us can say that we have had to kill the parent of the woman we love or demand the execution of our lover in order, precisely, to make that lover respect us?

But it is the rumor that Thésée has died that moves the play to its complication: what was previously entirely forbidden suddenly becomes possible; the framework of the family vanishes and creates an almost utopian liberation of desire. While Thésée's death does not solve Hippolyte's worry that he has not earned the maturity of heroic status, Hippolyte is now free to declare his love for Aricie. But Phèdre is equally free to offer her love to her stepson.

Phèdre's declaration to Hippolyte, though closely modeled on a passage of Seneca's *Phaedra* (also known as *Hippolytus*), Racine's brilliant French rendering of Phèdre's almost hallucinatory fusion of the father and the son into a pure, fantastic object of her desire in the second act is no doubt one of the most perfect moments in the entire history of French drama, indeed of French poetry. Though its rhythm, rhyme, and nuanced semantic play are beyond the reach of a reader who does not know French, Phèdre's outpouring to the shocked Hippolyte allows any audience to see how desire can rewrite history and restructure the image of a family. Hippolyte politely offers (does he really believe what he says?) Phèdre a rhetorical fig-leaf to cover the embarrassing semi-revelation she has just made in saying that Thésée is not dead "because he is alive in you." ("puisqu'il respire en vous.")[8] The son suggests that this vision of himself as his father is just the "prodigious effect of your love" ("Je vois de votre amour l'effet prodigieux") and Phèdre springs from this into an erotic fantasy in which all of the bad traits of her womanizing husband are erased.[9] We often think of fantasy as a desire projected into the future, but Phèdre delves into the past, saying that her husband, when he first came to Crete when he was to be sacrificed with other Athenian youth to the Minotaur, looked exactly like Hippolyte. She then successively peels away at the received image of the past, asking why Hippolyte himself (though too young) had not come with the other heroes, then supposes that he had come, that her sister Ariadne had given him rather than Thésée the thread that allowed escape from the labyrinth—and then revises the fantasy still more to say that she herself, Phèdre, would have taught him the twists and turns of the tunnels, not content with giving him a thread. She would have accompanied him and would have, with him, either survived, or perished.

This gradual baring of her desire through the dream of the labyrinth is, of course, at multiple points conveyed through a sexual allegory. The labyrinth that she would guide him through appears clearly to be the labyrinth of her own body as well as that of the complexities of any amorous relationship, and the last word of her speech, *perdue* (lost), suggests sin, the loss of virtue, and potential damnation. Even Hippolyte, supposed to be unsophisticated in the ways of love and the discourse of women, exclaims with shock at this obliteration of the patrilineal family: "Gods! What do I hear? Madame, do you forget / That Thésée is my Father, and that he is your Spouse?" ("Dieux! Qu'est-ce que j'entends? Madame, oubliez-vous / Que Thésée est mon Père, et qu'il est votre Époux?") It is highly significant that Hippolyte does not just say "no." Instead he expresses his refusal by reasserting the two key roles—father and husband—through which Thésée regulates their lives. In a way, Thésée serves as a shield to protect Hippolyte from the scary, intense desire that he now sees, a desire that would appear all the more striking to Racine's contemporaries in that dramatic heroines were, in the seventeenth century, expected to express their erotic love only within the deeply coded language of passive compliance. In this respect, Chimène's declaration of love in Corneille's *Le Cid* is exemplary. Her passionate love for Rodrigue had expressed itself by the simple statement, "Go, I do not hate you." ("Va, je ne te hais point.") It is in this literary context that Phèdre's aggressive stance (she later grabs Hippolyte's sword) explodes the patriarchal family.

By a sudden reversal, however, Thésée does come back and finds himself shunned by son and wife alike, shaken as they are by their awareness that they have violated the law that is now restored. This kind of return could, of course, occur in a comedy, but tragedies are plays haunted by death and display the fragility not just of happiness but of life itself. In this case, moreover, it is not only life that is labile but even the barrier that prevents the return of the dead. Does Thésée return simply from an ordinary voyage? Or does he actually return from the world of the dead? Phèdre suggests as much when she imputes to him an attempt to seduce the wife of the god of the underworld ("Who goes to dishonor the bed of the God of the Dead" ["Qui va du Dieu des Morts déshonorer la couche"]). This possibility of the return of the dead to demand justice or revenge may not at first seem like a matter within the scope of the topic that concerns us here, tragedy and the family. And yet, according to a tradition going back into remote antiquity, it is the family, not the broader society and not the state, that is responsible for burying the dead with all proper rituals. In *Hamlet*, the ghost of the deceased king Hamlet returns to demand that his son take care of unfinished business, and that business consists of punishing those who violated the laws of matrimony and brotherly duty. The French stage of the seventeenth century is less and less inclined to stage "literal" ghosts, but the boundary between life and death still requires careful attention. Much of *Le Cid* was about the proper burial of Chimène's father, who, she points out, cannot rest until he is avenged. Racine is a master in the artful duplicity of providing both rational, naturalistic accounts of what happens and at the same time leaving open the possibility that supernatural agencies are at work.

Such an overdetermined causality is apparent in the dénouement of *Phèdre*, when Thésée, believing his son to have been guilty of raping Phèdre, disinherits and curses him. We recall that Hippolyte does not defend himself against the charge, believing that his innocence should be all too apparent. Instead, he arranges to flee with Aricie, pausing only to marry her on the tombs of his ancestors. In the final crescendo of violence, the most banal accounts of adolescent love and the most transcendent, supernatural, and mythological tales unite in a flickering scene of heroic struggle and annihilation. This is a "scene" that the theater audience never sees, nor could it (except in imagination).[10] Hippolyte rides along the shore of Troezen in his chariot to meet Aricie. A creature rises out of the sea, spooking the horses. Hippolyte, who has never had a heroic encounter before, attempts to fight the monster, but he cannot control his horses. He falls, tangled in the reins, and is smashed to a bloody pulp on the rocks and reeds.

As in *Phèdre*, family conflicts of all sorts fill Racine's tragedies, where sons and daughters are locked in rivalry with their parents (as in *Andromaque*) and with their siblings (as in *La Thébaïde* and *Bajazet*), but in the seventeenth century there is another tendency that shaped tragedy in ways that reduced the role of the family. With the French in the lead, society and in particular literature, took a turn toward the *galant* concept that is virtually untranslatable and that has many shades of meaning, but that, with regard to the theater conveys the idea of highly stylized renderings of male-female amorous interaction with particular emphasis on politeness and refined conversation. The *galant* in tragedy did not spring forth overnight but gradually increases from the time of Corneille's *Le Cid* onward. In the latter play, which few would describe as in itself *galant*, the playwright gives a very central role to the two young protagonists and distinguishes between their views of love and the views of their parents. In a notable exchange, Rodrigue (he who will later be known as *le Cid*) hears his father say dismissively that "Love is only a pleasure, and honor is a duty." ("L'amour n'est qu'un Plaisir, l'honneur est un devoir.") This deprecating view of love is entirely different from Rodrigue's, but the entanglement

FIGURE 7.3: *Phèdre and Hippolyte*, illustrated by Charles Le Brun, engraved by Sebastien Leclerc. Bibliothèque nationale de France, département Réserve des livres rares, RES-YF-3213.

of codes of value between the older and younger generations leads to the tragic impasse of the plot.

As the *galant* trend became increasingly important, the family recedes to the background and in some cases disappears entirely. Instead, the male and female characters begin to assume a distinct autonomy with regard to their family. The dwindling of the family in such works follows logically from the concepts advanced by the writers of that proto-feminist movement sometimes known as the *précieuses*, among whom are Madeleine de Scudéry and Marie-Madeleine de Lafayette, who opposed marriage while favoring male-female love within a category of "tender friendship" (*tendre amitié*). Marriage, as these women perceived it, was in most cases coerced by fathers or even by the extended family of uncles and other members of an aristocratic clan. This negative conception of marriage implies the possibility (or at least the fantasy) of a male-female union free from familial considerations. Perhaps the best-known example of a *galant* hero is the Pyrrhus of Racine's *Andromaque*, who treats Hector's captive widow with such politeness that even within the play itself Pyrrhus' mentor Phœnix mocks him for it. Even Racine points out in his preface that he had "softened somewhat the ferocity" of the character.

However, the *galant* is much more pronounced in tragedies such as Quinault's *La Mort de Cyrus* (1658–9) and Thomas Corneille's *Timocrate* (1656), which was the most popular French tragedy of the seventeenth century. The title of Quinault's play suggests heroism. Cyrus "the great," founder of the Persian empire in the sixth century BCE remains, alongside Alexander, the paragon of military prowess. After a series of spectacular conquests, he is said (by Herodotus) to have died in battle against the Massagetae, led by their queen Tomyris. The idea of a victorious female-led army had evident appeal for a feminist public and readership, and one could imagine versions of this story in which a tough and aggressive Cyrus was out-generaled by a woman with superior strategic talents and daring. This is, however, not the story that Quinault chose to present. Instead, both Tomyris and Cyrus commit suicide because they are caught up in an impossible love—in short, the height of the *galant*, in which an intense love exceeds all other considerations. Earlier playwrights like Shakespeare, Pierre Corneille, and the contemporary Jean Racine wrote tragedies in which love had a decisive and central position, but in their major plays love is usually intertwined with familial and political considerations. What is striking in *La Mort de Cyrus* is that Thomiris is entirely independent of any members of her family—in fact, she seems to have none. Even more striking, within the millennia-old tradition of tragic revenge, is that the death of Thomiris' son, which occurs before the play opens, makes no difference whatsoever to the queen even though Cyrus was the man who killed that son. Quinault does not present his Thomiris as an Amazonian warrior. Actual battles are left to her general Odatirse, who has captured Cyrus. The issue to resolve, as the play begins, is the expected marriage of the widowed Thomiris to her brother-in-law Clodamante (as her deceased husband commanded), though from the very first verses of the opening scene it is clear that she is secretly in love with someone else. The general hopes that he is the one the queen prefers, and to that end—to drive a wedge between her apparent duty to marry Clodamante and her amorous desires—Odatirse sets forth a doctrine of irrational love:

> What pleases is only that which should please,
> And allowing ourselves to be aroused by a pure instinct,
> We love, without knowing what makes us love.
> In such a state one loves much less

What should be loved than what seems lovable.
(Ce qui plaît n'est rien moins que ce qui devrait plaire,
Et par un pur instinct nous laissant enflammer,
Nous aimons, sans savoir ce qui nous fait aimer.
On aime beaucoup moins en un état semblable
Ce qui doit être aimé que ce qui semble aimable.)

5.270–4[11]

Odatirse is dismayed to learn that the queen loves Cyrus, suspected of killing her son treacherously when he was in Cyrus' custody. She, however, believes that her son committed suicide and did not die by Cyrus' order—though before learning of this new version of her son's death she had ordered that Cyrus be executed by being drowned in blood of his Persian subjects. All of this is laid out in the first act. Subsequently the double-dealing Odatirse throws up obstacles to the marriage of the queen and the captive Cyrus because Odatirse wishes to marry Thomiris himself and become king. The culmination of the general's scheming consists of rebelliously telling Thomiris that Cyrus can be released unharmed on the condition that she marry Odatirse. She does so, Odatirse holds up his end of the bargain and has Cyrus released from his chains, but Cyrus, outraged at Odatirse's coercion of Thomiris, slays the general. The queen, at first not suspecting Cyrus, orders that the killer be found and executed. Despite her dislike of her new spouse, she feels obliged as ruler to punish the murderer of the newly promoted king ("To avenge my husband, begin now to believe / That it is enough, without loving him, to love glory itself." ["Pour venger mon mari, commence ici de croire / Qu'il suffit, sans l'aimer, que l'on aime la gloire."]).[12] This outcome looks a bit like the situation of Corneille's Chimène in *Le Cid*, where she feels obliged to demand that the king punish Rodrigue with death for having killed her father in a duel. However, Quinault has removed from his play the social and familial framework that give a certain plausibility to Chimène's actions. Thomiris is queen and has no father or any other superior whom she must please. She loathed Odatirse, and the validity of her marriage itself could be called into question insofar as her consent was coerced. In any event, Odatirse is dead, she is free to act as she wishes (Odatirse had himself earlier in the play pointed out that the queen, who was already a widow in the first act, was not bound in any way by the wishes of her late husband), and she loves and admires Cyrus. Nonetheless, she orders his execution and then swallows poison, and Cyrus stabs himself to death. In short, Quinault has constructed a suicidal love story that has a rather bizarre resemblance to *Romeo and Juliet* insofar as the two principal characters commit suicide not in spite of but because of a reciprocated love.

Although Voltaire's tragedy *Zaïre* (1732) is not *galant* in giving a prominent role to the amorous interaction of the main characters, it does follow the trend of giving a particularly dark view of the family as a tyrannical institution extending its influence through the generations. In other words, it shares with the *galant* the valorization of the emancipated individual, capable of accepting or rejecting marriage and freed from dynastic considerations. In *Zaïre* the characters are not brought low because of an ancestral sin that in some mysterious way transmits itself from father to son, nor because of a social requirement that the family avenge any and all wrongs done to members. Instead *Zaïre* indicts a more basic, universal expectation that members of the family will replicate and perpetuate the values and beliefs of the family forever. In other words, the individuality of family members can only be a failure or a crime. Whereas in Quinault's *La Mort de Cyrus* the main characters had already emancipated themselves from the family so that tragedy derives from conflict between love and society, in *Zaïre* the eponymous heroine finds herself, like Shakespeare's Juliet, caught between the man she loves and a family that adamantly refuses to accept her right to free herself from the traditions of her ancestors. This core conflict between family and individual could, on a casual reading, be somewhat lost in the context of a clash of civilizations, insofar as the heroine's family is Christian and her lover is Muslim, but religion per se is not the cause of conflict.

To recall the story of this once-popular work (it continued to be performed regularly at the Comédie-Française until 1936), the young slave Zaïre lives within the seraglio of the sultan of Jerusalem, Orosmane, where her friend and confidant Fatime, a Christian, frequently reminds Zaïre that her parents (whom she lost at birth) may have been of that faith. In fact, Zaïre has among her few belongs a cross that has apparently been with her since infancy. Fatime and Zaïre have begun to doubt the promise made by a French crusader, Nérestan, that he would return to ransom the two women and ten French knights. Nérestan, himself a captive, was released provisionally for this purpose more than two years before and has not reappeared. Meanwhile, the sultan has asked Zaïre to marry him, and, astoundingly, plans to have no other wives. He distains the Asian practice of polygamy. Zaïre, for her part, has very relativist views of religious belief. She tells Fatime that such belief is simply the result of circumstance and upbringing. She would have been a polytheist in India, a Christian in Paris, and may as well be a Muslim where she is, in Jerusalem. Just as Zaïre and Orosmane are to marry, Nérestan returns from France with enough money to purchase the freedom of the two women and ten French knights, but does not have enough to obtain his own freedom. Always generous, Orosmane grants freely Nérestan his freedom and goes much further: the sultan declines to take any ransom money and instead of granting freedom to ten Christian prisoners he frees a hundred. There are only two whom Orosmane will not surrender to the Frenchman: Zaïre and the old, deposed French king of Jerusalem, Lusignan, who has been held in solitary confinement during the twenty years since the defeat of the Christian forces. The French captives think it dishonorable to leave without their elderly leader, but at this apparent impasse Zaïre comes to announce that she has obtained from Orosmane Lusignan's freedom. Until this point in the last scene of the second act, it seems that we are watching Nérestan's disappointment at finding that Zaïre, with whom he shared the years in captivity, will not follow him back to France as his future wife (this is implied, but not fully expressed). Suddenly the situation changes, as Lusignan discovers that Nérestan and Zaïre are the children he had lost when the Crusader kingdom of Jerusalem was defeated. This euphoric moment is reversed, however, when Lusignan discovers that Zaïre has been raised as a Muslim. At the spectacle of Nérestan's vehement outrage, Zaïre promptly declares that she is now a Christian.

This affirmation of "being Christian" (her father ordered her to say "I am Christian" ["Je suis chrétienne"] is entirely empty of any doctrinal sense.[13] Zaïre quickly makes it clear to her brother that she does not know what that means in terms of obligations ("His law which I seek, and that is unknown to my heart" ["sa loi que je cherche, et que mon cœur ignore"]).[14] Nérestan, though raised as a Christian, is almost equally clueless and declines to tell her about the faith: "Should I be the one to speak of it? Less instructed than faithful, / I am only a soldier, and all I have is zeal." ("Est-ce à moi d'en parler? Moins instruit que fidèle, / Je ne suis qu'un soldat, et je n'ai que du zèle.")[15] That the designation "Christian" is a term of group identity, rather than a reference to doctrinal content, becomes soon after even more obvious when Zaïre tells Nérestan that she loves

Orosmane and was planning to marry him. This information unleashes a violent tirade from Nérestan, who tells Zaïre that she deserves to die because she is a disgrace to her family ("Wretched disgrace to the blood from which you come." ["Opprobre malheureux du sang dont vous sortez."]).[16] He demands that she show her loyalty to an ethnic group ("Promise King Louis, to Europe, and to your father, / To God who already speaks to your sincere heart, / Not to make this odious marriage" ["Promets au roi Louis, à l'Europe, à ton père, / Au Dieu qui déjà parle à ce cœur si sincère, / De ne point accomplir cet hymen odieux"]).[17] Zaïre, in short, is the property of her family and through that family belongs to a set of controlling institutions and symbols.

Orosmane, for his part, does not seem to be invested in this kind of ethnic bigotry. Instead, what bothers him is the suspicion that Zaïre is in love with Nérestan—the sultan is ignorant of the newly-discovered kinship. Finally, in an incident entirely consonant with the Aristotelian model of a killing that happens because of a lack of correct information, Orosmane, thinking that she is going to meet a lover, stabs Zaïre to death while she is going to meet her brother so that she can be baptized. When he discovers his misapprehension, Orosmane commits suicide with the same dagger, after having given instructions for the safe departure of the French prisoners.

What is at issue in this tragedy built out of modules of the classical tragic repertory is the comparison between the generous and enlightened Orosmane, who is concerned only with the happiness of the woman he loves, and the tradition-obsessed, clan-centered French, for whom "religion" is only a code-word for submission to the family group. It seems, indeed, that Orosmane would even have allowed Zaïre to become Christian. When he learned that she was not planning to meet a lover but instead be baptized, the sultan shows no offense at this religious preference of hers. Instead, he indicates only his dismay that he killed a woman who truly loved him: "Zaïre! She loved me? Is it really true, Fatime? / His sister? ... I was beloved?" ("Zaïre! Elle m'aimait? Est-il bien vrai, Fatime? / Sa sœur? ... J'étais aimé?")[18] We could look at Voltaire's work as a kind of thought experiment playing (as so much French drama after 1637 does) with the variables of Corneille's *Cid*. Suppose, Voltaire seems to be saying to us, that Rodrigue and Chimène, rejecting the self-destructive codes of feudal family honor, had been able to live in peace as an autonomous, nuclear couple. That seems to be what Orosmane and Zaïre aspire to do. The sultan, for his part, has overcome the traditions of his family and his ethnic group, rejecting polygamy and treating the French with kindness. He is a *galant* individual who is in love with an unemancipated woman who remains subservient to her family.

# THE END OF TRAGEDY AND THE RISE OF THE "DRAMA"

The end of the eighteenth century, the period of the French Revolution, saw a burst of writings that theorize the tragic. These writings grow out of the Quarrel of the Ancients and the Moderns in France and the rise of Idealist and Romantic philosophy in Germany.[19] Both of these currents of thought tended towards the view that modern dramatic writing far surpassed that of the ancient Greeks. Friedrich Schiller wrote that Pierre Corneille's *Le Cid* was "undeniably in point of intrigue the masterpiece of the tragic stage" and further claimed that "Greek art never rose to [the] supreme serenity of tragic emotion, because neither their national religion, nor even the philosophy of the Greeks lighted their step on this advanced road."[20] Given this attitude toward the tragic tradition it is hardly surprising that numerous writers of the Enlightenment finally decided that some new term was necessary for the kind of serious drama that suited modernity.

A little more than two decades after *Zaïre*, Denis Diderot created the work that, as we see in retrospect, was the first major challenge to "tragedy" as it had existed in European culture for two centuries, his comedy *Le Fils naturel, ou les Epreuves de la vertu* (*The Illegitimate Son, or the Trials of Virtue*, 1757). The story itself is rather trite, based, like so many tragedies and comedies of the past on a plot that could be inflected towards a "happy" or an "unhappy" ending. In fact, it is a bourgeois variation on *Zaïre*. A man, Dorval, is unwittingly in love with his sister, thus betraying his best friend and disappointing the woman who loves Dorval. All is straightened out when Dorval and Rosalie's long-lost father appears after decades of absence. This play and particularly the influential critical dialogue that accompanied its publication, *Entretiens sur Le Fils naturel*, marked a turning-point in the history of serious drama. Diderot calls for a new kind of drama that would be neither comedy nor tragedy.[21] It could be called, he says, "domestic and bourgeois tragedy" ("la tragédie domestique et bourgeoise") or "the serious genre" ("le genre sérieux").[22] It would, like tragedy, concern the family, but it would level the social and economic classes, showing that regardless of social status, "The same situation . . . could have inspired the same discourse." ("La même situation . . . eût inspiré le même discours.")[23] The general idea of this shift would not only be to replace the princes and emperors of tragedy but to replace also the central aesthetic unit, which for tragedy, he says, is words and for the new genre is "impressions."[24] The result would be a theatrical experience closer to the actual world of the audience and thus more emotionally moving. We are here a far cry from the *galant* of Quinault and Thomas Corneille. The emphasis should, according to Diderot, be on real people and real situations.

A decade later in his *Essai sur le genre dramatique sérieux* (*Essay on the serious dramatic genre*, 1768), Beaumarchais imagines those who disdain this new type of theatrical creation as exclaiming "Tragi-comedy, bourgeois Tragedy, tearful Comedy—we don't know what name to give to these monstrous productions." ("Tragi-comédie, Tragédie bourgeoise, Comédie larmoyante, on ne sait quel nom donner à ces productions monstrueuses.")[25] He defends the new plays that turn away from "tragedy" with three main points. First, the new works make the public weep, whereas tragedy awakens in the audience primarily "involuntary indignation against their cruel gods" ("une indignation involontaire contre leurs dieux cruels") who victimize innocent people. Second, the new plays are more realistic and on a human scale. In tragedy, everything is excessive and unnatural: "passions always unbridled, crimes always atrocious . . . as far from nature as they are unheard of in our customs." ("les passions toujours effrénées, les crimes toujours atroces.") In such blood-drenched stories, "we only reach the end through poisonings, murder, incest, and parricide." ("et l'on n'arrive à la catastrophe que par l'empoisonnement, l'assassinat, l'inceste ou le parricide.")[26] Third, if everything in human life is predetermined by fate, then there is nothing to learn from tragedy, or if we learn something, it is only to be worse: "if we drew a moral lesson from such a genre, it would be awful." ("Si l'on tirait une moralité d'un pareil genre de spectacle, elle serait affreuse.") In keeping with the second of these objections—the outsized scale of tragedy—Beaumarchais considers that the heroic dimension of tragedy—its insistence on representing the misfortunes or crimes of heroes, demi-gods, and princes—prevents audiences from feeling their pathos. But identification with "the unhappiness of a good man" ("malheur d'un honnête homme") causes the spectator to leave the theater better than when he entered. In terms of the traditional Aristotelian theorization of tragedy, Beaumarchais by far emphasizes "pity" over "fear" and does so by insisting copiously and repetitively on weeping, which is what the audience is expected to do during the performance. The *drame* proposes a kind of weeping-therapy, which, oddly enough, intersects with Aristotle's obscure but certainly therapeutic concept of catharsis.

In Beaumarchais' conception, the *drame* and its reception by the public are intimately related to the status of the family, and particularly to the good or bad conduct of the father of the family: "It is certain that he who has dispossessed his father, had his son locked away, who lives divorced from his wife, who disdains his humble family origins, who loves no one, and who, in short, publicly flaunts his hard heart, can only perceive in this type of play [the *drame*] a bitter criticism of his conduct and a public reproach of his hardness." ("Il est certain que celui qui fit interdire son père, enfermer son fils, qui vit dans le divorce avec sa femme, qui dédaigne son obscure famille, qui n'aime personne, et qui fait, en un mot, profession publique de mauvais cœur, ne peut voir dans ce genre de spectacle qu'une censure amère de sa conduite, un reproche public de sa dureté.")[27] The family-centered quality of the *drame* appears in other of the many alternative terms the author uses for it, the *Tragédie domestique*. For such a play, content and form are inextricably related. The aim of representing ordinary people, in their families, as they really are, requires that the *drame* be written in prose rather than in verse: "the serious genre, ... required to show us people absolutely as they are, cannot afford the slightest departure from the language, the customs, or the dress of those it puts on the stage." ("le genre sérieux... devant nous montrer les hommes absolument tels qu'ils sont, ne peut pas se permettre la plus légère liberté contre le langage, les mœurs ou le costume de ceux qu'il met en scène.")[28] In describing the drama of *Eugénie* (1762) itself, the author insists on its familial context, in pointing out that the construction of the plot should display the unhappiness of the protagonist: "I am going therefore to surround her in such a way that her father, her lover, her aunt, her brother, and even strangers, do not take a single step, and do not say a single word that does not worsen the unhappiness which I wish to overwhelm her." ("je vais donc tellement l'entourer, que son père, son amant, sa tante, son frère, et jusqu'aux étrangers, tout ce qui aura quelque relation avec cette victime dévouée, ne fasse pas un pas, ne dise pas un mot qui n'aggrave le malheur dont je veux l'accabler aujourd'hui.")[29]

Michel-Jean Sedaine's *Le Philosophe sans le savoir* (1765) appeared only two years before Beaumarchais' *Eugénie* (1767), which was the occasion of the latter's reflections on the new drama. *Le Philosophe sans le savoir* is an excellent example of what happened to serious drama in the course of the eighteenth century. As one editor has written, "Despite the fact that the word 'comédie' appears on the title-page ... Sedaine's masterpiece is the best example ever produced of the so-called *drame bourgeois*."[30] What makes this play particularly useful for understanding the shifts in society and the family between the seventeenth and eighteenth centuries is the fact that, intentionally or not, *Le Philosophe sans le savoir* offers a point-by-point contrast to Corneille's paradigmatic *Le Cid*. Moreover, the term "tragedy" is specifically uttered by one of the main characters in Sedaine's play, and we can be assured that the author was highly conscious of writing in a genre that specifically rejects the ideological framework of the aristocratic tragedies of the previous century.

*Le Philosophe sans le savoir* stages a story that takes place within twenty-four hours, the standard duration of most seventeenth-century plays, both comedies and tragedies, and the story is quite simple. Everything happens on the eve and then the morning of the day on which the wealthy merchant, Monsieur Vanderk, is about to celebrate the wedding

# LE PHILOSOPHE
## *SANS LE SAVOIR*,
### COMÉDIE EN PROSE,
### ET EN CINQ ACTES,

Repréſentée par les Comédiens Français ordinaires
du Roi, le 2 Novembre 1765.

Par *Monſieur* S E D A I N E.

*A PARIS*,
Chez CLAUDE HERISSANT, Libraire-Imprimeur, rue Neuve Notre-Dame, à la Croix d'or.

M. DCC. LXVI.

*Avec Approbation & Privilege du Roi.*

FIGURE 7.4: Front page of *Le Philosophe sans le savoir* (1766). Wikimedia Commons.

of his daughter. There is, however, some concern that Vanderk's son is first absent and then rather distracted, with something troubling on his mind. Finally, his father learns that his son has had a quarrel in a coffee house and challenged someone to a duel. The cause of the dispute was an insulting reference to merchants made by a member of the military aristocracy. It is only on hearing of this intended duel that the father reveals to his son that they are both themselves aristocrats, that the name Vanderk is one that the father adopted in his youth when he was befriended by a generous Dutch trader, and that the father had himself fought a duel in his own youth (the result of which was that he had killed his adversary and had to flee France). Although the father does not wish his son to participate in the duel, he agrees that one must honor all one's verbal agreements ("when one has taken on a commitment towards the public, one must act on it, although it is contrary to reason, and even to nature" ["quand on a pris un engagement vis-à-vis du public, on doit le tenir, quoiqu'il en coûte à la raison, et même à la nature"]).[31] The son leaves to fight the duel and in the meanwhile the elder Vanderk cashes a letter of credit for a stranger (a Protestant aristocrat) quickly and without taking any commission—thus demonstrating outstanding probity and generosity, a new form of nobility in the merchant class that appears in the play to be at least equivalent to the officially sanctioned military and judicial aristocracies. Finally, the younger Vanderk returns from the duel, in which he showed himself willing to fight but during which he made peace with his adversary, who, for his part, also apologized for having given offense. It turns out that the gentleman whom the elder Vanderk had helped is the father of the younger Vanderk's opponent. Thus, in the end not only are individuals reconciled but, allegorically, aristocracy and bourgeoisie as well.

There are many aspects of Sedaine's play that link it to the tradition of tragedy. The protagonists are aristocrats (even though this fact does not appear at the outset of the action) and they engage in mortal combat to defend their family honor. More specifically, if we compare this play to Corneille's *Le Cid*, the son assumes the obligation of a duel to defend his father's reputation, rather than his own—thus illustrating the way tragedy inflicts often arbitrary obligations from one generation upon another. The term "tragedy" occurs in the dialogue between the Vanderks father and son in a moment of dramatic irony, which the public understands but not the father. The son, in a brief soliloquy (reminiscent of Rodrigue's monologic *stances* in *Le Cid*) debates within himself the reasons for the duel, realizing the great unhappiness he will bring upon his family on this otherwise particularly happy day, the day of his sister's wedding. His father enters, seeing his son striding back and forth as he wrestles internally with his dilemma, and asks what he is doing. The son replies, "I was speechifying; I was acting the hero." ("Je déclamais; je faisais le héros.") Upon which the father asks, "You won't act out tomorrow some stage play, a tragedy?" ("Vous ne représenterez pas demain quelque pièce de théâtre, une tragédie?")[32] So Sedaine makes it clear that what the son is about to do is appropriate for a tragedy, while at the same time pointing mockingly toward tragedy as the imposition of a hyperbolic, declamatory tradition upon real life.

While clearly reminding his audience of the tradition of tragedy, Sedaine displays a huge difference. First of all, whereas in early modern tragedy violence occurs within the family and among friends, in *Le Philosophe sans le savoir* the family (including the domestic servants) is entirely harmonious and without any conflict whatsoever. All danger of violence concerns the world outside the family. Second, in the main tragic tradition, children in some way inherit the propensity to violence from their parents. In *Le Cid* the father orders his son to fight a duel to defend the family honor and makes it clear that failure to do so would entail disinheritance. In Sedaine's play, on the contrary, the father has concealed from his son the aristocratic origin of the family precisely in order to prevent the perpetuation of the violent custom of dueling. Finally, the very fact that the elder Vanderk has taken, out of gratitude, the name and social condition of a man to whom he was unrelated, shows a new attitude toward the family itself. The Vanderk family is one that is based on diligent and honest commercial activity, and neither on inherited wealth nor prestige. A whole set of assumptions on which tragedy was based are here discarded, and yet Sedaine's play is a serious one, in which people risk their lives, and not one that it meant simply to amuse.

Thirteen years after the performance of Sedaine's play, Friedrich Schiller's *The Robbers* was published anonymously.[33] In the first words of his preface to *The Robbers* (1781), Schiller pointedly rejected the term tragedy: "This play is to be regarded merely as a dramatic narrative (*eine dramatische Geschichte*) in which, for the purpose of tracing out the innermost workings of the soul, advantage has been taken of the dramatic method, without otherwise conforming to the stringent rules of theatrical composition." ("Man nehme dieses Schauspiel für nichts Anderes, als eine dramatische Geschichte, die Vortheile der dramatischen Methode, die Seele gleichsam bei ihren geheimsten Operationen zu ertappen, benutzt, ohne sich übrigens in die Schranken eines Theaterstücks einzuzäunen.")[34] Yet translations of this play soon called it a "tragedy," and this is not surprising in view of the many ways the play refers to earlier tragedies and their characters and the way Schiller places the central tragic acts of parricide and fratricide at the center of the plot.[35] The story of *The Robbers* resembles the contemporaneous Gothic romances of Horace Walpole, Clara Reeve, and Ann Radcliffe, though without their supernatural elements. Two aristocratic brothers, Karl and Franz von Moor, are in love with the same woman, their cousin Amelia. Karl is a wayward, rebellious young man who has left home and taken up with a band of robbers, of which he has become the leader. His grotesque and dissolute brother Franz remains at home with their father, Count Maximilian von Moor, whose death Franz from the very first scene of the play is trying to provoke, first by reading a letter alleging all sorts of misdeeds on Karl's part in the hope of killing his father with a heart attack (the letter was forged by Franz) and then by a false report that Karl died through suicidal daring on the battlefield. Franz's attempt to provoke his father's death by purely psychological means includes, in the messenger's report of Karl's death, the purported dying words, that "[my father] is avenged—let him rejoice. Tell him that his curse drove me into battle and into death; that I fell in despair." ("Er ist gerochen, er mag sich weiden. Sag' ihm, sein Fluch hätte mich gejagt in Kampf und Tod, ich sei gefallen in Verzweiflung!")[36] The ruse comes close to success; Count von Moor screams and lacerates his face, exclaiming, "Woe, woe! my curse drove him into death! He fell in despair!" ("Wehe, wehe! Mein Fluch ihn gejagt in den Tod! gefallen in Verzweiflung!") The father identifies himself as the killer of his own son: "I am the father who slew his noble son! . . . Monster, monster that I am!" ("Ich bin der Vater, der seinen großen Sohn erschlug. . . Mich zu rächen, rannte er in Kampf und Tod! Ungeheuer, Ungeheuer!") In fact, the count realizes that Franz is the one who promoted his paternal alienation from Karl and seizes Franz by the neck, attempting in reality to kill the other son. In this fit of rage, the father dies—or so it seems. With the count out of the picture, Franz becomes count and plans to force Amelia to marry him, though she loathes Franz and has sworn eternal love for Karl. This leads to the strikingly macabre threat: "Franz shall be the dread phantom ever lurking behind the image of your loved, like the field-dog that guards the subterranean treasure. I will drag you to church by the hair, and sword in hand wring the nuptial vow from your soul!" ("Das Schreckbild Franz soll hinter dem Bild deines Lieblings im Hinterhalt lauern, gleich dem Verzauberten Hund, der auf unterirdischen Goldkästen liegt Kapelle schleifen, den Degen in der Hand dir den ehlichen Schwur aus der Seele pressen, dein jungfräuliches Bette im Sturm ersteigen und deine stolze Scham mit noch größerem Stolze besiegen.")[37] In announcing his plan to rape Amelia, Franz presents himself as a "phantom" even though he is alive, and Karl is supposed to be dead. This is a small reminder of a concept that unites tragedies, early modern tragic stories (*histoires tragiques*), Gothic romance, and Schiller's drama: families live in fear of the haunting that lurks within families in such a way that simply killing family members is not enough. They can return whether in physical reality or in dreams to torment other family members.[38] In fact, Karl does return, in disguise, and unleashes his band of robbers on the castle. Franz dies (though in the performance version of the script, his fate is unknown once he is turned over to the robbers to be judged), and Karl finds that his father did not really die but was imprisoned in a dungeon after his apparent natural (though provoked) death. But there is no happy ending. Although Karl would like to leave behind his life as an outlaw and marry Amelia, the robbers are outraged that he would leave them and violate his oath to the band. When he prepares to leave with them, Amelia begs him to kill her, rather to leave her in her grief, then plans to kill herself. Karl finally shoots and kills her, before he is carried away, unconscious, by the robbers.

Schiller's play, like many "dramas" (or *drames*) is overtly and insistently didactic, much more so than the earlier tragedies of the mid-to-late seventeenth century. One of the main issues is religion, both in its beliefs and institutions. While Karl is in part a Robin Hood figure willing to punish towns for their hypocrisy and bigotry, Franz is an atheistic materialist, who finds all social conventions, including honor, to be absurd. Schiller ties the religious theme—a critique of Enlightenment skepticism—with the tradition of tragedy in a striking scene in which Franz, during a night of bad dreams, fright, and delirious but repressed guilt, argues with the local clergyman. Franz asks, "which are the greatest sins—which excite him [God] to the most terrible wrath?" ("Was ist die größte Sünde, und die ihn am grimmigsten aufbringt?") The pastor replies, "I know but two. But men do not commit these, nor do men even dream of them.... Parricide is the name of the one; fratricide of the other." ("Ich kenne nur zwei. Aber sie werden nicht von Menschen begangen, auch ahnden sie Menschen nicht.... Vatermord heißt die eine, Brudermord die andere.")[39] In this scene near the end of the play, Schiller points to the same acts that were central to Aristotle's teaching of the ways to awaken the most intense emotions appropriate for tragedy.

It seems fitting to end our reflections on tragedy and the family in the Enlightenment with one of the best-known dramatic works of all time and one that announces the revolutionary changes that society and literature underwent at the turn of the nineteenth century. In 1781 the same year that Schiller published *The Robbers*, the first performance of Beaumarchais' *La Folle journée, ou le Mariage de Figaro* took place. Although this play appeared (like Sedaine's *Le Philosophe sans le savoir*) with the generic designation "comedy," its seriousness reveals it to be part of the shift away from the dominance of "tragedy" as the pre-eminent genre of serious drama, and it pursues, as Sedaine earlier did, the critique of the social basis on which tragedy as a genre had for so long been based.

The plot of *Le Marriage de Figaro* is both too complicated and too well known to require much explanation here. It is important, however, to say something about the concept of "family" that we have until now taken largely for granted. In tragedy, since Greek antiquity, the term family has usually signified something much broader than the small group of people included under that designation in the English-speaking world today. It included those related by blood (biology, genetics), by marriage, and by friendship-alliance (*philoi*) but also included servants. Indeed, the terms "family" and "house" are interchangeable throughout the periods in which tragedy was the pre-eminent theatrical genre. This is precisely why it is important to consider how the character of Figaro emerges in Beaumarchais' play as the protagonist. In tragedies such as *Phèdre*, Phèdre's nurse Œnone and Hippolyte's mentor Théramène have important roles, as does the advisor Narcisse in Racine's *Britannicus*. They could even be construed by a vernacular expression such as "handler," as when we speak of the ever-present and entirely necessary assistants without whom an important personage would be left disoriented. But such persons are only appendages of the higher-ranking individuals whom they serve and advise. Similar individuals play even more exuberant and active roles in classical comedy; and so, the Figaro of Beaumarchais' earlier play *Le Barbier de Séville* (1775) is the most clever and active character in that play, but acts essentially on behalf of his employer, Count Almaviva. With *Le Marriage de Figaro* that subordinate position is questioned and the household of tragedy, within which the domestics are appendages of their lords, flattens out into the household of drama. The vertical hierarchy of birth gives way to an individualism of merit.

In *Le Marriage de Figaro*, Count Almaviva, now married to Rosine, whom he had courted in *Le Barbier de Séville*, is planning to seduce Figaro's fiancée Susanne. There is much scheming and counter-scheming, and the effect is to show that despite the difference in rank, Figaro and the Count are basically just two men, each acting for what he considers his own interests. Figaro's long, incendiary monologue is often chosen as an exemplary statement of the mood of the non-aristocracy, the *tiers état*, at the eve of the French Revolution. The servant now declares (in absentia, in a rhetorical apostrophe) to the Count: "Just because you are a great Lord, you think you are a great genius. . . nobility, wealth, rank, official responsibilities; all that makes a man proud! What did you do to get so many things? You took the trouble to be born, and nothing more." ("Parce que vous êtes un grand Seigneur, vous vous croyez un grand génie . . . noblesse, fortune, un rang, des places; tout cela rend fier! Qu'avez-vous fait pour tant de biens? Vous vous êtes donné la peine de naître, et rien de plus.") Further, with regard to the role of family in constructing an individual's identity, Beaumarchais created for Figaro a last-minute, visibly parodic family identity through his recognition in extremis as the son of a woman he was contractually (because of a monetary debt) obliged to marry. Figaro is thus free to marry his beloved Suzanne and avoids incest. In this way the foundation of tragedy, birth into a household, with the attendant risks of misrecognition of family members, consequent violence, and incest, are doubly attacked: through Figaro's confrontation with the Count and through Figaro's vastly implausible discovery of his birth.

On the eve of the French Revolution, as the *drame* and other variant genres eclipse tragedy as the locus of serious theatrical creation, the family does not disappear, but its shape and status are far different from what they were a century and a half before. Virtue, merit, and sentimentality are henceforth the decisive terms of interaction of kin and friends.

# CHAPTER EIGHT

# Gender and Sexuality

*Sexuality and Gender in Enlightenment Tragedy*

JENNIFER ROW

When considering the relationship between tragedy, sexuality, and gender in the late early modern period (1650–1800) it is crucial to underscore that we can either consider this relation as either one of a "mirror" or one of a "motor." In the first case, we might treat early modern theater as the symptom of or as the reflection of a larger culture undergoing great change in terms of sexual identities, proclivities, intimacies, and gendered expression. This is a period bookended by a range of unruly bodies and sexual types, beginning with the poetic celebration of overt homoeroticism and the platonic masculine ideal in the mid-seventeenth century, and ending with the rule-breaking, sexually excessive Enlightenment libertine who emerges towards the end of the eighteenth century. At the same time, however, instead of solely locating examples of these kinds of bodies and desires as *mirrored* in the tragic texts of the early modern period, we can also consider drama as a *motor* of change, a provoker or instigator of new forms of relation.

The genre of tragedy itself was undergoing great shifts, from the regimented dramatic rules of French Classicism that took inspiration from Aristotelian theater theory to the Restoration stage in England, tasked with re-building dramatic culture after the theaters were re-opened. Some of the developments in the field of drama included strict rules, as in the French case, as to what could and could not be represented onstage. Christopher Wheatley summarizes that early modern theories concerning the purpose and regulations of tragedy tended to draw from Horace's philosophies of poetry (that it should be "both instructional and delightful") and from Aristotle's *Poetics*, (that the audience should find that "experience of pity and fear pleasurable in itself") to highlight that tragedy was imagined to have a didactic capacity as well as a capacity to incite a particular emotional response (pleasure, fear, pity, or horror) in the audience.[1] Taken together, the Horatian and Aristotelian theories of the theater yielded different configurations of gender and sexuality regulations onstage depending on the social mores and politics of each nation and culture. Prior to the 1660 Restoration, English Renaissance theater uniquely employed male actors and young prepubescent boys took the female roles. For scholars of queer early modern theater, the fact that many of the tenderest love scenes in English tragedy took place between two biologically male actors means that the performance context and conditions lent themselves easily to homoerotic subtexts. Therefore, pre-Restoration English theater structurally acknowledged and "hid in plain sight" the male–male connections that were so crucial both to society and to the filial rhetoric so necessary for the subject-sovereign relation, as we will explore later. In France, while female actresses were not only permitted, but also celebrated, sexuality was restricted in a less obvious sense: the banishment of the representation of corporeality onstage, in the total elimination of death, pregnancy, eating, or sex, fell under the French rules of propriety (the *bienséances*). The theater might therefore be seen as a "motor" in its capacity to stimulate the imaginations of the public and to incite the desires in the bodies of the spectators, called upon to supplement the unrepresentable and the unrepresented with their own fantasies and imaginations. Tragedy operates as a disciplinary "motor" insofar as it propelled and shaped what proper desires, relations, and intimacies ought to look like.

A first section examines gender and considers the relationship between gender and performance as well as the impact of several sub-genres of tragedy whose very plots and forms hinged on the representation of specific kinds of women (mothers, queens, widows, and victims). Sexuality is the focus of the second section, in which we consider the relevance and importance of the term "queer" as well as a few different sexual "types" as represented in Enlightenment tragedy, all the while keeping in mind that the tragic genre itself was far from monolithic across time periods and national traditions. Throughout, we shall see that due to theater's dual nature as a motor and a mirror, it stands as a powerful site to produce and *re*-produce both the norms of sex and desire as well as a spectrum of marginalized, aberrant positions.

# GENDER

The analysis of tragedy seems almost inextricable from the analysis of feminism and gender: the death of virgins, the tearful sacrifices of virtuous wives, the murderous intent of queens are all familiar and recognizable hallmarks of tragedy, as Nicole Loraux suggests in *Tragic Ways of Killing a Woman*. Loraux analyzes Attic tragedies to underscore that while women in ancient Greece were historically banned from the public sphere and relegated to the silent domain of the household, female characters died spectacular deaths onstage, eliciting pity and tears from the audience. At the same time, the tragic tales served to shore up the "heroic" nature of male action, thus ensuring that tragedy and tragic tropes cemented a gender binary between passive, pitiable women and active, assured men.

Classical Greek tragedy is particularly relevant to the period at hand (1650–1800) which begins with many scholars call the "Neoclassical" period in France due to the playwrights' self-professed relationship to the theater of the ancient past. This tie to antiquity has two major impacts on the representation of sexuality and gender. The first builds on the aforementioned theories of the theater (Horatian and Aristotelian); the implications for the tragic genre on sexuality, then, is that sexuality could either be presented in a way intended for didactic instruction, towards a moral end, or the representation of transgressive desires and deviant gender positions could be used to shock and delight audiences. Secondly, tragedies sought to rewrite or reinterpret the classical myths and plays. This is not necessarily to say that neoclassical tragedy or Enlightenment tragedy exactly mirrored the gender dynamics of sacrificial female victimhood. But the relationship between femininity and death is, of course deeply prevalent. French neoclassical tragedies such as Racine's *Iphigénie* (1674) and Corneille's *Medée* (1635) take up the same mythology as depicted in the works of Euripides, Aeschylus, and Sophocles and recount the tragic murders and suicides of the female characters.

## GENDER: SACRIFICIAL VICTIM

*Iphigénie*, to explore one example, centers on the sacrifice of the eponymous daughter of Clytemnestra and Agamemnon. Agamemnon has been informed by an oracle that the gods desire the sacrifice of his beloved daughter in order to garner favorable winds to launch the Greek ships forth to Troy. For Agamemnon, sacrificing his child will secure the glory of the Trojan War, but her death will shatter his family. If he refuses to sacrifice Iphigénie, he risks political mutiny from his allies and from his army. And yet, far from being an exact copy of the Euripidean original, Racine's play includes the innovation of the character of Ériphile, Iphigénie's enemy-friend who does not know who her parents are. The addition of Ériphile allows Racine to present a richer, more complicated portrait of female sexuality, for the two women can be considered mirror images of one other.

Iphigénie is brought to the site of sacrifice, lured by the false promise of marriage to her beloved Achille, which is but a deception and a trap. In her devotion to her filial duty, and in the pleasures of submission to the law, Iphigénie easily exchanges her desire for her future lover with the desire to please her father, and the doubled nature of the altar (the locus of both marriage and of sacrifice) facilitates this equivalence. Indeed, Iphigénie's motivations are easily summed up in a single line regarding both Achille and her father: "His glory, his love, my father, my duty." ("Sa gloire, son amour, mon père, mon devoir.")[2] For Iphigénie, the pleasures of submission to duty is the condition of her daughterly identity. In contrast, Ériphile takes pleasure in undermining Iphigénie's escape and sowing the seeds of disorder by pitting Achille against Agamemnon. Thus, as the inversed mirror of Iphigénie, for Ériphile, it is the destruction of the law is what gives her pleasure. Similarly, as the inverse to Iphigénie, the anarchic relation to the law stems from her lack of knowledge regarding her parentage and/or filial position. In the final scene it is Ériphile, instead of Iphigénie, who is revealed to be the true sacrificial victim, a role that Ériphile relishes to take on, for it affirms her own identity (and solves the mystery of her obscure parentage).[3]

As Thomas Laqueur has argued, early seventeenth-century popular and medical beliefs concerning gender adhered to a "one-sex" model inherited from Galen, a Greek second-century physician.[4] Galen's model of human sexuality envisioned female reproductive organs as the inverted (inside-out) version of the biologically "superior" male's penis and testes. As the character Suzanne in the popular pornographic dialogue *L'école des filles* states, "As for the girl, I don't know how her body is made, but I've heard tell that she has an engine on the inside, formed like that of the boy." ("Pour la fille je ne sçais comment elle est faite, mais on dit qu'elle a un engine par dedans, fait comme celui du garcon.")[5] Under the one-sex model, men and women were viewed as two endpoints on a continuum rather than being categorically different genders or sexes. This model began to fall away by the end of the seventeenth century. "Within this new framework," writes Helen E.M. Brooks, "male and female bodies existed in a horizontal, incommensurable relationship and were understood to be anatomically and qualitatively different. For the first time, the sexed body became the primary site of identity and difference and was drawn on to determine and constrain men's and women's social roles and behaviors, economic activities and sexual desires."[6] It is significant to note that such potential fungibility between the male and the female allowed for both anxiety and playfulness. On a rhetorical level, we find this slipperiness evident even in the language regarding tears and emotions which were believed to have a weakening, womanly impact. In John Dryden's *All for Love*, which we will analyze shortly, (the general and ruler) Marc Antony is criticized for being too susceptible to love and shamed as "thus altered from the lord of half mankind, / Unbent, unsinewed, made a woman's toy."[7]

FIGURE 8.1: Illustration of Act 4 of *Iphigénie*. Photo by Lebrecht Music & Arts/Alamy.

## GENDER: QUEENS

Women were not unilaterally denigrated, however. Despite social prejudices and misogynies, French neoclassical theater welcomed women as active participants in the theater world. Celebrated female actresses (such as Mademoiselle Duparc and Marie de Champmeslé) enjoyed a cult of celebrity and were famed for their acting prowess. La Champmeslé in particular also played the role of mistress and muse to Jean Racine, and he wrote some of his greatest female roles (Phèdre, Bérénice) explicitly for her. In seventeenth-century France, women also wrote for the stage (as the research of Perry Gethner has revealed) and playwrights such as Catherine Bernard (1662–1712) even were awarded prizes from the Académie française and saw her plays staged at the Comédie-Française, to great acclaim.

One of Bernard's tragedies, *Laodamie, Reine d'Epire* (1689) was met with resounding success during her day. The play centers on the queen, Laodamie, who faces difficult choices regarding the uncertain future of her country. She is betrothed to neighboring prince Attale, and their loveless marriage would ensure the security of her country. However, she is deeply in love with Gélon, the people's favorite and the intended future spouse of her younger sister Nérée. She must choose between breaking her sister's heart and ruling alongside Gélon, or allowing Nérée and Gélon to marry, thus weakening her political position. Laodamie is accidentally killed in a crowd uprising, while trying to protect Gélon, and she remains, until the end, a queen dedicated to the best interests of her country and a caring sister concerned for the best interests of her younger sibling. According to Theresa Varney Kennedy, Laodamie exhibits strengths as a "deliberative heroine" who contradicts the popular viewpoints of female-led governments at the time. Derval Conroy argues that seventeenth-century political writings, "particularly those concerning Salic Law [forged links between] gynæcocracy (government by women) and disorder."[8] Misogynistic tropes typical of the period are deployed in order to cement this association: depicting women as prevaricators, governing through emotion rather than intelligence, and avaricious for power; in contradistinction, sovereignty itself is billed as a uniquely masculine enterprise, requiring reason, cool-headedness, and emotional strength. It is therefore all the more unique to find a tragedy that not only depicts a female-led kingdom, but also spotlights the female ruler in such a way that does not denigrate or essentialize her governance abilities due to her sex. Conroy writes that *Laodamie* defies such misogynistic rhetoric insofar as "The kernel of the disorder is displaced away from the female sovereign and lies instead with her rebellious people. More specifically, it lies with the association of sovereignty with the traditionally male virtue of military prowess. Each time her possible marriage and the popular demands are referred to, it is not framed in terms of the need for male rationale [. . .] instead, it is evoked specifically and uniquely in terms of military strength."[9] It is therefore even more fitting that Laodamie does not die by any of the "traditional" means of Loraux's other tragic female figures—by knife or by hanging, whether in tragic murder or suicide—but rather, she is killed by the disorder of her own people, rendering her a uniquely deliberative and political heroine to the very end.

## GENDER: MOTHERS AND WIDOWS

The widow occupied a unique place in early modern culture. As Christian Biet underscores, the female sex was considered the weaker one and juridically had a similar status to (that of) a child, insofar as the woman needed to submit to the decisions and governance of either her father (as an unmarried woman) or to her husband. The widow held a paradoxical position of agency; while she was expected to remarry, she was no longer under her father's control and therefore held no small degree of autonomy.

> However, since the seventeenth century, women increasingly escaped the regulation exercised by their families or their husbands. Their freedom of choice following the death of their spouse, initially limited, became more and more relaxed [. . .] the widow had the choice between two ideals: the ideal of the faithful wife to her husband beyond

death, even to the point of renouncing the living world to follow her spouse to the tomb, and the idea of the virtuous woman who remarries as quickly as possible, while following the preferences of her family, in order to not remain in the sinful state of being alone, that is to say in danger of being free.

(Or, depuis le XVIIe siècle, les veuves échappent de plus en plus à la tutelle exercée par leur famille ou celle de leur mari. Leur liberté d'action après la mort de leur conjoint, d'abord limitée, devient de plus en plus large [. . .] la veuve eut le choix entre deux idéaux: l'idéal de la femme fidèle à son mari par-delà la mort et à même de renoncer au monde pour suivre son époux dans la tombe, et l'idéal de la femme vertueuse se remariant au plus vite, en suivant de préférence l'avis de sa famille, afin de ne pas rester dans le péché d'être seule, c'est à dire en danger d'être libre.)[10]

Jean Racine's 1667 *Andromaque* depicts this dilemma succinctly. In the aftermath of the Trojan War, the widowed Andromaque and her infant son Astyanax have been taken captive by Pyrrhus, the king of Épirus. Yet, it is actually the captor, Pyrrhus, who is the real prisoner, hopelessly shackled to his unrequited burning love for Andromaque. Tired of waiting, Pyrrhus threatens Andromaque with a blackmail ultimatum: either marry him or he will surrender her child to Orestes and the Greeks, who demand that the infant be handed over and executed, for fear that the boy will grow up to become like his famed warrior father Hector. Orestes' diplomatic mission to retrieve Astyanax, however, is only a pretext to return to Épire to win the heart of Hermione. While Hermione is betrothed to Pyrrhus and loves him desperately, Pyrrhus continues to long for Andromaque. His advances remain ignored, as she insists on remaining faithful to the memory of her beloved Hector. When faced with the choice to either remarry her captor Pyrrhus or to allow her son Astyanax to be executed, Andromaque responds to this terrible ultimatum with delay and hesitation. Andromaque's lagging delay to make a decision, extending over three acts of the play, has long puzzled scholars. It is Andromaque's stalling that Roland Barthes criticizes, writing: "Faced with contradictory obligations, Andromaque fails to turn to her maternal side (and if she had thought maternally, would she have hesitated even for a moment?)" ("Devant la contradiction de son devoir, ce n'est nullement sa maternité qu'Andromaque consulte [et si elle l'avait consultée, aurait-elle hésité un instant?])"[11] However, the very space of the hesitation, and the anxieties that it provokes in a domino-like effect, underscore Biet's point that the un-remarried widow was perceived as a threat to the social order.

Andromaque finally decides to marry Pyrrhus in order to save her son, and then to kill herself in order to escape the shame of marriage to her captor. However, by the end of the play, an angry mob of Greeks rises up, kill Pyrrhus, and crown Andromaque queen. Significantly, by the play's end, Andromaque has inhabited a range of roles that were typically assigned to women—mother, widow, wife, but also grieving daughter of Troy as well as unexpected queen. But Racine ingeniously employs this spectrum of feminine roles as a foil to augment the tragedy and pathos of the situation. For example, Andromaque comments on how she is only allowed to see her son once per day:

> I'm on my way to where my son is kept.
> Since once a day you suffer me to see
> All I have left of Hector and of Troy,
> I meant, my lord, to weep with him awhile:
> I have not held him in my arms today.

(Je passais jusqu'aux lieux, où l'on garde mon fils.
Puisqu'une fois le jour vous souffrez que je voie
Le seul bien qui me reste, et d'Hector et de Troie,
J'allais, Seigneur, pleurer un moment avec lui,
Je ne l'ai point encore embrassé d'aujourd'hui.)[12]

She therefore uses her position as mother to highlight the inhumanity of captivity: that unlike a "natural" situation in which a mother could caress her child as she wished, the structure of captivity and the regulation and surveillance of her motherly touch strips her of humanity. Therefore, the proposition that Pyrrhus offers—that she love him and marry him—can make no logical sense to her under these conditions of inhumanity. The play aptly illustrates the great demands early modern society placed on women to perfectly inhabit multiple contradictory, gender positions. It is thanks to the poetic language of Racine that the far-off plights of historical or mythological characters, and the gendered burdens that they face, feel especially relevant even today.

## SEXUALITY: QUEER TERMS

In Isaac de Benserade's 1634 tragi-comedy *Iphis et Iante*, the young married couple's love appears to be doomed. Iphis' male appearance is but a concealment strategy devised by Iphis' own mother to save Iphis' life; Iphis is biologically female and her father has vowed to kill any of his female offspring. Thus, when Iphis and Iante fall in love, are wed, and progress towards their tantalizing, timorous nuptial night, the play is ripe with implications concerning same-sex female desire.[13] Iphis says to Iante, fearful of revealing the truth of her biological sex:

This marriage that transforms crime to innocence
Gives full rein to my youthful desires.
I love and even if I possess, in this delay
Do you not suspect my secret torment?
(L'hymen qui convertit le crime en innocence
À mes jeunes désirs donne toute licence,
J'aime et si je possède, en ce retardement
Ne vous doutez-vous pas de mon secret tourment?)

—4.1[14]

The same-sex wedding night would not have seemed scandalous to the seventeenth-century audience, not only because of the authority of its classical source (taken from Ovid's *Metamorphoses*) but also because of a changing context in which sexuality and gender expression was only beginning to be sedimented in identity categories, and the lines between obscenity and propriety were only beginning to be traced out. Furthermore, as Joseph Harris underscores, early modern audiences were deeply confused over if sexuality between women was even possible: "Fragmentary in form and contradictory in content, discussions of the topic [of early modern lesbianism] reflect the period's great difficulty in understanding and assimilating inter-female desire ... While some medical writings associated lesbianism with 'prodigies' such as hermaphrodites or other unexplained phenomena that disrupt the natural order, other thinkers attributed it to a [Sapphic] tradition."[15] Therefore, the social legitimacy of representing same-sex desire onstage, especially between women, hovered somewhere between acceptance (because it was unthinkable that women could even desire women) and scandalous titillation.

The general social and political climate was changing during the period 1650–1800 with regards to what one might anachronously call homosexuality in contemporary terms. On the one hand, it was a period of increased regulation and punishment. Historian Katherine Crawford notes that the sixteenth and seventeenth centuries saw changing and competing notions of non-normative intimacies, or sodomy: "A capital offense in early modern France (although not often prosecuted), sodomy was conceptualized as a sin against nature. It encompassed a range of nonreproductive sexual acts that included masturbation as well as acts involving two men, a person and an animal, or a man and a woman if performed in such a way as to prevent conception."[16] The problem with the declaration of sodomy as going "against nature" is that the very sense of what was "natural" was also ambiguous. For example, even for theologian Jean Benedicti, writing in 1610 against sodomy, he struggles to pinpoint the exact "unnatural" quality to the act (or to the sin): "This sin is against the natural order because it is committed against the sexual order, a sin that is more grievous than having relations with one's sister, or even with one's own mother."[17] In an earlier period, Rictor Norton notes that in England, the Buggery Act of 1533 declaimed that "the detestable and abominable Vice of Buggery committed with mankind or beast" was a felony; the consequence of the crime of "buggery" (meaning anal penetration) was execution, often by hanging, but this English statute was only intermittently prosecute.[18] On the other hand, despite the vitriolic legal rhetoric against buggery or same-sex acts, the early modern social culture was ripe with homoerotic affection both platonically sublimated and corporeally realized. King Louis XIV's own brother enjoyed many "boy favorites" ("mignons"). While sexual behaviors were either met with a blind eye or encroaching scrutiny, many prominent courtiers frequently cross-dressed, such as the l'Abbé de Choisy, who published scandalous memoirs of his trysts "dressed as a woman" ("habillé en femme") and later served on the French ambassadorial mission to Siam in 1685.[19] Thus, we can conclude that gender and sexuality were in a state of relative fluidity, but such fluidity was nevertheless in tension with increasing prosecution.

"Queer" is a term that highlights particularities of sexuality as represented in early modern tragedy. Although "queer" itself is a modern term and concept, scholars have made the case for applying it to the early modern period. Michel Foucault contended in the *History of Sexuality* that prior to the late 1890s same-sex intimacy fell within the realm of simply deviant acts; after a certain point the "homosexual was now a species" ("l'homosexuel est maintenant une espèce")[20] as the discursive category/label emerged to concretely identify and name the "type" of person who would engage in such deviance.[21] However, as historians and scholars have underscored, this did not mean that same-sex intimacy did not exist prior to the date; it simply failed to register as such.

Queer theory differs from lesbian and gay studies insofar as the latter field has tended to recover lesbian and gay subjectivities, positions, social conditions, and sub-cultures from art, literature, and history. In contrast, "queer" can be thought of as a strategic critique of hetero-normativity. In other words, queer challenges the presumed good of heterosexual relations and the imagined normalcy of the heterosexual family unit. A queer analysis becomes most salient in neoclassical tragedy for many reasons; as a *positional* intervention, "queer" does not rely on the post 1890s identities of "lesbian" and "gay" to bring to the fore a range of other possibilities of what sexual attraction could look like; such ontological indeterminacy leaves open the field of possibility of what it can accomplish (destabilizing the socio-political order). In other words, "queer" takes Eve Sedgwick's approach that we "can't know in advance" what same-sex desire looked like in this time period, and we have to leave open the conditions of analysis that let emerge "the open mesh of possibilities, gaps, overlaps, dissonances and resonances, lapses and excesses of meaning when the constituent elements of anyone's gender, of anyone's sexuality aren't made (or can't be made) to signify monolithically."[22]

One approach that scholars of early modern sexuality have taken is to rely upon the terms and social categories of the past. Jonathan Goldberg, building on the work of historian Alan Bray, for example, highlights that the category of "sodomy" in the Renaissance (roughly 1540–1650) did not necessarily name the same-sex act that we know today. Far from being self-evident, it was a catch-all category that included "anything that threatens alliance – any sexual act, that is, that does not promote the aim of married procreative sex (anal intercourse, fellatio, masturbation, bestiality)."[23] In short, it was a term that marked a potential disturbance to the socio-sexual order of things. Rather than the transgression residing in the person, the aberrance of the act most clearly comes into focus when the person being accused "traitors, heretics or the like, at the very least, disturbers of the social order that alliance—marriage arrangements—maintained."[24] The expansive nature of "sodometrie" as Goldberg notes, resides in the ways that its slipperiness can be "mobilized in more than one direction."[25]

This is not to say that every aberrant relationship is necessarily sodomitical. It is important to highlight that same-sex desires and sodomitial intimacies were not necessarily the same thing. Certainly, there were erotics that were associated with a disruption to the social order, but same-sex desire could also serve to—paradoxically—knit together the order of society, a society that was founded on the relationships, respect, and reliance between men. Jeffrey Masten analyzes the prolific term of endearment "sweet" between male friends (as in Horatio's "Goodnight, Sweet Prince" farewell speech to Hamlet) to propose that "the rhetoric of these relationships is centrally concerned with describing ideally persons of absolute identicality, indistinguishability, and interchangeability."[26] In this latter framework, male–male friendships in particular bolster up the social fabric as well as model the behavior of love and adoration that was expected between sovereign and subject.

## SEXUALITY: SODOMITICAL AND HOMOSOCIAL

In John Dryden's *All for Love* (1677), the loves of Marc Antony illustrate both the "sodomitical" and the "homosocial" forms of queer desire. Antony appears as but a shadow of the great military and world leader that he once was. He is consistently torn between yielding to his passion for the Egyptian queen Cleopatra and the knowledge that he must leave her and resume the mantle of his sovereign duties and his family in Rome. Antony's friend Ventidius says, speaking to the eunuch Alexas:

> She has left him
> The blank of what he was.
> I tell thee, eunuch, she has quite unmanned him.
> Can any Roman see, and know him now,
> Thus altered from the lord of half mankind,
> Unbent, unsinewed, made a woman's toy[27]

Love, in this tragedy, and especially adulterous love for a foreign queen, is presented as emasculating and threatening to the socio-political order. In this light, even though the *relation* is on the surface "heterosexual," the force of their attraction has sodomitical resonance.

Dryden's tragedy also illuminates the force of homosocial bonds. At a crucial turning point, Antony reminisces about his friendship with his male friend Dolabella:

> He loved me too:
> I was his soul, he lived not but in me.
> We were so closed within each other's breasts,
> The rivets were not found that joined us first.
> That does not reach us yet: we were so mixed
> As meeting streams, both to ourselves were lost;
> We were one mass; we could not give or take
> But from the same, for he was I, I he[28]

To the contemporary reader, Antony's language expresses a rhetoric of a deeply felt love for Dolabella. However, ought we interpret this as an expression of deep friendship? Is there erotic desire present? How do we understand the historical specificity of the kind of love or intimacy that Antony conveys? Antony is swayed throughout the drama by two male friends, Ventidius (his former general) and Dolabella, who profess their (intimate and admiring) love for him and use this love to convince him to leave or commit to Cleopatra. Initially, Antony is presented in the throes of depression, "his heart a prey to black despair" (I, 61) and sleeping the morning away. Ventidius tries to rouse him to action; his deep empathy to Antony's shame elicits tears in the eyes of both men:

> V: Look, Emperor, this is no common dew.
> I have not wept this forty year, but no
> My mother comes afresh into my eyes;
> I cannot help her softness.
> ...
> A: Sure, there's contagion in the tears of friends:
> See, I have caught it too. Believe me, 'tis not
> for my own griefs, but thing—Nay, father
> V: Emperor.
> A: Emperor![29]

In this tender moment shared by the two, the outpouring of tears supersedes Ventidius' rhetoric. While Ventidius admits to a womanly, emotional "softness," it is a moment of gendered vulnerability that serves to suture the two men together. It is the intensity of their mutual sorrow and recognition of deep sameness in their affective positions that finally propels Antony to rouse himself and to move on. The re-recognition of a fallen emperor is crucial here, both politically and sexually.

## SEXUALITY: POLITICS

It is key to recall that Dryden wrote *All for Love* in 1677, during his simultaneous tenure as England's first poet laureate and Historiographer Royal. Themes in his plays were inextricable from his own position within the royal court. Previously, in 1642, with a civil war looming on the horizon, the rising Puritan faction in Parliament had succeeded in banning the staging of plays in the theater. Indeed, the "lasciviousness" that the Parliament's order condemns traces in reverse the trajectory of French theater: in France, the art form previously associated with bawdiness and charlatans was elevated to an apparatus of the Absolutist French state, whereas the imperiled English government leveraged the castigation of the theater form in order to boost an austerely conservative, Puritanical, and anti-monarchical position. The specters of deviant sexuality and the incitement of aberrant desires haunt the Puritanical positions vis-à-vis theater, in both cases, for the theater is imagined as a force that could tame sexuality (through the orderly conduct under the *bienséances*) or as a force that needed to be banished in order to outright suppress sexuality.

Following the execution of the monarch Charles I in 1649, after a bloody and bitter civil war, his son, the future Charles II, managed to escape to France, where he remained during the decade of parliamentary rule. Once Charles II was restored to power in 1660, many of his governance choices seemed to reflect his cousin Louis XIV's Absolutist style, including and not limited to the uses of theater. David Bruce Kramer underscores that Charles had developed not only a pleasurable appreciation of the genre of neoclassical tragedy, but also an understanding of its potential power and force: "Like [Cardinal] Richelieu, [Charles] took an active interest in the writing and production of plays; the king reviewed manuscripts, made detailed 'suggestions' for revision, deigned to adopt at least one play as 'his' [. . .] and personally settled disputes in the theatrical company he took under his protection."[30] The English transition from monarchy to parliamentary government and back created a paradoxical temporality in which the current governance system of re-established monarchy was simultaneously painted as restored progress *and* as outmoded forms of ruling. To aid in this shift, the theater as well as paratextual writings such as prefaces and critical pamphlets served to smooth the transition. However, the theater was not simply a manifested spectacle of glorious monarchy; theater relied upon the dramatic representation of specific kinds of gender and sexual relationships *in order to secure* the affective political orientation to monarchy.

Most crucially, *All for Love* and several other plays in the category of "heroic tragedy" promote a certain form of male–male love in order to re-establish political order. Brandon Chua suggests, following Mitchell Greenberg, that "filiation" and patriarchal forms of governance were particular values that are leveraged by restored royal power:

> seventeenth-century kingship [in France and England] depended upon an intensely emotional bond between rulers and subjects, relying heavily on a paternalistic rhetoric that naturalized political subjection by figuring the king as a loving father and representative of the common good. Royalist polemic identified familial affection as the main casualty of the illegitimate opposition put up by a restless parliament that had managed to forget its filial obligations to the king.[31]

Thus, (in *All for Love*), when Antony pays respects to the chronologically older Ventidius by calling him "father," it is significant that Ventidius invokes "Emperor" as a reply, exchanging the generational relationship (the affection between the older Ventidius and the younger Antony) for a formalized, political one. In the reversal of the honorifics, he imbues his declaration of homage—"Emperor"—with the "filial obligations" owed to the king.

Such subtleties of language highlight an aspect of gender and tragedy that would have been quite apparent to the early modern audience. Greenberg argues, analyzing the French context under King Louis XIV, that the "patriarchal, paternalistic rhetoric that played so large a role in the imaginary construction of the image of the monarch" is rooted primarily in passionate, emotional attachment to the king.[32] Tragedy's role in producing and securing the orderliness of patriarchal identities and bonds is crucial.

## SEXUALITY: *GLOIRE* AND SAMENESS

In France, for authors such as Pierre Corneille (1606–84), the harnessing of passionate attachments to a patriarchal power is not merely incidental. Like Dryden, Corneille was in the service of a monarch, more specifically in Cardinal Richelieu's Les Cinq Auteurs, a group of five authors who would realize Richelieu's vision of developing theater as a spectacular and orderly extension of sovereign power. While the collaboration was not sustained successfully, it is apparent that Corneille did adopt a particular investment in a masculine, patriarchal worldview of politics, and one that is highlighted in his tragedies. In his *Trois Discours Sur le Poème Dramatique* he writes,

> When we stage a simple love story among kings, and these tales risk no danger, either to their life or to the State, I do not think that although the characters are illustrious, the action is elevated enough to be a tragedy. Its dignity demands some great interest of state, or some passion more noble and more male than love, such as ambition or vengeance; and it should provoke fears greater than the loss of a mistress.

> (Lorsqu'on met sur scène une simple intrigue d'amour entre des rois et qu'ils ne courent aucun péril, ni de leur vie, ni de leur Etat, je ne crois pas que bien que les personnes soient illustres, l'action le soit assez pour s'élever jusqu'à la tragédie. Sa dignité demande quelque grand intérêt d'Etat, ou quelque passion plus noble et plus mâle que l'amour, telles que sont l'ambition ou la vengeance, et veut donner à craindre des malheurs plus grands, que la perte d'une maîtresse.)[33]

For Corneille, love is not worthy of being the sole plot point of a tragedy; tragedy needs to address passions of a grander scale, which he revealingly terms "more noble and more male." Love, in the Cornellian universe and as typical of many seventeenth-century French tragedies, was seen as an *obstacle* to manly glory and imagined to have a "softening" or emasculating force. It is often in Corneille's plays that characters heroically conquer their love in favor of maintaining their *gloire* (a word that exceeds mere "glory" and encompasses the notions of reputation, legacy, self-worth, and more). The action, then, is not *about* love, but rather about how love's softening force must be surmounted in order to direct attention and energies towards other passions. For example, in Corneille's *Le Cid* (1637) Chimène must confront her beloved Rodrigue, who has just killed Chimène's father in a duel in order to maintain the sense of family honor and pride. She says, "Though offending me, you prove worthy too; I must, by your death, prove worthy yet of you." ("Tu t'es en m'offensant montré digne de moi, Je me dois par ta mort montrer digne de toi.")[34] To unravel this complicated chiasmus and the uniquely gendered notion of *gloire* for Corneille, Rodrigue has successfully suppressed his feelings of love for his betrothed Chimène in order to undertake the more "noble" duty of defending his father's honor (and killing Chimène's father). In so doing, his grand gesture of repudiating soft love makes him, paradoxically, "worthy" of Chimène's affection. However, she also believes that her love makes her weak, soft, and less honorable, as she describes the fact that she too must conquer her amorous feelings for Rodrigue in order to honorably pursue justice and vengeance against him (as her father's murderer).

Corneille's *Polyeucte* (1642), set in Armenia in 230 CE, depicts the force of both the disruptive sodomitical and the sameness of the homosocial to destabilize a fragile governance context. As a colony of Rome, Armenia is managed by a Roman governor, Félix. In order to secure his foothold in the region, Félix has married his daughter Pauline off to an Armenian noble, Polyeucte, despite the fact that Pauline's heart truly belongs to Sévère, a war hero and favorite of the emperor. Félix's power is challenged when his son-in-law, Polyeucte, converts to Christianity at the behest of his friend and fellow Armenian, Néarque. The two men rush into the Roman temple, smash the idols of the pagan gods, and are promptly condemned to death for such a blasphemous transgression against the state. While Néarque is executed quickly, Polyeucte's life hangs in the balance while Pauline pleads with her father to intervene and to save him. Finally, Polyeucte's eager embrace of martyrdom inspires those around him to convert to Christianity, as they too face their imminent deaths.

FIGURE 8.2: Engraving for the frontispiece of the original 1643 version of *Polyeucte*. A Roman officer who was converted to Christianity and later martyred, smashing pagan idols in a temple. Bibliotheque nationale de France. Photo by Culture Club/Hulton Archive/Getty Images.

The play's queerness derives from the nature of Néarque and Polyeucte's relationship, described as an aberrant friendship that leads to religious and social destabilization. As Néarque convinces Polyeucte to convert in secrecy, the two men consistently posit the baptism and their relationship (to God, or perhaps to each other) as being of utmost importance, far more significant than Polyeucte's recent marriage. The opposition between heterosexual marriage and a queer same-sex friendship is even remarked-upon by other characters. Stratonice, Pauline's friend, suggests that Néarque ripped Polyeucte from Pauline's arms. Pauline's husband's conversion is depicted explicitly as a seduction:

> Néarque seduced him
> This disgraceful fruit is begotten of their old friendship
> This traitor, rather, in despite of himself
> Tearing Polyeucte from your arms, drove him to baptism.
> Behold this secret, so mysterious
> That even your inquiring love could not draw from him.
> (Néarque l'a séduit:
> De leur vieille amitié c'est là l'indigne fruit.
> Ce perfide tantôt, en dépit de lui-même,
> L'arrachant de vos bras, le traînait au baptême.
> Voilà ce grand secret et si mystérieux
> Que n'en pouvait tirer votre amour curieux.)[35]

In her discourse, Stratonice directly counter-opposes the love that Pauline can provide ("from your arms" ["de vos bras"]) with another type of generative love (amitié) that Néarque's seduction is founded upon. Painted as such, the conversion does not merely enact a change in religious or social identity, but also explicitly swaps out marital love for the "disgraceful fruit" ("l'indigne fruit") begotten of same-sex friendships.

Corneille's dramatization of the martyr tale presents the men's bonds through the subtle, repeated ways that Néarque and Polyeucte seek sameness and togetherness rather than separation and difference, similar to Jeffrey Masten's and Laurie Shannon's argument regarding the force of sameness in the Renaissance. Shannon writes, regarding Shakespearean comedy, that "in affective terms, affiliation, affinity, and attraction normally proceed on a basis of likeness, a principle of resemblance strong enough to normalize relations between members of one sex above relations that cross sexual difference."[36] Polyeucte answers Néarque's accusations of weak Christian faith by insisting upon the sameness of their passionate experiences. He says, "You don't understand me: the very same ardor burns within me / And desire only increases when the effect disappears." ("Vous me connaissez mal: la même ardeur me brûle / Et le désir accroît quand l'effet se recule.")[37]

Later, Polyeucte will even repeat Néarque's identical words back to him. When the governor Félix has Néarque executed, he asks, "And our Polyeucte saw his life cut short?" ("Et notre Polyeucte a vu trancher sa vie?") He hopes that witnessing the horrific spectacle of his friend's death will prompt Polyeucte to retract his conversion to Christianity. Albin responds, "He saw him, but alas, with an envious eye / He burns to follow him instead of backing away." ("Il l'a vu, mais hélas! Avec un oeil d'envie. / Il brûle de le suivre au lieu de reculer.")[38] Same-sex love and attachment provoke—and transcend—the most fatal and fearful displays of state violence and power.

The magnetizing force of sameness between men and the queer intimacy that it generates is deeply destabilizing on the political level. In the case of French neoclassical tragedy, we can discern a strong difference from English Restoration tragedy in which homosocial behavior and bonds between men are not valorized in the same way as they were in *All for Love*; same-sex ties in *Polyeucte* trouble the political and patriarchal order of state, society, and family. In *Polyeucte*, Pauline and Polyeucte's marriage was intended to be a securing, orderly force; the fact that Polyeucte declines his role as husband in order to follow his friend Néarque to martyrdom only redoubles the queerly sodomitical (disruptive) nature of their intense friendship.

## SEXUALITY: *HONNÊTE* AND GENDERED SALONS

When considering the role of same-sex desire, or queer erotics in tragedy, it is important to keep in mind the fact that not all forms of desire, and even "deviant" desire were monolithically coherent. In a slighter earlier period, under the reign of Charles I (1625–49), Queen Henrietta Maria introduced a vibrant salon culture into the court. According to Erica Veevers and John Fransceschina, "relations between men and women were governed by an ideal of *honnête amité*, based on mutual respect, not passion. . . . This philosophy assisted in the production of a species of homosocial theater called cavalier drama, a systematic dramatization of the action Greek romance, inhabited by Platonic characters declaiming in long, sententious speeches written in florid cadenced prose, feminist in tendency, serious, refined in tone."[39] One example of this cavalier drama, replete with intense friendships (both same-sex and cross-gender) is William Davenant's *Love and Honor* (1634) in which two men and one woman all draw upon their gallant love for the captive Evandra to justify their desires to sacrifice themselves so that she might be freed.

The cover of purely platonic friendships allowed playwrights to slide in allusions to intense male–male love. The declamations of deep respect and affection between friends becomes indistinguishable from the rhetoric of lovers. At the same time, the cross-gendering of salon culture allowed a cover to the real-life charge of same-sex intimacies. According to Lewis Seifert and Rebecca Wilkin, "The pressure on male friends to avoid homoerotic insinuations created an imperative of heterosociality of which the salon was a major beneficiary. Male friends deflected suspicions of sodomy through observable interaction with women."[40] Thus, we see even within one small historicized sub-culture of same-sex friendship and respect, the particularities of those codes of conduct impacted not only the themes of the theater, but the ways that relationships could and could not be represented.

## SEXUALITY: VIOLENCES

Neoclassical French tragedy and Restoration English tragedy used homosociality and queer/sodomitical themes in order to highlight certain ideals of gender or to emphasize political passions. However, sexual themes in these earlier tragedies can *grosso modo* be considered a technique to illustrate, whether as a means of modeling relations within patriarchal sovereignty, allegorizing political or social deviance, or fostering homosocial ties. In French seventeenth-century theater, sexuality itself, we recall, was not permitted to be represented per se onstage due to the constraints of the *bienséances*. The most explicit sexual literature appeared not onstage, but rather in other genres, such as poetry or short dialogues. By the beginning of the eighteenth century, however, sexuality became more commonly represented in the theater, and began to take on more explicitly debauched or violent representations onstage.

Since at least the Edict of Nantes (1598) the Catholic League had targeted *libertinage*, a term coined to indicate heresy and debauchery—a debauchery that was often flagrantly in defiance (or liberated from) the constraints of Church dogma. In France, Théophile de Viau, a known "sodomite," libertine and licentious poet was subject to the first obscenity trial in 1623 and was burned in effigy; his own sexual and homoerotic poetry was used as evidence against him. De Viau's own tragedy, *Pyrame et Thisbe* (1623), however, follows the conventions of propriety that governed neoclassical French tragedy. The tragedy tells the story of the star-crossed lovers Pyrame and Thisbe, whose obstacles to romantic happiness include warring families and the jealous love of the king for Thisbe. Planning to flee, lovers miss each other at their meeting point, and a series of misinterpreted cues and crossed signals results in the couple's double suicide. While the tone of this drama is remarkably subdued compared to de Viau's other poetry in which he jokes about sodomy and sexually transmitted diseases, one might also speculate that the Ovidian story of impossible love, forbidden by society, had strong resonances for him.

The surprising difference between a relatively tame drama and a more licentious philosophy also appears in the writings of the Marquis de Sade. Sade's name has become a familiar placeholder, even in contemporary popular culture, of a type of desire associated with blatant perversity and violence in eroticism. His 1795 *Philosophie dans le boudoir*, while not a drama per se, is written in the form of a dialogue and depicts the sexual corrupting and education of a young girl, incited to submit to and then to perpetrate increasingly violent and perverse sexual acts. As is the case for many erotic dialogues (for example, Aretino's *Ragionamento* [1534] or the *L'escole des filles* [1655]), the viewer is situated in a position of a voyeur, and part of the erotic pleasure is the theater-like setting of a dialogue, that offers the impression of peeping into an intimate scene staged specifically for the reader/viewer's enjoyment.[41] For Sade, the reason for such sexualized violence is not merely pure titillation. John Phillips points out that Sade's novels (and not his dramas) draw upon the tradition of Greek tragedy, in which pity and terror are staged in order to elicit catharsis.

Sade's radical philosophy is grounded in an extreme sense of freedom, a freedom that is liberated from the constraints of "reason" (that might operate on the body in the guise of Church decrees, politics, or other normative ideologies). If the Church has held up sins "against nature" as the litmus test against which all sexual transgressions were measured, including the sin of sodomy, then Sade flips such logic on its head by arguing that the category of "nature" has been constructed and deployed in order to reinforce procreative hegemonies, but it is not a moral thing in and of itself. For Sade the most "natural" is actually the sexual drive for carnal knowledge, not the artificial, restrictive suppression of the instincts. Therefore, fantasies should be enacted and pushed to their most pleasurable extremes; this, according to Sade, is what the ideal sexual body should strive for, not the end goal of reproduction within the normative family unit. The tone of Sade's dialogues is often witty and almost satirical; descriptions of what bodies can do to other bodies is shocking, but they are intercalated with philosophical asides about the liberation of the instincts. In contrast, Thomas Wynn and others have pointed out that Sade's own theater (including over a dozen plays) can be thought of as "disappointingly conventional."[42] Just as the conventionality of de Viau's *Pyrame et Thisbe* did reinforce, however fleetingly, the nature of a forbidden love that might have appealed to de Viau, similarly on Sade's stage the erotics of spectatorship might be located in "an imaginary space (psychic, physical and temporal), sequence or scenario in which specific acts may be performed."[43]

Sade offers a useful counterpart to compare to the spectacles of sexual violence characteristic of the late seventeenth-century English she-tragedy. Female actresses were increasingly allowed onstage after the Restoration and were initially a marvel for the crowds. While actresses were no longer a novelty by 1680, they were a "powerful sexual presence on the stage," according to Jean Marsden.[44] "The pathetic play, with its scenes of female suffering, incorporated the titillation of sex comedies popular in previous decades but avoided the aggressive sexuality displayed by women in the earlier plays, thus bringing the stage characters closer to popular ideals of feminine behavior."[45] Thus, even as sexuality and the female body was increasingly represented onstage, it was a representation designed to curtail and discipline the expression of sexuality, not liberate it from moral ideals of behavior as Sade's philosophies strove for.

The she-tragedy was a peculiar genre of tragedy in late Restoration England that focused on "a new kind of heroine, whose victimization provides the essential material of the plot and whose defenselessness specifically contrasts with the defiance of the passionate and ambitious female characters in the preceding heroic play."[46] In the she-tragedy the heroine is usually depicted as innocent, weak, and kind. Thomas Otway's *The Orphan*, to give one example, depicts the plight of Monima, the orphan who weds Castalio, the son of her guardian. She unwittingly commits adultery when on her wedding night her husband's debaucherous identical twin, Polydore, tricks her into sleeping with him instead. Her sexual transgression prompts a triple suicide; she poisons herself in shame and the two brothers die by the sword. The she-tragedy also conveys a penetrating, almost perverse interest in the representation of the trembling, innocent female body and a hyper-scrutinization of female sexual desire, with the end goal of both rhetoric and of the plot the sustained victimization of the female protagonist.

As Monima begs Castalio to tell her what is wrong, his reply is rife with highly misogynistic language that paints women as dangerous and hints at anxieties over maintaining masculine ideals:

> 'Tis here—'tis in my head—'tis in my heart—
> 'Tis every where: it rages like a madness,
> And I most wonder how my reason holds.
> No more, Monimia, of your sex's arts:
> They're useless all—I'm not that pliant tool;
> I know my charter better—I am man,
> Obstinate man, and will not be enslav'd![47]

In response, Monima describes her devotion to him in almost doglike or masochistic terms, desiring her abasement to him on her knees:

> Oh, kill me here, or tell me my offence!
> I'll never quit you else; but, on these knees,
> Thus follow you all day, till they're worn bare,
> And hang upon you like a drowning creature.[48]

Violence accomplishes a theatrical erotics here, but it is a violence that serves to reify the hierarchies and essentialist nature of masculinity and femininity, by denigrating women as either poisonous vixens or as innocent little birds, and by inviting the voyeuristic spectatorship of a theater that objectifies and commodifies female suffering. For Laura Brown "the defenseless woman of this distinctive dramatic form is thus a figure that fuses a variety of ideological concerns, from domestic virtue and female passivity to rape, social chaos and fetishization."[49] This is an enjoyment of violence that differs from the kind of sexual violence depicted by Sade, notably on the level of agency. In the she-tragedies, women are rarely, if ever, presented as agents of their own violent suffering; they are solely victims. In contrast, for Sade, violent sexuality is what ignites agency. "Rather than treat violence as the expression of a pre-constituted and autonomous self," argues Wynn, "one may distinguish a kind of subjection (which might be called subjectification) in which violence plays a creative or generative function"; for Sade violence is a wound (whether emotional or physical) that is the *site* of the subject, for the sensorium of pain itself awakens the body from the (numbing) constraints of the "moral" and alerts one to the contingent nature of subjectivity.[50]

## SEXUALITY: EXOTIC

Voltaire's *Zaïre* (1732), merges the suffering female protagonist of the she-tragedy with the structure of French neoclassical tragedy (written in verse, obeying the rules of propriety, limiting the action to take place in the span of one day, etc.) In the play, Voltaire depicts the plight of Zaïre, a French Christian who has been raised since infancy in the harem of Orosmane. The play is set against the backdrop of the thirteenth-century Crusades, in which the Christian French soldiers are attempting to wrest control of Jerusalem from the sultan. Onstage, however, the violence is more internal than explicit. Zaïre, poised to marry the sultan Orosmane, is unaware of her origins or her true identity; the only clue to her past is a wooden cross that was discovered on her person as a baby.

When the mysterious Nérestan returns to ransom the freedom of Zaïre and other enslaved Christians, a series of sudden reversals unfolds. Nérestan is shocked to discover that Zaïre does not wish to be freed; she will stay with her beloved Orosmane in Jerusalem. Furthermore, the one political prisoner whom Orosmane refuses to release is the deposed Christian king Lusignan, who has languished in a sunless cell for the past twenty years and must there remain due to his potential disruption to Orosmane's absolute authority. To her great surprise, Zaïre learns that Lusignan is none other than her father and Nérestan is actually her brother. Her family is devastated to realize that she will be marrying the Muslim sultan. Nérestan urges her to be rebaptized in Christianity and subsequently die for her faith, as a martyr. Meanwhile, Orosmane, unaware of the family ties that were revealed, suspects that the surreptitious on-goings between Zaïre and Nérestan indicate a romantic betrayal. The whole tragedy ends in an *Othello*-like turn, in which the racialized Muslim lover (Orosmane) is overcome by his suspicion of Zaïre's faithfulness, reinforcing the stereotype of the jealous Arab. When Zaïre rushes to meet Nérestan at night for a secret baptism, Orosmane misinterprets the meeting as a romantic tryst, and murders Zaïre in a fit of jealousy, crying out, "Miserable Zaïre, you shall not have pleasure/enjoyment!" ("Misérable Zaïre, tu ne jouiras pas.")[51] As Caroline Weber has shown, both the Muslim lover and Christian brother "recoil from her incomprehensible desire—the obscene enjoyment she would ostensibly attain through the simultaneous entertainment of mutually exclusive symbolic claims—and so work pitilessly toward its elimination."[52] Much like the she-tragedy genre, scrutiny of female sexuality contributes to the main plot, and the tragic element stems from the innocent woman's undeserving punishment.

As I have argued elsewhere, the play's drama hinges on the word *infidèle*, a term that triggers a chiasmus between faith and bond. That is to say: the love that binds Orosmane and Zaïre generates a certain type of lover's fidelity but a religious infidelity (she is aligned

FIGURE 8.3: The actor Lekain (1729–78) as Orosmane in the tragedy *Zaïre*, as performed in 1767. Drawn by Simon Bernard Lenoir (1729–91). Collection of Musée du Louvre, Paris. Photo by Fine Art Images/Heritage Images/Hulton Fine Art Collection/Getty Images.

with the *infidèle*, and violates her Christian heritage).[53] The ties that bind Zaïre to her religious faith—tenuously represented by the cross that she bears and Lusignan's narrative—cast her love to Orosmane as a national, racial, and cultural treason, or being another kind of *infidèle*. And part of the construction of Zaïre's suffering in being wrongfully accused of being *infidèle* is the careful depiction of her kindness and innocence, similar to Monima's personality. Jean-Jacques Rousseau even says, in his praise for *Zaïre* in his *Lettre à d'Alembert*:

> I would be interested to find someone, man or woman, who would dare to brag after leaving a performance of *Zaïre* that they were well-innoculated against love. For my part, I believe that I hear every spectator saying in his heart at the end of the tragedy: Ah, if only I were given a Zaïre, I would do my best so that I should not have to kill

her. If women tirelessly flock to this enchanting play and make the men come see it too, I do not believe that it's to strengthen their resolve not to imitate the example of the heroine's sacrifice that turns out so poorly for her, but it is because of all of the tragedies that are in the theater, no other demonstrates with more charm the power of love and the empire of beauty.

(Je serois curieux de trouver quelqu'un, homme ou femme, qui s'osât vanter d'être sorti d'une représentation de *Zaïre*, bien prémuni contre l'amour. Pour moi, je crois entendre chaque Spectateur dire en son cœur à la fin de la Tragédie: ah! qu'on me donne une Zaïre, je ferai bien en sorte de ne la pas tuer. Si les femmes n'ont pu se lasser de courir en foule à cette pièce enchanteresse et d'y faire courir les hommes, je ne dirai point que c'est pour s'encourager par l'exemple de l'héroïne à n'imiter pas un sacrifice qui lui réussit si mal; mais c'est parce que, de toutes les tragédies qui sont au théâtre, nulle autre ne montre avec plus de charmes le pouvoir de l'amour et l'empire de la beauté.)[54]

For Rousseau, even the most hardhearted spectator, steeled against pitiable scenes or mushy romance, would be (nevertheless) provoked to imaginative fantasy, "beyond the spectator's control." Male spectators are prompted to view themselves in Orosmane's place; they position themselves as paternalistic caretakers of a Zaïre without succumbing to the weakness of (racialized) jealousy or religious zeal. Zaïre's pureness of virtue supposedly elicits such gentlemanly compassion. An equivalent gesture of the play inspiring a man to save a helpless woman—one's own personal Zaïre—is invited by such rhetoric.

Finally, plays like *Zaïre* and Racine's *Bérénice* (1670) and *Bajazet* (1672) use foreign locations (or, often a Middle Eastern identity) in order to highlight racial and racist beliefs of the period concerning sexual difference. For the foreigner, sexual transgression is more likely, and fits of emotion, anger, and jealousy reflect the prevalent stereotypes of racialized others as "less civilized". Thus, any analysis of theater's investment in the representation of violence, especially sexualized violence, must necessarily also take into account the early modern geopolitics and the importance of racialized identities.

## CONCLUSION

One discovers that the relationship between early modern tragedy and gender and sexuality is far from being a tale of mirrored representation. Certainly, many tragedies contain themes pertaining to sex and gender, including highly gendered mythologies and histories, or sexualized encounters. But theater was itself a site that produced and negotiated richly different forms of sexual intimacy, including sodometric relationships that destabilized the social order, or homosocial ties that sutured amicable networks and connections between men. Later Enlightenment theater also ignited new forms of misogyny and racialized discourse, specifically through its depictions of gender and sexuality. While tragedy itself is an ancient and some might even argue, timeless form, it is also an art that has never ceased tarrying with the intensities and flows of gender and sexual identity.

Tragedy becomes a site that can reinforce certain normative ideas regarding expectations of gendered behavior (of a mother or a widow). However, it is not entirely a hegemonic disciplinary force; it also allows for surprising moments of troubling the norm, whether in the representation of queer intimacy or the thoughtful deliberation of a queen. It is only when we can carefully read against the grain and contextualize the particular sexual and gendered mores of the epoch that we can unearth the complexities of gender and sexuality in tragedy in the late early modern period.

# NOTES

## Introduction

1. André Green, *The Tragic Effect: The Oedipus Complex in Tragedy*, trans. A. Sheridan (Cambridge: Cambridge University Press, 1979), 7–8.
2. Steven Mullaney, *The Place of the Stage: License, Play and Power in Renaissance England* (Chicago: The University of Chicago Press, 1988).
3. Mullaney, *The Place of the Stage*, 142.
4. Louis XIV, *Mémoires*, ed. J. Longnon (Paris: Tallandier, 1978), 33. "But you must try to picture for yourself the prevailing conditions: formidable insurrections throughout the realm both before and after my majority; a foreign war where because of these internal troubles France had lost considerable advantages.... Countless plots in the Realm ... at my own court there was little disinterested loyalty, and because of that those of my subjects who appeared the most submissive were as worrisome to me and as feared as the most rebellious." Cf. also: Michel de Certeau, *La Fable Mystique*, vol. 2 (Paris: Gallimard, 1982), 32. "Such was the situation in the seventeenth century. Divisive conflicts called into question heteronomous social formations. The fatal splitting of the former religious unity gradually shifted onto the State the responsibility of representing for all members of society a reference point of stable unity. A concept of unity gradually emerged based on an inclusionary strategy, subtended by a subtle interplay of hierarchies and mediations."
5. Franco Moretti, *Signs Taken for Wonders: On the Sociology of Literary Forms* (London, Verso, 2005), 43.
6. Louis Althusser, *Lenin and Philosophy and Other Essays*, trans. B. Brewster (London, MR Press, 1971), 162.
7. Académie française, *Des sentiments de l'Académie française sur la tragi-comédie du Cid: essai sur la compétence des hommes de l'art et du public en matière de goût* (Paris: Panckoucke, 1840), 21.
8. Pierre Corneille, "Discours de l'utilité et des partis du poème dramatique," in *Trois discours sur le poème dramatique*, 1660.
9. The expression is Foucault's. Michel Foucault, *La volonté de savoir*, vol. 1 (Paris: Gallimard, 1976), 65.
10. Serge Doubrovsky, *Corneille et la dialectique du héros* (Paris: Gallimard, 1963).
11. Lucien Goldmann, *Le Dieu caché: Etude sur la vision tragique dans les "Pensées" de Pascal et dans le théâtre de Racine* (Paris: Gallimard, 1955).
12. Roland Barthes, *Sur Racine*, trans. R. Howard (New York: Hill and Wang, 1964), viii.
13. Anne Ubersfeld, *Le théâtre et la cité: de Corneille à Kantor* (Brussels: Aissa-Iaspa, 1991), 10.
14. To this list we must add a first tragedy, *La Thebaïde* (1664) then *Alexandre le Grand* (1665), which in turn was followed by his only comedy, *Les Plaideurs* (1668). Finally, the two biblical tragedies *Esther* (1689) and *Athalie* (1691) complete his dramatic output.
15. Philip Lewis, "Sacrifice and Suicide: Some Afterthoughts on the Career of J. Racine" (paper presented at North American Society for Seventeenth-Century French Literature,

7th Conference, Baton Rouge, LA, 1985), ed. S.A. Zebouni (Paris; Seattle: Papers on French Seventeenth Century Literature, 1986), 58–9. See also: Mitchell Greenberg, *Racine: From Ancient Myth to Tragic Modernity* (Minneapolis: University of Minnesota Press, 2010).
16. Corneille's *Œdipe* was first performed in 1659.
17. Marie Delcourt, *Œdipe ou la légende du conquérant* (Paris: Faculté de philosophie et lettres, 1944), 108.
18. Louis Racine, *Vie de Racine* (Paris: Les Belles Lettres, 1999), 137.
19. Sigmund Freud, *The Interpretation of Dreams* in *The Standard Edition of the Complete Psychological Works of Sigmund Freud*, vol. 4, ed. J. Strachey (London: The Hogarth Press and the Institute of Psychoanalysis, 1953), 262.
20. See, for instance, Marie-Hélèna Huet, *Rehearsing the Revolution: The Staging of Marat's Death, 1793–1797* (Berkeley: University of California Press, 1982) and Susan Maslan, *Revolutionary Acts: Theater, Democracy, and the French Revolution* (Baltimore: Johns Hopkins University Press, 2005).
21. Blair Hoxby, *What Was Tragedy? Theory and the Early Modern Canon* (Oxford: Oxford University Press, 2015).
22. Joshua Billings, *Genealogy of the Tragic: Greek Tragedy and German Philosophy* (Princeton: Princeton University Press, 2014).

## Chapter One

1. Many thanks to Joanne Brueton for the translation.
2. See Christian Biet, "L'avenir des illusions ou le théâtre et l'illusion perdue," *Littératures classiques: L'illusion au XVIIe siècle* 44 (Winter 2002).
3. Walter Benjamin, *The Origin of German Tragic Drama*, trans. John Osborne (London: NLB, 1977 [1925]).
4. Antoine Furetière, "Scaffold," in the *Universal Dictionary*, 1690.
5. César de Saint-Réal, *De l'usage de l'histoire*, ed. René Démoris and Christian Meurillon (Lille: Presses de l'Université de Lille, 1980 [1672]).
6. Pierre Corneille, "Discourse on Tragedy and on the Ways of Composing it in Accordance with Plausibility and Necessity," in *Discourse on the Dramatic Poem*, in *Trois discours sur le poème dramatique* [1660], 110.
7. See Christian Biet, *Œdipe en monarchie, tragédie et théorie juridique à l'Age classique* (Paris: Klincksieck, 1994).
8. Johann Wolfgang Goethe, "On epic and dramatic poetry," in *Correspondence Between Schiller and Goethe, from 1794 to 1805*, vol. 1, trans. George H. Calvert (New York and London: Wiley and Putnam, 1845), 387.
9. Friedrich Schiller, "Letter to Goethe, 26th December 1797," in *Correspondence*, 386.
10. Bertold Brecht, "Notes on the *Threepenny Opera*," in *The Threepenny Opera* (New York: Grove Press, 1949), 99.

## Chapter Two

1. A fuller version of this article will appear in *The Seventeenth Century*. I am grateful to Mitchell Greenberg and Richard Maber for their generosity in allowing me to publish my work in these two locations.
2. He had abandoned it following the failure of *Pertharite* in 1652.

3. La Grange, *Registre*, ed. B.E. Young and G.P. Young, 2 vols. (Paris: Droz, 1947). La Grange abandoned his summary in 1685.
4. Ibid., vol. 1, 25–7.
5. Jan Clarke, *The Guénégaud Theatre in Paris (1673–1680). Volume One: Founding, Design and Production* (Lewiston-Queenston-Lampeter: Edwin Mellen, 1998), 3–56.
6. Jan Clarke, "Part 3: 1680–1715," in *French Theatre in the Neo-Classical Era*, ed. William D. Howarth (Cambridge: Cambridge University Press, 1997), 285–90.
7. Georges Monval, *Le Premier Registre de La Thorillière (1663–1664)* (Geneva: Slatkine, 1969); William Leonard Schwartz, "Light on Molière in 1664 from *Le Second Registre de La Thorillière*," *PMLA* 53 (1938): 1054–75; Sylvie Chevalley, "Le 'Registre d'Hubert,' 1672–1673," *Revue d'histoire du théâtre* 25 (1973): 1–132.
8. Jan Clarke, *The Guénégaud Theatre in Paris (1673–1680). Volume Two: the Accounts Season by Season* (Lewiston-Queenston-Lampeter: Edwin Mellen, 2001).
9. "The Comédie-Français Registers Project," http://cfregisters.org/en/ (accessed June 1, 2018).
10. Henry Carrington Lancaster, *A History of French Dramatic Literature in the Seventeenth Century*, 9 vols. (Baltimore: Johns Hopkins University Press, 1929–42); S. Wilma Deierkauf-Holsboer, *Le Théâtre de l'Hôtel de Bourgogne*, 2 vols. (Paris: Nizet, 1968–70). On the meaning of *répertoire* in French, see Christian Biet, "Introduction: la question du répertoire au théâtre," *Littératures classiques* 95 (2018): 7–14 (7–8); and Agathe Sanjuan, "Lecture du répertoire dans les archives de la Comédie-Française," *Littératures classiques* 95 (2018): 45–54 (45). In English, *repertory* is sometimes used as a synonym for *répertoire*, but primarily refers to the performance of works in rotation and is used as a modifier ("repertory company," "repertory actor"). Throughout this article, *répertoire* refers to the catalogue of plays that can be performed by a given troupe.
11. John Lough, *Paris Theatre Audiences in the Seventeenth and Eighteenth Centuries* (Oxford: Oxford University Press, 1957).
12. Jan Clarke, "Music at the Guénégaud Theatre, 1673–1680," *Seventeenth-Century French Studies* 12 (1990): 89–110.
13. Samuel Chappuzeau, *Le Théâtre français* (1674), ed. Christopher J. Gossip (Tübingen: Gunter Narr, 2009), 104–5.
14. Ibid., 204–5.
15. Jan Clarke, "Les Conséquences pour la troupe de Molière de ses voyages à la cour, 1667–1672," in *Molière à la cour: les Amants magnifiques en 1670*, ed. Laura Naudeix, forthcoming.
16. See William L. Wiley, *The Early Public Theatre in France* (Cambridge, MA: Harvard University Press, 1960).
17. Jan Clarke, "Le Spectateur au Palais Royal et à l'Hôtel Guénégaud," in *Le Spectateur de théâtre à l'Âge Classique: XVII$^e$ et XVIII$^e$ siècles*, ed. Bénédicte Louvat-Molozay and Franck Salaün (Montpellier: L'Entretemps, 2008).
18. Barbara G. Mittman, *Spectators on the Paris Stage in the Seventeenth and Eighteenth Centuries* (Ann Arbor MI: UMI Research Press, 1984).
19. Boyer's tragedy *Judith* was so successful in 1695 that women occupied seats onstage for the first time, much to the amusement of the men in the audience (Clarke, "Part 3: 1680–1715," 371).
20. Clarke, *Guénégaud*, vol. 1, 248.
21. Maurice Descotes, *Le Public de théâtre et son histoire* (Paris: Presses Universitaires de France, 1964), 130.
22. Tristan's *Mariane* was given three times in second position in 1666–7, following Molière's *Misanthrope* (once) and Pierre Corneille's *Sertorius* (twice) (Jan Clarke, "Tristan dans les registres," *Cahiers Tristan l'Hermite* 37 [2015]: 23–45 [28]).

23. Jan Clarke, "Molière's Double Bills," *Seventeenth-Century French Studies* 20 (1998): 29–44.
24. See also Sophie Marchand, "Réflexions sur le succès théâtral à partir des nouvelles perspectives ouvertes par la base de données des registres de la Comédie-Française," *Littératures classiques* 95 (2018): 67–76 (69).
25. Chappuzeau, *Le Théâtre français*, ed. Gossip, 104.
26. Ibid., 169.
27. The proportion of old plays only dropped below 75 percent in 1667–8 (59 percent).
28. See below for Racine's *Thébaïde*, *Psyché* by Molière, Pierre Corneille, and Quinault, and *Circé* by Donneau De Visé and Thomas Corneille. The only play whose summer creation I can not explain is Louvart's *Mort d'Alexandre*.
29. Figures relate solely to public performances in Paris. Court and other private performances will be examined briefly later. Free public performances (for example to celebrate a royal birth) are also omitted.
30. Sara Harvey, "La Genèse stratifiée du répertoire de la Comédie-Française entre 1680 et 1730," *Littératures classiques* 95 (2018): 89–103 (94).
31. Jules Bonnassies, *La Comédie-Française: histoire administrative (1658–1757)* (Paris: Didier, 1874), 134.
32. Jan Clarke, "La Création d'un répertoire national: la Comédie-Française de 1680 à 1689," *Littératures classiques* 95 (2018): 77–88 (88).
33. "Naissance de la critique dramatique," https://www2.unil.ch/ncd17/index.php?extractCode=1043 (accessed June 13, 2018).
34. Jan Clarke, "Pierre Corneille dans les répertoires des troupes de Molière et de l'Hôtel Guénégaud," *Revue d'histoire littéraire de la France*, 106 (2006): 571–98.
35. François Boquet, *La Troupe de Molière et les deux Corneille à Rouen en 1658* (Paris: A. Claudin, 1858).
36. Molière, *Oeuvres complètes*, ed. Georges Couton, 2 vols. (Paris: Gallimard, 1971), vol. 1, xxvii.
37. Molière, *Oeuvres complètes*, ed. Georges Forestier and Claude Bourqui, 2 vols. (Paris: Gallimard, 2010), vol. 1, 1101.
38. *Oedipe* (1659), *Sophonisbe* (1663), *Othon* (1664), and *Agésilas* (1666) to the Hôtel de Bourgogne, and *La Conquête de la Toison d'or* (1661) and *Sertorius* (1662) to the Marais.
39. Hugh Gaston Hall, "Le Répertoire de l'Illustre Théâtre des Béjart et de Molière," *Australian Journal of French Studies* 30 (1993): 276–91. Hall points out that a portrait of Molière by Mignard shows him in the role of Pompée. (See Figure 2.1.)
40. C.E.J. Caldicott, *La Carrière de Molière entre protecteurs et éditeurs* (Amsterdam-Atlanta, GA: Rodopi, 1998), 31.
41. Virginia Scott, *Molière: a Theatrical Life* (Cambridge: Cambridge University Press, 2000), 93; and Virginia Scott, *Women on the Stage in Early Modern France 1540–1750* (Cambridge: Cambridge University Press, 2010), 150–5.
42. Molière's *L'Étourdi* was first performed in Paris in November 1658.
43. Molière, *Oeuvres complètes*, ed. Couton, vol. 1, 340.
44. "Naissance de la critique dramatique," https://www2.unil.ch/ncd17/index.php?extractCode=1043 (accessed September 10, 2018).
45. Constant Venesoen, "Molière tragédien," *XVIIe Siècle* (1969): 25–34.
46. He is not named among the cast members for Racine's *Alexandre* in 1665 (Georges Forestier, *Jean Racine* [Paris: Gallimard, 2006], 237).
47. Sabine Chaouche, *L'Art du comédien: déclamation et jeu scénique en France à l'âge classique (1629–1680)* (Paris: Honoré Champion, 2013), 298.

48. According to John Lough, ten to fifteen performances represented a modest success, fifteen to twenty-two or three a striking success, while figures in the thirties and forties were exceptional (Lough, *Paris Theatre Audiences*, 52).
49. "Naissance de la critique dramatique," https://www2.unil.ch/ncd17/index.php?extractCode=1335 (accessed June 13, 2018).
50. Pierre Corneille dedicated a madrigal to "a lady who played Night in the play *Endimion*" ("une dame qui représentait La Nuit en la Comédie d'Endymion"), usually supposed to have been Mlle Du Parc (Pierre Corneille, *Oeuvres complètes*, ed. Georges Couton [Paris: Gallimard, 1980–7], vol. 3, 102).
51. La Grange does not identify the author of this play. However, Roger Duchêne attributes it to Gilbert and describes it as a tragedy. Roger Duchêne, *Molière* (Paris: Fayard, 1998), 269.
52. Clarke, "Pierre Corneille dans les répertoires," 582–3.
53. Forestier, *Jean Racine*, 191–9. Roger Duchêne (Duchêne, *Molière*, 344) claims that Racine's play was programmed to compete with a work by Boyer at the Hôtel de Bourgogne, which argument is convincingly countered by Forestier. The two troupes did, though, compete this season with two comedies entitled *La Mère coquette*: by Quinault at the Hôtel de Bourgogne and De Visé at the Palais-Royal (ibid., 443–4).
54. Forestier, *Jean Racine*, 199.
55. This work must not be confused with Louvart's *Mort d'Alexandre*, performed at the Comédie-Française in 1684–5.
56. Forestier, *Jean Racine*, 237–8.
57. La Grange, *Registre*, ed. Young and Young, vol. 1, 81. Authors of new main plays were generally remunerated by means of two shares in the takings during the play's first run.
58. Forestier, *Jean Racine*, 241–5.
59. Duchêne, *Molière*, 479. This is the work of which Boileau famously wrote, "I saw *Agésilas*. / Alas!"
60. La Grange, *Registre*, ed. Young and Young, vol. 1, 88.
61. Chappuzeau, *Le Théâtre français*, ed. Gossip, 102.
62. Forestier, *Jean Racine*, 251.
63. Corneille, *Oeuvres complètes*, ed. Couton, vol. 3, 1533.
64. Ibid.
65. This work must not be confused with a tragedy with the same title by La Chappelle, given at the Comédie-Française in 1681–2.
66. Chappuzeau, *Le Théâtre français*, ed. Gossip, 98.
67. La Grange, *Registre*, ed. Young and Young, vol. 1, 118.
68. These plays are both referred to in the account books as "Bérénice." To avoid confusion, I have used *Tite et Bérénice* for Corneille's tragedy and the shorter form for Racine's work.
69. Duchêne, *Molière*, 591–2.
70. Forestier, *Jean Racine*, 384–7.
71. Ibid., 399.
72. Mlle Champmeslé had joined the Hôtel de Bourgogne from the Marais in 1670. Georges Mongrédien and Jean Robert, *Les Comédiens français du XVII$^e$ siècle: dictionnaire biographique* (Paris: Centre National de la Recherche Scientifique, 1981), 53.
73. Corneille, *Oeuvres complètes*, ed. Couton, vol. 3, 1606.
74. Ibid., 1312.
75. Sylvie Chevalley, "Les deux *Bérénice*," *Revue d'histoire du théâtre* 22 (1970): 91–124.
76. Henry Carrington Lancaster, *Actors' Roles at the Comédie Française according to the Répertoire des comédies françaises qui se peuvent jouer en 1685* (Baltimore: Johns Hopkins University Press, 1953), 5, 19.

77. Molière, *Oeuvres complètes*, ed. Forestier and Bourqui, vol. 2, 1483.
78. La Grange, *Registre*, ed. Young and Young, vol. 1, 124–6.
79. Jan Clarke, "Repertory and Revival at the Guénégaud Theatre, 1673–1680," *Seventeenth-Century French Studies* 10 (1988): 136–53; Jan Clarke, "Another look at the Comédie-Française as the 'Maison de Molière,'" *Nottingham French Studies* 33 (1994): 71–82 (78–9).
80. The *Dictionnaire de l'Académie Française* of 1694 defines *ambigu* as a "meal where meat and fruit are served at the same time" ("repas où l'on sert en mesme temps la viande & le fruit, ensorte qu'on ne sçauroit dire si c'est un souper ou une collation"). https://artflsrv03.uchicago.edu/philologic4/publicdicos/query?report=bibliography&head=ambigu (accessed July 31, 2018).
81. The Guénégaud also gave performances of Pierre Corneille's "heroic comedy" ("comédie héroique") *Pulchérie*, created at the Marais in 1672: four in 1673–4 and two in 1675–6, 1676–7, and 1677–8.
82. Thomas Corneille, *Circé*, ed. Jan Clarke (Exeter: University of Exeter, 1989), ii.
83. Jan Clarke, *The Guénégaud Theatre in Paris (1673–1680). Volume Three: the Demise of the Machine Play* (Lewiston-Queenston-Lampeter: Edwin Mellen, 2007), 65–92.
84. Ibid., 102–34.
85. Guy Boquet, "Naissance d'une troupe, genèse d'un répertoire," *Revue d'histoire du théâtre* 32 (1980): 105–26 (121–2).
86. As with the two *Bérénice*, I have used *Phèdre et Hippolyte* for Pradon's play and the shorter title for Racine's work.
87. Forestier, *Jean Racine*, 531, 550–2.
88. Clarke, *Guénégaud* vol. 2, 289–90.
89. This work must be distinguished from the *Coriolan* by an anonymous author created at the Comédie-Française in 1688–9.
90. Lancaster, *History*, vol. 4, 140–2.
91. I have followed Sylvie Chevalley in assuming this work to be that of Corneille (Chevalley, "Les deux *Bérénice*," 94).
92. Alexandre Joannidès, *La Comédie-Française de 1680 à 1900: dictionnaire général des pièces et des auteurs* (1901) (New York: Burt Franklin, 1971), 57.
93. Philippe Quinault, *Astrate*, ed. Edmund J. Campion (Exeter: University of Exeter, 1980), vii–viii.
94. Joannidès, *La Comédie-Française de 1680 à 1900*, 81.
95. La Grange, *Registre*, ed. Young and Young, vol. 1, 218.
96. I have again followed Sylvie Chevalley in assuming that, following the transfer of Mlle Champmeslé, it was the tragedies previously given at the Hôtel de Bourgogne that were performed at the Guénégaud and at the Comédie-Française, unless otherwise specified (Chevalley, "Les deux *Bérénice*," 94). Of these works, *Camma* alone did not subsequently form part of the repertoire of the Comédie-Française in our period.
97. Sylvie Chevalley, "Les Derniers Jours de l'Hôtel de Bourgogne," *Revue d'histoire du théâtre* 17 (1965): 404–7.
98. *Rodogune* was described by Corneille in 1676 as having been revived recently, which can only have been at the Hôtel de Bourgogne (Corneille, *Oeuvres complètes*, ed. Couton, vol. 3, 1313).
99. "*Le Nouveau Mercure Galant, octobre, tome 8, 1677, p. 200–243*," http://obvil.sorbonne-universite.site/corpus/mercure-galant/MG-1677-10?q=iphigénie#mark1 (accessed August 4, 2018).
100. Lancaster, *History*, vol. 4, 155–6.
101. La Grange, *Registre*, ed. Young and Young, vol. 1, 237.

102. "*Mercure Galant*, septembre 1681 [tome 9], p. 366–379," http://obvil.sorbonne-universite.site/corpus/mercure-galant/MG-1681-09?q=oreste#mark1 (accessed August 6, 2018). On the partiality of the *Mercure galant*, see Clarke, *Guénégaud* vol. 3, 48–57.
103. Chevalley, "Les Derniers Jours de l'Hôtel de Bourgogne."
104. "*Mercure Galant*, juin [tome 6], 1679, p. 279–285," accessed August 13, 2018, http://obvil.sorbonne-universite.site/corpus/mercure-galant/MG-1679-06?q=belonde#mark1. This document enables us to add *Polyeucte* to the list of plays given at the Hôtel de Bourgogne.
105. Since 1688–9 is the end of the period under examination, subsequent seasons have not been trawled for information. Where it is stated that plays were given in repertory, this means in this context "up to 1688–9."
106. For example, when first revived, the sequence of performances was as follows: July 22, *Endimion*; July 23, *Fâcheux* (by Molière) and *Crispin bel esprit* (by La Tuillerie); July 24 and 25, *Endimion*; July 26, *Mère coquette* (by Quinault); July 27, *Endimion*. Henry Carrington Lancaster, *The Comédie-Française 1680–1701: Plays, Actors, Spectators, Finances* (Baltimore and London: Johns Hopkins University Press and Oxford University Press, 1941), 30.
107. Corneille, *Oeuvres complètes*, ed. Couton, vol. 2, 1396–7.
108. In his obituary of Thomas, De Visé claimed to have collaborated with him on a number of spectacular works, but only those that had been successful: "*Mercure Galant*, janvier 1710 [tome 1], p. 270–299," accessed August 13, 2018, http://obvil.sorbonne-universite.site/corpus/mercure-galant/MG-1710-01#MG-1710-01_270.
109. Clarke, *Guénégaud* vol. 3, 277–383. It is no doubt significant that *La Pierre philosophale* flopped in February 1681 and *Endimion* was revived in July.
110. According to La Grange, the machines for *Andromède* cost 12,921 *livres*, whereas the expenses for the preparation of *Circé* had been 10,842 *livres* (La Grange, *Registre*, ed. Young and Young, vol. 1, 171, 300).
111. De Visé's *comédie-héroïque*, *Le Mariage de Bacchus et d'Ariane*, created at the Marais in 1672, and given five performances in 1685–6 might also be included here. As we have seen, the Comédie-Française would return to machine tragedy again in 1705, with its revival of *Circé* with a new prologue and *intermèdes* by Dancourt.
112. Jean de La Fontaine, *Oeuvres diverses*, ed. Jean Marmier (Paris: Gallimard, 1968), 483.
113. Assuming these roles reverted to Mlle Champmeslé on the merger, with Mlle Bellonde as second choice if she were elsewhere or indisposed. Alain Couprie, *La Champmeslé* (Paris: Fayard, 2003), 230.
114. Pierre Corneille's last theatrical work was *Suréna* in 1674, while Racine abandoned the professional stage in 1677, following the production of *Phèdre*.
115. Victor Fournel, "Contemporains et successeurs de Racine: les poètes tragiques décriés, Le Clerc, l'abbé Boyer, Pradon, Campistron," *Revue d'histoire littéraire de la France* 27 (1920): 233–58.
116. Catherine Bernard's *Laodamie* has been omitted because it was subsequently revived at the Comédie-Française after 1689.
117. As Sara Harvey notes, "the creations of tragedies are more difficult to maintain in the long term." ("les créations de tragédies se maintiennent plus difficilement sur le long terme.") Harvey, "La Genèse stratifiée du répertoire," 96.
118. Clarke, *Guénégaud* vol. 1, 200–7.
119. "*Le Nouveau Mercure Galant*, janvier–mars, tome 1, 1677, p. 47–54IV," http://obvil.sorbonne-universite.site/corpus/mercure-galant/MG-1677-03?q=rodogune#mark1 (accessed August 30, 2018).
120. Corneille, *Oeuvres complètes*, ed. Couton, vol. 3, 1313.

121. "*Le Nouveau Mercure Galant*, octobre, tome 8, 1677, p. 200–243," http://obvil.sorbonne-universite.site/corpus/mercure-galant/MG-1677-10?q=iphigénie#mark1 (accessed August 4, 2018).
122. "*Mercure Galant*, mars [tome 3], 1678, p. 379–381," http://obvil.sorbonne-universite.site/corpus/mercure-galant/MG-1678-03?q=corneille#mark1 (accessed August 4, 2018). This must have been at the Hôtel de Bourgogne because *Polyeucte* was not added to the Guénégaud repertoire until June 1681.
123. "*Mercure Galant*, août [tome 9], 1679, p. 259–359," http://obvil.sorbonne-universite.site/corpus/mercure-galant/MG-1679-09?q=sertorius#mark1 (accessed August 6, 2018). Marie-Louise d'Orléans had married Charles II of Spain by proxy on August 30.
124. "*Mercure Galant*, septembre 1681 [tome 9], p. 366–379," http://obvil.sorbonne-universite.site/corpus/mercure-galant/MG-1681-09?q=oreste#mark1 (accessed August 6, 2018). *Oreste* by Le Clerc and Boyer was created at the Comédie-Française on October 10, 1681.
125. "Mercure Galant, avril 1681 [tome 4], p. 327–344," http://obvil.sorbonne-universite.site/corpus/mercure-galant/MG-1681-04?q=sigaral#mark1 (accessed August 6, 2018).
126. "Mercure Galant, mai [tome 5], 1682, p. 190–196," http://obvil.sorbonne-universite.site/corpus/mercure-galant/MG-1682-05?q=venceslas#mark1 (accessed August 6, 2018).
127. Bibliothèque-Musée de la Comédie-Française, R14, Registre 1682–1683, 291v.
128. See, for example, William S. Brooks and P.J. Yarrow, *The Dramatic Criticism of Elizabeth Charlotte, duchesse d'Orléans* (Lewiston-Queenston-Lampeter: Edwin Mellen, 1996), 101.
129. Note that the last two were not performed at court in this period.
130. Bibliothèque-Musée de la Comédie-Française, 1AA 1680–1700, 1AA 1683, 3–7. Extracts from these letters were first published by Sylvie Chevalley in Chevalley, "Les deux *Bérénice*," 94–6.
131. Pierre Pasquier, *Le Mémoire de Mahelot: mémoire pour la décoration des pièces qui se représentent par les Comédiens du Roi* (Paris: Champion, 2005), 219, 337.
132. Harvey, "La Genèse stratifiée du répertoire," 97–8.

## *Chapter Three*

1. For France, see Martine de Rougemont, *La Vie théâtrale en France au XVIII$^e$ siècle* (Paris: Champion, 1988), 279–313; Max Fuchs, *La Vie théâtrale en province au XVIII$^e$ siècle* (Paris: Droz, 1933); Rahul Markovits, *Civiliser l'Europe. Politiques du théâtre français au XVIII$^e$ siècle* (Paris: Fayard, 2014) and Lauren Clay, *Stagestruck: The Business of Theater in Eighteenth-Century France and its Colonies* (Ithaca: Cornell University Press, 2013). For England, see John C. Greene, *Theatre in Dublin, 1745–1820: A Calendar of Performances* (Bethlehem, PA: Lehigh University Press, 2012) and Elizabeth Maddock Dillon, *New World Drama: The Performative Commons in the Atlantic World, 1649–1849* (Durham: Duke University Press, 2014).
2. Henri Louis Lekain, *Réflexions destinées à êtres mises sous les yeux de nos seigneurs les Premiers Gentilshommes de la Chambre*, quoted in Sabine Chaouche, *La Mise en scène du répertoire à la Comédie-Française (1680–1815)* (Paris: Champion, 2013), vol. 1, 148.
3. See the database of the Comédie-Française Registers Project, http://cfregisters.org.
4. Lauren Clay, "The Strange Career of Voltaire, Bestselling Playwright of Eighteenth-Century France," in *The Eighteenth-Century French Stage Online*, ed. Sylvaine Guyot and Jeffrey Ravel (Cambridge: MIT Press, 2018), online.
5. Quoted in Chaouche, *La Mise en scène de repertoire à la Comédie-Française (1680–1815)*, vol. 1, 147.
6. Ibid., 169.

7. Jacqueline Razgonnikoff, "Les Théâtres nationaux à l'écoute de la vie du peuple. Créations et réactions, d'une scène à l'autre (Théâtre de la Nation et Théâtre de la République)," *Studi Francesi* 169, 57.1 (2013): 27–39.
8. Martial Poirson, "Introduction," in *Le Théâtre sous la Révolution française. Politique du répertoire (1789–1799)*, ed. Martial Poirson (Paris: Desjonquères, 2008), 34.
9. Pierre Frantz, "Le Moment Voltaire," in *The Eighteenth-Century French Stage Online*.
10. Judith Milhous, "Theater companies and regulation," in *The Cambridge History of British Theatre*, ed. Joseph Donohue (Cambridge: Cambridge University Press, 2005), vol. 2, 122–3.
11. George Winchester Stone, "The Making of the Repertory," in *The London Theater World, 1660–1800*, ed. Robert D. Hume (Carbondale: Southern Illinois University Press, 1980), 194–5.
12. Charles Beecher Hogan, *Shakespeare in the Theatre, 1701–1800* (Oxford: Clarendon Press, 1952).
13. Judith Milhous, "Reading Theater History from Account Books," in *Players, Playwrights, Playhouses: Investigating Performance, 1660–1800*, ed. Michael Cordner and Peter Holland (Basingstoke: Palgrave Macmillan, 2007), 126.
14. Robert D. Hume, "Theatres and Repertory," in *The Cambridge History of British Theatre*, vol. 2, 68.
15. Henri-Louis Lekain, *Mémoires, publiés par son fils aîné* (Paris: Colnet, Debray, Mongie, 1801), 104.
16. Laurence Marie, *Inventer l'acteur. Émotions et spectacle dans l'Europe des Lumières* (Paris: PUPS, 2019).
17. Eugène Green, *La Parole baroque* (Paris: Desclée de Brouwer, 2001); Sabine Chaouche, *L'Art du comédien. Déclamation et jeu scénique en France à l'âge classique (1629–1680)* (Paris: Champion, 2001).
18. David Garrick, *The Journal of David Garrick* (New York: Modern Language Association of America, 1939), quoted in Laurence Marie, *Inventer l'acteur*, 232.
19. Pierre Frantz, *L'Esthétique du tableau dans le théâtre du XVIII$^e$ siècle* (Paris: Puf, 1998).
20. Fiona Ritchie, *Women and Shakespeare in the Eighteenth Century* (Cambridge: Cambridge University Press, 2014), 113–14.
21. Martine de Rougemont, *La Vie théâtrale*, 135–41.
22. Michel-Jean Sedaine, Preface to *Maillard*.
23. "Letter from November 17, 1760," in *Correspondance*, ed. Theodore Besterman, vol. 6 (Paris: Gallimard, 1981), 93.
24. *La Scène en contrechamp. Anecdotes françaises et traditions de jeu au siècle des Lumières*, ed. Sabine Chaouche (Paris: Champion, 2005), 133.
25. Joseph de La Porte and Jean Marie Bernard Clément, *Anecdotes dramatiques* I (Paris: Veuve Duchesne, 1775), 563.
26. Antoine Lilti, *The Invention of Celebrity*, trans. Lynn Jeffress (Cambridge: Polity Press, 2017).
27. Judith Milhous, "Reading Theater History from Account Books," 123.
28. See for example the *Mémoires secrets de Bachaumont*, January 1762.
29. Joseph Roach, "Public Intimacy: The Prior History of 'It,'" in *Theatre and Celebrity in Britain, 1660–2000*, ed. Mary Luckhurst and Jane Moody (Basingstoke and New York: Palgrave, 2005), 24–5.
30. Chris Rojek, *Celebrity* (London: Reaktion, 2001).
31. Felicity Nussbaum, *Rival Queens: Actresses, Performance, and the Eighteenth-Century British Theater* (Philadelphia: University of Pennsylvania Press, 2010), 80–1.

32. Thomas Thomson, "Celebrity and Rivalry: David [Garrick] and Goliath [Quin]," in *Theatre and Celebrity*, 135–6.
33. Judith Milhous, "Company Management," in *The London Theater World, 1660–1800*, ed. Robert D. Hume (Carbondale: Southern Illinois University Press, 1980), 22; Claude Alasseur, *La Comédie-Française au XVIII<sup>e</sup> siècle* (Paris: Mouton, 1967).
34. Felicity Nussbaum, *Rival Queens*, 51.
35. Judith Milhous, "Reading Theater History from Account Books," 118.
36. Daniel Roche, *Humeurs vagabondes. De la circulation des hommes et de l'utilité des voyages* (Paris: Fayard, 2003), 859–921.
37. Tragedy, however, represented a very small percentage of the repertoire performed in European courts. See Rahul Markovits, *Civiliser l'Europe*, 97–8.
38. Alain Viala, *Naissance de l'écrivain. Sociologie de la littérature à l'âge classique* (Paris: Minuit, 1985).
39. Gregory Brown, *A Field of Honor: The Identities of Writers, Court Culture and Public Theater in the French Intellectual Field from Racine to the Revolution* (New York: Columbia University Press, 2002), 18.
40. See Déborah Blocker, *Instituer un "art." Politiques du théâtre dans la France du premier XVII<sup>e</sup> siècle* (Paris: Champion, 2009).
41. Martial Poirson, "L'auteur dramatique: vedette contrariée du premier champ théâtral (XVII–XVIII<sup>e</sup> siècles)," in *Le Sacre de l'acteur. Émergence du vedettariat théâtral de Molière à Sarah Bernhardt*, ed. Florence Filippi, Sara Harvey, and Sophie Marchand (Paris: Armand Colin, 2017), 112.
42. Brown, *A Field of Honor*, 153–63.
43. Viala, *Naissance*, 183–238.
44. The account given by Boursault, at the start of *Artémise et Poliante* (1670), of the play's premiere is eloquent on this point. On Racine's career, see Alain Viala, *Racine. La stratégie du caméléon* (Paris: Seghers, 1990).
45. See Robert Darnton, "The Facts of Literary Life in Pre-Revolutionary France," in *The Political Culture of the Old Regime*, ed. Keith Michael Baker (Oxford: Pergamon, 1989), 261–91; Brown, *A Field of Honor*, 57–8.
46. Paulina Kewes, *Authorship and Appropriation. Writing for the Stage in England, 1660–1710* (Oxford: Clarendon Press, 1998), esp. 12–31.
47. Michael R. Booth et al., eds., *The Revels History of Drama in English. 1750–1880*, vol. 4 (London: Methuen, 1975), 43 sqq.
48. Misty Anderson, "Women Playwrights," in *The Cambridge Companion to British Theatre. 1730–1830*, ed. Jane Moody and Daniel O'Quinn (Cambridge: Cambridge University Press, 2007), 145–58.
49. Roger Chartier, *Publishing Drama in Early Modern Europe* (London: British Library, 1999), 51–73.
50. See Georges Forestier, *Jean Racine* (Paris: Gallimard, 2006), 258 sqq.
51. Logan Connors, *Dramatic Battles in Eighteenth-century France. Philosophes, anti-philosophes and polemical theatre* (Oxford: Voltaire Foundation, 2012), 219–26.
52. Sophie Marchand, "'L'Auteur! L'auteur!' ou quand l'auteur se donne en spectacle. Rites de reconnaissance, évolution du rapport de force et définition du fait théâtral dans la seconde moitié du XVIII<sup>e</sup> siècle," in *Diversité et modernité du théâtre du XVIII<sup>e</sup> siècle*, ed. Guillemette Marot-Mercier and Nicholas Dion (Paris: Hermann, 2014), 41–60.
53. On this point, see Jeffrey Ravel, "Le théâtre et ses publics. Pratiques et représentations du parterre à Paris au XVIII<sup>e</sup> siècle," *Revue d'histoire moderne et contemporaine* 49.3 (2002): 92.

54. For France, John Lough, *Paris Theatre Audiences in the Seventeenth and Eighteenth Centuries* (Oxford: Oxford University Press, 1957); Henri Lagrave, *Le Théâtre et le public à Paris de 1715 à 1750* (Paris: Klincksieck, 1972); Rougemont, *La Vie théâtrale en France*, chs. 3 and 9; Jeffrey S. Ravel, *The Contested Parterre. Public Theater and French Political Culture (1680–1791)* (Ithaca-London: Cornell University Press, 1999). For England, Harry William Pedicord, *The Theatrical Public in the Time of Garrick* (Carbondale: Southern Illinois University Press, 1954); Leo Hughes, *The Drama Patrons. A Study of the Eighteenth-Century London Audience* (Austin: University of Texas Press, 1971); Frances M. Kavenik, *British Drama. 1660–1779. A Critical History* (New York: Twayne, 1995), 1–25.
55. Samuel Pepys, *The Diary of Samuel Pepys (1660–68)*, ed. Robert Latham and William Matthews (Berkeley: University of California Press, 1970–83), vol. 8, 71–2; vol. 9, 195.
56. Ravel, "Le théâtre et ses publics," 102–5.
57. Kristina Straub, "The Making of an English Audience: The case of the footmen's gallery," in *The Cambridge Companion to British Theatre. 1730–1830*, 131–43.
58. On the history of the notion of "audience" in seventeenth-century France, see Hélène Merlin-Kajman, *Public et littérature en France au XVII$^e$ siècle* (Paris: Les Belles Lettres, 1994).
59. Sylvaine Guyot and Clotilde Thouret, "Des émotions en chaîne: représentation théâtrale et circulation publique des affects au XVII$^e$ siècle," *Littératures classiques* 68 (2009): 225–41.
60. See especially Pierre François Godard de Beauchamps, *Recherches sur les théâtres de France* (Paris: Prault, 1735).
61. "Preface," quoted in Emmett L. Avery, *The London Stage, Part 2: 1700–1729* (Carbondale: Southern Illinois UP, 1960), clxvii.
62. Ibid., cxiv, clxii–clxiii.
63. *Journal de politique et de littérature* (juillet 1777), 307–8.
64. On all of this, see Ravel.
65. Martial Poirson, "Le spectacle est dans la salle. Siffler n'est pas jouer," *Dix-huitième siècle* 149 (2017): 57–74.
66. Pierre Frantz, "Les échos de la Révolution," in *Le Théâtre français du XVIII$^e$ siècle*, ed. Pierre Frantz and Sophie Marchand (Paris: L'Avant-Scène, 2009), 507–15.
67. Sophie Marchand, *Théâtre et pathétique au XVIII$^e$ siècle. Pour une esthétique de l'effet dramatique* (Paris: Champion, 2009).
68. Charles Élie, marquis de Ferrières, *Mémoires du marquis de Ferrières* (Paris: Baudouin frères, 1821), quoted in Razgonnikoff, "Les Théâtres nationaux," 28.
69. Charles-Guillaume Étienne, Alphonse Martainville, *Histoire du théâtre français depuis le commencement de la Révolution jusqu'à la réunion générale* (Paris: Barba, 1802), 34.

## Chapter Four

1. See Christian Meier, *The Political Art of Greek Tragedy*, trans. Andrew Webber (Baltimore: Johns Hopkins University Press, 1993), 166 and Demonsthenes, *On the False Embassy*, 247.
2. Christian Meier, "Greek Drama and Political Theory," in *The Political Art of Greek Tragedy*, 74. See also Jonathan Strauss, *Private Lives, Public Deaths: Antigone and the Invention of Individuality* (New York: Fordham University Press, 2013), 16–17.
3. Jean-Pierre Vernant and Pierre Vidal-Naquet, *Myth and Tragedy in Ancient Greece*, trans. Janet Lloyd (New York: Zone Books, 1990), 27.
4. Sophocles, *Œdipus at Colonus*, ll. 969–73.

5. As Gabriela Basterra has written, "[i]f the protagonists of tragedy cooperate with their own death, . . . they do so in order to occlude the fact that the gods themselves are at fault" *Seductions of Fate: Tragic Subjectivity, Ethics, Politics* (New York: Palgrave MacMillan, 2004), 5. Cf. 30–4.
6. I have argued elsewhere that the concepts of self and other were fluid in fifth-century Athens and that Greek tragedies from this period express the frustrated desire to invent the human individual. But this very aspiration marks a profound concern about self and other—and the apportioning of guilt between them—even if their definitions and contours were unclear. See Jonathan Strauss, *Private Lives*, 16–48.
7. René Girard, *La Violence et le sacré* (Paris: Albin Michel, 1990), 458–9.
8. Martin Heidegger, *Introduction to Metaphysics*, trans. Gregory Field and Richard Polt (New Haven: Yale University Press, 2000), 166.
9. Walter Benjamin, *The Origin of German Tragic Drama*, trans. John Osborne, intro. George Steiner (New York: Verson, 2009).
10. Kant, "An Old Question Raised Again. . ." trans. Lewis Beck et al., in *The Conflict of the Faculties: Der Streit der Fakultäten*, trans. Mary J. Gregor (New York: Abaris, 1979), 153.
11. See Louis-Henri de Loménie, *Mémoires inédits de Louis-Henri de Loménie, comte de Brienne Secrétaire d'État sous Louis XIV*, ed. F. Barrière, vol. 2 (Paris: Ponthieu et Cie., 1828), 158 (my translation).
12. Jean-Marie Apostolidès, "Idéologie concretisée," in *La Roi-machine: Spectacle et politique au temps de Louis XIV* (Paris: Minuit, 1980). See also Louis Marin, *Le Portrait du roi* (Paris: Minuit, 1981) for a semiotics of royal power in sixteenth-century France, and Claire Goldstein, *Vaux and Versailles: The Appropriations, Erasures, and Accidents That Made Modern France* (Philadelphia: University of Pennsylvania Press, 2008), for a reading of Versailles and its gardens as physical representations of monarchy. Michel Foucault describes the "éclat des supplices," or the spectacularly semiotic nature of punishments as expressions of royal power that was codified in Louis XIV's *ordonnance de 1670*; see *Surveiller et punir: Naissance de la prison* (Paris: Gallimard [NRF], 1975), 36–72. "Le supplice," he writes, "a donc une fonction juridico-politique. Il s'agit d'un cérémonial pour reconstituer la souveraineté un instant blessée. Il la restaure en la manifestant dans tout son éclat. L'exécution publique, aussi hâtive et quotidienne qu'elle soit, s'insère dans toute la série des grands rituels du pouvoir éclipsé et restauré . . .; par-dessus le crime qui a méprisé le souverain, elle déploie aux yeux de tous une force invincible" ("Torture has a juridical and political function. It is a ceremonial to restore a wounded sovereignty. It restores sovereignty by showing it off in all its glory. Public execution, as hasty and banal as it may be, fits into the entire series of great rituals of power eclipsed and restored . . .; over and above the crime that has mocked the sovereign, it displays invincible force before the eyes of all") (52).
13. See *Vaux and Versailles*, 156–74. In describing one such guidebook by Claude Denis, Goldstein writes: "As he attempts to elucidate the meaning of the statues, paintings, and sculptural décor, Denis instructs the reader or visitor in the proper relationship vis-à-vis Versailles. One enters with 'a respectful step' and observes with 'a modest gaze.' The power and sublime *je ne sais quoi* of Versailles are transmitted and created with his choice of descriptive words" (160).
14. Pierre Corneille, *Trois Discours sur le poème dramatique*, ed. Bénédicte Louvat and Marc Escola (Paris: Flammarion, 1999), 70–1.
15. Corneille, *Trois discours*, 72–3.
16. Hélène E. Bilis, *Passing Judgment: The Politics and Poetics of Sovereignty in French Tragedy from Hardy to Racine* (Toronto: University of Toronto Press, 2016), ix.

17. Bilis, *Passing Judgment*, 3–4.
18. John D. Lyons, *The Tragedy of Origins: Pierre Corneille and Historical Perspective* (Stanford, CA: Stanford University Press, 1996), xii.
19. Lyons, *Origins*, xiii–iv.
20. Nicole Loraux writes: "By its very nature, tragedy entails an *opposition of two discourses*, an *agon logon*," in *L'Invention d'Athènes: Histoire de l'oraison funèbre dans la "cité classique"* (Paris: Payot, 1981), 217.
21. Lyons, *Origins*, 3 (cf. xiv–xv).
22. Corneille, *Le Cid*, 5.7.30.
23. Lyons, *Origins*, 9. Mitchell Greenberg makes a similar observation about *Le Cid* and Corneille's later *Cinna*, arguing that they both represent the emergence of a centralized monarch and the archaic or heterosynchronous resistance to his authority in *Subjectivity and Subjugation in Seventeeth-Century Drama and Prose: The Family Romance of French Classicism* (Cambridge: Cambridge University Press, 1992), 54–60.
24. Corneille, *Le Cid*, 5.7.39–47.
25. Ibid., 5.7.15–16.
26. Greenberg, *Subjectivity*, 19.
27. Ibid., 22.
28. Lyons, *Origins*, 181–4.
29. Greenberg, *Subjectivity*, 19–20, 125–6.
30. Jean Racine, *Britannicus*, ed. F.M. Warren (New York: Henry Holt and Company, 1909), 5.8.1764.
31. Jacques Brunschwig, "Aristote et l'effet Perrichon," in *La Passion de la Raison: Hommage à Fernand Alquié*, ed. Jean-Luc Marion and Jean Deprun (Paris: Presses Universitaires de France, 1983), 376.
32. Heidegger, *Introduction to Metaphysics*, 157. For an extensive treatment of this question in the politics, culture, and tragedies of fifth-century BCE Athens, see Strauss, *Private Lives*, especially 5–8.
33. Through a reading of Lacan's essay on the "mirror stage," Greenberg understands subjectivity as the individual's integration into a symbolic system structured around the nominal law of a paternal figure (19–20). The monarch embodies that paternal figure: "As the prince becomes the center of History, the main agent of human affairs, so too does he become the symbol of subjectivity as the focal point of legal, grammatical, and sexual authority" (49).
34. "A punctum ... quod esset firmum & immobile": Descartes, *Méditations métaphysiques. Objections et réponses suivies de quatre lettres*, ed. Jean-Marie Beyssade and Michelle Beyssade (Paris: Garnier-Flammarion 1979), 78.
35. Fragment 265 (Brunschwicq 348) in Blaise Pascal, *Œuvres complètes*, ed. Jacques Chevalier (Paris: Gallimard [Pléiade], 1954), 1150.
36. Greenberg, *Subjectivity*, 153.
37. Jean Touchard, ed., *Histoire des Idées Politiques* (Paris: Presses Universitaires de France, 1959), 342.
38. Ernst H. Kantorowicz, *The King's Two Bodies: A Study in Medieval Political Theology*, intro. by Conrad Leyser, preface by William Chester Jordon (Princeton: Princeton University Press, 2016).
39. Greenberg, *Subjectivity*, 3.
40. *Pascal's Pensées*, trans. W.F. Trotter, intro. T.S. Eliot (New York: Dover Publications, 2003 [1958]), 84. Translation modified to fit the purpose of the text. The original text comes from Fragment 230 (Brunschwicq 294) in Pascal, *Œuvres complètes*, 1150.

41. Ernst Cassirer, *The Philosophy of the Enlightenment*, trans. Fritz C.A. Koelln and James Pettegrove (Princeton, New Jersey: Princeton University Press, 1951), 7–8.
42. Denis Diderot, d'Alembert et al., eds. *Encyclopédie ou Dictionnaire raisonné des sciences, des arts et des métiers, par une société de gens de lettres*, vol. 5 (Paris: Briasson, David l'aîné, Le Breton, & Durand, 1751), 116.
43. Diderot and d'Alembert, *Encyclopédie*, 132.
44. Louis-Antoine-Léon de Saint-Just, "De la nature," in *Œuvres completes*, ed. Anne Kupiec and Miguel Abensour (Paris: Gallimard [Folio], 2004), 1067.
45. Ibid.
46. Emmet Kennedy et al. *Theater, Opera, and Audiences in Revolutionary Paris: Analysis and Repertory* (Westport, CT: Greenwood Press, 1996), 87.
47. See ibid., 57 and 87.
48. Ibid., 60.
49. Ibid., 57.
50. Ibid., 53.
51. Ibid., 51.
52. Ibid., 57.
53. Marie-Joseph Chénier, "*Charles IX*," in *Théâtre de M.-J. Chénier* (Paris: Foulon et Cie, 1818), 5.2.182.
54. Chénier, "*Caïus Gracchus*," ibid., 1.4.390.
55. Chénier, "*Charles IX*," ibid., 2.3.140.
56. Ibid., 5.4.189.
57. Chénier, "*Caïus Gracchus*," ibid., 1.2.382.
58. Ibid., 1.4.381.
59. Ibid., 2.2.400.
60. See, for example, where Drusus addresses the assembled populace: "What! The representatives of Roman greatness [i.e., the senators], have they then earned your hatred?" ("Quoi! Les représentans de la grandeur romaine [i.e., les sénateurs] / Ont-ils donc en effet mérité votre haine?") Ibid., 2.2.398; "You, descendants of Mars, come, in the name of the laws, and retake your rights from these usurpers and may a people who are king in name at last cease to be slaves: it is time to subjugate a senate that defies you; it is time to abolish the distinctions of rank." ("Vous, descendans de Mars, venez, au nom des lois, / Sur des usurpateurs reconquérir vos droits. / Qu'un peuple roi de nom cesse enfin d'être esclave: / Il est temps d'abaisser un sénat qui vous brave;/Il est temps d'abolir la distance des rangs.") Ibid., 1.4.392.
61. Kant, "An Old Question. . ." 152–3. See also Marie-Hélène Huet, *Rehearsing the Revolution: The Staging of Marat's Death 1793–1797*, trans. Robert Hurley (Berkeley: University of California Press, 1982).
62. Jules Michelet, *Histoire de la Révolution française*, vol. 2 (Paris: Gallimard [Pléiade], 1952), 174 (quoted and translated by Huet, *Rehearsing the Revolution*, 1).
63. Huet, *Rehearsing the Revolution*, 30.
64. Jean-Jacques Rousseau, "Lettre à d'Alembert," in *Œuvres complètes de J. J. Rousseau*, ed. Ch. Lahure, vol. 1 (Paris: Hachette, 1856), 178.
65. Ibid., 188–90.
66. Ibid., 260.
67. Ibid., 263.
68. Ibid.
69. Saint-Just, "Carnet," in *Œuvres*, 1128–9.
70. Ibid., 1129.

71. Susan Maslan, *Revolutionary Acts: Theater, Democracy, and the French Revolution* (Baltimore, MD: Johns Hopkins University Press, 2005), 3.
72. See ibid., 34 and 68.
73. Maximilien Robespierre, *Pour le bonheur et pour la liberté: Discours*, ed. Yannick Bosc, Florence Gauthier, and Sophie Wahnich (Paris: La Fabrique, 2000), 196.
74. Saint-Just, "Discours sur le jugement de Louis XVI," in *Œuvres*, 482.
75. Diderot and d'Alembert, *Encyclopédie*, 116.
76. "Sur les principes de morale politique qui doivent guider la Convention Nationale dans l'administration intérieure de la République, Séance du 17 pluviôse, an II [February 5, 1794]," in *Œuvres de Maximilien Robespierre*, ed. Marc Bouloiseau and Albert Soboul, vol. 10 (Paris: Presses Universitaires de France, 1967), 354.
77. G.W.F. Hegel, *The Phenomenology of Spirit*, trans. A.V. Miller, Foreword and Analysis by J.N. Findlay (Oxford: Oxford University Press, 1981 [1977]), 360. For an extended analysis of this passage, see Jonathan Strauss, *Subjects of Terror: Hegel, Nerval, and the Modern Self* (Stanford, CA: Stanford University Press, 1998), 12–16.
78. Ibid., "[T]he government, for its part, has nothing specific and outwardly apparent by which the guilt of the will opposed to it would be demonstrated. . . . *Being suspected*, therefore, takes the place, or has the significance and effect, of *being guilty*."
79. Basterra, *Seductions of Fate*, 63 and 67–105.
80. Ibid., 1 and 14–37.
81. Quoted in Bilis, xii. Bilis herself writes about "the role theater played in legitimizing political power" in seventeenth-century France (x).

## Chapter Five

1. Louis Riccoboni, *Reflexions historiques et critiques sur les differens theatres de l'Europe. Avec les Pensées sur la Declamation* (Paris: de l'imprimerie de Jacques Gerin, quay des Augustins, 1738), vii.
2. Riccoboni, *Reflexions*, 105. For more on this anecdote, Christopher Semk, *Playing the Martyr. Theater and Theology in Early Modern France* (Bucknell University Press, 2017), 1–4.
3. On the work of Dutch and German theorists, see James R. Parente, *Religious Drama and the Humanist Tradition. Christian Theater in Germany and in the Netherlands, 1500–1680* (Leiden: Brill, 1987).
4. M. Fumaroli, "*Sacerdos sive rhetor, orator sive histrio*: rhétorique, théologie et moralité du théâtre en France de Corneille à Molière," in *Héros et orateurs* (Genève: Droz, 1990), 449–91.
5. Christian Delmas, *Mythologie et mythe dans le théâtre français: 1650–1676* (Geneve: Droz, 1985), 8.
6. François Hédelin, abbé d'Aubignac. *La Pratique du Théâtre*, ed. Hélène Baby (Paris: Honoré Champion, 2011), 450.
7. Lynette R. Muir, *Love and Conflict in Medieval Drama: The Plays and Their Legacy* (New York: Cambridge University Press, 2007), 4–5.
8. D'Aubignac, *La Pratique*, 265. Cf Aristotle, *Poetics* 1449a10-15.
9. D'Aubignac, *La Pratique*, 703–4.
10. Laurent Thirouin, *L'Aveuglement salutaire. Le réquisitoire contre le théâtre dans la France classique* (Paris : Honoré Champion, 1997), 12.
11. Fabien Cavaillé, "Les temps du théâtre. Organisation et déroulement de la séance," in *La Représentation théâtrale en France au XVIIe siècle*, ed. Pierre Pasquier and Anne Surgers (Paris: Armand Colin, 2011), 38–9.

12. Samuel Chappuzeau, *Le Théâtre français* (Paris: chez Michel Mayer, 1674).
13. Cavaillé, "Les temps du théâtre," 40.
14. D'Aubignac, *La Pratique*, 407.
15. Léon de Saint-Jean, *Les Divins paradoxes de l'Eucharistie* (Brussels: Jean Mommart, 1663), 184.
16. Bossuet, Jacques-Béninge. *Maximes et réflexions sur la comédie* (Paris: Jean Anisson, 1694), 13.
17. Tertullian, *On Spectacles*, X.95.
18. Armand de Bourbon Conti. *Traité de la comédie et des spectacles selon la tradition de l'Eglise tirée des Conciles et des Saints Pères* (Paris: chez Louis Billaine, 1667), 45–6.
19. Pierre Nicole. *Les Imaginaires, ou lettres sur l'hérésie imaginaire* (Liège: Adolphe Beyers, 1667), 425.
20. Marie-Thérèse Mourey, "Littérature, politique et religion en Silésie au XVIIe siècle: La guerre des mots et ses arcanes," *Dix-septième siècle* 273, no. 4 (2016): 649–60.
21. Pierre Corneille, "Trois Discours sur le poème dramatique," in *Œuvres complètes* III (Paris: Gallimard, 1987), 118.
22. Jean-Pierre Perchellet, *L'Héritage classique. La tragédie entre 1680 et 1814.* (Paris: Honoré Champion, 2004), 281.
23. Jean Racine, *Phèdre*, 5.6.1498–1570.
24. See most recently M. da Vinha, A. Maral, and N. Milovanovic, eds., *Louis XIV. L'image et le mythe* (Rennes-Versailles: PUR-CRCV, 2014). See also Peter Burke, *The Fabrication of Louis XIV* (New Haven: Yale University Press, 1994).
25. Pierre de Villiers, "Entretiens sur les tragédies de ce temps" (1675), in Jean Racine, *Œuvres complètes*, ed. Georges Forestier, vol. 1 (Paris: Gallimard, 1999), 787.
26. François Fénelon, "Lettre à l'Académie," in *Œuvres complètes* 2 (Paris: Gallimard, 1997), 1169.
27. Ibid., 1172.
28. Charles de Saint-Évremond, "De la tragédie ancienne et moderne," in *Œuvres choisies de Saint-Évremond* (Paris: Didot, 1852), 136–44.
29. Gérard Sabatier, *Versailles, ou la disgrâce d'Apollon* [1999] (Versailles-Rennes: CRCV-PUR, 2016).
30. See Robert S. Miola, *Early Modern Catholicism: An Anthology of Primary Sources* (Oxford: OUP, 2007), 329.
31. Jean-Marie Valentin, *Le Théâtre des Jésuites dans les pays de langue allemande (1554–1680)*. 3 vols. (Bern, 1978). See also Fidel Rädle, "Jesuit Theatre in Germany, Austria, and Switzerland," in *Neo-Latin Drama in Early Modern Europe*, ed. Jan Bloemendal and Howard Norland (Leiden-Boston: Brill, 2013), 185–292.
32. Louis J. Oldani and Victor R. Yanitelli, "Jesuit Theater in Italy: Its Entrances and Exit," *Italica* 76.1 (Spring 1999), 24.
33. Henry Carrington Lancaster, *A History of French Dramatic Literature in the Seventeenth Century. Part IV: The Period of Racine. 1673–1700*, 2 volumes (Baltimore: Johns Hopkins University Press, 1940), Vol. 1, 327.
34. See Henry Carrington Lancaster, *Sunset: A History of Parisian Drama in the Last Years of Louis XIV* (Baltimore: Johns Hopkins University Press, 1945) 82–98. Cf. Mireille Herr, *Les Tragédies bibliques au XVIIIe siècle* (Paris-Genève: Champion-Slatkine, 1988).
35. Derek Hughes, *Culture and Sacrifice* (Cambridge: Cambridge University Press, 2007), 103.
36. Lancaster, *French Dramatic Literature*, Part 4, Vol 1, 318.

37. Louis Racine, *Mémoires sur la vie de Jean Racine*, 2 vols. (Lausanne-Genève: Chez Marc-Michel Bousquet et Cie, 1747), Vol 1, 239.
38. Lancaster, *French Dramatic Literature*, Part 4, Vol 1, 332.
39. Jacques-Béninge Bossuet, "Oraison funèbre de Michel le Tellier," in *Œuvres* (Paris: Gallimard, 1961), 183.
40. Anne-Marguerite Petit du Noyer, *Mémoires de Madame Du Noyer, première partie* (Amsterdam, par la Compagnie, 1760), 378.
41. Anthony Gable, "Tragedy, Discontent and the Question of Kingship 1685–1715," *Seventeenth-Century French Studies* 9 (1987), 168–91, 182.
42. Jérôme Brillaud, "La Jouissance de la vérité ou le plaisir tragique selon le Chancelier d'Aguesseau" *French Studies* 62, no. 2 (April 2008): 150–61.
43. Jérôme Brillaud, "La Coupe d'Atrée: Crébillon et la réinvention du théâtre tragique au 18ᵉ siècle," *Dalhousie French Studies* 78 (2007): 35–7.
44. Perchellet, *L'Héritage classique*, 335.
45. Voltaire, *Oedipe*, 4.1.951–2.
46. Caroline Weber, "Voltaire's 'Zaïre': Fantasies of Infidelity, Ideologies of Faith," *South Central Review* 21, no. 2 (2004): 57.
47. Sophie Marchand, *Théâtre et pathétique au XVIIIe siècle : pour une esthétique de l'effet dramatique* (Paris: Honoré Champion, 2009).
48. See Pannill Camp, *The First Frame: Theatre Space in Enlightenment France* (Cambridge: Cambridge University Press, 2014).
49. Diderot, "De la poésie dramatique," in *Œuvres esthétiques*, ed. P. Vernière (Paris: Classiques Garnier, 1994), 231.
50. Paul Friedland, *Political Actors: Representative Bodies and Theatricality in the Age of the French Revolution* (Ithaca: Cornell University Press: 2003), 86–9. See also James H. Johnson, *Listening in Paris: A Cultural History* (Berkeley: University of California Press, 1995).
51. An ample account of this evening is given by Marvin Carlson, *Voltaire and the Theater of the Eighteenth Century* (Westport and London: Greenwood Press, 1998), 151–3.
52. Hugh Barr Nisbet, *Gotthold Ephraim Lessing: His Life, Works, and Thought* (Oxford: Oxford University Press, 2015), 218.
53. Friedrich Schiller, "Theater Considered as a Moral Institution" (1784), in *Essays Aesthetical and Philosophical* (London: George Bell & Sons, 1910), 334. See also Theodore Ziolkowski, *Scandal on Stage: European Theater as Moral Trial* (Cambridge: Cambridge University Press, 2009), 15–17.
54. Michael J. Sosulski, *Theater and Nation in Eighteenth-Century Germany* (Aldershot and Burlington: Ashgate, 2007). See also Blair Hoxby, *What Was Tragedy?: Theory and the Early Modern Canon* (Oxford: Oxford University Press, 2015), 14–16.
55. Michael Green, "Kheraskov and the Christian Tragedy," *California Slavic Studies* 9 (1967): 1–25.
56. Elise Kimerling Wirtschafter, *The Play of Ideas in Russian Enlightenment Theater* (DeKalb, IL: NIU Press, 2003), 175.
57. Annelle Curulla, "False Frocks: Chénier's *Charles IX* and the Debate on Religious Costume in Parisian Theater, 1789–901," *Restoration and 18th-Century Theatre Research* 29, no. 1 (2014): 97–116.
58. Chénier, "Discours préliminaire," in *Théâtre*, 250.
59. See Christoph Schmitt-Maaß, Stefanie Stockhorst, and Doohwan Ahn, eds., *Fénelon in the Enlightenment: Traditions, Adaptations, and Variations* (Amsterdam: Brill, 2014).

## Chapter Six

1. Pedro José Bermúdez de la Torre y Solier, *Triunfos del Santo Oficio Peruano. Relacion panegyrica, historica, y politica del auto publico de fè celebradoen [Lima] 23. de diziembre del Año de 1736* (Lima: Imprenta Real, 1737), fol. 17v ("Relacion Panegyrica, Historica, y Politica," foliation is non-consecutive). Except where I cite to an English edition, all translations are mine.
2. Nicolás Flores' "Relación del auto grande de la Inquisición que se celebró en la Plaza Grande de Lima el día 23 de diciembre del año de 1736," in Jerry Williams, "A New Text in the Case of Ana de Castro: Lima's Inquisition on Trial," *Dieciocho: Hispanic Enlightenment*, 24:1 (2001), 49–51, 56–8. On the untranslatable word *"desengaño"* (here, both "disillusionment" and "revelation") see Mercedes Allendesalazar, "Desengaño," in Barbara Cassin, ed. *The Dictionary of Untranslatables: A Philosophical Lexicon* (Princeton: Princeton University Press, 2014), 206–210.
3. Bermúdez, *Triunfos*, fol. 17v.
4. See the description of the 1639 Lima *auto*, reproduced in Jerry M. Williams, ed. *Theatre of Infamy: Autos de Fe in Peru. Inquisition, Trial, and Sentencing Records, 1639–1749* (Potomac, MD: Scripta Humanistica, 2015), 50 (and 318–19 on Bermúdez' reiteratation of similar sixteenth-century arguments).
5. See, for instance, Guillaume de Ségla, *Histoire tragique, et arrests de la Cour de Parlement de Tholose* (Paris: Robinot, 1613); François de Rosset, *Les histoires tragiques de nostre temps* (Cambray: Jean de la Riviere, 1614); *Sad and Bloody Newes from Yorkshire* (London: Edwards, 1663); *Chamberlain's Tragedy* (N.p., n.p., c.1671).
6. Rosset, *De groote schouw-plaets der jammerlijcke bloed-en-moord geschiedenissen*, trans. Simon de Vries (Utrecht: Johannes Ribbius, 1670).
7. *Memoirs of the Two Last Years of the Reign of that Unparallell'd Prince, of Ever Blessed Memory, King Charles I* (London: Robert Clavell, 1702), 251; John Gauden, *The Bloody Court, or, The Fatall Tribunall* ([London]: G. Horton, [1660?]), title page; Andrew Marvell, *The Poems and Letters of Andrew Marvell*, 3rd edition, vol. 1, ed. H.M. Margoliouth (Oxford: Clarendon Press, 1971), 92.
8. François Babié de Bercenay, *Correspondance politique et confidentielle inédite, de Louis XVI* (Paris: Debray, 1803), 118; "Observations on the Unhappy Reverse of Fortune Experienced by the Late Queen of France," *Lady's Magazine* 24 (December 1793), 624.
9. *Fin tragique de Louis XVI* (Paris: n.p., 1793); *Fin tragique de la reine de France Maria Antoneta* ([Paris?; London?, n.p., 1793?]).
10. *The Triumphs of Divine Justice, over Bloody and Inhumane Murtherers and Adulterers* (London: H. Nelme, 1697), title page.
11. Drawing and quartering (etc.) in fact persisted well into the nineteenth century (the last breaking was in Prussia in 1841) but were enacted only on corpses.
12. The first book of Reynold's *Triumphs* appeared in 1621. The frontispiece appeared in 1635 in the first complete edition.
13. *The Holy Bible Conteyning the Old Testament and the New: Newly Translated* (London: Robert Barker, 1611). sig. A5r. *Blood for Blood: Or Murthers Revenged* by "T. M." (Oxford, 1661) (a retelling of Reynolds) adds several recent execution narratives.
14. *A Full and the Truest Narrative of the Most Horrid, Barbarous Unparalled Murder, Committed on the Person of John Knight, [. . .] by the Desperate and Bloody Hand of Nathaniel Butler* (London: n.p., 1657), 6.
15. See Reynolds, *Triumphs*, I, XVII, XVIII, XXIV, XXVIII.
16. Ibid., title page.

17. Henning Grosse, *Tragica, seu, Tristum historium de poenis criminalibus et exitu horribili* ([Eisleben]: Henning Grosse, 1598), title page; Rosset, *Histoires* (title page).
18. For these words in titles, see, for instance: Rosset, *Histoires*; Reynolds, *Triumphs*; Henry Arthington, *The Seduction of Arthington by Hacket* (London: Thomas Man, 1592); *Discours tragique et pitoyable sur la mort d'une jeune damoiselle* (Paris: A. Du Brueil, 1597).
19. *England's Black Tribunall* (London: J. Playfield, 1660), 167.
20. Ibid., 163, 166.
21. Ibid., 164–6, 168–9 (italics removed).
22. Ibid., 167.
23. *The True and Perfect Speeches of Colonel John Gerhard upon the Scaffold at Tower-Hill [and] the Speech of the Portugal Ambassadors Brother upon the Scaffold* (London: C. Horton, 1654), 8.
24. *England's Black Tribunall*, 167.
25. Ibid.
26. Ibid., 160.
27. Ibid.
28. *True and Perfect Speeches*, 8.
29. Joseph Sevin, Comte de Quincy, *Mémoires du Chevalier du Quincy*, vol. 1 (Paris: Librairie Renouard, 1898), 115.
30. Ibid.
31. Nicolas de Gueudeville, *L'Esprit des cours de l'Europe*, vol. 1 (The Hague: François L'Honoré, 1699), 155.
32. François Gayot de Pitaval, *Causes célèbres et intéressantes, avec les jugemens qui les ont décidées*, vol. 4 (Paris: T. Legras, 1735), 30.
33. Anne Marguerite Petit Du Noyer, *Letters from a Lady at Paris to a Lady at Avignon*, 2nd edition, vol. 2 (London: W. Mears and J. Browne, 1716), 37 (letter 24). Published as quasi-fictional letters but clearly reflecting first-hand experience.
34. Ibid., 37–8.
35. Gueudeville, *L'Esprit*, vol. 1, 166.
36. Du Noyer, *Letters*, vol. 2, 37–8.
37. Ibid., vol. 2., 38.
38. François Gastaud, *Oraison funèbre de Madame Tiquet* (Cologne: P. L'Enclume, 1699), 21, 23–4.
39. Ibid., 24.
40. Ibid., 18, 20.
41. Ibid., 25.
42. Ibid., 4, 18–19.
43. Ibid., 27.
44. Ibid., 26.
45. Pierre Barthès, "Les heures perdues de Pierre Barthès, maître répétiteur en Toulouse," unpublished notebooks, Rosalis (Bibliothèque numérique de Toulouse), notebook 5, 145. (Notebook number precedes page number in my citations.)
46. Ibid., notebook 5, 68. (Describing the execution of the Grenier brothers, the last Huguenots executed in France.)
47. Ibid., notebook 4, 1.
48. António José da Silva, *Vida do Grande Dom Quixote de la Mancha*, translated in Lúcia Helena Costigan, *Through Cracks in the Wall: Modern Inquisitions and New Christian Letrados in the Iberian Atlantic World* (Boston: Brill, 2010), 184. Translation modified.

49. Ibid.
50. Bernard Mandeville, *An Enquiry into the Causes of the Frequent Executions at Tyburn* (London: J. Roberts, 1725), 6.
51. Ibid., 19.
52. Ibid., 20–3.
53. Ibid., 25.
54. Ibid., 25–6.
55. Ibid., 42, 25.
56. Ibid., 32.
57. Ibid., 25.
58. Ibid., 37.
59. Ibid.
60. Ibid., 18.
61. Ibid., 25.
62. Ibid., 24.
63. Ibid., 36.
64. Ibid., 5–6.
65. Ibid., 43.
66. Ibid., 41–2.
67. Ibid., 41.
68. Ibid., 42.
69. Ibid.
70. Ibid.
71. See, e.g., Pieter Spierenburg, *The Spectacle of Suffering: Executions and the Evolution of Repression: From a Pre-Industrial Metropolis to the European Experience* (Cambridge: Cambridge University Press, 1984), ix–x.
72. Mandeville, *Enquiry*, 43.
73. Ibid., 20.
74. Ibid., 42.
75. Ibid., 36.
76. Ibid.
77. Ibid.
78. Ibid.
79. Ibid., 43.
80. Ibid., 24, 41–2.
81. Ibid., 42, 45.
82. All Bermúdez quotes below are from his *Triunfos*, fol. 17r–17v.
83. Flores, "Relación," 57–8.
84. René Descartes, *The Passions of the Soul and Other Late Philosophical Writings* (Oxford: Oxford University Press, 2015), 25.
85. Ibid., 29.
86. René Rapin, *Reflections on Aristotle's Treatise of Poesie* (London: H. Herringman, 1674), 115–16.
87. Jean-Baptiste Du Bos, *Critical Reflections on Poetry, Painting, and Music*, vol. 1 (London: John Nourse, 1748), 9.
88. Ibid., 10.
89. Anthony Ashley Cooper, 3rd Earl of Shaftesbury, *Characteristics of Men, Manners, Opinions, Times*, vol. 2 (London: John Darby, 1711), 64–5.
90. Ibid.

91. Ibid.
92. Francis Hutcheson, *An Inquiry into the Original of our Ideas of Beauty and Virtue* (London: W. and J. Innys, et al., 1725), sig. A7r.
93. Ibid., 217.
94. Ibid., 219–20.
95. Hutcheson, *An Essay on the Nature and Conduct of the Passions and Affections* (London: John Smith and William Bruce, 1728), 237.
96. See Richard Ward, ed. *A Global History of Execution and the Criminal Corpse* (Houndmills, Basingstoke, Hampshire: Palgrave Macmillan, 2015), 3–4, for a helpful summary. In London, executions multiplied five-fold in the second half of the eighteenth century. Between 1770 and 1868, crowds of 3000–7000 were standard, crowds of 35,000 were common, and some executions drew crowds of nearly 100,000 (V.A.C. Gatrell, *The Hanging Tree: Execution and the English People 1770–1868* [Oxford: Oxford University Press, 1994], 7, 616–19).
97. See Spierenburg, *Spectacle*, 72–3; John McManners, *Death and the Enlightenment: Changing Attitudes to Death among Christians and Unbelievers in Eighteenth-Century France* (Oxford: Clarendon Press, 1981), 389.
98. See Caroline Walker Bynum, *The Resurrection of the Body in Western Christianity, 200–1336* (New York: Columbia University Press, 1995). Officially, resurrection did not in fact depend on the state of the body at death, but many believed it did.
99. Quoted in Richard J. Evans, *Rituals of Retribution: Capital Punishment in Germany, 1600–1987* (Oxford: Oxford University Press, 1996), 122.
100. Quoted in Spierenburg, *Spectacle*, 72–3. For similar examples in France, see François Lebrun, *Les Hommes et la mort en Anjou aux 17e et 18e siècles: essai de démographie et de psychologie historiques* (Paris: Mouton, 1971), 420.
101. Quoted (as apocryphal) in Gatrell, *Hanging Tree*, 318n31.
102. See Steven Wilf, "Imagining Justice: Aesthetics and Public Executions in Late Eighteenth-Century England," (1993), 57. (Also see 63–75 on Hanway, Turner, and Skinner).
103. Jonas Hanway, *The Defects of Police the Cause of Immorality, and the Continual Robberies Committed, Particularly in and about the Metropolis* (London: J. Dodsley, and Brotherton and Sewell, 1775), 243 (emphasis added).
104. Ibid., 244.
105. Ibid., 246.
106. Ibid., 245.
107. For a helpful corrective, see Simon Devereaux, "Recasting the Theatre of Execution: The Abolition of the Tyburn Ritual," *Past & Present* 202, no. 1 (February 2009), 127–74. As Devereux notes (140), many towns removed executions from the city outskirts to jails near city centers: Chelmsford in 1785; Oxford in 1787; Liverpool in 1788; and York and Aylesbury in 1805. Devereux (151–4) notes an additional motivation for the change: the urban working classes could attend executions without missing an entire work day.
108. Barnard Turner and Thomas Skinner, *An Account of Some Alterations and Amendments Attempted in the Duty and Office of the Sheriff of the County of Middlesex and Sheriffs of the City of London* (London, Stephen Clark, 1784), 24.
109. Ibid., 26.
110. Ibid., 24.
111. Ibid.
112. Ibid., 17.
113. Ibid., 27–8.
114. Ibid., 28.

115. Ibid., 29.
116. Ibid., 30.
117. See, similarly, Hanway, *Defects*, 242, 245.
118. Edmund Burke, *A Philosophical Enquiry into the Origin of our Ideas of the Sublime and Beautiful*, ed. Adam Phillips (Oxford: Oxford University Press, 1990), 43. (Were the audience to learn of execution in an adjoining square, "the emptiness of the theatre would [. . .] proclaim the triumph of the real sympathy.")
119. John Villette, *A Genuine Account of the Behaviour, Confession, and Dying-Words of William Hawke and William Jones* (London: H. Turpin, et al., 1774), 22.
120. James Thacher, *A Military Journal During the American Revolutionary War, from 1775 to 1783* (Boston: Richardson & Lord, 1823), 272. (Describing the 1780 execution of John André.)
121. *The Last Dying Words, Speech, and Confession of the 5 Malefactors who were Executed at Tyburn near York.* ([York?], n.p., [1792?]).
122. *An Account of the Life, Death, and Writings, of the Rev. Dr. Dodd* (London: n.p., 1777), 56.
123. See, however, McManners, *Death*, 380, for examples of late retributive discourse, and Immanuel Kant's *Metaphysics of Morals* (1797) for a non-theological revival of retributism.
124. John Villette, *A Genuine Account of the Behaviour and Dying-Words of Daniel Perreau and Robert Perreau* (London: the Author, [1776?]), 20.
125. Barthès, *Heures perdues* [1764], notebook 5, 164.
126. Cesare Beccaria, *On Crimes and Punishments*, trans. David Young (Indianapolis, IN: Hackett, 1986), 49–50.
127. Ibid., 49, 52.
128. Ibid., 47, 49, 52.
129. Ibid., 50–1.
130. Ibid., 47, 51.
131. Ibid., 37, 47, 49.
132. Ibid., 49.
133. Ibid., 81.
134. Ibid., 7.
135. Ibid.
136. Ibid.; Cesare Beccaria, *Dei delitti e delle pene*, ed. Gianni Francioni and Luigi Firpo (Milan: Mediobanca, 1984), 26.
137. Beccaria, *On Crimes*, 7.
138. Ibid.
139. Ibid., 51.
140. Ibid., 50.
141. Denis Diderot, *Oeuvres complètes*, ed. Jules Assezat and Maurice Tourneux, vol. 4 (Paris: Garnier Frères, 1875), 68.
142. *The Malefactor's Register; or, the Newgate and Tyburn Calendar*, vol. 1 (London: Alexander Hogg, 1779), vi–vii.
143. Jeremy Bentham, *Panopticon: or, the Inspection-House* (Dublin: Thomas Byrne, 1791), 29, 169–70. Julie Stone Peters, "Penitentiary Performances: Spectators, Affecting Scenes, and Terrible Apparitions in the Nineteenth-Century Model Prison," in *Law and Performance*, ed. Austin Sarat, Lawrence Douglas, and Martha Merrill Umphrey (Amherst, MA: University of Massachusetts Press, 2018), 18–67.
144. Ibid., 172.
145. Ibid., 173.

146. Ibid.
147. Ibid.
148. George Steiner, *The Death of Tragedy*, 2nd edition (New Haven: Yale University Press, 1996), 127–8.
149. George Jacob Holyoake, *Public Lessons of the Hangman* (London: F. Farah, 1864), 3. (Describing the impact of cheap theater on the execution "mob.")
150. Bercenay, *Correspondance*, 79.
151. Henry Essex Edgeworth de Firmont, *Memoirs of the Abbé Edgeworth: Containing his Narrative of the Last Hours of Louis XVI* (London: Rowland Hunter, 1815), 84.
152. *Fin tragique de Louis XVI*.
153. "A Sermon Preached Before the Lords Spiritual and Temporal," *The British Critic*, vol. 1 (May 1793), 27–8. (Preached on the anniversary of Charles I's execution.)
154. "Marie Antoinette, Tragédie," *Mercure de France*, vol. 3, no. 13 (1800–1), 19.
155. Gotthold Ephraim Lessing, *Werke und Briefe in zwölf Bänden*, ed. Wilfried Barner and Klaus Bohnen, vol. 11.1 (Frankfurt an Main: Deutscher Klassiker Verlag, 1987), 118–19. (Letter to Nicolai and Mendelssohn.)
156. Benjamin Rush, *An Enquiry into the Effects of Public Punishments upon Criminals and upon Society* (Philadelphia: Joseph James, 1787), 6.
157. Ibid.
158. Ibid., 7.
159. See Rush, *Essays Literary, Moral and Philosophical* (Philadelphia: Thomas & Samuel Bradford, 1798), 82. (Writing primarily of novel-reading.)
160. Rush, *Medical Inquiries and Observations, upon the Diseases of the Mind* (Philadelphia: Kimber & Richardson, 1812), 67.
161. Ibid.
162. Ibid., 68.
163. Raymond Williams, *Modern Tragedy* (London: Chatto & Windus, 1966), 83.
164. Ibid., 77.
165. Ibid.
166. Ibid.
167. Ibid., 81.
168. Ibid., 77.

## Chapter Seven

1. Plato, *The Republic*, trans. Benjamin Jowett (Cleveland: World Pub. Co., 1946), Book 3, 91.
2. Plato, *Republic*, Book 10, 364–5.
3. Elizabeth Belfiore, "Wine and Catharsis of the Emotions in Plato's Laws," *The Classical Quarterly* (New Series) 36, no. 2 (January 1, 1986): 421.
4. Aristotle, *The Poetics of Aristotle: Translation and Commentary*, trans. Stephen Halliwell (Chapel Hill: University of North Carolina Press, 1987), 46.
5. Pierre Corneille, *Trois discours sur le poème dramatique*, ed. Bénédicte Louvat and Marc Escola (Paris: Flammarion, 1999), 72.
6. Samuel Johnson, *Rambler* 125 (May 28, 1751).
7. John D. Lyons, "Racine's Silent Places," in *L'éloquence du silence sur la scène théâtrale du 17e et 18e siècles*, ed. Hélène Bilis and Jennifer Tamas (Paris: Garnier, 2014), 217–37.
8. Jean Racine, *Phèdre*, 4.5.632.
9. Ibid., 4.5.631.

10. European theatre of this period made ambitious use of stage machinery to display monsters and divinities, but the subtle and complex events of Hippolyte's demise would no doubt have been reduced to a laughable carnival display if *Phèdre* had been a *pièce à machines*. More importantly, the rich ambiguity that is so important, would have squashed into a flat literalness.
11. Philipe Quinault, *La Mort de Cyrus*, 5.270–4.
12. Ibid., 5.1377–8.
13. Voltaire, *Zaïre*, 5.692.
14. Ibid., 5.792.
15. Ibid., 5.799–800.
16. Ibid., 5.833.
17. Ibid., 5.887–9.
18. Ibid., 5.1593–4.
19. Joshua Billings, *Genealogy of the Tragic: Greek Tragedy and German Philosophy* (Princeton: Princeton University Press, 2014).
20. Friedrich Schiller, "On the Tragic Art," in *Aesthetical and Philosophical Essays* (New York: Harvard Publishing Company, 1895), 346–67.
21. Denis Diderot, *Œuvres*, ed. Laurent Versini, vol. 4, 1131–90 (Paris: Robert Laffont "Bouquins," 1996), 1164. See Nicholas Cronk, ed., "Études sur 'Le Fils naturel' et 'Entretiens sur le Fils naturel'" (Oxford: Voltaire Foundation, 2000).
22. Diderot, *Œuvres*, 1155, 1166.
23. Ibid., 1143.
24. Ibid., 1284.
25. Pierre Augustin Caron de Beaumarchais, *Théatre. Lettres relatives à son théatre*, ed. Maurice Allem and Pléiade Paul-Courant (Paris: Gallimard, 1957), 6.
26. Beaumarchais, 9.
27. Ibid., 13.
28. Ibid., 15.
29. Ibid., 18.
30. Michel-Jean Sedaine, *Le Philosophe sans le savoir*, ed. Graham E. Rodmell (Durham: University of Durham, 1987), 15.
31. Ibid., 2.8.
32. Ibid., 1.4.
33. Friedrich Schiller, *Early Dramas*, trans. by Samuel Taylor Coleridge (London: 1901).
34. Schiller, *The Robbers. A Tragedy* (London: G.G. and J. Robinson, 1797), 133.
35. Ibid.
36. Ibid., 1.2.
37. Ibid., 3.1.
38. John D. Lyons, *Tragedy and the Return of the Dead*, Rethinking the Early Modern (Evanston, IL: Northwestern University Press, 2018).
39. Schiller, *The Robbers*, 5.1.

## Chapter Eight

1. Christopher J. Wheatley, "Tragedy," in *The Cambridge Companion to English Restoration Theatre*, ed. Deborah Payne Fisk (Cambridge: Cambridge University Press, 2000), 72. One major impact of Aristotle on French neoclassical tragedy is the fact that drama was expected to follow the unity of time, place, and action (that the play's plot could only transpire during one day, one location, and without extraneous subplots).

2. Jean Racine, *Iphigénie*, 1.2.595.
3. Jennifer Row, "*Iphigénie*, Jean Racine," in *The Literary Encyclopedia*, vol. 1.5.2.03: *French Writing and Culture of the Seventeenth Century: Classical and Baroque, 1600–1700*. http://www.litencyc.com/php/sworks.php?rec=true&UID=4399
4. Thomas Laqueur, *Making Sex: Body and Gender from the Greeks to Freud*, reprint edn. (Cambridge, MA: Harvard University Press, 1992).
5. Michel Millot. *L'ecole des filles*, ed. Pascal Pia (n.p., La Bibliothèque privée, 1969), 19. All translations are mine unless otherwise stated.
6. Helen E.M. Brooks, "Sexuality and Gender: Changing Identities," in *A Cultural History of Theatre in the Age of Enlightenment*, ed. Mechele Leon (London: Bloomsbury Academic, 2017), 57.
7. John Dryden, *All for Love*, ed. N.J. Andrew (New York: Bloomsbury Methuen Drama, 2004), 1.178–9.
8. Derval Conroy, "The displacement of disorder: gynæcocracy and friendship in Catherine Bernard's Laodamie (1689)," in *Papers on French Seventeenth-Century Literature 67* (Tübingen: Narr Franke Attempto), 2007. The Salic Law, commissioned by the first Frankish king Clovis around 500 CE, excluded females from inheriting property or titles.
9. Ibid.
10. Theresa Varney Kennedy, *Women's Deliberation: The Heroine in Early Modern French Women's Theater (1650–1750)* (Abingdon: Routledge, 2018), 216.
11. Roland Barthes, *Sur Racine* (Paris: Éditions du Seuil, 1963). I offer here a good translation in *On Racine*, trans. Richard Howard, 1st edition (University of California Press, 1992), 81.
12. Jean Racine, *Andromaque*, 1.4.260–4. The translation offered here is from John Edmunds, *Four French Plays: Cinna, the Misanthrope, Andromache, Phaedra* (London: Penguin Classics, 2013).
13. For further reflection on the temporality of desire in *Iphis et Iante*, see also Jennifer Row, "Queer Time on the Early Modern Stage: France and the Drama of Biopower," *Exemplaria* 29, no. 1 (Winter 2017).
14. Isaac de Benserade, *Iphis et Iante* ([Paris]: [LAMPSAQUE], 2000), 94.
15. Joseph Harris, "Disruptive Desires: Lesbian Sexuality in Isaac de Benserade's Iphis et Iante (1634)," *Seventeenth-Century French Studies* 24, no. 1 (2002): 156.
16. Katherine B. Crawford, "Love, Sodomy, and Scandal: Controlling the Sexual Reputation of Henry III," *Journal of the History of Sexuality* 12, no. 4 (2003): 514.
17. Jeffrey Merrick and Bryant T. Ragan, *Homosexuality in Early Modern France: A Documentary Collection* (Oxford: Oxford University Press, 2001), 3.
18. Rictor Norton, "Homosexuality," in *A Cultural History of Sexuality in the Enlightenment*, ed. Julie Peakman (London: Bloomsbury, 2012), 61.
19. For more on this, see Mitchell Greenberg, *Baroque Bodies: Psychoanalysis and the Culture of French Absolutism* (Ithaca: Cornell University Press, 2001), 122–4.
20. Michel Foucault, *An Introduction*, Vol. 1 of *The History of Sexuality*, trans. Robert Hurley, reissue edition (New York: Vintage, 1978), 43.
21. An excellent discussion on ways of engaging with the alterity of sexuality in the past can be found in Ari Friedlander's introduction to "Desiring History and Historicizing Desire," *Journal of Early Modern Cultural Studies* 16, no. 2 (Spring 2016).
22. Eve Kosofsky Sedgwick, *Tendencies* (Abingdon: Routledge, 1994), 8.
23. Jonathan Goldberg, *Sodometries: Renaissance Texts, Modern Sexualities*. 1st edition (New York: Fordham University Press, 2010), 19.
24. Ibid.
25. Ibid., xv.

26. Jeffrey Masten, *Queer Philologies: Sex, Language and Affect in Shakespeare's Time* (Philadelphia, PA: University of Pennsylvania Press, 2016), 73–4.
27. Dryden, *All for Love*, 1.172–9.
28. Ibid., 3.90–7.
29. Ibid., 1.261–74.
30. David Bruce Kramer, *The Imperial Dryden: The Poetics of Appropriation in Seventeenth Century England* (Athens, GA: University of Georgia Press, 1994), 22.
31. Brandon Chua, *Ravishment of Reason: Governance and the Heroic Idioms of the Late Stuart Stage, 1660–1690* (Lewisburg, PA: Bucknell University Press, 2014), 11.
32. Greenberg, *Baroque Bodies*, 8.
33. Pierre Corneille, *Œuvres complètes*, vol. 1, ed. Georges Couton, new edn (Paris: Gallimard, 2003), 124.
34. Pierre Corneille, *Le Cid*, 3.4.931–2. The translation here is A.S. Kline's: https://www.poetryintranslation.com/PITBR/French/LeCidActIII.php#anchor_Toc168900825
35. Pierre Corneille, *Polyeucte*, 3.2.807–12.
36. Laurie Shannon, "Nature's Bias: Renaissance Homonormativity and Elizabethan Comic Likeness," *Modern Philology* 98, no. 2 (2000): 187.
37. Corneille, *Polyeucte*, 1.1.41–2.
38. Ibid., 3.4.958–9.
39. John Franceschina, *Homosexualities in the English Theatre: From Lyly to Wilde* (Westport, CT: Greenwood Press, 1997), 94.
40. Lewis Seifert and Rebecca Wilkin, *Men and Women Making Friends in Early Modern France* (Farnham: Ashgate Publishing, Ltd., 2015), 12.
41. See Greenberg's chapter "Classicism's Pornographic Body: *L'Ecole des filles, L'académie des dames,*" in *Baroque Bodies* (Ithaca: Cornell University Press, 2001).
42. Thomas Wynn, "Sade's Theatre: Pleasure, Vision, Masochism," *SVEC 2007*, no. 2 (Oxford: Voltaire Foundation, 2007), 3.
43. Ibid., 6.
44. Jean I. Marsden, "Spectacle, Horror and Pathos," in *The Cambridge Companion to English Restoration Theatre*, ed. Deborah Payne Fisk (Cambridge: Cambridge University Press, 2000), 182.
45. Ibid.
46. Laura Brown, *Ends of Empire: Women and Ideology in Early Eighteenth-Century English Literature* (Ithaca: Cornell University Press, 1993), 65
47. Thomas Otway, "The Orphan," in *The British Drama; a Collection of the Most Esteemed Tragedies, Comedies, Operas, and Farces, in the English Language* (Thomas Cowperthwait & Co., 1824), IV, 434.
48. Ibid.
49. Brown, *Ends of Empire*, 66.
50. Thomas Wynn, "Violence, vulnerability and subjectivity in Sade," in *Representing violence in France 1760–1820* (Oxford: Voltaire Foundation, 2013), 143.
51. Voltaire, *Zaïre*, 5.7.1514.
52. Caroline Weber, "Voltaire's "Zaïre": Fantasies of Infidelity, Ideologies of Faith," *South Central Review* 21, no. 2 (Summer 2004): 44.
53. I offer a further analysis of emotions and the role of sexuality and incarceration in *Zaïre* in "Alternative Intimacies, Carceral Sympathy and Sexuality in Voltaire's *Zaïre*," *Le Monde français du dix-huitième siècle* 2, no. 1 (2017).
54. Jean-Jacques Rousseau, *Lettre a d'Alembert Sur Les Spectacles* (Paris: Flammarion, 2003), 105–6.

# BIBLIOGRAPHY

Académie française. *Des sentiments de l'Académie française sur la tragi-comédie du Cid: essai sur la competence des hommes de l'art et du public en matière de goût*. Paris: Panckoucke, 1840. https://gallica.bnf.fr/ark:/12148/bpt6k5653977d/f8.image.texteImage

[An] *Account of the Life, Death, and Writings, of the Rev. Dr. Dodd*. London: n.p., 1777.

Alasseur, Claude. *La Comédie-Française au XVIIIe siècle*. Paris: Mouton, 1967.

Allendesalazar. "Desengaño." In *The Dictionary of Untranslatables: A Philosophical Lexicon*, edited by Barbara Cassin, 206–210. Princeton: Princeton University Press, 2014.

Althusser, Louis. *Lenin and Philosophy and Other Essays*. Translated by B. Brewster. London: MR Press, 1971.

"Ambigu." *The Dictionnaire de l'Académie Française of 1694*. https://artflsrv03.uchicago.edu/philologic4/publicdicos/query?report=bibliography&head=ambigu (accessed July 31, 2018).

Apostolidès, Jean-Marie. "Idéologie concretisée." In *La Roi-machine: Spectacle et politique au temps de Louis XIV*. Paris: Minuit, 1980.

Aristotle. *The Poetics of Aristotle: Translation and Commentary*. Translated by Stephen Halliwell. Chapel Hill: University of North Carolina Press, 1987.

Arthington, Henry. *The Seduction of Arthington by Hacket especiallie with some tokens of his vnfained repentance and submission. Written by the said Henrie Arthington, the third person, in that wofull tragedie*. London: Thomas Man, [1592].

Avery, Emmett L. *The London Stage, Part 2: 1700–1729*. Carbondale: Southern Illinois University Press, 1960.

Babié de Bercenay, François. *Correspondance politique et confidentielle inédite, de Louis XVI*. Paris: Debray, 1803.

Barthès, Pierre. "Les heures perdues de Pierre Barthès, maître répétiteur en Toulouse." Unpublished notebooks. Rosalis (Bibliothèque numérique de Toulouse). https://rosalis.bibliotheque.toulouse.fr/cgi-bin/hub?a=q&txq=Barth%C3%A8s%2c+Pierre+%281704-1781%29&fqc=&fqf=DO&fqv=&results=1&r=1&qt=0&t=2&e=fr-20--1--txt-heures+perdues------TE--0----

Barthes, Roland. *On Racine*. Translated by Richard Howard, 1st edition. University of California Press, 1992.

Barthes, Roland. *Sur Racine*. Paris: Éditions du Seuil, 1963.

Barthes, Roland. *Sur Racine*. Translated by Richard Howard. New York: Hill and Wang, 1964.

Basterra, Gabriela. *Seductions of Fate: Tragic Subjectivity, Ethics, Politics*. New York: Palgrave MacMillan, 2004.

Beccaria, Cesare. *Dei delitti e delle pene*. Edited by Gianni Francioni and Luigi Firpo. Milan: Mediobanca, 1984.

Beccaria, Cesare. *On Crimes and Punishments*. Translated by David Young. Indianapolis, IN: Hackett, 1986.

Belfiore, Elizabeth. "Wine and Catharsis of the Emotions in Plato's Laws." *The Classical Quarterly* (New Series) 36, no. 2 (January 1, 1986): 421.

Benjamin, Walter. *The Origin of German Tragic drama*. Translated by John Osborne. London: NLB, 1977 [1925].

Benjamin, Walter. *The Origin of German Tragic Drama*. Translated by John Osborne, Introduction by George Steiner. New York: Verson, 2009.

Benserade, Isaac de. *Iphis Et Iante*. LAMPSAQUE, 2000.

Bentham, Jeremy. *Panopticon: or, the Inspection-House*. Dublin: Thomas Byrne, 1791.

Bermúdez de la Torre y Solier, Pedro José. *Triunfos del Santo Oficio Peruano. Relacion panegyrica, historica, y politica del auto publico de fè celebrado en [Lima] 23. de diziembre del Año de 1736*. Lima: Imprenta Real, 1737.

Bernard, Catherine. *Brutus* [1690]. Edited by Derval Conroy. In *Théâtre de femmes de l'Ancien Régime, XVIIe–XVIIIe siècle*, edited by Aurore Evain, Perry Gethner, and Henriette Goldwyn, 175–182. Saint-Étienne: Publications de l'Université de Saint-Étienne, 2011.

Bernard, Catherine. Vol. 3 of *Théâtre des femmes de l'Ancien Régime*. Edited by Derval Conroy. Classiques Garnier, 2011.

Besterman, Théodore, ed. "Letter from November 17, 1760." In Vol. 3 of *Correspondance*, 93. Paris: Gallimard, 1981.

Bibliothèque-Musée de la Comédie-Française, 1AA 1680–1700, 1AA 1683, 3–7.

Bibliothèque-Musée de la Comédie-Française, R14, Registre 1682–1683, 291v.

Biet, Christian. "Introduction: la question du répertoire au théâtre." *Littératures classiques* 95 (2018): 7–14: 7–8.

Biet, Christian. "La Veuve et l'idéal Du Mari Absolu. Célimène et Alceste." *Cahiers Du Dix-Septième* 7, no. 1 (Spring 1997): 215–26.

Biet, Christian. "L'avenir des illusions ou le théâtre et l'illusion perdue." *Littératures classiques: L'illusion au XVIIe siècle* 44 (Winter 2002).

Biet, Christian. *Œdipe en monarchie, tragédie et théorie juridique à l'Age classique*. Paris: Klincksieck, 1994.

Biet, Christian, ed. *Théâtre de la cruauté et récits sanglants en France (XVIe–XVIIe siècles)*. Paris: Laffont, 2006.

Bilis, Hélène E. *Passing Judgment: The Politics and Poetics of Sovereignty in French Tragedy from Hardy to Racine*. Toronto: University of Toronto Press, 2016.

Billings, Joshua. *Genealogy of the Tragic: Greek Tragedy and German Philosophy*. Princeton: Princeton University Press, 2014.

Blocker, Déborah. *Instituer un "art." Politiques du théâtre dans la France du premier XVII$^e$ siècle*. Paris: Champion, 2009.

*Blood for Blood: or Murthers Revenged*. Oxford, 1661.

Bonnassies, Jules. *La Comédie-Française: histoire administrative (1658–1757)*. Paris: Didier, 1874.

Booth, Michael R. et al. *The Revels History of Drama in English. 1750–1880*. Vol. 4. London: Methuen, 1975.

Boquet, François. *La Troupe de Molière et les deux Corneille à Rouen en 1658*. Paris: A. Claudin, 1858.

Boquet, Guy. "Naissance d'une troupe, genèse d'un répertoire." *Revue d'histoire du théâtre* 32 (1980): 105–26.

Bossuet, Jacques-Béninge. "Maximes et réflexions sur la comédie." Paris: Jean Anisson, 1694.

Bossuet, Jacques-Béninge. "Oraison funèbre de Michel le Tellier." In *Œuvres*, edited by Abbé Bernard Velat Yvonne Champailler, 163–90. Paris: Gallimard, 1961.

Brecht, Bertold. "Notes on the *Threepenny Opera*." In *The Threepenny Opera*, 99. New York: Grove Press, 1949.

Brillaud, Jérôme. "La Coupe d'Atrée: Crébillon et la réinvention du théâtre tragique au 18ᵉ siècle." *Dalhousie French Studies* 78 (2007): 35–42.

Brillaud, Jérôme. "La Jouissance de la vérité ou le plaisir tragique selon le Chancelier d'Aguesseau." *French Studies* 62, no. 2 (April 2008): 150–61.

Brooks, Helen E.M. "Sexuality and Gender: Changing Identities." In *A Cultural History of Theatre in the Age of Enlightenment*, edited by Mechele Leon. London: Bloomsbury Academic, 2017.

Brooks, William S., and P.J. Yarrow. *The Dramatic Criticism of Elizabeth Charlotte, duchesse d'Orléans*. Lewiston-Queenston-Lampeter: Edwin Mellen, 1996.

Brown, Gregory. *A Field of Honor: The Identities of Writers, Court Culture and Public Theater in the French Intellectual Field from Racine to the Revolution*. New York: Columbia University Press, 2002.

Brown, Laura. *Ends of Empire: Women and Ideology in Early Eighteenth-Century English Literature*. Ithaca: Cornell University Press, 1993.

Brunschwig, Jacques. "Aristote et l'effet Perrichon." In *La Passion de la Raison: Hommage à Fernand Alquié*, edited by Jean-Luc Marion and Jean Deprun, 376. Paris: Presses Universitaires de France, 1983.

Burke, Edmund. *A Philosophical Enquiry into the Origin of our Ideas of the Sublime and Beautiful*. Edited by Adam Phillips. Oxford: Oxford University Press, 1990.

Burke, Peter. *The Fabrication of Louis XIV*. New Haven: Yale University Press, 1994.

Bynum, Caroline Walker. *The Resurrection of the Body in Western Christianity, 200–1336*. New York: Columbia University Press, 1995.

Caldicott, C.E.J. *La Carrière de Molière entre protecteurs et éditeurs*. Amsterdam-Atlanta GA: Rodopi, 1998.

Camp, Pannill. *The First Frame: Theatre Space in Enlightenment France*. Cambridge: Cambridge University Press, 2014.

Carlson, Marvin. *Voltaire and the Theater of the Eighteenth Century*. Westport and London: Greenwood Press, 1998.

Cassirer, Ernst. *The Philosophy of the Enlightenment*. Translated by Fritz C.A. Koelln and James Pettegrove. Princeton, NJ: Princeton University Press, 1951.

Cavaillé, Fabien. "Les temps du théâtre. Organisation et déroulement de la séance." In *La Représentation théâtrale en France au XVIIe siècle*, edited by Pierre Pasquier and Anne Surgers, 37–41. Paris: Armand Colin, 2011.

[The] *Chamberlain's Tragedy: or, The Cook-Maid's Cruelty; Being a True Account How She in the Heat of Passion, Murder'd Her Fellow-Servant*. N.p.: [1671?].

Chaouche, Sabine. Vol. 1 of *La Mise en scène du répertoire à la Comédie-Française (1680–1815)*. Paris: Champion, 2013.

Chaouche, Sabine. ed. *La Scène en contrechamp. Anecdotes françaises et traditions de jeu au siècle des Lumières*, 133. Paris: Champion, 2005.

Chaouche, Sabine. *L'Art du comédien. Déclamation et jeu scénique en France à l'âge classique (1629–1680)*. Paris: Honoré Champion, 2001.

Chaouche, Sabine. *L'Art du comédien: déclamation et jeu scénique en France à l'âge classique (1629–1680)*. Paris: Honoré Champion, 2013.

Chappuzeau, Samuel. *Le Théâtre français*. Paris: chez Michel Mayer, 1674.

Chappuzeau, Samuel. *Le Théâtre français* (1674). Edited by Christopher J. Gossip. Tübingen: Gunter Narr, 2009.

Chartier, Roger. *Publishing Drama in Early Modern Europe*. London: British Library, 1999.
Chénier, Marie-Joseph. "Discours préliminaire." Preface to *Fénelon, ou Les Religieuses de Cambrai*. In *Théâtre*, edited by Ambrus Gauthier and Francois Jacob. Paris: Flammarion, 2002.
Chénier, Marie-Joseph. *Théâtre de M.-J. Chénier*. Paris: Foulon et Cie, 1818.
Chevalley, Sylvie. "Le 'Registre d'Hubert.' 1672–1673." *Revue d'histoire du théâtre* 25 (1973): 1–132.
Chevalley, Sylvie. "Les Derniers Jours de l'Hôtel de Bourgogne." *Revue d'histoire du théâtre* 17 (1965): 404–407.
Chevalley, Sylvie. "Les deux *Bérénice*." *Revue d'histoire du théâtre* 22 (1970): 91–124.
Chua, Brandon. *Ravishment of Reason: Governance and the Heroic Idioms of the Late Stuart Stage, 1660–1690*. Lewisburg, PA: Bucknell University Press, 2014.
Clarke, Jan. "Another look at the Comédie-Française as the 'Maison de Molière.'" *Nottingham French Studies* 33 (1994): 71–82.
Clarke, Jan. "La Création d'un répertoire national: la Comédie-Française de 1680 à 1689." *Littératures classiques* 95 (2018): 77–88.
Clarke, Jan. "Le Spectateur au Palais Royal et à l'Hôtel Guénégaud." In *Le Spectateur de théâtre à l'Âge Classique: XVIIe et XVIIIe siècles*, edited by Bénédicte Louvat-Molozay and Franck Salaün. Montpellier: L'Entretemps, 2008.
Clarke, Jan. "Les Conséquences pour la troupe de Molière de ses voyages à la cour, 1667–1672." In *Molière à la cour: les Amants magnifiques en 1670*, edited by Laura Naudeix, forthcoming.
Clarke, Jan. "Molière's Double Bills." *Seventeenth-Century French Studies* 20 (1998): 29–44.
Clarke, Jan. "Music at the Guénégaud Theatre, 1673–1680." *Seventeenth-Century French Studies* 12 (1990): 89–110.
Clarke, Jan. "Part 3: 1680–1715." In *French Theatre in the Neo–Classical Era*, edited by William D. Howarth. Cambridge: Cambridge University Press, 1997.
Clarke, Jan. "Pierre Corneille dans les répertoires des troupes de Molière et de l'Hôtel Guénégaud." *Revue d'Histoire Littéraire de la France*, 106 (2006): 571–98.
Clarke, Jan. "Repertory and Revival at the Guénégaud Theatre, 1673–1680." *Seventeenth-Century French Studies* 10 (1988): 136–53.
Clarke, Jan. "Tristan dans les registres." *Cahiers Tristan l'Hermite* 37 (2015): 23–45.
Clarke, Jan. *The Guénégaud Theatre in Paris (1673–1680). Volume One: Founding, Design and Production*. Lewiston-Queenston-Lampeter: Edwin Mellen, 1998.
Clarke, Jan. *The Guénégaud Theatre in Paris (1673–1680). Volume Two: the Accounts Season by Season*. Lewiston-Queenston-Lampeter: Edwin Mellen, 2001.
Clarke, Jan. *The Guénégaud Theatre in Paris (1673–1680). Volume Three: the Demise of the Machine Play*. Lewiston-Queenston-Lampeter: Edwin Mellen, 2007.
Clay, Lauren. *Stagestruck. The Business of Theater in Eighteenth-Century France and its Colonies*. Ithaca: Cornell University Press, 2013.
Clay, Lauren. "The Strange Career of Voltaire, Bestselling Playwright of Eighteenth-Century France." In *The Eighteenth-Century French Stage Online*, edited by Sylvaine Guyot and Jeffrey Ravel. Cambridge: MIT Press, 2018. Online.
"[The] Comédie-Français Registers Project." http://cfregisters.org/en/ (accessed June 1, 2018).
Connors, Logan. *Dramatic Battles in Eighteenth-century France. Philosophes, anti-philosophes and polemical theatre*. Oxford: Voltaire Foundation, 2012.

Conroy, Derval. "The displacement of disorder: gynæcocracy and friendship in Catherine Bernard's Laodamie (1689)." In *Papers on French Seventeenth-Century Literature* 67, 443–64. Tübingen: Narr Franke Attempto, 2007.

Conti, Armand de Bourbon. *Traité de la comédie et des spectacles selon la tradition de l'Eglise tirée des Conciles et des Saints Pères*. Paris: Louis Billaine, 1667.

Cooper, Anthony Ashley, 3rd Earl of Shaftesbury. *Characteristics of Men, Manners, Opinions, Times*. 3 vols. London: John Darby, 1711.

Corneille, Pierre. "Discourse on Tragedy and on the Ways of Composing it in Accordance with Plausibility and Necessity." In *Trois discours sur le poème dramatique* [1660].

Corneille, Pierre. *Le Cid*. Translated by A.S. Kline. https://www.poetryintranslation.com/PITBR/French/LeCidActIII.php#anchor_Toc168900825 (accessed January 17, 2019).

Corneille, Pierre. *Œuvres complètes*. Edited by Georges Couton. New edn. Paris: Gallimard, 2003.

Corneille, Pierre. *Oeuvres complètes*. Edited by Georges Couton. Paris: Gallimard, 1980–87.

Corneille, Pierre. "Trois Discours sur le poème dramatique." In *Œuvres complètes* III. Paris: Gallimard, 1987.

Corneille, Pierre. *Trois Discours sur le poème dramatique*. Edited by Bénédicte Louvat and Marc Escola. Paris: Flammarion, 1999.

Corneille, Thomas. *Circé*. Edited by Jan Clarke. Exeter: University of Exeter, 1989.

Costigan, Lúcia Helena. *Through Cracks in the Wall: Modern Inquisitions and New Christian Letrados in the Iberian Atlantic World*. Boston: Brill, 2010.

Couprie, Alain. *La Champmeslé*. Paris: Fayard, 2003.

Crawford, Katherine B. "Love, Sodomy, and Scandal: Controlling the Sexual Reputation of Henry III." *Journal of the History of Sexuality* 12, no. 4 (2003): 513–42.

Cronk, Nicholas, ed. "Études sur 'Le Fils naturel' et 'Entretiens sur le Fils naturel.'" Oxford: Voltaire Foundation, 2000.

Curulla, Annelle. "False Frocks: Chénier's *Charles IX* and the Debate on Religious Costume in Parisian Theater, 1789–901." *Restoration and 18th-Century Theatre Research* 29, no. 1 (Summer 2014): 97–116.

d'Aubignac, François Hédelin, abbé. *La Pratique du Théâtre*. Edited by Hélène Baby. Paris: Honoré Champion, 2011.

Da Vinha, Mathieu, A. Maral, and N. Milovanovic, eds. *Louis XIV. L'image et le mythe*. Rennes-Versailles: PUR-CRCV, 2014.

Darnton, Robert. "The Facts of Literary Life in Pre-Revolutionary France." In *The Political Culture of the Old Regime*, edited by Keith Michael Baker, 261–91. Oxford: Pergamon, 1989.

de Beauchamps, Pierre François Godard. *Recherches sur les théâtres de France*. Paris: Prault, 1735. "Préface."

de Beaumarchais, Pierre Augustin Caron. *Théatre. Lettres Relatives à Son Théatre*. Edited by Maurice Allem and Paul-Courant, Pléiade. Paris: Gallimard, 1957.

de Certeau, Michel. Vol. 1 of *La Fable Mystique*. Paris: Gallimard, 1982.

de La Fontaine, Jean. *Oeuvres diverses*. Edited by Jean Marmier. Paris: Gallimard, 1968.

de La Porte, Joseph, and Jean Marie Bernard Clément. Vol. 1 of *Anecdotes dramatiques*. Paris: Veuve Duchesne, 1775.

de Loménie, Louis-Henri. Vol. 2 of *Mémoires inédits de Louis-Henri de Loménie, comte de Brienne Secrétaire d'État sous Louis XIV*. Edited by F. Barrière. Paris: Ponthieu et Cie., 1828.

de Rougemont, Martine. *La Vie théâtrale en France au XVIIIᵉ siècle*. Paris: Champion, 1988.

de Saint-Évremond, Charles. "De la tragédie ancienne et moderne." In *Œuvres choisies de Saint-Évremond*, 136–44. Paris: Didot, 1852.

de Saint-Jean, Léon. *Les Divins paradoxes de l'Eucharistie*. Brussels: Jean Mommart, 1663.

de Saint-Just, Louis-Antoine-Léon. "De la nature." In *Œuvres completes*, edited by Anne Kupiec and Miguel Abensour, 1067. Paris: Gallimard [Folio], 2004.

de Saint-Réal, César. *De l'usage de l'histoire*. Edited by René Démoris and Christian Meurillon. Lille, Presses de l'Université de Lille, 1980 [1672].

de Viau, Theophile. *Les Amours Tragiques de Pyrame et Thisbe*. Paris: Flammarion, 2015.

de Villiers, Pierre. "Entretiens sur les tragédies de ce temps." [1675] In Jean Racine, Vol. 1 of *Œuvres complètes*, edited by Georges Forestier, 786–92. Paris: Gallimard, 1999.

Deierkauf-Holsboer, S. Wilma. *Le Théâtre de l'Hôtel de Bourgogne*. 2 vols. Paris: Nizet, 1968–70.

Delcourt, Marie. *Œdipe ou la légende du conquérant*. Paris: Faculté de philosophie et lettres, 1944.

Delmas, Christian. *Mythologie et mythe dans le théâtre français: 1650–1676*. Geneve: Droz, 1985.

Descartes, René. *Méditations métaphysiques. Objections et réponses suivies de quatre lettres*. Edited by Jean-Marie Beyssade and Michelle Beyssade. Paris: Garnier-Flammarion, 1979.

Descartes, René. *The Passions of the Soul and Other Late Philosophical Writings*. Oxford: Oxford University Press, 2015.

Descotes, Maurice. *Le Public de théâtre et son histoire*. Paris: Presses Universitaires de France, 1964.

Devereaux, Simon. "Recasting the Theatre of Execution: The Abolition of the Tyburn Ritual." *Past & Present* 202, no. 1 (February 2009): 127–74.

Dickens, Charles. *Selected Letters of Charles Dickens*. Edited by David Paroissien. London: Macmillan Press, 1985.

Diderot, Denis. "De la poésie dramatique." In *Œuvres esthétiques*, edited by P. Vernière. Paris: Classiques Garnier, 1994.

Diderot, Denis. *Oeuvres complètes*. Edited by Jules Assezat and Maurice Tourneux. Paris: Garnier Frères, 1875–7.

Diderot, Denis. Vol. 4 of *Œuvres*. Edited by Laurent Versini. Paris: Robert Laffont "Bouquins," 1996.

Diderot, Denis, d'Alembert, et al., eds. Vol. 5 of *Encyclopédie ou Dictionnaire raisonné des sciences, des arts et des métiers, par une société de gens de lettres*. Paris: Briasson, David l'aîné, Le Breton, & Durand, 1751.

Dillon, Elizabeth Maddock. *New World Drama: The Performative Commons in the Atlantic World, 1649–1849*. Durham: Duke University Press, 2014.

*Discours tragique et pitoyable sur la mort d'une jeune Damoiselle âgée de dix-sept à dix-huit ans, exécutée dans la ville de Padouë au mois de décembre dernier 1596. Avec les regrets qu'elle a faict avant sa mort. Traduit d'italien en François*. Paris: A. Du Brueil, 1597.

Donohue, Joseph, ed. *The Cambridge History of British Theatre*. Cambridge: Cambridge University Press, 2005.

Doubrovsky, Serge. *Corneille et la dialectique du héros*. Paris: Gallimard, 1963.

Dryden, John. *All for Love*. Edited by N.J. Andrew. New York: Bloomsbury Methuen Drama, 2004.

Du Bos, Jean-Baptiste. *Critical Reflections on Poetry, Painting, and Music*. 3 vols. London: John Nourse, 1748.

du Noyer, Anne-Marguerite Petit. *Letters from a Lady at Paris to a Lady at Avignon*. 2nd edn. 2 vols. London: W. Mears and J. Browne, 1716.

du Noyer, Anne-Marguerite Petit. *Mémoires de Madame Du Noyer, première partie*. Amsterdam: par la Compagnie, 1760.

Duchêne, Roger. *Molière*. Paris: Fayard, 1998.

Dupas, Matthieu. "La sodomie dans l'affaire Théophile de Viau: questions de genre et de sexualité dans la France du premier xviie siècle." *Les Dossiers du Grihl*, no. 2010.1 (March 2010).

Edgeworth de Firmont, Henry Essex. *Memoirs of the Abbé Edgeworth: Containing his Narrative of the Last Hours of Louis XVI*. London: Rowland Hunter, 1815.

*England's Black Tribunall*. London: Printed for J. Playfield, 1660.

Étienne, Charles-Guillaume, and Alphonse Martainville. *Histoire du théâtre français depuis le commencement de la Révolution jusqu'à la réunion generale*. Paris: Barba, 1802.

Evans, Richard J. *Rituals of Retribution: Capital Punishment in Germany, 1600–1987*. Oxford: Oxford University Press, 1996.

Fénelon, François. "Lettre à l'Académie." [1714] In Vol. 2 of *Œuvres complètes*, edited by Jacques Le Brun, 1169–92. Paris: Gallimard, 1997.

Ferrières, Charles Élie, marquis de. *Mémoires du marquis de Ferrières*. Paris: Baudouin frères, 1821.

*Fin tragique de la reine de France Maria Antoneta*. [Paris? ; London?]: n.p., [1793?]. Bibliothèque Nationale de France. http://catalogue.bnf.fr/ark:/12148/cb40252529f

*Fin tragique de Louis XVI*. Paris: n.p., [1793]. Bibliothèque Nationale de France. http://catalogue.bnf.fr/ark:/12148/cb41509130v

Flores, Nicolás. *Relación del auto grande de la Inquisición que se celebró en la Plaza Grande de Lima el día 23 de diciembre del año de 1736*. New York: Pantheon Books, 1997.

Forestier, Georges. *Jean Racine*. Paris: Gallimard, 2006.

Foucault, Michel. *An Introduction*. Vol. 1 of *The History of Sexuality*. Translated by Robert Hurley. Reissue edn. New York: Vintage, 1978.

Foucault, Michel. *Discipline and Punish: the Birth of the Prison*. New York: Pantheon Books, 1977.

Foucault, Michel. Vol. 1 of *La volonté de savoir*. Paris: Gallimard, 1976.

Foucault, Michel. *Surveiller et punir: Naissance de la prison*. Paris: Gallimard [NRF], 1975

Fournel, Victor. "Contemporains et successeurs de Racine: les poètes tragiques décriés, Le Clerc, l'abbé Boyer, Pradon, Campistron." *Revue d'Histoire littéraire de la France* 27 (1920): 233–58.

Franceschina, John. *Homosexualities in the English Theatre: From Lyly to Wilde*. Westport, CT: Greenwood Press, 1997.

Frantz, Pierre. "Le Moment Voltaire." In *The Eighteenth-Century French Stage Online*.

Frantz, Pierre. "Les échos de la Révolution." In *Le Théâtre français du XVIII$^e$ siècle*, edited by Pierre Frantz and Sophie Marchand, 507–15. Paris: L'Avant-Scène, 2009.

Frantz, Pierre. *L'Esthétique du tableau dans le théâtre du XVIII$^e$ siècle*. Paris: Puf, 1998.

Freud, Sigmund. "The Interpretation of Dreams." In Volume 4 of *The Standard Edition of the Complete Psychological Works of Sigmund Freud (1900): The Interpretation of Dreams (First Part)*, edited by J. Strachey, 262. London: The Hogarth Press and the Institute of Psychoanalysis, 1953.

Friedland, Paul. *Political Actors: Representative Bodies and Theatricality in the Age of the French Revolution*. Ithaca: Cornell University Press, 2003.

Friedlander, Ari. "Desiring History and Historicizing Desire." *JEMCS*, 16.2 (2016).

Fuchs, Max. *La Vie théâtrale en province au XVIII$^e$ siècle*. Paris: Droz, 1933.

*[A] [Full] and the Truest Narrative of the Most Horrid, Barbarous and Unparalled Murder, Committed on the Person of John Knight, [. . .] by the Desperate and Bloody Hand of Nathaniel Butler*. London: n.p., 1657.

Fumaroli, Marc. *Héros et orateurs*. Genève: Droz, 1990.
Furetière, Antoine. "Scaffold." In the *Universal Dictionary*, 1690.
Gable, Anthony. "Tragedy, Discontent and the Question of Kingship 1685–1715." *Seventeenth-Century French Studies* 9 (1987): 168–91.
Garrick, David. *The Journal of David Garrick*. New York: Modern Language Association of America, 1939.
Gastaud, François. *Oraison funèbre de Madame Tiquet*. Cologne: P. L'Enclume, 1699.
Gatrell, V.A.C. *The Hanging Tree: Execution and the English People 1770–1868*. Oxford: Oxford University Press, 1994.
Gauden, John. *The Bloody Court, or, The Fatall Tribunall*. [London]: G. Horton, [1660?].
Girard, René. *La Violence et le sacré*. Paris: Albin Michel, 1990.
Goethe, Johann Wolfgang. "On epic and dramatic poetry." In Vol. 1 of *Correspondence Between Schiller and Goethe, from 1794 to 1805*, translated by George H. Calvert, 387. New York and London: Wiley and Putnam, 1845.
Goldberg, Jonathan. *Sodometries: Renaissance Texts, Modern Sexualities*. 1st edn. New York: Fordham University Press, 2010.
Goldmann, Lucien. *Le Dieu caché: Etude sur la vision tragique dans les "Pensées" de Pascal et dans le théâtre de Racine*. Paris: Gallimard, 1955.
Goldstein, Claire. *Vaux and Versailles: The Appropriations, Erasures, and Accidents That Made Modern France*. Philadelphia: University of Pennsylvania Press, 2008.
Green, André. *The Tragic Effect: The Oedipus Complex in Tragedy*. Translated by A. Sheridan. Cambridge: Cambridge University Press, 1979.
Green, Eugène. *La Parole baroque*. Paris: Desclée de Brouwer, 2001.
Green, Michael. "Kheraskov and the Christian Tragedy." *California Slavic Studies* 9 (1967): 1–25.
Greenberg, Mitchell. *Baroque Bodies: Psychoanalysis and the Culture of French Absolutism*. Ithaca: Cornell University Press, 2001.
Greenberg, Mitchell. *Racine: From Ancient Myth to Modern Tragedy*. Minneapolis: University of Minnesota Press, 2010.
Greenberg, Mitchell. *Subjectivity and Subjugation in Seventeenth-Century Drama and Prose: The Family Romance of French Classicism*. Cambridge, UK: Cambridge University Press, 1992.
Greene, John C. *Theatre in Dublin, 1745–1820: A Calendar of Performances*. Bethlehem, PA: Lehigh University Press, 2012.
Grosse, Henning. *Tragica, seu, Tristium historium de poenis criminalibus et exitu horribili*. [Eisleben]: Henning Grosse, 1598.
Gueudeville, Nicolas. *L'Esprit des cours de l'Europe*. 19 vols. The Hague: François L'Honoré, 1699–1710.
Guyot, Sylvaine and Clotilde Thouret. "Des émotions en chaîne: représentation théâtrale et circulation publique des affects au XVII$^e$ siècle." *Littératures classiques* 68 (2009): 225–41.
Hall, Hugh Gaston. "Le Répertoire de l'Illustre Théâtre des Béjart et de Molière." *Australian Journal of French Studies* 30 (1993): 276–91.
Hanway, Jonas. *The Defects of Police the Cause of Immorality, and the Continual Robberies Committed, Particularly in and about the Metropolis*. London: J. Dodsley, and Brotherton and Sewell, 1775.
Harris, Joseph. "Disruptive Desires: Lesbian Sexuality in Isaac de Benserade's Iphis et Iante (1634)." *Seventeenth-Century French Studies* 24, no. 1 (2002): 151–63.

Harvey, Sara. "La Genèse stratifiée du répertoire de la Comédie-Française entre 1680 et 1730." *Littératures classiques* 95 (2018): 89–103: 94.

Hegel, G.W.F. *The Phenomenology of Spirit*. Translated by A.V. Miller, Foreword and Analysis by J.N. Findlay. Oxford, UK: Oxford University Press, 1981 [1977].

Heidegger, Martin. *Introduction to Metaphysics*. Translated by Gregory Field and Richard Polt. New Haven: Yale University Press, 2000. 166.

Herr, Mireille. *Les Tragédies bibliques au XVIIIe siècle*. Paris-Genève: Champion-Slatkine, 1988.

Hogan, Charles Beecher. *Shakespeare in the Theatre, 1701–1800*. Oxford: Clarendon Press, 1952.

Holyoake, George Jacob. "Public Lessons of the Hangman." *Morning Star*, November 16, 1864, 52–54.

[The] *Holy Bible Conteyning the Old Testament, and the New: Newly Translated*. London: Robert Barker, 1611.

Hoxby, Blair. *What Was Tragedy? Theory and the Early Modern Canon*. Oxford: Oxford University Press, 2015.

Huet, Marie-Hélène. *Rehearsing the Revolution: The Staging of Marat's Death 1793–1797*. Translated by Robert Hurley. Berkeley: University of California Press, 1982.

Hughes, Derek. *Culture and Sacrifice*. Cambridge: Cambridge University Press, 2007.

Hughes, Leo. *The Drama Patrons. A Study of the Eighteenth-Century London Audience*. Austin: University of Texas Press, 1971.

Hutcheson, Francis. *An Essay on the Nature and Conduct of the Passions and Affections*. London: John Smith and William Bruce, 1728.

Hutcheson, Francis. *An Inquiry into the Original of our Ideas of Beauty and Virtue*. London: W. and J. Innys, et al., 1725.

Joannidès, Alexandre. *La Comédie-Française de 1680 à 1900: dictionnaire général des pièces et des auteurs* (1901). New York: Burt Franklin, 1971.

Johnson, James H. *Listening in Paris: A Cultural History*. Berkeley: University of California Press, 1995.

Johnson, Samuel. *Rambler* 125 (May 28, 1751).

Kant, Immanuel. "An Old Question Raised Again. . ." Translated by Lewis Beck et al. In *The Conflict of the Faculties: Der Streit der Fakultäten*, translated by Mary J. Gregor, 153. New York: Abaris, 1979.

Kant, Immanuel. *Metaphysics of Morals*.

Kantorowicz, Ernst H. *The King's Two Bodies: A Study in Medieval Political Theology*. Introduction by Conrad Leyser, Preface by William Chester Jordon. Princeton: Princeton University Press, 2016.

Kavenik, Frances M. *British Drama. 1660–1779. A Critical History*. New York: Twayne, 1995.

Kennedy, Emmet, et al. *Theater, Opera, and Audiences in Revolutionary Paris: Analysis and Repertory*. Westport, CT: Greenwood Press, 1996.

Kennedy, Theresa Varney. *Women's Deliberation: The Heroine in Early Modern French Women's Theater (1650–1750)*. Abingdon: Routledge, 2018.

Kewes, Paulina. *Authorship and Appropriation. Writing for the Stage in England, 1660–1710*. Oxford: Clarendon Press, 1998.

Kramer, David Bruce. *The Imperial Dryden: The Poetics of Appropriation in Seventeenth Century England*. Athens, GA: University of Georgia Press, 1994.

La Grange. *Registre*, 2 vols. Edited by B.E. Young and G.P. Young. Paris: Droz, 1947

Lagrave, Henri. *Le Théâtre et le public à Paris de 1715 à 1750*. Paris: Klincksieck, 1972.

Lancaster, Henry Carrington. *A History of French Dramatic Literature in the Seventeenth Century*. 9 vols. Baltimore: Johns Hopkins University Press, 1929–42.

Lancaster, Henry Carrington. *Actors' Roles at the Comédie Française according to the Répertoire des comédies françaises qui se peuvent jouer en 1685*. Baltimore: Johns Hopkins University Press, 1953.

Lancaster, Henry Carrington. *Sunset: A History of Parisian Drama in the Last Years of Louis XIV*. Baltimore: Johns Hopkins University Press, 1945.

Lancaster, Henry Carrington. *The Comédie-Française 1680–1701: Plays, Actors, Spectators, Finances*. Baltimore and London: Johns Hopkins Press and Oxford University Press, 1941.

Laqueur, Thomas. *Making Sex: Body and Gender from the Greeks to Freud*. Reprint edn. Cambridge, MA: Harvard University Press, 1992.

[The] *Last Dying Words, Speech, and Confession of the 5 Malefactors who were Executed at Tyburn near York*. [York?], [1792?].

"*Le Nouveau Mercure Galant*, janvier–mars, tome 1, 1677, p. 47–54[IV]." http://obvil.sorbonne-universite.site/corpus/mercure-galant/MG-1677-03?q=rodogune#mark1 (accessed August 30, 2018).

"*Le Nouveau Mercure Galant*, octobre, tome 8, 1677, p. 200–243." http://obvil.sorbonne-universite.site/corpus/mercure-galant/MG-1677-10?q=iphigénie#mark1 (accessed August 4, 2018).

Lebrun, François. *Les Hommes et la mort en Anjou aux 17e et 18e siècles: essai de démographie et de psychologie historiques*. Paris: Mouton, 1971.

Lekain, Henri-Louis. *Mémoires, publiés par son fils aîné*. Paris: Colnet, Debray, Mongie, 1801.

Lekain, Henri Louis. *Réflexions destinées à êtres mises sous les yeux de nos seigneurs les Premiers Gentilshommes de la Chambre*. In Sabine Chaouche, *La Mise en scène du répertoire à la Comédie-Française (1680–1815)*, vol. 1, 148. Paris: Champion, 2013.

Lessing, Gotthold Ephraim. *Werke und Briefe in zwölf Bänden*. Edited by Wilfried Barner and Klaus Bohnen. 12 vols. Frankfurt am Main: Deutscher Klassiker Verlag, 1985–2003.

Lewis, Philip. "Sacrifice and Suicide: Some Afterthoughts on the Career of J. Racine." Paper presented at North American Society for Seventeenth-Century French Literature, 7th Conference, Baton Rouge, LA, 1985. Edited by S.A. Zebouni, 58–9. Paris; Seattle: Papers on French Seventeenth Century Literature, 1986.

*Life and Trial of F. H. de la Motte*. London: T. Truman, [1781].

Lilti, Antoine. *The Invention of Celebrity*. Translated by Lynn Jeffress. Cambridge: Polity Press, 2017.

Loraux, Nicole. *L'Invention d'Athènes: Histoire de l'oraison funèbre dans la "cité classique."* Paris: Payot, 1981.

Loraux, Nicole. *Tragic Ways of Killing a Woman*. Translated by Anthony Forster. Cambridge, MA: Harvard University Press, 1987.

Lough, John. *Paris Theatre Audiences in the Seventeenth and Eighteenth Centuries*. Oxford: Oxford University Press, 1957.

Louis XIV, King of France. *Mémoires*. Edited by J. Longnon. Paris: Tallandier, 1978.

Lyons, John D. "Racine's Silent Places." In *L'éloquence Du Silence Sur La Scène Théâtrale Du 17e et 18e Siècles*, edited by Hélène Bilis and Jennifer Tams, 217–37. Paris: Garnier, 2014.

Lyons, John D. *The Tragedy of Origins: Pierre Corneille and Historical Perspective*. Stanford, CA: Stanford University Press, 1996.

Lyons, John D. *Tragedy and the Return of the Dead*. Rethinking the Early Modern. Evanston, IL: Northwestern University Press, 2018.

Mandeville, Bernard. *An Enquiry into the Causes of the Frequent Executions at Tyburn.* London: J. Roberts, 1725.

Marchand, Sophie. "'L'Auteur! L'auteur!' ou quand l'auteur se donne en spectacle. Rites de reconnaissance, évolution du rapport de force et définition du fait théâtral dans la seconde moitié du XVIII<sup>e</sup> siècle." In *Diversité et modernité du théâtre du XVIII<sup>e</sup> siècle*, edited by Guillemette Marot-Mercier and Nicholas Dion, 41–60. Paris: Hermann, 2014.

Marchand, Sophie. *Théâtre et pathétique au XVIIIe siècle: pour une esthétique de l'effet dramatique.* Paris: Honoré Champion, 2009.

Marchand, Sophie. "Réflexions sur le succès théâtral à partir des nouvelles perspectives ouvertes par la base de données des registres de la Comédie-Française." *Littératures classiques* 95 (2018): 67–76: 69.

"Marie Antoinette, Tragédie." *Mercure de France* 3, no. 13 (1800–1): 18–21.

Marie, Laurence. *L'Art de l'acteur. Inventions du spectacle dans l'Europe des Lumières.* Paris: PUPS, 2017.

Marin, Louis. *Le Portrait du roi.* Paris: Minuit, 1981.

Markovits, Rahul. *Civiliser l'Europe. Politiques du théâtre français au XVIII<sup>e</sup> siècle.* Paris: Fayard, 2014.

Marsden, Jean I. "Spectacle, Horror and Pathos." In *The Cambridge Companion to English Restoration Theatre*, edited by Deborah Payne Fisk. Cambridge: Cambridge University Press, 2000.

Marvell, Andrew. *The Poems and Letters of Andrew Marvell.* 3rd edn. Edited by H.M. Margoliouth. Oxford: Clarendon Press, 1971.

Maslan, Susan. *Revolutionary Acts: Theater, Democracy, and the French Revolution.* Baltimore: Baltimore, MD: Johns Hopkins University Press, 2005.

Masten, Jeffrey. *Queer Philologies: Sex, Language and Affect in Shakespeare's Time.* Philadelphia, PA: University of Pennsylvania Press, 2016.

McManners, John. *Death and the Enlightenment: Changing Attitudes to Death among Christians and Unbelievers in Eighteenth-Century France.* Oxford: Clarendon Press, 1981.

Meier, Christian. *The Political Art of Greek Tragedy.* Translated by Andrew Webber. Baltimore: Johns Hopkins University Press, 1993.

*Mémoires secrets de Bachaumont*, January 1762.

*Memoirs of the Two Last Years of the Reign of that Unparallell'd Prince, of Ever Blessed Memory, King Charles I.* London: Robert Clavell, 1702.

"*Mercure Galant*, août [tome 9], 1679, p. 259–359." http://obvil.sorbonne-universite.site/corpus/mercure-galant/MG-1679-09?q=sertorius#mark1 (accessed August 6, 2018).

"*Mercure Galant*, avril 1681 [tome 4], p. 327–344." http://obvil.sorbonne-universite.site/corpus/mercure-galant/MG-1681-04?q=sigaral#mark1 (accessed August 6, 2018).

"*Mercure Galant*, janvier 1710 [tome 1], p. 270–299." http://obvil.sorbonne-universite.site/corpus/mercure-galant/MG-1710-01#MG-1710-01_270 (accessed August 13, 2018).

"*Mercure Galant*, juin [tome 6], 1679, p. 279–285." http://obvil.sorbonne-universite.site/corpus/mercure-galant/MG-1679-06?q=belonde#mark1 (accessed August 13, 2018).

"*Mercure Galant*, mai [tome 5], 1682, p. 190–196." http://obvil.sorbonne-universite.site/corpus/mercure-galant/MG-1682-05?q=venceslas#mark1 (accessed August 6, 2018).

"*Mercure Galant*, mars [tome 3], 1678, p. 379–381." http://obvil.sorbonne-universite.site/corpus/mercure-galant/MG-1678-03?q=corneille#mark1 (accessed August 4, 2018).

"*Mercure Galant*, septembre 1681 [tome 9], p. 366–379." http://obvil.sorbonne-universite.site/corpus/mercure-galant/MG-1681-09?q=oreste#mark1 (accessed August 6, 2018).

Merlin-Kajman, Hélène. *Public et littérature en France au XVII<sup>e</sup> siècle*. Paris: Les Belles Lettres, 1994.

Merrick, Jeffrey, and Bryant T. Ragan. *Homosexuality in Early Modern France: A Documentary Collection*. Oxford: Oxford University Press, 2001.

Michelet, Jules. Vol. 2 of *Histoire de la Révolution française*. Paris: Gallimard [Pléiade], 1952.

Milhous, Judith. "Company Management." In *The London Theater World, 1660–1800*, edited by Robert D. Hume. Carbondale: Southern Illinois University Press, 1980, 22.

Milhous, Judith. "Reading Theater History from Account Books." In *Players, Playwrights, Playhouses: Investigating Performance, 1660–1800*, edited by Michael Cordner and Peter Holland, 126. Basingstoke: Palgrave Macmillan, 2007.

Millot, Michel. *L'ecole des filles*. Edited by Pascal Pia. n.p., La Bibliothèque privée, 1969.

Miola, Robert S. *Early Modern Catholicism: An Anthology of Primary Sources*. Oxford: Oxford University Press, 2007.

Mittman, Barbara G. *Spectators on the Paris Stage in the Seventeenth and Eighteenth Centuries*. Ann Arbor, MI: UMI Research Press, 1984.

Molière. *Oeuvres complètes*. 2 vols. Edited by Georges Couton. Paris: Gallimard, 1971.

Molière. *Oeuvres complètes*. 2 vols. Edited by Georges Forestier and Claude Bourqui. Paris: Gallimard, 2010.

Mongrédien, Georges, and Jean Robert. *Les Comédiens français du XVII<sup>e</sup> siècle: dictionnaire biographique*. Paris: Centre National de la Recherche Scientifique, 1981.

Monval, Georges. *Le Premier Registre de La Thorillière (1663–1664)*. Geneva: Slatkine, 1969

Moody, Jane, and Daniel O'Quinn, eds. *The Cambridge Companion to British Theatre. 1730–1830*. Cambridge: Cambridge University Press, 2007.

Moretti, Franco. *Signs Taken for Wonders: On the Sociology of Literary Forms*. London: Verso, 2005.

Mourey, Marie-Thérèse. "Littérature, politique et religion en Silésie au XVIIe siècle: La guerre des mots et ses arcanes." *Dix-septième siècle* 273, no. 4 (2016): 649–60.

Muir, Lynette R. *Love and Conflict in Medieval Drama: The Plays and Their Legacy*. New York: Cambridge University Press, 2007.

Mullaney, Steven. *The Place of the Stage: License, Play and Power in Renaissance* England. Chicago: The University of Chicago Press, 1988.

"Naissance de la critique dramatique." https://www2.unil.ch/ncd17/index.php?extractCode=1043 (accessed June 13, 2018 and September 10, 2018).

[The] *Newgate Calendar: The Malefactors' Bloody Register*. Vol. 1. London, n.p., 1774.

Nicole, Pierre. *Les Imaginaires, ou lettres sur l'hérésie imaginaire*. Liège: Adolphe Beyers, 1667.

Nisbet, Hugh Barr. *Gotthold Ephraim Lessing: His Life, Works, and Thought*. Oxford: Oxford University Press, 2015.

Norton, Rictor. "Homosexuality." In *A Cultural History of Sexuality in the Enlightenment*, edited by Julie Peakman. London: Bloomsbury, 2012.

Nussbaum, Felicity. *Rival Queens: Actresses, Performance, and the Eighteenth-Century British Theater*. Philadelphia: University of Pennsylvania Press, 2010.

"Observations on the Unhappy Reverse of Fortune Experienced by the Late Queen of France." *Lady's Magazine* 24 (Dec. 1793), 623–4.

Oldani, Louis J., and Victor R. Yanitelli. "Jesuit Theater in Italy: Its Entrances and Exit." *Italica* 76.1 (Spring 1999): 18–32.

Otway, Thomas. "The Orphan." In *The British Drama; a Collection of the Most Esteemed Tragedies, Comedies, Operas, and Farces, in the English Language*. Thomas Cowperthwait & Co., 1824.

Parente, James R. *Religious Drama and the Humanist Tradition. Christian Theater in Germany and in the Netherlands, 1500–1680*. Leiden: Brill, 1987.

Pascal, Blaise. *Œuvres complètes*, Fragment 265, Brunschwicq 348. Edited by Jacques Chevalier. Paris: Gallimard [Pléiade], 1954.

*Pascal's Pensées*. Translated by W.F. Trotter, Introduction by T.S. Eliot. New York: Dover Publications, 2003 [1958].

Pasquier, Pierre. *Le Mémoire de Mahelot: mémoire pour la décoration des pièces qui se représentent par les Comédiens du Roi*. Paris: Champion, 2005.

Pedicord, Harry William. *The Theatrical Public in the Time of Garrick*. Carbondale: Southern Illinois University Press, 1954

Pepys, Samuel. *The Diary of Samuel Pepys (1660–68)*, edited by Robert Latham and William Matthews. Berkeley: University of California Press, 1970–83.

Perchellet, Jean-Pierre. *L'Héritage classique. La tragédie entre 1680 et 1814*. Paris: Honoré Champion, 2004.

Peters, Julie Stone. "Penitentiary Performances: Spectators, Affecting Scenes, and Terrible Apparitions in the Nineteenth-Century Model Prison." In *Law and Performance*, edited by Austin Sarat and Martha Umphrey, 18–67 Amherst, MA: University of Massachusetts Press, 2018.

Pitaval, François Gayot de. *Causes célèbres et intéressantes, avec les jugemens qui les ont décidées*. 20 vols. Paris: T. Legras, 1734–43.

Plato. *Republic*. Translated by Benjamin Jowett. Cleveland: World Pub. Co., 1946.

Poirson, Martial. "Introduction." In *Le Théâtre sous la Révolution française. Politique du répertoire (1789–1799)*, edited by Martial Poirson, 34. Paris: Desjonquères, 2008.

Poirson, Martial. "L'auteur dramatique: vedette contrariée du premier champ théâtral (XVII–XVIIIe siècles)." In *Le Sacre de l'acteur. Émergence du vedettariat théâtral de Molière à Sarah Bernhardt*, edited by Florence Filippi, Sara Harvey, and Sophie Marchand, 112. Paris: Armand Colin, 2017.

Poirson, Martial. "Le spectacle est dans la salle. Siffler n'est pas jouer." *Dix-huitième siècle* 149 (2017): 57–74.

Quinault, Philippe. *Astrate*. Edited by Edmund J. Campion. Exeter: University of Exeter, 1980.

Quinault, Philippe. *La Mort de Cyrus*. 1658–9.

Quincy, Joseph Sevin, comte de. *Mémoires du Chevalier de Quincy*. 3 vols. Paris: Librairie Renouard, 1898–1901.

Racine, Jean. "Andromaque." Translated by John Edmunds. In *Four French Plays: Cinna, the Misanthrope, Andromache, Phaedra*. London: Penguin Classics, 2013.

Racine, Jean. *Britannicus*. Edited by F.M. Warren. New York: Henry Holt and Company, 1909.

Racine, Jean. *Théâtre complet*. Edited by Alain Viala and Sylvaine Guyot. Paris: Classiques Garnier, 2014.

Racine, Louis. *Mémoires sur la vie de Jean Racine*, 2 volumes. Lausanne-Genève: Marc-Michel Bousquet et Cie, 1747.

Racine, Louis. *Vie de Racine*. Paris: Les Belles Lettres, 1999.

Rädle, Fidel. "Jesuit Theatre in Germany, Austria, and Switzerland." In *Neo-Latin Drama in Early Modern Europe*, edited by Jan Bloemendal and Howard Norland, 185–292. Leiden-Boston: Brill, 2013.

Rapin, René. *Reflections on Aristotle's Treatise of Poesie*. London: H. Herringman, 1674.
Ravel, Jeffrey S. *The Contested Parterre. Public Theater and French Political Culture (1680–1791)*. Ithaca-London: Cornell University Press, 1999.
Ravel, Jeffrey S. "Le théâtre et ses publics. Pratiques et représentations du parterre à Paris au XVIIIe siècle." *Revue d'histoire moderne et contemporaine* 49-3 (2002): 92.
Razgonnikoff, Jacqueline. "Les Théâtres nationaux à l'écoute de la vie du peuple. Créations et réactions, d'une scène à l'autre (Théâtre de la Nation et Théâtre de la République)." *Studi Francesi* 169, 50.1 (2013): 27–39.
Reynolds, John. *The Triumphs of Gods Revenge Against the Crying and Execrable Sinne of (Wilful and Premeditated) Murther*. 3rd edn. London: William Lee, 1657.
Riccoboni, Louis. *Reflexions historiques et critiques sur les differens theatres de l'Europe. Avec les Pensées sur la Declamation*. Paris: Jacques Gerin, 1738.
Ritchie, Fiona. *Women and Shakespeare in the Eighteenth Century*. Cambridge: Cambridge University Press, 2014.
Roach, Joseph. "Public Intimacy: The Prior History of 'It.'" In *Theatre and Celebrity in Britain, 1660–2000*, edited by Mary Luckhurst and Jane Moody, 24–5. Basingstoke and New York: Palgrave, 2005.
Robespierre, Maximilien. *Pour le bonheur et pour la liberté: discours*. Edited by Yannick Bosc, Florence Gauthier, and Sophie Wahnich. Paris: La Fabrique, 2000.
Roche, Daniel. *Humeurs vagabondes. De la circulation des hommes et de l'utilité des voyages*. Paris: Fayard, 2003.
Rojek, Chris. *Celebrity*. London: Reaktion, 2001.
Rosset, François de. *De groote schouw-plaets der jammerlijcke bloed-en-moord geschiedenissen*. Edited by Simon de Vries. Utrecht: Johannes Ribbius, 1670.
Rosset, François de. *Les histoires tragiques de nostre temps: Où sont contenuës les morts funestes & lamentables de plusieurs personnes, arrivées par leurs ambitions, amours desreiglees, sortileges, vols, rapines*. Cambray: Jean de La Riviere, 1614.
Rousseau, Jean-Jacques. "Lettre à d'Alembert." In *Œuvres complètes de J. J. Rousseau*, edited by Ch. Lahure, vol. 1, 178. Paris: Hachette, 1856.
Rousseau, Jean-Jacques. *Lettre à d'Alembert Sur Les Spectacles*. Paris: Flammarion, 2003.
Row, Jennifer. "Alternative Intimacies, Carceral Sympathy and Sexuality in Voltaire's *Zaïre*." *Le Monde français du dix-huitième siècle* 2, no. 1 (2017).
Row, Jennifer. "*Iphigénie*, Jean Racine." In *The Literary Encyclopedia*, volume 1.5.2.03: *French Writing and Culture of the Seventeenth Century: Classical and Baroque, 1600–1700*. http://www.litencyc.com/php/sworks.php?rec=true&UID=4399
Row, Jennifer. "Queer Time on the Early Modern Stage: France and the Drama of Biopower." *Exemplaria* 29, no. 1 (Winter 2017).
Rush, Benjamin. *An Enquiry into the Effects of Public Punishments upon Criminals and upon Society*. Philadelphia: Joseph James, 1787.
Rush, Benjamin. *Essays Literary, Moral and Philosophical*. Edited by Michael Meranze. Schenectady, NY: Union College Press, 1988.
Rush, Benjamin. *Medical Inquiries and Observations, upon the Diseases of the Mind*. Philadelphia: Kimber & Richardson, 1812.
Sabatier, Gérard. *Versailles, ou la disgrâce d'Apollon*. [1999] Versailles-Rennes: CRCV-PUR, 2016.
*Sad and Bloody Newes from Yorkshire*. London: Edwards, 1663.

Sanjuan, Agathe. "Lecture du répertoire dans les archives de la Comédie-Française." *Littératures classiques* 95 (2018): 45–54.
Sedaine, Michel-Jean. *Le Philosophe sans le savoir*. Edited by Graham E. Rodmell. Durham: University of Durham, 1987.
Schiller, Friedrich. "Letter to Goethe, 26th December 1797." In Vol. 1 of *Correspondence Between Schiller and Goethe, from 1794 to 1805*, translated by George H. Calvert, 386. New York and London: Wiley and Putnam, 1845.
Schiller, Friedrich. "On the Tragic Art." In *Aesthetical and Philosophical Essays*, 346–67. New York: Harvard Publishing Company, 1895.
Schiller, Friedrich. "Theater Considered as a Moral Institution." [1784] Translated by John Sigerson and John Chambless. Schiller Institute, Washington, D.C., 2002–5. http://www.schillerinstitute.org/transl/schil_theatremoral.html
Schiller, Friedrich. *Early Dramas*. Translated by Samuel Taylor Coleridge. London: 1901.
Schiller, Friedrich. *The Robbers. A Tragedy*. London: G.G. and J. Robinson, 1797.
Schmitt-Maaß, Christoph, Stefanie Stockhorst, and Doohwan Ahn, eds. *Fénelon in the Enlightenment: Traditions, Adaptations, and Variations*. Amsterdam: Brill, 2014.
Schwartz, William Leonard. "Light on Molière in 1664 from *Le Second Registre de La Thorillière*." *PMLA* 53 (1938): 1054–75.
Scott, Virginia. *Molière: a Theatrical Life*. Cambridge: Cambridge University Press, 2000.
Scott, Virginia. *Women on the Stage in Early Modern France 1540–1750*. Cambridge: Cambridge University Press, 2010.
Sedgwick, Eve Kosofsky. *Tendencies*. Abingdon: Routledge, 1994.
Ségla, Guillaume de. *Histoire tragique, et arrests de la Cour de Parlement de Tholose*. Paris: Robinot, 1613.
Seifert, Lewis C. "Théophile de Viau et l'herméneutique de l'amitié masculine." *Dix-septième siècle* 258, no. 1 (Mar. 2013): 107–16.
Seifert, Lewis, and Rebecca Wilkin. *Men and Women Making Friends in Early Modern France*. Farnham: Ashgate Publishing, Ltd., 2015.
Semk, Christopher. *Playing the Martyr. Theater and Theology in Early Modern France*. Bucknell University Press, 2017.
"[A] Sermon Preached Before the Lords Spiritual and Temporal." Vol. 1 of *The British Critic* (May 1793), 25–8.
Shannon, Laurie. "Nature's Bias: Renaissance Homonormativity and Elizabethan Comic Likeness." *Modern Philology* 98, no. 2 (2000): 183–210.
Sosulski, Michael J. *Theater and Nation in Eighteenth-Century Germany*. Aldershot and Burlington: Ashgate, 2007.
Spierenberg, Pieter. *The Spectacle of Suffering: Executions and the Evolution of Repression: From a Pre-Industrial Metropolis to the European Experience*. Cambridge: Cambridge University Press, 1984.
Steiner, George. *The Death of Tragedy*. 2nd edn. New Haven: Yale University Press, 1996.
Stone, George Winchester. "The Making of the Repertory." In *The London Theater World, 1660–1800*, edited by Robert D. Hume. Carbondale: Southern Illinois University Press, 1980.
Strauss, Jonathan. *Private Lives, Public Deaths: Antigone and the Invention of Individuality*. New York: Fordham University Press, 2013.
Strauss, Jonathan. *Subjects of Terror: Hegel, Nerval, and the Modern Self*. Stanford, CA: Stanford University Press, 1998.

"Sur les principes de morale politique qui doivent guider la Convention Nationale dans l'administration intérieure de la République, Séance du 17 pluviôse, an II [February 5, 1794]." In Vol. 10 of *Œuvres de Maximilien Robespierre*, edited by Marc Boulouiseau and Albert Soboul, 354. Paris: Presses Universitaires de France, 1967.

Thacher, James. *A Military Journal During the American Revolutionary War, from 1775 to 1783*. Boston: Richardson & Lord, 1823.

Thirouin, Laurent. *L'Aveuglement salutaire. Le réquisitoire contre le théâtre dans la France classique*. Paris: Honoré Champion, 1997.

Thomson, Thomas. "Celebrity and Rivalry: David [Garrick] and Goliath [Quin]." In *Theatre and Celebrity*, 135–6.

Touchard, Jean, ed. *Histoire des Idées Politiques*. Paris: Presses Universitaires de France, 1959.

[The] *True and Perfect Speeches of Colonel John Gerhard upon the Scaffold at Tower-Hill [and] the Speech of the Portugal Ambassadors Brother upon the Scaffold*. London: C. Horton, 1654.

Turner, Barnard and Thomas Skinner. *An Account of Some Alterations and Amendments Attempted in the Duty and Office of the Sherriff of the County of Middlesex and Sheriffs of the City of London*. London: n.p., 1784.

Ubersfeld, Anne. *Le théâtre et la cité: de Corneille à Kantor*. Brussels, Aissa-Iaspa, 1991.

Valentin, Jean-Marie. *Le Théâtre des Jésuites dans les pays de langue allemande (1554–1680)*. 3 volumes. Bern, 1978.

Venesoen, Constant. "Molière tragédien." *XVIIe Siècle* (1969): 25–34.

Vernant, Jean-Pierre and Pierre Vidal-Naquet. *Myth and Tragedy in Ancient Greece*. Translated by Janet Lloyd. New York: Zone Books, 1990.

Viala, Alain. *Naissance de l'écrivain. Sociologie de la littérature à l'âge classique*. Paris: Minuit, 1985.

Viala, Alain. *Racine. La stratégie du caméléon*. Paris: Seghers, 1990.

Villette, John. *A Genuine Account of the Behaviour and Dying-Words of Daniel Perreau and Robert Perreau*. London: the author, [1776?].

Villette, John. *A Genuine Account of the Behaviour, Confession, and Dying-Words of William Hawke and William Jones*. London: H. Turpin, et al., 1774.

Ward, Richard, ed. *A Global History of Execution and the Criminal Corpse*. Houndmills, Basingstoke, Hampshire: Palgrave Macmillan, 2015.

Weber, Caroline. "Voltaire's 'Zaïre': Fantasies of Infidelity, Ideologies of Faith." In *South Central Review* 21, no. 2 (2004): 42–62.

Wheatley, Christopher J. 'Tragedy." In *The Cambridge Companion to English Restoration Theatre*, edited by Deborah Payne Fisk. Cambridge: Cambridge University Press, 2000.

Wiley, William L. *The Early Public Theatre in France*. Cambridge, MA: Harvard University Press, 1960.

Wilf, Steven. "Imagining Justice: Aesthetics and Public Executions in Late Eighteenth-Century England." Faculty Articles and Papers 283, 1993. http://digitalcommons.uconn.edu/law_papers/283

Williams, Jerry M. "A New Test in the Case of Ana de Castro: Lima's Inquisition on Trial." *Dieciocho: Hispanic Enlightenment* 24, no. 1 (2001): 11–20.

Williams, Jerry M., ed. *The Theatre of Infamy: Autos de Fe in Peru. Inquisition, Trial, and Sentencing Records, 1639–1749*. Potomac, MD: Scripta Humanistica, 2015.

Williams, Raymond. *Modern Tragedy*. London: Chatto & Windus, 1966.

Wines, Enoch Cobb. *The State of Prisons and of Child-Saving Institutions in the Civilized World*. Cambridge MA: University Press, 1880.

Wirtschafter, Elise Kimerling. *The Play of Ideas in Russian Enlightenment Theater*. DeKalb, IL: NIU Press, 2003.
Wynn, Thomas. "Sade's Theatre: Pleasure, Vision, Masochism." In *SVEC 2007*, no. 2 (2007). Oxford: Voltaire Foundation, 2007.
Wynn, Thomas. "Violence, vulnerability and subjectivity in Sade." In *Representing violence in France 1760–1820*, 139–160. Oxford: Voltaire Foundation, 2013.
Ziolkowski, Theodore. *Scandal on Stage: European Theater as Moral Trial*. Cambridge: Cambridge University Press, 2009.

# INDEX

Note: Page numbers in *italics* refer to graphs and illustrations.

abortive sympathy 145, 146
absolutism 1–2, 3–4, 95
acting practice 70–3
acting treatises 75
actors 70–7. *See also individual actors*
    Society of Dramatic Actors 78
actresses 70–7, 170–1, 183. *See also individual actresses*
*Adélaide Du Guesclin* (Voltaire) 74
*Agamemnon* (Boyer) 51
*Alexandre* (Racine) 46–7, 69
*All for Love* (Dryden) 175–7
Althusser, Louis 4
*Amours de Diane et d'Endimion* (Gilbert) 46, 54
*Amours de Vénus et d'Adonis* (De Visé) 55
*Andromaque* (Racine) 14, 156, 172–3
*Andromède* (Corneille, P.) 54, 113, *113*
Aristotle 104, 148, 167
Arouet, François-Marie. *See* Voltaire (François-Marie Arouet)
*Athalie* (Racine) 16, 69, 115–16
*Atrée et Thyeste* (Crébillion) 118
*Attila* (Corneille, P.) 47
audience 81–6, 111
*Aureng-Zebe* (Dryden) 149–51
authorship 77–81. *See also* playwrights
*auto-de-fé* 125

baroque theatre 5
Barthès, Pierre 131
Barthes, Roland 13
Basterra, Gabriela 104
Beaumarchais, Pierre Augustin, Caron de 36, 160–1
    *La Folle journée, ou le Mariage de Fogaro* 165–6
Beccaria, Cesare 140–1
Béjart, Madeleine 44
Belfiore, Elizabeth 148
Benedicti, Jean 174
Benserade, Isaac de 173

Bentham, Jeremy 142–3
*Bérénice* (Racine) 77
Bermúdez, Pedro José de la Torre y Solier 125, 134–5
Bernard, Catherine 171
Biet, Christian 171–2
Bilis, Hélène E. 92
Billings, John 20
Bossuet, Jacques-Bénigne 111, 114
Brecht, Berthold 31, 32, 37
*Britannicus* (Racine) 95
Britard, Jean-Baptiste *8*
Brooks, E.M. 169
Brown, Gregory 77
Brown, Laura 183–4
Brueys, David-Augustin de 117
Brunschwig, Jacques 95
*Brutus* (Voltaire) 74, 85, 99
buggery 174
Burke, Edmund 139

Cain, Henri Louis. *See* Lekain (Henri Louis Cain)
*Caïus Gracchus* (Chénier) 100, 102
Caldicott, C.E.J. 44
capital punishment 27–8
Cassirer, Ernst 97–8
Catholic Church 35, 108
cavalier drama 181
censorship 66–7, 85
Chappuzeau, Samuel 40, 42, 47
Charles I 1, 126, 177
Charles II 177
*Charles IX* (Chénier) 85, 86, 99–100, 122–3
Chénier, Marie-Joseph 99
Christian theatre 115–17
Christianity 35, 108, 111–12, 114, 129, 130, 131, 158
Chua, Brandon 177
*Cinna ou la clémence d'Auguste* (Corneille, P.) 9–10, *11*, 69
*Circé* (Thomas Corneille, De Visé) 49

Clairon, Mlle Claire 2, 70, 71, 74, 76, 79
Comédie-Française 39, 40, 44, 53–60, 66
    audience 81, 84–5
    number of performances of individual tragedies 56, 57
    playwrights 77–8
    private performances 61, 62
    programming 42, 67, 69
    registers 68
    salaries 76
    seating capacity 81
comedy 42–3, 160
commercialization 65–70
compassion 137. *See also* sympathy
Conroy, Derval 171
contemporary theatre 23, 32
Corneille, Pierre 5–10, *6*, 39
    *Andromède* 54, 113, *113*
    *Attila* 47
    capital punishment 28
    *Cinna ou la clémence d'Auguste* 9–10, *11*, 69
    Comédie-Française 67
    *Horace* 7–8, 69, 73
    *La Toison d'or* (Corneille, P.) 54–5
    *Le Cid* 7, 69, 92–4, 153, 159, 163–4, 178
    *Médée* 6–7, 50, 168
    *Nicomède* 149, *150*
    politics 91–2
    *Polyeucte* 67, 69, 179–81
    *Psyché* 48, 49, 55
    publications 80
    scaffold theatre 24
    *Sertorius* 46
    *Three Discourses on the Tragic Poem* 148–9, 178
    *Tite et Bérénice* 47–8
    tragedies 44
Corneille, Thomas 46, 67, 69
    *Circé* 49
    *La Mort d'Achilles* 49
    *Timocrate* 28–31
Corneillian dilemma 8
court performances 46–7, 61–2, *63*, *64*
Crawford, Katherine 174
cruelty 23–8. *See also* violence

Danton, Georges 101
d'Aubignac, François Hédelin, Abbé 109–10
*David Garrick as Richard III* 72
De Viau, T. 182
De Visé, Donneau 44, 49, 52, 55

death of tragedy 143
Delcourt, Marie 14
democracy 102, 104
Descartes, René 136
desire 152–4
Diderot, Denis 19–20, 98, 141–2, 160
*Don Quixote* (da Silva) 131–2
drama 159–66
dramatic poems 36
dramatic projection 35–7
Drury Lane 66, 81
Dryden, John 18, *19*, 80
    *All for Love* 175–7
    *Aureng-Zebe* 149–51
Du Bos, Abbé Jean-Baptiste 136
Du Noyer, Anne-Marguerite 130–1
Duchêne, Roger 47

emotions 147–8
England 4, *5*, 18, 65, 66–7, 69, 80, 89
epic poems 36
epic theatre 31–7
erotic love 114
*Esther* (Racine) 16, 115–16
*Eugénie* (Beaumarchais) 161
executions 125–6, 127, 129–31, 132–4, 207n96
    Louis XVI 1, 126, 143–4
    Marie Antoinette 144–5
    spectators 134–7, 138–40
    support for 140–2
experimental theatre 25–8

family 2–3, 4
    as the center of the tragic plot 147–59
    in drama 159–66
fashion 76
female playwrights 17
Fénelon, François 114–15
*Fénelon, ou les religieuses de Cambrai* (Chénier) 123
Forestier, Georges 47
Foucault, Michel 174, 198n12
French Revolution 1, 20, 69, 90–1, 98–9, 101
    censorship 66, 85
    representation 102–4, 105
Freud, Sigmund 15

*galant* concept 154–9
Galen 169
Garrick, David 72, 74, 75, 76, 77
gender 9, 89, 167–73

gendered salons 181
Gerard, John 129, 130
German dramatic poetry 36
German romanticism 20
Germany 109–10
Girard, René 89
*gloire* 178
God 4, 127, 129, 130
Goethe, Johann Wolfgang von 36
Goldberg, Jonathan 175
Green, André 3
Greenberg, Mitchell 94, 95–6, 177–8, 199n33
Guénégaud company. *See* Hôtel Guénégaud
guilt 88, 89, 95, 101, 104

*Hamlet* (Shakespeare) 74
Hanway, Jonas 138
Harris, Joseph 173
Harvey, Sara 42–3
Hegel, G.W.F. 103–4
Heidegger, Martin 89, 95
Henry IV 26
homosexuality 173–4, 175
homosocial bonds 176, 180–1
homosocial theatre 181
Horace 167
*Horace* (Corneille, P.) 7–8, 69, 73
Hôtel de Bourgogne 39, 40, 51, 52–3, 107, 110
    private performances 46–7, 61
Hôtel Guénégaud 39, 40, 42, 44, 49–53
    number of performances of individual tragedies 52, 56, 57
    private performances 61
    seating capacity 81
Huét, Marie-Hélène 101
human tragedy 117–18
Hutcheson, Francis 137

ideology 4
*Idle 'Prentice Executed at Tyburn, The* (Hogarth) *133*
Illustre Théâtre 39
*Iphigénie* (Racine) 113–14, 168, 169, *170*
*Iphis et Iante* (Benserade) 173
Islam 35, 120
Italy 40, 90, 109, 116

Jansenism 10–13
*Jephté ou la Mort de Seïla* (Venel) 116
Jesuits 5–6, 116
judgment of the parterre 81
justice 88, 95, 96–7, 100, 101, 131–2, 133

Kant, Immanuel 91
Kramer, David Bruce 177

La Champmeslé, Marie Desmare 47, 50, 51, *51*, 55, 71, 74, 170
*La Folle journée* (Beaumarchais) 165–6
La Fontaine, Jean de 55
La Grange 39–40, 46–7, 50, 61
*La Mort d'Achilles* (Corneille, T.) 49
*La Mort de Cyrus* (Quinault) 156–8
*La Thébaïde* (Racine) 46, 69
*La Toison d'or* (Corneille, P.) 54–5
language 5
*Laodamie, Rein d'Empire* (Bernard) 171
Laqueur, Thomas 169
laws of nature 97–8
*Le Cid* (Corneille, P.) 7, 69, 92–4, 153, 159, 163–4, 178
*Le Fils natural* (Diderot) 20, 160
*Le Marriage de Figaro* (Beaumarchais) 165–6
*Le Philosophe sans le savoir* (Sedaine) 161–4
Lekain (Henri Louis Cain) 66, 70, 71, 73, 74, 76–7
*Les Comédiens-Français* 71
lesbianism 173
Lessing, G. 20, 121
*L'Honnête Criminel* (Falbair) 122
*libertinage* 182
location 26
Lope de Vega, F. 4–5
Loraux, Nicole 168
Louis XIV 3–4, *90*, 91, 96, 178, 187n4
Louis XV 78
Louis XVI 39, 101, 103, 126
    Christian theatre 115–17
    execution 1, 126, 143–4
love 32–3, 114–15, 152–6, 176, 178. *See also galant* concept
Lully, J.B. 15, 39, 40
Lyons, John 92

machine plays 40
madness 145
Mandeville, Bernard 132–4, 135
Marais 39, 40
Marie Antoinette 126, 144–5
marriage 156
Marsden, Jean 183
Maslan, Susan 102, 103
Masten, Jeffrey 175
*Médée* (Corneille, P.) 6–7, 50, 168
Meier, Christian 87

Mercier, L.S. 79–80
"Miseries and Misfortunes of War, The" (engraving) 30
Molière 45, 49
    troupe 39–40, 42, 44–9, 54
        number of performances of individual tragedies 48
        private performances 61
Moretti, Franco 4
mothers 171–3
Mullaney, Steven 3
mythology 108, 112–14

*Nathan der Weise* (Lessing) 121
neo-classical tragedy 33
*Nicomède* (Corneille, P.) 149, *150*
Norton, Rictor 174

*Oedipe* (Voltaire) 35, 118–19
Oedipus 14, 15, 35
one-sex model 169
opera 15
*Oresteia* (Aeschylus) 88
*Orphan, The* (Otway) 183

Pascal, Blaise 10–11, 96–7
passions 136
pathos 85
Pepys, Samuel 83
performances
    private 46–7, 61–2, *63*, 64
    rhythm of 40, 110
*Phèdre* (Racine) 14–15, 66, 69, 113, 114, 115, 152–4, *155*, 166
pity 139. *See also* sympathy
Plato 147–8
platonic friendships 181
playwrights 74, 77–81, 84. *See also* female playwrights; *individual playwrights*
poetry 36
polis 87–9
political engagement 122–3
political legitimacy 87–9, 92, 96–7, 98
    *Britannicus* (Racine) 95
    *Caïus Gracchus* (Chénier) 100
    *Charles IX* (Chénier) 99–100
    *Le Cid* (Corneille, P.) 92–4
    representation 102–4, 105
politics 34–5
    and sexuality 176–8
*Polyeucte* (Corneille, P.) 67, 69, 179–81
Poquelin, Jean Baptiste. *See* Molière

Port Royal des Champs 13
power 94
premieres 81
press 76, 86
private performances 46–7, 61–2, *63*, 64
programming 41–4, 66–70, 78
*Psyché* (Pierre Corneille, Molière, Quinault) 48, 49, 55
psychosexual relations 94–5
punishment 125–7, 140–3. *See also* executions; tragic scaffold paradigm
Puritans 177
*Pyrame et Thisbe* (de Viau) 182

queer theory 174–5
queerness 180–1
Quinault, Philippe 15, 48, 50, 54, 69, 77
    *La Mort de Cyrus* 156–8

Racine, Jean 11–12, *12*, 13–17, 39
    *Alexandre* 46–7, 69
    *Andromaque* 14, 156, 172–3
    *Athalie* 16, 69, 115–16
    *Bérénice* 77
    *Britannicus* 95
    Comédie-Française 67
    *Esther* 16, 115–16
    Hôtel Guénégaud 49–50
    *Iphigénie* 113–14, 168, 169, *170*
    *La Thébaïde* 46, 69
    *Lettre à l'auteur des Hérésies imaginaires et des deux Visionnaires* 80
    love 31
    Marie Desmare La Champmeslé 74
    *Phèdre* 14–15, 66, 69, 113, 114, 115, 152–4, *155*, 166
    psychosexual relations 94–5
religion 35, 107, 108. *See also* Christianity
    in Enlightenment critique 118–20
    *Nathan der Weise* (Lessing) 121
    *Robbers, The* (Schiller) 165
    and the state 121–2
    theatre's emancipation from 109–10
    *Zaïre* (Voltaire) 35, 158–9
religious antitheatrical polemic 111–12
religious theatre 115–17
religious tragedies 112
repertoire 42–4, 65–70
    Comédie-Française 53–60
    Hôtel Guénégaud 49–53
    Molière's troupe 44–6, 47, 48–9, 54
representation 102–4, 105

Riccoboni, Luigi 107
Richelieu, Cardinal (Armand Jean du Plessis) 5, 7, 77, 178
*Robbers, The* (Schiller) 164–5
Robespierre, Maximilien 103
Rousseau, Jean-Jacques 101–2, 185–6
Royal School of Declamation 74
Rush, Benjamin 145
Russia 121–2

sacrifice 169
Sade, Marquis de 182
Saint-Évremond, Charles de 115, 117
Saint-Just, Louis-Antoine-Léon 98, 102, 103
sameness 180–1
same-sex desire 173–5
same-sex friendships. *See* homosocial bonds
*Sarah Siddons as Lady Macbeth* 75
scaffold paradigm. *See* tragic scaffold paradigm
scaffold theatre 24, 25–8
Schiller, Friedrich 36, 121, 159
  *Robbers, The* 164–5
Scott, Virginia 44
secular rituals 110–11
secularism 117–18
Seifert, Lewis 181
*Sertorius* (Cornielle, P.) 46
sexuality 167–8, 169. *See also* psychosexual relations
  exotic 184–6
  gendered salons 181
  *gloire* and sameness 178–81
  politics 176–8
  queer terms 173–5
  sodomitical and homosocial 175–6
  violences 181–4
Shaftesbury, Anthony Ashley Cooper, Third Earl of 137
Shakespeare, William 20, 70, 74
shame 143
Shannon, Laurie 180
she-tragedies 183–4
social hierarchy 82–3, 148–9
Society of Dramatic Actors 78
sodomy 174, 175–6, 182
sovereignty 2
space 26
Spain 4–5, 89–90
state
  legitimacy 87–9, 92, 96–7, 98
  *Britannicus* (Racine) 95
  *Caïus Gracchus* (Chénier) 100
  *Charles IX* (Chénier) 99–100
  *Le Cid* (Corneille, P.) 92–4
  representation 102–4, 105
Steiner, George 143
subjectivity 95–6, 104, 199n33
sympathy 137, 139–40, 145, 146

tender friendship 156
theatre
  baroque 5
  Christian 115–17
  contemporary 23, 32
  cruelty in 23–8
  as a dialectical space 3
  emancipation from religion 109–10
  epic 31–7
  homosocial 181
  religious antitheatrical polemic 111–12
  scaffold 24, 25–8
  secular rituals 110–11
  as a site of contradiction 22–3
  and sovereignty 2
  and the state 101–2, 121–2
theatre companies 39–40
  Comédie-Française 39, 40, 53–60, 66
    audience 81, 84–5
    number of performances of individual tragedies 56, 57
    playwrights 77–8
    private performances 61, 62
    programming 42, 67, 69
    registers 68
    salaries 76
    seating capacity 81
  Drury Lane 66, 81
  Hôtel de Bourgogne 39, 40, 51, 52–3
    private performances 46–7, 61
  Hôtel Guénégaud 39, 40, 42, 44, 49–53
    number of performances of individual tragedies 52, 56, 57
    private performances 61
    seating arrangements 81
  Molière's troupe 39–40, 42, 44–9
    number of performances of individual tragedies 48
    private performances 61
  private performances 61–2, 63, 64
  programming 41–4
  rhythm of performances 40, 110
theatre design 41
Théâtre Français 69

*Théâtre Français, Mr Talma dans Brutus* (engraving) 73
theatre institutions 65–70
theatre of excess 25–8
theatrical seasons 40
*Timocrate* (Corneille, T.) 28–31
Tiquet, Angelique Carlier 130
*Tite et Bérénice* (Corneille, P.) 47–8
tolerance 122–3
torture 137–8
*tragédie sans amour* (tragedy withou love) 114–15
tragedy xi
  cruelty in 23–8
  death of 143
  effect of French Revolution on 20
  effect of German writers on 20
  end of 85, 159–66
  as epic theatre 31–7
  in judicial executions 125–6
  league table of private performances 63, 64
  league table of relative popularity 58, 59, 60
  percentage of performances involving 43
  political engagement 122–3
  and politics 89
*Tragic Effect, The* (Green) 3
tragic scaffold paradigm 126, 127–31
  challenges to 131–5
*Traité sur la tolerance* (Voltaire) 122

*Triumphs of Gods Revenge* (Reynolds) 127, *128*

Ubersfeld, Anne 13

Vernant, Jean-Pierre 87
Villiers, Pierre de 114
violence 23–8, 181–4
virtue 34
Voltaire (François-Marie Arouet) *17*, 18–19, 22, 78–9
  *Adélaide Du Guesclin* 74
  *Brutus* 74, 85, 99
  censorship 66
  Mlle Clairon 74, 79
  *Oedipe* 35, 118–19
  *Traité sur la tolerance* 122
  William Shakespeare 20
  *Zaïre* 18, 35, 67, 119–20, 157–9, 184–6

Weber, Caroline 184
Wheatley, Christopher 167
widows 171–3
Wilkin, Rebecca 181
Williams, Raymond 145–6
women 170–3. *See also* actresses; female playwrights
Wordsworth, William 91

*Zaïre* (Voltaire) 18, 35, 67, 119–20, 157–9, 184–6